Taste of Home
ULTIMATE
CHICKEN
COOKBOOK

TASTE OF HOME BOOKS • RDA ENTHUSIAST BRANDS, LLC • MILWAUKEE, WI

Taste of Home
ULTIMATE
CHICKEN
COOKBOOK

© 2022 RDA Enthusiast Brands, LLC.
1610 N. 2nd St., Suite 102
Milwaukee, WI 53212-3906

Visit us at **tasteofhome.com** for other
Taste of Home books and products.

International Standard Book Number:
978-1-62145-773-2

Executive Editor: Mark Hagen
Senior Art Director: Raeann Thompson
Senior Editor: Christine Rukavena
Senior Designer: Jazmin Delgado
Designer: Carrie Peterson
Deputy Editor, Copy Desk: Dulcie Shoener
Copy Editor: Cathy Jakicic

Cover
Photographer: Dan Roberts
Set Stylist: Stacey Genaw
Food Stylist: Josh Rink

Pictured on front cover:
Rotisserie-Style Chicken, p. 22
Pictured on spine:
Tex-Mex Chicken Strips, p. 39
Pictured on back cover:
Roast Chicken with Creole Stuffing, p. 163;
Ginger-Cashew Chicken Salad, p. 76; Mexican Chicken
Fajita Pizza, p. 53; Mexican-Inspired Chicken Soup,
p. 113; Falafel Chicken Burgers with Lemon Sauce,
p. 274; Sticky Honey Chicken Wings, p. 63

Printed in USA
1 3 5 7 9 10 8 6 4 2

CONTENTS

AT-A-GLANCE ICONS

Icons throughout the book indicate dishes
that are table-ready in 30 minutes or less,
that are better-for-you choices or that use
your favorite countertop appliances.

MORE WAYS TO CONNECT WITH US:

THE ULTIMATE CHICKEN BASICS

CHICKEN & DUMPLINGS, PAGE 101

EVERYBODY LOVES CHICKEN! FOR SATISFYING, THRIFTY AND VERSATILE MEALS, NOTHING BEATS A DELICIOUS BIRD.

We all are winners when luscious chicken dinners are on the menu. And with *Ultimate Chicken Cookbook*, it's never been simpler to make a great dish. You'll learn to make chicken extraordinary with the 300+ finger-licking good recipes in this book.

From classics, such as chicken and dumplings (page 101), to tasty, new international sensations like banh mi (page 182), you'll find the best chicken recipe for any occasion. So ring the dinner bell and call everyone to the table. Winner winner, chicken dinner!

CHOOSING CHICKEN

Read on for smart tips and key terms to help when you're shopping for chicken.

Quality Matters

When buying chicken, always be sure to look for:

- Fresh, moist meat. The skin color of chicken ranges from white to deep yellow. Color is an indication of the chicken's diet, not its freshness.

- A package with no holes, tears or excessive liquid, which may indicate improper handling and storage.

- A sell-by date on the package that is later than the day of your purchase. If it is the same date, use the meat that day or freeze it for later.

HOW MUCH TO PURCHASE?

TYPE	SERVINGS PER POUND
WHOLE CHICKEN	1 to 2
CHICKEN PIECES (BONE-IN, SKIN-ON)	2 to 3
CHICKEN BREASTS (BONELESS SKINLESS)	3 to 4
CORNISH GAME HENS	1 to 2 (PER HEN)

LEARN THIS TRICK FOR COOKING CHICKEN EVEN FASTER
Just hover your camera here.

GLAZED SPATCHCOCKED CHICKEN, PAGE 199

A GLOSSARY TO CLUCK ABOUT

Broiler/Fryer: A chicken that's about 7 weeks old and weighs 2½ to 4½ lbs.

Chicken Leg: The attached drumstick and thigh.

Chicken Quarter: A quarter of the chicken, which may be the leg or breast quarter. The leg quarter contains the drumstick, thigh and portion of the back. The breast quarter contains the breast, wing and portion of the back.

Cornish Game Hen: A small broiler/fryer that is less than 30 days old and weighs 1¼ to 1½ lbs.

Contains Broth/Self-Basted: Poultry has been injected or marinated with a solution of water, broth or stock that contains some form of fat, such as butter, as well as spices and other flavor enhancers.

Cut-Up Chicken: A broiler/fryer that has been cut into two breast halves, two thighs, two drumsticks and two wings. It may or may not have the back.

Drumettes & Wingettes: The first and second section of a chicken wing, respectively. You can purchase these frozen for easy preparation. To cut your own, see page 63.

Drumstick: Lower portion of the leg.

Free-Range/Free-Roaming: The animal was not confined to a chicken house but was allowed access to the outdoors.

Fresh: Uncooked poultry that has never been commercially stored below 26°.

Giblets: The heart, liver, neck and gizzard, usually packed inside the whole uncooked bird.

Natural: No artificial flavors, colors, chemical preservatives or other artificial or synthetic ingredients.

Organic: Raised by a producer certified by the National Organic Program in compliance with USDA regulations for organic products.

Roaster: A chicken between 3 and 5 months old, weighing 5 to 7 lbs.

Spatchcocked: A whole bird that has had its backbone removed and has been split open and flattened so that it cooks more evenly when grilled, broiled, or roasted.

Split Chicken: A broiler/fryer that has been cut in half lengthwise.

Stewing Chicken: Often a former egg-layer, over 10 months old, 5 - 7 lbs.

HELPFUL POULTRY HOW-TO'S

HOW TO REFRIGERATE, FREEZE & THAW YOUR CHICKEN DISHES

This handy guide will have you stockpiling like a pro in no time.

Refrigerating

- **After returning home** from the grocery store, be sure to place your raw chicken in the fridge or freezer right away. It should not be sitting out on the counter for any length of time. Store raw chicken no more than two days in the refrigerator before cooking or freezing.
- **For food safety,** store chicken on the bottom shelf of the refrigerator. That way, any juices that might leak out of the package are less likely to contaminate other foods in the fridge.
- **Keep chicken in its original packaging** and place it on a rimmed tray to contain drips. Or, wrap it tightly in food wrap or a resealable bag.

Freezing

- To safely freeze uncooked chicken, wrap it tightly in freezer paper or food wrap. Then, wrap it in a layer of aluminum foil. (Or, leave uncooked chicken in the manufacturer's packaging.) Place the foil-wrapped or commercially packed chicken in a freezer bag and seal.
- You can safely freeze uncooked chicken for up to a whole year(!). Here are the time frames for other popular poultry options.

FOOD	MONTHS
CHICKEN CASSEROLES	2-3
CHICKEN SOUPS & STEWS	2-3
CHICKEN SAUSAGES	1-2
COOKED CHICKEN PIECES	4
GROUND CHICKEN	4
UNCOOKED CHICKEN PIECES	9
WHOLE CHICKEN OR GAME HEN	12

Thawing

Here's how to thaw food safely.

Refrigerator Defrosting

- Place a tray under the meat to catch any liquid.
- Defrosting time will vary depending on the weight and thickness of the poultry.
- For bone-in parts or a small whole chicken, allow at least one to two days.
- For a large whole chicken, allow 24 hours for every 4 pounds.

Cold-Water Defrosting

- Place the poultry in a leakproof resealable bag and seal.
- Submerge the sealed bag in cold tap water.
- Change the water every 30 minutes.

Microwave Defrosting

- Microwaving works best for the last-minute thawing of small items.
- Unwrap the food and place it in a microwave-safe dish.
- Separate pieces as soon as you're able, or stir frozen casseroles or soups to help them thaw faster.
- Thoroughly cook or reheat the food immediately after defrosting.

SAFE, SMART HANDLING

Chicken food safety isn't complicated. Just follow a few key rules.

Food Safety Takeaways

- Keep a separate cutting board for handling uncooked poultry.

- Wash hands, utensils and surfaces thoroughly after contact with uncooked poultry.

- Don't allow other foods to touch uncooked poultry or any surface that has touched it—*especially* foods that won't receive any further cooking (such as lettuce or sliced tomato).

- Wet alert! Did you know there's actually no reason you should rinse chicken in the sink? In fact, those splishes and splashes can raise the risk of spreading dangerous bacteria in your kitchen.

See what to do instead of rinsing poultry. Just hover your camera here.

- Clean and sanitize the thermometer probe after each use.

CHICKEN ALFREDO WITH GRILLED APPLES, PAGE 210

HOW-TO

Cut a Chicken in Half

- Using a large knife or kitchen shears, carefully cut out and remove the backbone.
- Resting the tip of the knife on the cutting board for leverage, cut through the breastbone in a firm motion. Or use kitchen shears to carefully cut through the breastbone.
- Rearrange the skin to neatly cover the chicken breast during cooking.

TURN UP THE HEAT

Each cut of chicken has its own minimum-temperature requirement to ensure food safety. To check the temperature, insert a thermometer into the center or thickest portion of the cut, being careful not to touch bone.

165°
ground chicken

165°
boneless chicken breast

165°
stuffing inside
a whole bird

170°
bone-in chicken breast

170°
boneless chicken thighs

170°-175°
whole chicken as
measured in the
thickest part of thigh

170°-175°
chicken legs, drumsticks
and bone-in thighs

BEST COOKING METHODS FOR EACH CUT

CUT/TYPE	BROIL	FRY	GRILL	ROAST/BAKE	SAUTE	BRAISE
BREAST, CUBES OR STRIPS	•	•	•		•	
BREAST, BONE-IN	•	•	•	•		•
BREAST, BONELESS	•	•	•	•	•	
BROILER/FRYER, WHOLE			•	•		
BROILER/FRYER, HALVES	•		•	•		
DRUMSTICKS	•	•	•	•		•
THIGHS	•	•	•	•		•
WINGS	•	•	•	•		
ROASTING CHICKEN			•	•		
STEWING CHICKEN						•
GAME HENS, WHOLE			•	•		
GAME HENS, HALVES	•		•	•		

HOW-TO
Adapt Chicken Recipes
Here's how to get great results with your favorite countertop appliances.

Air Fryers work great for fried and roasted/baked recipes.

Slow Cookers are an alternative to stovetop or oven braising.

Pressure Cookers shine with roasted/baked and braised dishes.

ROASTING POULTRY

TYPE OF POULTRY (UNSTUFFED)	WEIGHT	COOKING TIME (MINUTES PER LB.)	OVEN TEMP.	DONENESS
BROILER/FRYER CHICKEN	3 to 4 lbs.	23 to 25	350°	170°-175° (IN THIGH)
ROASTING CHICKEN, WHOLE	5 to 7 lbs.	23 to 25	350°	170°-175° (IN THIGH)
CORNISH GAME HENS	1¼ to 1½ lbs.	50 to 60 (MINUTES TOTAL)	350°	180°

BAKING CHICKEN PIECES

CUT	WEIGHT	COOKING TIME	OVEN TEMP.	DONENESS
CHICKEN BREAST, BONE-IN	6 to 8 oz. each	30 to 40	350°	170°
CHICKEN BREAST, BONELESS	4 oz. each	20 to 30	350°	165°
CHICKEN LEGS	8 oz. each	40 to 50	350°	170°-175°
CHICKEN THIGHS	4 oz. each	40 to 50	350°	170°-175°
CHICKEN DRUMSTICKS	4 oz. each	35 to 45	350°	170°-175°
CHICKEN WINGS	2 to 3 oz. each	30 to 40	350°	Juices Run Clear

GRILLING POULTRY

CUT	WEIGHT OR THICKNESS	HEAT	COOKING TIME
BROILER/FRYER, WHOLE	3 to 4 lbs.	Medium/Indirect	1 to 1¼ hours
ROASTER, WHOLE	5 to 6 lbs.	Medium/Indirect	1¾ to 2¼ hours
MEATY BONE-IN PIECES, BREAST HALVES, LEGS, QUARTERS	1¼ to 1½ lbs.	Medium/Indirect or Medium/Direct	40 to 50 min. 16 to 30 min.
BONE-IN THIGHS, DRUMSTICKS, WINGS	3 to 7 oz. each	Medium-Low/Direct or Medium/Indirect	15 to 30 min. 20 to 30 min.
BREAST HALVES, BONELESS	6 oz. each	Medium/Direct	6 to 10 min.
KABOBS	1-in. cubes	Medium/Direct	10 to 15 min.
CORNISH GAME HENS	1½ to 2 lbs.	Medium/Indirect	45 to 55 min.

Successful Roasting

- To roast a whole bird, remove any giblets stored in a packet in the neck or body cavity. Save for another use, such as making gravy, if desired. Discard large pockets of fat in the neck area.

- Drain cavity of whole poultry and pat it dry with paper towels.

- Rub the inside of the cavity and neck area with salt.

- Brush the chicken's skin with oil or melted butter.

- Insert an oven-safe thermometer into the thickest part of thigh area of large birds without touching bone or fat. Or, for small and large birds, test for doneness with an instant-read thermometer. Never leave an instant-read thermometer in the oven.

- Roasting is a dry-heat method; no liquid should be added to the pan.

- If poultry browns too quickly, cover it with foil.

- Whole chickens continue to cook after being removed from the oven (this is called carry-over cooking). They should be removed from the oven at a minimum of 165°. However, if you prefer for the poultry to finish cooking at a higher temperature, remove it from the oven 5° to 10° below desired temperature.

- Let the chicken stand tented with foil 10 to 20 minutes (longer for larger birds) before removing any stuffing and carving.

Great Grilling

The cooking times given in the chart at left are for the doneness temperatures listed on page 10.

- For direct-heat grilling, turn food halfway through grilling time.

- Times are based on grilling with the lid of the grill closed.

ROTISSERIE-
STYLE CHICKEN,
PAGE 22

ALL-TIME
CLASSICS

FAVORITE CHICKEN POTPIE

Chock-full of chicken, potatoes, peas and corn, this autumn favorite makes two golden pies, so you can serve one at supper and save the other for a busy night. These potpies are perfect for company or a potluck.

—*Karen Johnson, Bakersfield, CA*

PREP: 40 min. • **BAKE:** 35 min. + standing
MAKES: 2 potpies (8 servings each)

- 2 cups diced peeled potatoes
- 1¾ cups sliced carrots
- 1 cup butter, cubed
- ⅔ cup chopped onion
- 1 cup all-purpose flour
- 1¾ tsp. salt
- 1 tsp. dried thyme
- ¾ tsp. pepper
- 3 cups chicken broth
- 1½ cups whole milk
- 4 cups cubed cooked chicken
- 1 cup frozen peas
- 1 cup frozen corn
- 4 sheets refrigerated pie crust

1. Preheat oven to 425°. Place potatoes and carrots in a large saucepan; add water to cover. Bring to a boil. Reduce heat; cook, covered, 8 10 minutes or until crisp-tender; drain.

2. In a large skillet, heat butter over medium-high heat. Add onion; cook and stir until tender. Stir in flour and seasonings until blended. Gradually stir in broth and milk. Bring to a boil, stirring constantly; cook and stir for 2 minutes or until thickened. Stir in the chicken, peas, corn and potato mixture; remove from heat.

3. Unroll 1 pie crust into each of two 9-in. pie plates; trim crusts even with rims. Add chicken mixture. Unroll remaining crusts; place over filling. Trim, seal and flute edges. Cut slits in tops.

4. Bake 35-40 minutes or until crust is lightly browned. Let stand 15 minutes before cutting.

Freeze option: Cover and freeze unbaked pies. To use, remove from freezer 30 minutes before baking (do not thaw). Preheat oven to 425°. Place pies on baking sheets; cover edges loosely with foil. Bake 30 minutes. Reduce oven setting to 350°; bake 70-80 minutes longer or until crust is golden brown and a thermometer inserted in center reads 165°.

1 piece: 475 cal., 28g fat (14g sat. fat), 74mg chol., 768mg sod., 41g carb. (5g sugars, 2g fiber), 15g pro.

TEST KITCHEN TIP

Feel free to use your favorite homemade pie crust in this recipe.

WATCH HOW WE DID IT
Just hover your camera here.

**FAVORITE
CHICKEN POTPIE**

🕐 SPICY CHICKEN NUGGETS

We devour these golden chicken nuggets at least once a week. If you want to tone down the heat, skip the chipotle pepper.
—*Cheryl Cook, Palmyra, VA*

- -

TAKES: 30 min. • **MAKES:** 6 servings

- 1½ cups panko bread crumbs
- 1½ cups grated Parmesan cheese
- ½ tsp. ground chipotle pepper, optional
- ¼ cup butter, melted
- 1½ lbs. boneless skinless chicken thighs, cut into 1½-in. pieces

1. Preheat oven to 400°. In a shallow bowl, mix bread crumbs, cheese and, if desired, chipotle pepper. Place butter in a separate shallow bowl. Dip chicken pieces in butter, then in crumb mixture, patting to help coating adhere.
2. Place chicken in a greased 15x10x1-in. baking pan; sprinkle with remaining crumb mixture. Bake 20-25 minutes or until chicken is no longer pink.
1 serving: 371 cal., 22g fat (10g sat. fat), 113mg chol., 527mg sod., 13g carb. (1g sugars, 1g fiber), 29g pro.

BUFFALO CHICKEN WINGS

BUFFALO CHICKEN WINGS

Hot wings got their start in Buffalo, New York, in the kitchen of a bar. Today, spicy wings and cool sauces are traditional game-day fare. Cayenne, chili sauce and spices keep these tangy buffalo chicken wings good and hot, just like the originals.
—*Nancy Chapman, Center Harbor, NH*

PREP: 10 min. • **COOK:** 10 min./batch
MAKES: about 4 dozen

- 5 lbs. chicken wings
  Oil for frying
- 1 cup butter, cubed
- ¼ cup Louisiana-style hot sauce
- ¾ tsp. cayenne pepper
- ¾ tsp. celery salt
- ½ tsp. onion powder
- ½ tsp. garlic powder
  Optional: Celery ribs and ranch dressing,

1. Cut chicken wings into 3 sections; discard wing-tip sections. In an electric skillet, heat 1 in. of oil to 375°. Fry wings in oil, a few at a time, for 3-4 minutes on each side or until chicken juices run clear. Drain on paper towels.
2. Meanwhile, in a small saucepan, melt butter. Stir in the hot sauce and spices. Place chicken in a large bowl; add sauce and toss to coat. Remove to a serving plate with a slotted spoon. Serve with celery and ranch dressing if desired.
Note: Uncooked chicken wing sections (wingettes) may be substituted for whole chicken wings.
1 piece: 126 cal., 12g fat (4g sat. fat), 25mg chol., 105mg sod., 0 carb. (0 sugars, 0 fiber), 5g pro.

🕐 BBQ & RANCH CHICKEN PIZZA

I wanted something different for dinner and came up with this pizza. The kids loved it, and so did my friends. Best of all, it's very quick with leftover chicken and convenience items. What's not to love?
—*Sue Sitler, Bloomsburg, PA*

- -

TAKES: 30 min. • **MAKES:** 8 servings

- 2 tubes (8 oz. each) refrigerated crescent rolls
- ½ cup hickory smoke-flavored barbecue sauce, divided
- ¼ cup prepared ranch salad dressing
- 3 cups cubed cooked chicken breasts
- 2 cups shredded pizza cheese blend

1. Preheat oven to 375°. Unroll both tubes of crescent dough and press onto the bottom and up the sides of an ungreased 15x10x1-in. baking pan, pressing perforations to seal. Bake 8-10 minutes or until lightly browned.
2. In a small bowl, mix ¼ cup barbecue sauce and the salad dressing; spread over crust. In another bowl, toss chicken with the remaining barbecue sauce. Arrange over top. Sprinkle with the cheese. Bake 15-20 minutes longer or until crust is golden brown and cheese is melted.
1 piece: 431 cal., 22g fat (5g sat. fat), 66mg chol., 875mg sod., 32g carb. (12g sugars, 0 fiber), 25g pro.

SAGE CHICKEN CORDON BLEU

It's nice to surprise the family with special meals like this during the week. I usually double the recipe so we can enjoy leftovers the next day.
—*Martha Stine, Johnstown, PA*

- -

PREP: 20 min. • **BAKE:** 40 min.
MAKES: 6 servings

- 6 boneless skinless chicken breast halves (4 oz. each)
- ½ to ¾ tsp. rubbed sage
- 6 slices thinly sliced deli ham
- 6 slices part-skim mozzarella cheese, halved
- 1 medium tomato, seeded and chopped
- ⅓ cup dry bread crumbs
- 2 Tbsp. grated Parmesan cheese
- 2 Tbsp. minced fresh parsley
- 4 Tbsp. butter, divided

1. Preheat oven to 350°. Flatten the chicken breasts with a meat mallet to ⅛-in. thickness; sprinkle with sage. Place ham, mozzarella cheese and tomato down the center of each; roll up chicken from a long side, tucking in ends. Secure with toothpicks.
2. In a shallow bowl, toss the bread crumbs with Parmesan cheese and parsley. In a shallow microwave-safe dish, microwave 3 Tbsp. butter until melted. Dip chicken in butter, then roll in crumb mixture. Place in a greased 11x7-in. baking dish, seam side down. Melt remaining butter; drizzle over top.
3. Bake, uncovered, until a thermometer inserted in the chicken rolls reads 165°, 40-45 minutes. Discard the toothpicks before serving.
1 serving: 328 cal., 17g fat (9g sat. fat), 112mg chol., 575mg sod., 8g carb. (2g sugars, 1g fiber), 35g pro.

SAGE CHICKEN CORDON BLEU

HOW-TO
Flatten Chicken Breasts
- To flatten boneless chicken breasts, place between two pieces of waxed paper or kitchen wrap.
- Starting in center and working out to the edges, pound lightly with the flat side of a meat mallet until the chicken is even in thickness—about ½ in. for larger cuts or as little as ⅛ in. for smaller chicken breasts.
- A small saucepan or skillet makes a fine stand-in if you don't have a meat mallet.

CHICKEN & WAFFLES

Adding mustard to the chicken coating lends a tang that's amazing with the savory waffles and sweet maple syrup.
—*John Ginn, Carlisle, PA*

PREP: 20 min. • **COOK:** 40 min.
MAKES: 8 servings

- 1 pkg. (6 oz.) stuffing mix
- 4 large eggs
- ¼ cup yellow mustard
- ½ cup all-purpose flour
- 1 tsp. salt
- 1 tsp. pepper
- 8 boneless skinless chicken thighs (about 2 lbs.)
  Oil for frying

WAFFLES
- 1¾ cups all-purpose flour
- 2 Tbsp. sugar
- 3 tsp. baking powder
- 1¾ cups 2% milk
- 2 large eggs, room temperature
- ½ cup butter, melted
- 2 tsp. vanilla extract
  Maple syrup

1. Prepare stuffing mix according to package directions; cool.
2. Meanwhile, in a shallow bowl, mix eggs and mustard. Place flour, salt and pepper in another shallow bowl. Dip chicken thighs in flour mixture to coat both sides; shake off excess. Dip in the egg mixture, then again in flour mixture, patting to help coating adhere.
3. In an electric skillet, heat ½ in. oil to 375°. Fry chicken thighs, a few at a time, until golden brown and a thermometer reads at least 170°, 2-3 minutes on each side. Drain on paper towels and keep warm.
4. Preheat waffle iron. In a large bowl, whisk flour, sugar and baking powder. In another bowl, whisk milk, eggs, butter and vanilla until blended. Add to the dry ingredients; stir just until moistened. Stir in prepared stuffing.
5. Bake the waffles according to the manufacturer's directions until golden brown. Serve with chicken and syrup.
1 piece of chicken with 2 waffles: 691 cal., 43g fat (16g sat. fat), 219mg chol., 1074mg sod., 44g carb. (7g sugars, 2g fiber), 32g pro.

CHICKEN DUMPLING SOUP

My husband was fooled by this low-fat recipe and I'm sure your family will be, too! A savory broth, hearty chicken and rich dumplings all add up to comforting flavor.
—*Brenda White, Morrison, IL*

PREP: 15 min. • **COOK:** 50 min.
MAKES: 4 servings

- 1 lb. boneless skinless chicken breasts, cut into 1½-in. cubes
- 3 cans (14½ oz. each) reduced-sodium chicken broth
- 3 cups water
- 4 medium carrots, chopped
- 1 medium onion, chopped
- 1 celery rib, chopped
- 1 tsp. minced fresh parsley
- ½ tsp. salt
- ¼ tsp. garlic powder
- ¼ tsp. poultry seasoning
- ¼ tsp. pepper

DUMPLINGS
- 3 large egg whites
- ½ cup 1% cottage cheese
- 2 Tbsp. water
- ¼ tsp. salt
- 1 cup all-purpose flour

1. In a Dutch oven coated with cooking spray, cook the chicken until no longer pink. Add broth, water, vegetables and seasonings. Bring to a boil. Reduce heat; simmer, uncovered, 30 minutes or until vegetables are tender.
2. Meanwhile, for dumplings, in a large bowl, beat the egg whites and cottage cheese until blended. Add water and salt. Stir in the flour and mix well.
3. Bring soup to a boil. Drop dumplings by tablespoonfuls onto the boiling soup. Reduce the heat; cover and simmer for 15 minutes or until a toothpick inserted in dumplings comes out clean (do not lift cover while simmering).
1½ cups: 363 cal., 4g fat (2g sat. fat), 73mg chol., 900mg sod., 39g carb. (0 sugars, 4g fiber), 42g pro.

CHICKEN & WAFFLES

FLAVORFUL LEMON CHICKEN

This easy and attractive meal is bound to become a staple with your family. It's made with everyday ingredients, so there's nothing complicated or fancy about this delicious recipe.
—*Elizabeth Hokanson, Arborg, MB*

PREP: 20 min. • **COOK:** 4¼ hours
MAKES: 6 servings

    1 tsp. dried oregano
   ½ tsp. seasoned salt
   ¼ tsp. pepper
    6 boneless skinless chicken breast
        halves (6 oz. each)
    2 tsp. chicken bouillon granules
   ¼ cup boiling water
    3 Tbsp. lemon juice
 1½ tsp. minced garlic
 1½ cups sour cream
    2 tsp. minced fresh parsley
        Hot cooked brown rice, optional

1. Combine the oregano, seasoned salt and pepper; rub over chicken. Place in a 3-qt. slow cooker.
2. In a small bowl, dissolve bouillon in boiling water. Stir in lemon juice and garlic. Pour over chicken. Cover and cook on low until chicken is tender, 4-5 hours.
3. Remove chicken and keep warm. Stir in sour cream and parsley; cover and cook until heated through, about 15 minutes. Serve chicken with sauce and, if desired, rice.

1 chicken breast half with about ⅓ cup sauce: 309 cal., 14g fat (8g sat. fat), 134mg chol., 509mg sod., 4g carb. (2g sugars, 0 fiber), 36g pro.

FLAVORFUL LEMON CHICKEN

🕐 CHOW MEIN CHICKEN

Whenever I get the craving for Chinese food, I look no farther than my own kitchen! This easy-to-make entree is ready in a matter of minutes.
—*Debbie Franzen, Sewickley, PA*

- -

TAKES: 30 min. • **MAKES:** 4 servings

2	celery ribs, chopped
1	medium onion, chopped
¼	cup butter
1	can (10¾ oz.) condensed cream of mushroom soup, undiluted
½	cup chicken broth
1	Tbsp. soy sauce
3	cups cubed cooked chicken
½	cup sliced fresh mushrooms
1	can (3 oz.) chow mein noodles
⅓	cup salted cashew halves

1. In a saucepan, saute celery and onion in butter until tender. Stir in soup, broth and soy sauce. Add cubed chicken and mushrooms; heat through.

2. Transfer to a greased 2-qt. baking dish. Sprinkle with chow mein noodles and cashews. Bake, uncovered, at 350° for 15-20 minutes or until the mixture is heated through.

1 serving: 578 cal., 36g fat (13g sat. fat), 127mg chol., 1283mg sod., 26g carb. (5g sugars, 3g fiber), 37g pro.

WHY YOU'LL LOVE IT...

"Very easy and delicious! Instead of baking it with the chow mein noodles or cashews on top, you can serve them on the side."

—ZUMMYB, TASTEOFHOME.COM

CHICKEN MARSALA EN CROUTE

CHICKEN MARSALA EN CROUTE

I love puff pastry and chicken Marsala, so I decided to combine the two. The result is a very special meal, perfect for a Sunday dinner or any special occasion. Be sure to keep the puff pastry chilled so it is easier to work with.

—*Lorraine Russo, Mahwah, NJ*

PREP: 35 min. + chilling • **BAKE:** 20 min.
MAKES: 4 servings

- 3 Tbsp. butter
- ½ lb. sliced baby portobello mushrooms
- 2 shallots, finely chopped
- 3 garlic cloves, minced
- 1 Tbsp. all-purpose flour
- ¼ cup beef broth
- ⅔ cup Marsala wine
- 4 boneless skinless chicken breast halves (5 oz. each)
- 1 Tbsp. large egg
- 1 Tbsp. water
- 1 sheet frozen puff pastry, thawed
- ½ tsp. salt
- ¼ tsp. pepper
  Fresh thyme, optional

1. In a large skillet, melt butter over medium-high heat; saute mushrooms and shallots until tender, 3-4 minutes. Add the garlic; cook and stir 1 minute longer. Stir in the flour until blended. Gradually stir in broth and wine; bring to a boil, stirring constantly. Reduce heat; simmer, uncovered, until slightly thickened, 2-3 minutes. Stir mixture occasionally. Remove to a bowl; cool slightly. Refrigerate, covered, until cold.

2. Preheat oven to 425°. Pound chicken breasts with a meat mallet to an even thickness. Whisk together the egg and water. On a lightly floured surface, roll pastry sheet into a 14-in. square. Cut into four 7-in. squares. Place 1 chicken breast on center of each square. If desired, fold narrow end under to fit pastry square; sprinkle with salt and pepper. Top each with 1 rounded Tbsp. mushroom mixture. Lightly brush the pastry edges with egg mixture. Fold pastry over filling; press edges with a fork to seal. Place on a rimmed parchment-lined baking sheet.

3. Brush tops with the egg mixture. Bake until pastry is golden brown and a thermometer inserted in chicken reads 165°, 18-23 minutes. Reheat the remaining mushroom mixture; serve with pastries. If desired, garnish with thyme.

1 pastry: 599 cal., 29g fat (10g sat. fat), 115mg chol., 703mg sod., 45g carb. (3g sugars, 5g fiber), 36g pro.

ROTISSERIE-STYLE CHICKEN

My mother used to fix this chicken when I lived at home. We called it "church chicken" because Mom would put it in the oven on Sunday morning before we left for church. When we returned home, the aroma of the roasted chicken would hit us as we opened the door.

—*Brian Stevenson, Grand Rapids, MI*

PREP: 15 min. + chilling
BAKE: 1¼ hours + standing
MAKES: 6 servings

2	tsp. salt
1¼	tsp. paprika
1	tsp. brown sugar
¾	tsp. dried thyme
¾	tsp. white pepper
¼	tsp. cayenne pepper
¼	tsp. pepper
1	broiler/fryer chicken (3 to 4 lbs.)
1	medium onion, quartered

1. Mix the first 7 ingredients. Rub over the outside and inside of the chicken. Place in a large dish. Cover and refrigerate 8 hours or overnight.

2. Preheat oven to 350°. Place chicken on a rack in a shallow roasting pan, breast side up. Tuck the wings under chicken; tie drumsticks together. Place onion pieces around chicken in pan.

3. Roast until a thermometer inserted in thickest part of thigh reads 170°-175°, 1¼-1½ hours. Baste occasionally with pan drippings. (Cover loosely with foil if chicken browns too quickly.)

4. Remove chicken from oven; tent with foil. Let stand 15 minutes before slicing.

5 oz. cooked chicken: 306 cal., 17g fat (5g sat. fat), 104mg chol., 878mg sod., 3g carb. (2g sugars, 1g fiber), 33g pro.

GET MORE CARVING BASICS
Just hover your camera here.

ROTISSERIE-STYLE CHICKEN

Carve a Chicken

Step 1: To ensure juiciness, let chicken stand at least 15 minutes before carving. Place chicken on a cutting board, ideally one with a well to catch any juices. Using a carving fork to stabilize the chicken, cut through the skin separating the leg from the body.

Step 2: Continue cutting down through the hip joint to remove the leg and thigh (also called a leg quarter) in one piece. Jiggle the leg to free it from the joint if necessary. Repeat on the second side.

Step 3: Separate the drumsticks from the thighs by cutting through the joint of each leg quarter.

Step 4: To remove the breast meat, first make a horizontal cut near the base of the chicken toward its center.

Step 5: Next, cut down along the breastbone, through to the horizontal cut that was just made. Remove the entire breast half. Rotate the chicken 180° and reposition the carving fork. Repeat on the second side to remove remaining breast half.

Step 6: Slice the chicken breast meat as desired.

Step 7: Pull the wings away from the body. For an attractive presentation, cut away and discard the wing tips.

Step 8: Plate chicken and serve.

CRISPY FRIED CHICKEN

This fried chicken can be served hot or pulled out of the fridge the next day as leftovers. Either way, folks love it.
—*Jeanne Schnitzler, Lima, MT*

- -

PREP: 15 min. • **COOK:** 15 min./batch
MAKES: 12 servings

- 4 cups all-purpose flour, divided
- 2 Tbsp. garlic salt
- 1 Tbsp. paprika
- 3 tsp. pepper, divided
- 2½ tsp. poultry seasoning
- 2 large eggs
- 1½ cups water
- 1 tsp. salt
- 2 broiler/fryer chickens (3½ to 4 lbs. each), cut up
   Oil for deep-fat frying

1. In a large shallow dish, combine 2⅔ cups flour, garlic salt, paprika, 2½ tsp. pepper and poultry seasoning. In another shallow dish, beat eggs and 1½ cups water; add 1 tsp. salt and the remaining 1⅓ cup flour and ½ tsp. pepper. Dip chicken in egg mixture, then place in flour mixture, a few pieces at a time. Turn to coat.

2. In a deep-fat fryer, heat oil to 375°. Fry chicken, several pieces at a time, until skin is golden brown and a thermometer inserted into chicken reads 165°, about 7-8 minutes on each side. Drain on paper towels.

5 oz. cooked chicken: 543 cal., 33g fat (7g sat. fat), 137mg chol., 798mg sod., 17g carb. (0 sugars, 1g fiber), 41g pro.

CRISPY FRIED CHICKEN

QUICK SWEET-AND-SOUR CHICKEN

On a really busy night, this quick entree, made with a frozen stir-fry vegetable mix and chicken nuggets, will hit the table— and the spot— in no time.
—*Mary Tallman, Arbor Vitae, WI*

TAKES: 25 min. • **MAKES:** 3 servings

- 1 pkg. (13.2 oz.) breaded chicken nuggets
- 1 pkg. (21 oz.) frozen sweet-and-sour stir-fry mix
- 1 pkg. (8.8 oz.) ready-to-serve brown rice
- 3 Tbsp. salted cashews

1. Cook chicken nuggets according to package directions. Meanwhile, in a large skillet, cook stir-fry mix, covered, over medium heat for 6-8 minutes or until heated through. Stir in chicken nuggets.

2. Microwave rice according to package directions. Serve with stir-fry mixture; sprinkle with cashews.

1 serving: 717 cal., 29g fat (8g sat. fat), 75mg chol., 1258mg sod., 83g carb. (31g sugars, 5g fiber), 28g pro.

BEST CHICKEN KIEV

From holiday suppers to potlucks, this is one of my most-requested meals. Folks love the mildly seasoned chicken roll-ups.
—*Karin Erickson, Burney, CA*

PREP: 15 min. + freezing • **BAKE:** 35 min.
MAKES: 6 servings

- ¼ cup butter, softened
- 1 Tbsp. minced chives
- 1 garlic clove, minced
- 6 boneless skinless chicken breast halves (8 oz. each)
- ¾ cup crushed cornflakes
- 2 Tbsp. minced fresh parsley
- ½ tsp. paprika
- ⅓ cup buttermilk

1. In a small bowl, combine the butter, chives and garlic. Shape into a 3x2-in. rectangle. Cover and freeze until firm, about 30 minutes.

2. Flatten each chicken breast to a ¼-in. thickness. Cut the butter mixture into six 1-in. pieces; place 1 piece in center of each chicken breast. Roll up chicken from a long side; tuck ends under. Secure with toothpicks.

3. In a shallow bowl, combine the cornflakes, parsley and paprika. Place buttermilk in another shallow bowl. Dip the chicken into buttermilk, then coat evenly with cornflake mixture.

4. Preheat oven to 425°; place the chicken in a greased 13x9 in. baking dish, seam side down. Bake, uncovered, 35-40 minutes or until chicken reaches an internal temperature of 170°. Discard the toothpicks.

Note: To substitute for each cup of buttermilk, use 1 Tbsp. white vinegar or lemon juice plus enough milk to measure 1 cup. Stir, then let stand 5 min. Or, use 1 cup plain yogurt or 1¾ tsp. cream of tartar plus 1 cup milk.

1 serving: 357 cal., 13g fat (6g sat. fat), 146mg chol., 281mg sod., 10g carb. (2g sugars, 0 fiber), 47g pro.

BEST CHICKEN KIEV

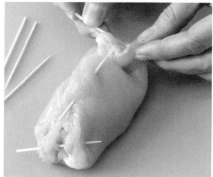

HOW-TO

Stuff Chicken Rolls
- Spread stuffing in center of flattened chicken breast.
- Roll up jelly-roll style, tucking in sides. Secure with toothpicks.

CHICKEN CACCIATORE

This dish makes a good Sunday dinner, since the recipe is so simple to prepare. It's inexpensive besides—and loaded with lots of vegetables.
—*Barbara Roberts, Courtenay, BC*

PREP: 15 min. • **COOK:** 1½ hours
MAKES: 6 servings

1 broiler/fryer chicken (3½ to 4 lbs.), cut up
¼ cup all-purpose flour
 Salt and pepper to taste
2 Tbsp. olive oil
2 Tbsp. butter

1 large onion, chopped
2 celery ribs, sliced
1 large green pepper, cut into strips
½ lb. sliced fresh mushrooms
1 can (28 oz.) tomatoes, drained and chopped
1 can (8 oz.) tomato sauce
1 can (6 oz.) tomato paste
1 cup dry red wine or water
1 tsp. dried thyme
1 tsp. dried rosemary, crushed
1 tsp. dried oregano
1 tsp. dried basil
3 garlic cloves, minced
1 Tbsp. sugar
 Hot cooked pasta
 Grated Parmesan cheese

1. Dust chicken with flour. Season with salt and pepper. In a large skillet, brown the chicken on all sides in oil and butter over medium-high heat. Remove the chicken to platter.
2. In the same skillet, cook and stir the onion, celery, pepper and mushrooms for 5 minutes. Stir in the tomatoes, tomato sauce, tomato paste, wine, herbs, garlic and sugar. Bring to a boil. Reduce heat; cover and simmer for 30 minutes.
3. Return chicken to skillet. Cover and simmer for 45-60 minutes or until the chicken is tender. Serve over pasta and sprinkle with Parmesan cheese.
Freeze option: Cool chicken mixture. Freeze in freezer containers. To use, partially thaw in refrigerator overnight. Heat through slowly in a covered skillet, stirring occasionally, until a thermometer inserted in chicken reads 165°.
1 serving: 517 cal., 25g fat (8g sat. fat), 112mg chol., 790mg sod., 28g carb. (13g sugars, 6g fiber), 39g pro.

MUSHROOM CHICKEN ALFREDO

All you need is one skillet to make this delicious, scaled-down dinner. It's an easy way to dress up packaged noodles and sauce. Plus, cleanup is a breeze.
—*Margery Bryan, Moses Lake, WA*

TAKES: 30 min. • **MAKES:** 3 servings

½ lb. boneless skinless chicken breasts, cut into 2-in. cubes
1 Tbsp. butter
1 cup sliced fresh mushrooms
1 small onion, sliced
1¾ cups water
½ cup 2% milk
1 pkg. (4.4 oz.) quick-cooking noodles and Alfredo sauce mix
 Minced fresh parsley, optional

1. In a large nonstick skillet, cook the chicken in butter for 6 minutes or until meat is no longer pink. Remove and keep warm. In the same skillet, saute mushrooms and onion until tender.
2. Stir in water and milk; bring to a boil. Stir in contents of noodles and sauce mix; boil for 8 minutes or until noodles are tender.
3. Return the chicken to the pan; heat through. Garnish with parsley if desired.
1⅓ cups: 317 cal., 11g fat (6g sat. fat), 105mg chol., 727mg sod., 30g carb. (6g sugars, 1g fiber), 24g pro. **Diabetic exchanges:** 2 starch, 2 lean meat, 1 fat.

DID YOU KNOW?

Mushrooms are one of the few plant sources of Vitamin D. Some growers expose their mushrooms to UV light to increase their vitamin D content.

CHICKEN PICCATA
WITH LEMON SAUCE

⏱ 🍎 POACHED CHICKEN

You can't beat poaching for chicken that is moist and tender. Once it's cooled, store extra in the freezer for quick meals.
—*James Schend, Pleasant Prairie, WI*

- -

TAKES: 25 min. • **MAKES:** 4 servings

- 4 boneless skinless chicken breast halves (6 oz. each)
- ½ cup white wine
  Aromatic ingredients: 6 whole peppercorns, 3 thyme sprigs, 1 rosemary sprig, 1 smashed garlic clove and 1 bay leaf
- 1 tsp. salt

In a skillet or saucepan just large enough to hold chicken in 1 layer, combine chicken, wine, aromatics and salt; add cold water to cover by 1 in. Bring liquid to a boil. Reduce the heat to low; simmer, covered, until a thermometer reads 170°, 15-20 minutes. Serve warm, or cool completely before refrigerating.
1 chicken breast half: 192 cal., 4g fat (1g sat. fat), 94mg chol., 141mg sod., 0 carb. (0 sugars, 0 fiber), 34g pro.
Diabetic exchanges: 5 lean meat.

🍎 CHICKEN PICCATA WITH LEMON SAUCE

Once you've tried this tangy yet delicate entree, you won't hesitate to make it for company. Seasoned with Parmesan and parsley, the chicken cooks up golden brown, then is drizzled with a light lemon sauce.
—*Susan Pursell, Fountain Valley, CA*

- -

PREP: 25 min. • **COOK:** 25 min.
MAKES: 8 servings

- 8 boneless skinless chicken breast halves (4 oz. each)
- ½ cup egg substitute
- 2 Tbsp. plus ¼ cup dry white wine or chicken broth, divided
- 5 Tbsp. lemon juice, divided
- 3 garlic cloves, minced
- ⅛ tsp. hot pepper sauce
- ½ cup all-purpose flour
- ½ cup grated Parmesan cheese
- ¼ cup minced fresh parsley
- ½ tsp. salt
- 3 tsp. olive oil, divided
- 2 Tbsp. butter

1. Flatten chicken to ¼-in. thickness. In a shallow dish, combine the egg substitute, 2 Tbsp. wine, 2 Tbsp. lemon juice, garlic and hot pepper sauce. In another shallow dish, combine the flour, Parmesan cheese, parsley and salt. Coat chicken with flour mixture, dip in egg substitute mixture, then coat again with flour mixture.
2. In a large nonstick skillet, brown 4 chicken breast halves in 1½ tsp. oil for 3-5 minutes on each side or until juices run clear. Remove and keep warm. Drain drippings. Repeat with the remaining chicken and oil. Remove and keep warm.
3. In the same pan, melt butter. Add the remaining wine and lemon juice. Bring to a boil. Boil, uncovered, until sauce is reduced by a fourth. Drizzle over chicken.
1 chicken breast half: 232 cal., 9g fat (4g sat. fat), 75mg chol., 346mg sod., 8g carb. (1g sugars, 0 fiber), 27g pro.
Diabetic exchanges: 3 lean meat, 1 fat, ½ starch.

🍎 BAKED CHICKEN PARMESAN

With this healthier version of chicken Parmesan, you won't even miss the extra fat and calories.
—*Margie Pharr, Belmont, MS*

PREP: 15 min. • **BAKE:** 30 min.
MAKES: 2 servings

- ¼ cup seasoned bread crumbs
- 2 Tbsp. grated Parmesan cheese
- ½ tsp. minced fresh basil
- 1 large egg white
- 2 boneless skinless chicken breast halves (6 oz. each)
- 2 tsp. cornstarch
- ¾ tsp. Italian seasoning
- ½ tsp. sugar
- ¼ tsp. garlic powder
- ⅛ tsp. Worcestershire sauce
  Dash pepper
- 1 can (14½ oz.) diced tomatoes, undrained
  Hot cooked pasta, optional

1. In a shallow bowl, combine the bread crumbs, Parmesan cheese and basil. In another shallow bowl, beat egg white until foamy. Dip chicken into the beaten egg white, then roll in crumb mixture; place in a 1-qt. baking dish coated with cooking spray. Bake, uncovered, at 350° for 30-35 minutes or until chicken juices run clear.
2. Meanwhile, in a small saucepan, combine the cornstarch, Italian seasoning, sugar, garlic powder, Worcestershire sauce, pepper and tomatoes until blended. Bring to a boil. Reduce heat; simmer, uncovered, for 15 minutes. Serve chicken and sauce with pasta if desired.
1 serving: 302 cal., 6g fat (2g sat. fat), 97mg chol., 580mg sod., 22g carb. (8g sugars, 4g fiber), 40g pro. **Diabetic exchanges:** 5 lean meat, 1 starch, 1 vegetable, ½ fat.

CHICKEN FAJITAS

🍎 CHICKEN FAJITAS

This chicken fajitas recipe is definitely on my weeknight dinner rotation. The marinated chicken in these popular wraps is mouthwatering. The fajitas go together in a snap and always get raves!
—*Julie Sterchi, Campbellsville, KY*

PREP: 20 min. + marinating
COOK: 10 min. • **MAKES:** 6 servings

- 4 Tbsp. canola oil, divided
- 2 Tbsp. lemon juice
- 1½ tsp. seasoned salt
- 1½ tsp. dried oregano
- 1½ tsp. ground cumin
- 1 tsp. garlic powder
- ½ tsp. chili powder
- ½ tsp. paprika
- ½ tsp. crushed red pepper flakes, optional
- 1½ lbs. boneless skinless chicken breasts, cut into thin strips
- ½ medium sweet red pepper, julienned
- ½ medium green pepper, julienned
- 4 green onions, thinly sliced
- ½ cup chopped onion
- 6 flour tortillas (8 in.), warmed
  Optional: Shredded cheddar cheese, taco sauce, salsa, guacamole, sliced red onions and sour cream

1. In a large bowl, combine 2 Tbsp. oil, lemon juice and seasonings; add the chicken. Turn to coat; cover. Refrigerate for 1-4 hours.
2. In a large cast-iron or other heavy skillet, saute peppers and onions in remaining oil until crisp-tender. Remove and keep warm.
3. Drain chicken, discarding marinade. In the same skillet, cook chicken over medium-high heat until no longer pink, 5-6 minutes. Return pepper mixture to pan; heat through.
4. Spoon filling down the center of tortillas. Add toppings as desired. Fold in half.
1 fajita: 369 cal., 15g fat (2g sat. fat), 63mg chol., 689mg sod., 30g carb. (2g sugars, 1g fiber), 28g pro. **Diabetic exchanges:** 3 lean meat, 2 starch, 2 fat.

CASHEW CHICKEN WITH GINGER

There are lots of recipes for cashew chicken, but my family thinks this one stands alone. We love the flavor from the fresh ginger and the crunch of the cashews. Plus, it's easy to prepare.
—*Oma Rollison, El Cajon, CA*

TAKES: 30 min. • **MAKES:** 6 servings

- 2 Tbsp. cornstarch
- 1 Tbsp. brown sugar
- 1¼ cups chicken broth
- 2 Tbsp. soy sauce
- 3 Tbsp. canola oil, divided
- 1½ lbs. boneless skinless chicken breasts, cut into 1-in. pieces
- ½ lb. sliced fresh mushrooms
- 1 small green pepper, cut into strips
- 1 can (8 oz.) sliced water chestnuts, drained
- 1½ tsp. grated fresh gingerroot
- 4 green onions, sliced
- ¾ cup salted cashews
  Hot cooked rice

1. Mix first 4 ingredients until smooth. In a large skillet, heat 2 Tbsp. oil over medium-high heat; stir-fry chicken until no longer pink. Remove from pan.
2. In same pan, heat remaining oil over medium-high heat; stir-fry mushrooms, pepper, water chestnuts and ginger until pepper is crisp-tender, 3-5 minutes. Stir broth mixture and add to pan with green onions; bring to a boil. Cook and stir until sauce is thickened, 1-2 minutes.
3. Stir in chicken and cashews; heat through. Serve with rice.
¾ cup chicken mixture: 349 cal., 19g fat (3g sat. fat), 64mg chol., 650mg sod., 18g carb. (6g sugars, 2g fiber), 28g pro.
Diabetic exchanges: 3 lean meat, 3 fat, 1 starch.

CASHEW CHICKEN WITH GINGER

🕐 CHICKEN SALAD CROISSANT SANDWICHES

Parmesan cheese and dill make this the most incredible chicken salad I've ever tasted. These sandwiches are a simple entree to serve at parties, showers or picnics.
—*Jaclyn Bell, Logan, UT*

- -

TAKES: 25 min. • **MAKES:** 4 servings

- 2 cups shredded cooked chicken breast
- 1 cup seedless red grapes, halved
- ½ cup chopped cashews
- 1 celery rib, chopped
- ⅓ cup grated Parmesan cheese
- 1 green onion, chopped
- ½ cup mayonnaise
- ⅓ cup buttermilk
- 2 tsp. lemon juice
- 1 tsp. dill weed
- 1 tsp. dried parsley flakes
- ¼ tsp. salt
- ¼ tsp. garlic powder
- ¼ tsp. pepper
- 4 croissants, split

In a small bowl, combine the first 6 ingredients. In another bowl, whisk mayonnaise, buttermilk, lemon juice and seasonings. Pour over chicken mixture; mix well. Spoon chicken salad onto croissant bottoms. Replace tops.
1 sandwich: 687 cal., 44g fat (13g sat. fat), 101mg chol., 881mg sod., 42g carb. (15g sugars, 3g fiber), 30g pro.

WHY YOU'LL LOVE IT...

"Yum! Loved the seasonings! It was a quick and easy way to make a delicious, special-occasion sandwich."
—KIMSPACC, TASTEOFHOME.COM

SWEET & TANGY BARBECUED CHICKEN

SWEET & TANGY BARBECUED CHICKEN

My family loves to grill in the summer, and this has become our hands-down favorite to share with friends. Every bite is full of flavor and the chicken is always tender and juicy.
—*Joy Yurk, Grafton, WI*

- -

PREP: 15 min. + marinating
GRILL: 30 min. • **MAKES:** 8 servings

2½	cups white wine
2	medium onions, finely chopped (1½ cups)
½	cup lemon juice
10	garlic cloves, minced
16	chicken drumsticks
3	bay leaves
1	can (15 oz.) tomato puree
¼	cup honey
1	Tbsp. molasses
1	tsp. salt
½	tsp. dried thyme
¼	tsp. cayenne pepper
¼	tsp. pepper
2	Tbsp. white vinegar

1. For marinade, in a large bowl, combine wine, onions, lemon juice and garlic. Pour 2 cups marinade into a large shallow dish. Add chicken; turn to coat. Cover and refrigerate 4 hours to overnight. Add bay leaves to remaining marinade; cover and refrigerate.

2. In a large saucepan, combine the tomato puree, honey, molasses, salt, thyme, cayenne, pepper and reserved marinade. Bring to a boil. Reduce heat; simmer, uncovered, 35-40 minutes or until liquid is reduced by half. Remove from heat. Remove bay leaves; stir in the vinegar. Reserve 1 cup sauce for serving; keep warm.

3. Drain chicken, discarding marinade in bag. Grill chicken, covered, on an oiled rack over indirect medium heat 15 minutes. Turn; grill 15-20 minutes longer or until a thermometer reads 170°-175°, brushing occasionally with remaining sauce. Serve chicken with reserved sauce.

2 drumsticks with 2 Tbsp. sauce: 334 cal., 12g fat (3g sat. fat), 95mg chol., 398mg sod., 18g carb. (13g sugars, 1g fiber), 30g pro.

MEXICAN CHICKEN
FAJITA PIZZA, PAGE 53

WEEKNIGHT *STAPLES*

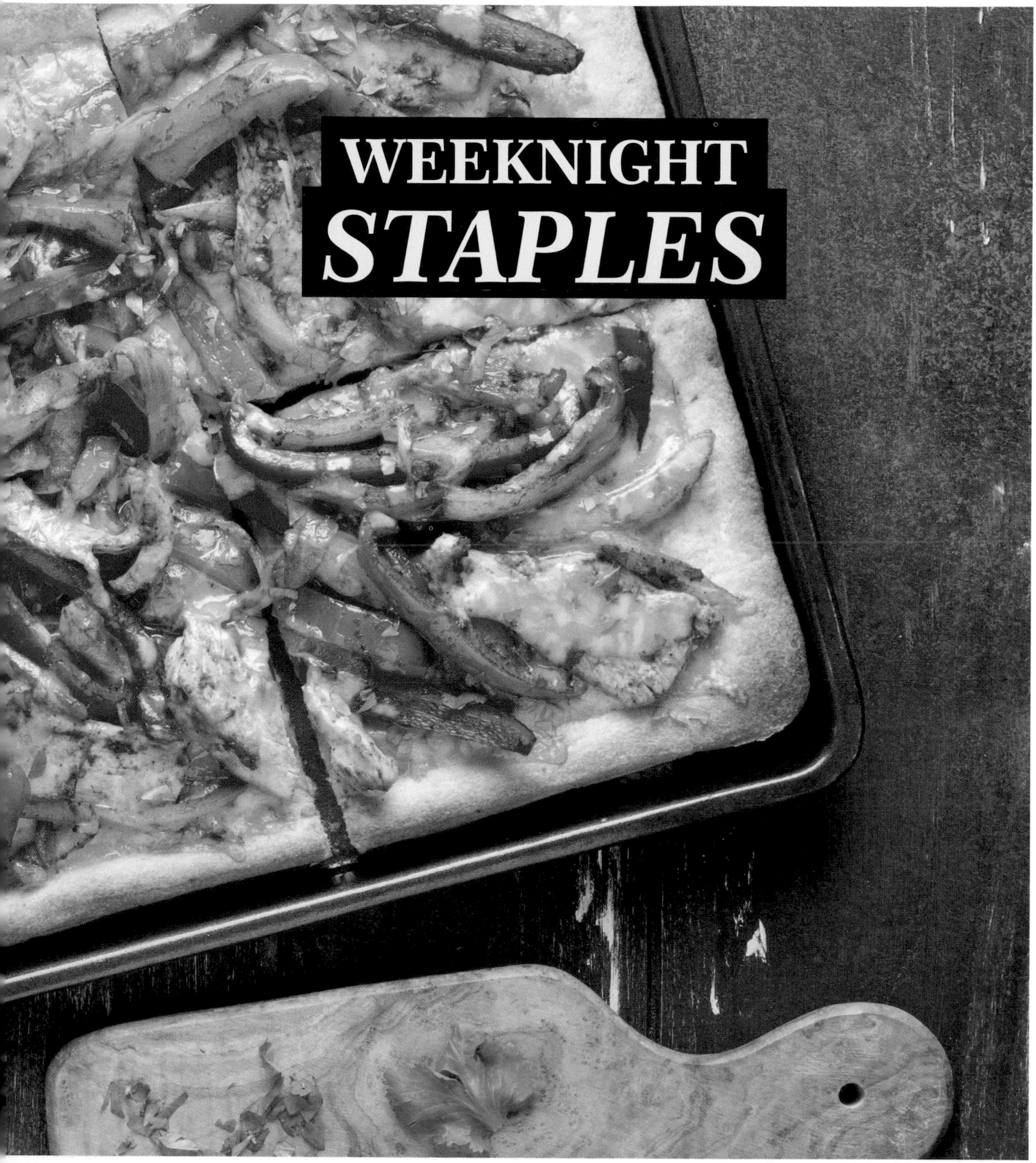

🕐 FETA-DILL CHICKEN BURGERS

I found fresh ground chicken at the butcher and gave it a whirl on our new grill. The result is these saucy burgers. Everybody went nuts—including my sister-in-law, an amazing cook!
—*Wendy Boughton, Victoria, BC*

TAKES: 25 min. • **MAKES:** 4 servings

- 1   large egg, lightly beaten
- 1   large shallot, minced
- 2   Tbsp. crushed Ritz crackers
- 2   Tbsp. minced fresh dill
- 3   garlic cloves, minced
- ¼   tsp. salt
- ¼   tsp. pepper
- 1   lb. ground chicken
- ½   cup finely crumbled feta cheese
- 2   Tbsp. canola oil
- 4   hamburger buns, split
      Optional: Refrigerated tzatziki sauce and sliced tomato

1. Combine first 7 ingredients. Add chicken; mix lightly but thoroughly. Gently stir in cheese.
2. Shape into four ½-in.-thick patties (mixture will be soft). Brush patties with oil. Grill, covered, over medium heat until a thermometer reads 165°, 5-6 minutes per side. Serve on buns. If desired, top with tzatziki sauce and sliced tomato.
1 burger: 414 cal., 22g fat (5g sat. fat), 129mg chol., 608mg sod., 27g carb. (4g sugars, 2g fiber), 27g pro.

🕐 🍎 CHICKEN STIR-FRY WITH NOODLES

A stir-fry on a cooking show caught my eye. I ran with the idea and loaded mine with veggies. Now it's our favorite hurry-up meal.
—*Beverly A. Norris, Evanston, WY*

TAKES: 30 min. • **MAKES:** 4 servings

- 8   oz. uncooked whole wheat spaghetti
- ½   head bok choy (about 1 lb.)
- 2   Tbsp. canola oil, divided
- 1   lb. boneless skinless chicken breasts, cubed
- 1   celery rib, sliced
- ½   cup coarsely chopped green pepper
- ½   cup coarsely chopped sweet red pepper
- ⅓   cup coarsely chopped onion
- 6   Tbsp. reduced-sodium teriyaki sauce

1. Cook spaghetti according to package directions; drain. Meanwhile, trim and discard root end of bok choy. Cut stalks into 1-in. pieces. Coarsely chop leaves.
2. In a large skillet, heat 1 Tbsp. oil over medium-high heat. Add chicken; stir-fry 5-7 minutes or until no longer pink. Remove from pan.
3. Stir-fry bok choy stalks, celery, peppers and onion in remaining oil 4 minutes. Add bok choy leaves; stir-fry 3-5 minutes longer or until leaves are tender. Stir in teriyaki sauce. Add the spaghetti and chicken; heat through, tossing to combine.
1½ cups: 434 cal., 11g fat (1g sat. fat), 63mg chol., 623mg sod., 53g carb. (10g sugars, 9g fiber), 35g pro.

🍎 BAKED LEMON CHICKEN

I found this recipe many years ago when my children were toddlers. I've changed it a little over the years to make it my own. Everyone in my family just loves it!
—*Aida Babbel, Bowen Island, BC*

PREP: 25 min. • **BAKE:** 25 min.
MAKES: 4 servings

- 3   Tbsp. all-purpose flour
- ¼   tsp. pepper
- 4   boneless skinless chicken breast halves (1½ lbs.)
- 2   Tbsp. vegetable oil
- 1   medium onion, chopped
- 1   Tbsp. butter
- 1   cup chicken broth
- 3   Tbsp. lemon juice
- 2   tsp. dried basil
- ½   tsp. dried thyme
- 4   lemon slices
- 2   Tbsp. minced fresh parsley
      Hot cooked rice, optional

1. In a shallow bowl, combine flour and pepper; dredge the chicken. Set remaining flour mixture aside. In a skillet, brown chicken in oil; transfer to an ungreased 9-in. square baking dish.
2. In a saucepan, saute onion in butter. Add reserved flour mixture; stir to form a thick paste. Gradually add broth, lemon juice, basil and thyme; mix well. Bring to boil; cook and stir for 2 minutes or until thickened and bubbly. Pour over the chicken. Top each half with a lemon slice. Sprinkle parsley. Cover and bake at 350° for 25-30 minutes or until the juices run clear. Serve over rice if desired.
1 chicken breast half: 312 cal., 14g fat (4g sat. fat), 103mg chol., 353mg sod., 9g carb. (2g sugars, 1g fiber), 36g pro.
Diabetic exchanges: 5 lean meat, ½ starch.

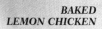

**SEE OUR
TEST
KITCHEN
MAKE IT**
Just hover your
camera here.

🕓 SPICY CHICKEN & BACON MAC

I've been working to perfect a creamy, spicy mac and cheese for years. After adding smoky bacon, chicken, jalapenos and spicy cheese, this is the ultimate! I use rotisserie chicken and precooked bacon when I'm pressed for time.
—*Sarah Gilbert, Beaverton, OR*

TAKES: 30 min. • **MAKES:** 6 servings

- 1½ cups uncooked cavatappi pasta or elbow macaroni
- 3 Tbsp. butter
- 3 Tbsp. all-purpose flour
- 1½ cups heavy whipping cream
- ½ cup 2% milk
- 1 tsp. Cajun seasoning
- ¼ tsp. salt
- ¼ tsp. pepper
- 2 cups shredded pepper jack cheese
- 2 cups shredded cooked chicken
- 6 bacon strips, cooked and crumbled
- 1 jalapeno pepper, seeded and chopped
- 1 cup crushed kettle-cooked potato chips or panko bread crumbs

1. Cook pasta according to package directions for al dente; drain. Preheat the broiler.
2. In a 10-in. cast-iron or other ovenproof skillet, heat the butter over medium heat. Stir in flour until blended; cook and stir until lightly browned, 1-2 minutes (do not burn). Gradually whisk in cream, milk, Cajun seasoning, salt and pepper. Bring to a boil, stirring constantly. Reduce heat; cook and stir until thickened, about 5 minutes. Stir in cheese until melted. Add pasta, chicken, bacon and jalapeno; cook and stir until heated through. Sprinkle chips over top.
3. Broil 3-4 in. from heat until chips are browned, about 30 seconds.

1 cup: 673 cal., 50g fat (28g sat. fat), 175mg chol., 705mg sod., 26g carb. (3g sugars, 1g fiber), 32g pro.

SPICY CHICKEN & BACON MAC

HERBED
BALSAMIC
CHICKEN

⏱ 🍎 HERBED BALSAMIC CHICKEN

Our kitchen is tiny and cramped, so we try to grill simple (but tasty) meals outside as often as possible during the summer months. Dried herbs work, but during the summer use fresh herbs for the best taste.
—*Kelly Evans, Denton, TX*

- -

TAKES: 30 min. • **MAKES:** 6 servings

½	cup balsamic vinegar
3	Tbsp. extra virgin olive oil
1	Tbsp. minced fresh basil
1	Tbsp. minced fresh chives
2	tsp. grated lemon zest
1	garlic clove, minced
¾	tsp. salt
¼	tsp. pepper
6	boneless skinless chicken thighs (1½ lbs.)

1. Whisk together all the ingredients except chicken. In a bowl, toss chicken with ⅓ cup vinegar mixture; let stand for 10 minutes.

2. Grill the chicken, covered, over medium heat or broil 4 in. from heat until a thermometer reads 170°, 6-8 minutes per side. Drizzle with remaining the vinegar mixture before serving.

1 chicken thigh with 2 tsp. sauce: 245 cal., 15g fat (3g sat. fat), 76mg chol., 358mg sod., 6g carb. (5g sugars, 0 fiber), 21g pro. **Diabetic exchanges:** 3 lean meat, 1½ fat.

🕐 BARBECUE CHICKEN QUESADILLAS

When my kids were small, I'd stuff leftover chicken into these oven-baked quesadillas.
—*Pam Martin, Canandaigua, NY*

TAKES: 25 min. • **MAKES:** 6 servings

- 3 cups shredded cooked chicken
- 1 can (4 oz.) chopped green chiles
- ½ cup salsa
- ⅓ cup barbecue sauce
- ¼ cup taco sauce
- 8 flour tortillas (8 in.)
- ¾ cup shredded sharp cheddar cheese
  Optional: Sour cream and additional salsa

1. Preheat oven to 450°. In a large bowl, toss together the first 5 ingredients.
2. Divide 4 tortillas between 2 baking sheets; spread with chicken mixture. Sprinkle with cheese; top with remaining tortillas.
3. Bake 6-8 minutes or until lightly browned and cheese is melted. Cut each quesadilla into 6 wedges. If desired, serve with sour cream and additional salsa.
4 wedges: 446 cal., 15g fat (5g sat. fat), 76mg chol., 815mg sod., 46g carb. (6g sugars, 3g fiber), 29g pro.

🕐 CHICKEN RANCH FLATBREADS

To get my son to try new things, I revamped this mini pizza. Mr. Picky ate it, so this is definitely family-friendly, even for those with fussy tastes.
—*Jenny Dubinsky, Inwood, WV*

TAKES: 25 min. • **MAKES:** 4 servings

- 4 whole wheat or white pita breads (6 in.)
- 2 cups chopped cooked chicken breast
- ¼ cup reduced-fat ranch salad dressing
- 2 plum tomatoes, thinly sliced
- 1 cup shredded part-skim mozzarella cheese
- 4 bacon strips, cooked and crumbled
- 1 tsp. dried oregano

1. Preheat oven to 400°. Place pita breads on a large baking sheet; bake 10-12 minutes or until lightly browned. Meanwhile, in a bowl, toss chicken with the dressing.
2. Top pitas with tomatoes and chicken mixture; sprinkle with the cheese, bacon and oregano. Bake 8-10 minutes or until cheese is melted.
1 pita pizza: 448 cal., 16g fat (6g sat. fat), 86mg chol., 888mg sod., 42g carb. (3g sugars, 5g fiber), 37g pro.

🕐 CRISPY ORANGE CHICKEN

These tangy nuggets go a long way. We eat them over noodles or rice, in sandwiches, and even on top of lettuce and cabbage.
—*Darlene Brenden, Salem, OR*

TAKES: 30 min. • **MAKES:** 4 servings

- 16 oz. frozen popcorn chicken (about 4 cups)
- 1 Tbsp. canola oil
- 2 medium carrots, thinly sliced
- 1 garlic clove, minced
- 1½ tsp. grated orange zest
- 1 cup orange juice
- ⅓ cup hoisin sauce
- 3 Tbsp. sugar
- ¼ tsp. salt
- ¼ tsp. pepper
  Dash cayenne pepper
  Hot cooked rice

1. Bake popcorn chicken according to package directions.
2. Meanwhile, in a large skillet, heat oil over medium-high heat. Add carrots; cook and stir until tender, 3-5 minutes. Add garlic; cook 1 minute longer. Stir in orange zest, juice, hoisin sauce, sugar and seasonings; bring to a boil. Reduce heat; simmer, uncovered, until thickened, 4-6 minutes, stirring constantly. Add chicken to pan; toss to coat. Serve with rice.
1 cup: 450 cal., 20g fat (3g sat. fat), 35mg chol., 1294mg sod., 56g carb. (25g sugars, 3g fiber), 14g pro.

BARBECUE CHICKEN QUESADILLAS

TEX-MEX CHICKEN STRIPS

TEX-MEX CHICKEN STRIPS

I was looking for a way to amp up the flavor of regular chicken strips, so I crushed up some leftover corn chips to create a crispy, flavorful coating.
—*Cyndy Gerken, Naples, FL*

TAKES: 30 min. • **MAKES:** 4 servings

- ½ cup finely crushed corn chips
- ¼ cup panko bread crumbs
- ¼ cup dry bread crumbs
- ¼ cup finely shredded Mexican cheese blend
- 5 tsp. taco seasoning
  Dash cayenne pepper
- ¼ cup butter, melted
- 1 lb. chicken tenderloins

1. Preheat oven to 400°. In a shallow bowl, mix the first 6 ingredients. Place butter in a separate shallow bowl. Dip chicken in butter, then roll in the crumb mixture to coat; press to adhere.
2. Place the chicken in a foil-lined 15x10x1-in. baking pan. Bake until a thermometer inserted into the chicken reads 165°, about 15 minutes, turning halfway through the cooking time.
3 oz. cooked chicken: 258 cal., 14g fat (7g sat. fat), 85mg chol., 351mg sod., 7g carb. (0 sugars, 0 fiber), 28g pro.

TEST KITCHEN TIP

This chicken would taste great chopped and served over taco salad. Also try these as dippers with salsa, guacamole, sour cream or ranch dressing.

⏱ 🍎 SPICY APRICOT-GLAZED CHICKEN

Looking for a new chicken idea? Skip the trip to the store and check the fridge first. I found chili sauce, mustard and apricot preserves for a sweet, hot flavor.
—*Sonya Labbe, West Hollywood, CA*

- -

TAKES: 20 min. • **MAKES:** 4 servings

- ⅓ cup apricot preserves
- ¼ cup chili sauce
- 1 Tbsp. hot mustard
- ¼ tsp. salt
- ⅛ tsp. pepper
- 4 boneless skinless chicken breast halves (4 oz. each)

1. Preheat broiler. In a small saucepan, combine the first 5 ingredients; cook and stir over medium heat until sauce is heated through.
2. Place chicken in 15x10x1-in. baking pan coated with cooking spray. Broil 3-4 in. from heat until a thermometer reads 165°, 6-8 minutes on each side. Brush occasionally with sauce during the last 5 minutes of cooking.
1 chicken breast half : 209 cal., 3g fat (1g sat. fat), 63mg chol., 476mg sod., 23g carb. (13g sugars, 0 fiber), 23g pro.

⏱ 🍎 CHORIZO SPAGHETTI SQUASH SKILLET

Get your noodle fix minus the pasta with this spicy one-dish meal. It's a fill-you-up dinner that's low in calories—which makes it a weeknight winner in my book!
—*Sherrill Oake, Springfield, MA*

- -

TAKES: 30 min. • **MAKES:** 4 servings

- 1 small spaghetti squash (about 2 lbs.)
- 1 Tbsp. canola oil
- 1 pkg. (12 oz.) fully cooked chorizo chicken sausage links or other sausage flavor of choice, sliced
- 1 medium sweet yellow pepper, chopped
- 1 medium sweet onion, halved and sliced
- 1 cup sliced fresh mushrooms
- 1 can (14½ oz.) no-salt-added diced tomatoes, undrained
- 1 Tbsp. reduced-sodium taco seasoning
- ¼ tsp. pepper
  Chopped green onions, optional

1. Halve squash lengthwise; discard seeds. Place squash on a microwave-safe plate, cut side down; microwave on high until tender, about 15 minutes. Cool slightly.
2. Meanwhile, in a large skillet, heat oil over medium-high heat; saute sausage, yellow pepper, onion and mushrooms until onion is tender, about 5 minutes.
3. Separate strands of squash with a fork; add to skillet. Stir in tomatoes and seasonings; bring to a boil. Reduce heat; simmer, uncovered, until the flavors are blended, about 5 minutes. If desired, top with green onions.
1½ cups: 299 cal., 12g fat (3g sat. fat), 65mg chol., 725mg sod., 34g carb. (12g sugars, 6g fiber), 18g pro. **Diabetic exchanges:** 2 starch, 2 lean meat, 1 vegetable, 1 fat.

CHORIZO SPAGHETTI SQUASH SKILLET

Chicken Sausage

Chicken sausages are readily available in most supermarkets. They come in a variety of favors, from classic Italian to apple-maple and chipotle-Monterey Jack cheese. Some chicken sausages are fresh (uncooked), while others are fully cooked. You might also find organic and natural sausages in your market. Chicken sausages generally have fewer calories and fat than pork sausages.

GARLIC CHICKEN WITH HERBS

🕐 🍎 GARLIC CHICKEN WITH HERBS

Pan-roasting garlic cloves transforms them into rich, creamy deliciousness. This chicken is fantastic with crusty Italian bread or mashed potatoes on the side.
—*Kathy Fleming, Lisle, IL*

- -

TAKES: 30 min. • **MAKES:** 4 servings

- 4 boneless skinless chicken thighs (about 1 lb.)
- ½ tsp. salt
- ¼ tsp. pepper
- 1 Tbsp. butter
- 10 garlic cloves, peeled and halved
- ¼ cup white wine or chicken broth
- 1½ tsp. minced fresh rosemary
- ½ tsp. minced fresh sage
- 1 cup chicken broth
   Hot cooked rice of your choice

1. Sprinkle chicken with salt and pepper. In a large skillet, heat the butter over medium-high heat; brown chicken on both sides. Remove from pan, reserving the drippings.
2. In same skillet, saute the garlic in drippings over medium-high heat until light golden brown. Add wine and herbs; bring to a boil, stirring to loosen the browned bits from pan. Cook until mixture is almost evaporated. Add broth and chicken; bring to a boil. Reduce heat; simmer, covered, until a thermometer inserted in chicken reads at least 170°, 10-12 minutes.
3. To serve, spoon pan juices over chicken. Serve with rice.
1 serving: 214 cal., 12g fat (3g sat. fat), 76mg chol., 487mg sod., 3g carb. (0 sugars, 0 fiber), 22g pro. **Diabetic exchanges:** 3 lean meat, ½ fat.

🕐 THAI SLOPPY JOE CHICKEN & WAFFLES

Since sloppy joes, chicken and waffles, and Thai food are all family favorites at my house, I decided to mix these three together and create a tasty dish. The crunchy slaw with Asian peanut dressing adds texture and flavor.
—*Arlene Erlbach, Morton Grove, IL*

- -

TAKES: 30 min. • **MAKES:** 6 servings

- ¼ cup creamy peanut butter
- ½ cup minced fresh cilantro, divided
- 6 Tbsp. teriyaki sauce, divided
- 3 Tbsp. chili sauce, divided
- 2 Tbsp. lime juice
- 2 cups coleslaw mix
- 1 lb. ground chicken
- ⅓ cup canned coconut milk
- 1 tsp. ground ginger
- ¾ tsp. garlic powder
- 6 frozen or homemade waffles
   Sliced green onions, optional

1. Place peanut butter, ¼ cup cilantro, 4 Tbsp. teriyaki sauce, 1 Tbsp. chili sauce and lime juice in a food processor; process until combined. Place coleslaw mix in a large bowl; add peanut butter mixture. Toss to coat; set aside.
2. In a large skillet, cook chicken over medium heat until no longer pink, 6-8 minutes, breaking it into crumbles; drain. Stir in coconut milk, ginger, garlic powder, remaining ¼ cup cilantro and 2 Tbsp. teriyaki sauce. Cook and stir until heated through.
3. Meanwhile, prepare waffles according to package directions. Top waffles with chicken mixture and coleslaw. If desired, sprinkle with green onions.
1 serving: 314 cal., 17g fat (5g sat. fat), 55mg chol., 1046mg sod., 24g carb. (7g sugars, 2g fiber), 18g pro.

THAI SLOPPY JOE
CHICKEN &
WAFFLES

MANGO SALSA CHICKEN WITH VEGGIE HASH

This hash has the fresh flavors of spring. Using precooked grilled chicken strips makes it come together quickly. And the veggies make the dish so pretty!
—Lori McLain, Denton, TX

- -

TAKES: 30 min. • **MAKES:** 4 servings

- 1 Tbsp. canola oil
- 2 cups chopped red potatoes (2-3 medium)
- 1 small sweet yellow pepper, chopped
- ½ cup chopped red onion
- 1½ cups cut fresh asparagus (1-in. pieces)
- 12 oz. frozen grilled chicken breast strips, partially thawed (about 2 cups)
- 1½ cups mango salsa, divided
- 1 Tbsp. chopped fresh cilantro Additional cilantro

1. In a large skillet, heat oil over medium-high heat; saute potatoes, pepper and onion until potatoes are lightly browned, 6-8 minutes. Add asparagus; cook and stir until potatoes are tender, 2-3 minutes. Stir in chicken, ¾ cup salsa and 1 Tbsp. cilantro; heat through, stirring occasionally.
2. Sprinkle with additional cilantro. Serve with remaining salsa.
1½ cups: 237 cal., 6g fat (1g sat. fat), 51mg chol., 1025mg sod., 20g carb. (3g sugars, 2g fiber), 24g pro.

TEST KITCHEN TIP
Red potatoes work well in hash because they hold their shape and add nice color. Leaving the skin on also adds fiber and saves prep time.

30-MINUTE COQ AU VIN

I love being able to fix a fancy gourmet dish in such a short amount of time and still have it turn out so delicious. To reduce fat, I use chicken tenderloin pieces or skinless chicken breasts.
—Judy VanCoetsem, Cortland, NY

- -

TAKES: 30 min. • **MAKES:** 6 servings

- ¼ cup all-purpose flour
- 1 tsp. dried thyme
- 1 tsp. salt, divided
- 6 boneless skinless chicken thighs (4 oz. each)
- 1 Tbsp. olive oil
- 6 cups quartered baby portobello mushrooms
- 2 cups sliced fresh carrots
- 3 pieces Canadian bacon, chopped
- 1 Tbsp. tomato paste
- 1 cup chicken broth
- 1 cup dry red wine Chopped fresh thyme, optional

1. In a shallow dish, combine flour, thyme and ½ tsp. salt. Dip chicken in flour mixture to coat both sides; shake off excess.
2. In a Dutch oven or high-sided skillet, heat oil over medium-high heat. Cook chicken until golden brown, 3-4 minutes per side. Remove from pan; keep warm.
3. In same pan, cook the mushrooms, carrots, bacon, tomato paste and the remaining ½ tsp. salt for 2 minutes. Add broth and wine; bring to a boil. Return chicken to pan; reduce heat. Cook until chicken reaches 170° and carrots are just tender, 8-10 minutes. If desired, top with chopped fresh thyme.
1 serving: 255 cal., 11g fat (3g sat. fat), 80mg chol., 648mg sod., 9g carb. (4g sugars, 2g fiber), 26g pro. **Diabetic exchanges:** 3 lean meat, ½ starch, ½ fat.

30-MINUTE COQ AU VIN

SAFELY HANDLE UNCOOKED CHICKEN
Just hover your camera here.

GARLICKY CHICKEN PIZZA

Tomatoes, olives and goat cheese really brighten up this white pizza. I like to cook extra chicken for this recipe while making another meal. Just make sure the tomatoes are well drained to make sure the crust stays nice and crispy.
—Teri Otte, Cannon Falls, MN

TAKES: 25 min. • **MAKES:** 6 servings

- 1 tube (13.8 oz.) refrigerated pizza crust
- 2 Tbsp. olive oil
- 2 garlic cloves, minced
- 1 can (14½ oz.) diced tomatoes, well drained
- 1 large onion, thinly sliced (about 1 cup)
- ⅓ cup pitted kalamata olives, halved
- 2 cups cubed or shredded cooked chicken
- 1⅓ cups crumbled goat cheese
- 1 tsp. minced fresh rosemary or ¼ tsp. dried rosemary, crushed
- ½ tsp. garlic salt
- ½ tsp. pepper

1. Preheat oven to 400°. Unroll and press dough onto bottom and ½ in. up sides of a greased 15x10x1-in. baking pan. Bake 8-10 minutes or until edges are lightly browned.
2. Mix oil and garlic; brush over crust. Top with the tomatoes, onion, olives, chicken and goat cheese. Sprinkle with the rosemary, garlic salt and pepper. Bake 10-12 minutes or until crust is golden.
1 piece: 418 cal., 19g fat (6g sat. fat), 73mg chol., 957mg sod., 39g carb. (7g sugars, 3g fiber), 25g pro.

CHICKEN & RED POTATOES

CHICKEN & RED POTATOES

Try this juicy and tender chicken-and-potato dish—with scrumptious gravy—tonight! Just fix it earlier in the day, then forget about it until mealtime.
—Michele Trantham, Waynesville, NC

PREP: 20 min. • **COOK:** 3½ hours
MAKES: 4 servings

- 3 Tbsp. all-purpose flour
- 4 boneless skinless chicken breast halves (6 oz. each)
- 2 Tbsp. olive oil
- 4 medium red potatoes, cut into wedges
- 2 cups fresh baby carrots, halved lengthwise
- 1 can (4 oz.) mushroom stems and pieces, drained
- 4 canned whole green chiles, cut into ½-in. slices
- 1 can (10¾ oz.) condensed cream of onion soup, undiluted
- ¼ cup 2% milk
- ½ tsp. chicken seasoning
- ¼ tsp. salt
- ¼ tsp. dried rosemary, crushed
- ¼ tsp. pepper

1. Place flour in a large bowl or dish. Add chicken, 1 piece at a time; toss to coat. In a large skillet, brown chicken in oil on both sides.
2. Meanwhile, place the potatoes, carrots, mushrooms and chiles in a greased 5-qt. slow cooker. In a small bowl, combine the remaining ingredients. Pour half of soup mixture over vegetables.
3. Transfer chicken to slow cooker; top with remaining soup mixture. Cover and cook on low for 3½-4 hours or until a thermometer reads 170°.
1 chicken breast half with 1½ cups vegetables: 451 cal., 15g fat (3g sat. fat), 105mg chol., 1046mg sod., 38g carb. (8g sugars, 4g fiber), 40g pro.

⏱ 🍎 GRILLED BROWN SUGAR-MUSTARD CHICKEN

I came up with this recipe in college and it's been a household staple ever since. It's a snap to throw together with ingredients I have on hand.
—*Kendra Doss, Colorado Springs, CO*

TAKES: 20 min. • **MAKES:** 8 servings

- ½ cup yellow or Dijon mustard
- ⅓ cup packed brown sugar
- ½ tsp. ground allspice
- ¼ tsp. crushed red pepper flakes
- 8 boneless skinless chicken thighs (about 2 lbs.)

1. In a large bowl, mix the mustard, brown sugar, allspice and pepper flakes. Remove ¼ cup mixture for serving. Add chicken to remaining mixture; toss to coat.

2. Grill chicken, covered, over medium heat or broil 4 in. from heat 6-8 minutes on each side or until a thermometer reads 170°. Serve with reserved mustard mixture.

1 chicken thigh with 1½ tsp. mustard mixture: 224 cal., 9g fat (2g sat. fat), 76mg chol., 597mg sod., 13g carb. (9g sugars, 1g fiber), 22g pro. **Diabetic exchanges:** 3 lean meat, 1 starch.

⏱ COUNTRY CHICKEN WITH GRAVY

Here's a lightened-up take on classic southern comfort food. It's been a hit at our house since the first time we tried it!
—*Ruth Helmuth, Abbeville, SC*

TAKES: 30 min. • **MAKES:** 4 servings

- ¾ cup crushed cornflakes
- ½ tsp. poultry seasoning
- ½ tsp. paprika
- ¼ tsp. salt
- ¼ tsp. dried thyme
- ¼ tsp. pepper
- 2 Tbsp. fat-free evaporated milk
- 4 boneless skinless chicken breast halves (4 oz. each)
- 2 tsp. canola oil

GRAVY
- 1 Tbsp. butter
- 1 Tbsp. all-purpose flour
- ¼ tsp. pepper
- ⅛ tsp. salt
- ½ cup fat-free evaporated milk
- ¼ cup condensed chicken broth, undiluted
- 1 tsp. sherry or additional condensed chicken broth
- 2 Tbsp. minced chives

1. In a shallow bowl, combine the first 6 ingredients. Place milk in another shallow bowl. Dip chicken in milk, then roll in cornflake mixture.

2. In a large nonstick skillet, cook the chicken in oil over medium heat until a thermometer reads 170°, 6-8 minutes on each side.

3. Meanwhile, in a small saucepan, melt butter. Stir in the flour, pepper and salt until smooth. Gradually stir in the milk, broth and sherry. Bring to a boil; cook and stir until thickened, 1-2 minutes. Stir in chives. Serve with chicken.

1 chicken breast half with 2 Tbsp. gravy: 274 cal., 8g fat (3g sat. fat), 72mg chol., 569mg sod., 20g carb. (6g sugars, 0 fiber), 28g pro. **Diabetic exchanges:** 3 lean meat, 1 starch, ½ fat.

WATCH THE 2-MINUTE VERSION
Just hover your camera here.

⏱ APPLE-MUSTARD CHICKEN TENDERS

My husband says this dish is sweet and a little bit sassy, just like me. I like to use Granny Smith apples for a bit of tartness. Winesaps are great for this recipe, too.
—*Linda Cifuentes, Mahomet, IL*

TAKES: 30 min. • **MAKES:** 6 servings

- 1½ **lbs. chicken tenderloins**
- ½ **tsp. salt**
- ¼ **tsp. pepper**
- 3 **Tbsp. butter**
- 2 **small Granny Smith apples, thinly sliced**
- ½ **cup packed brown sugar**
- ¼ **cup stone-ground mustard**

1. Sprinkle chicken with salt and pepper. In a large skillet, heat the butter over medium heat. Add the chicken; cook 4-6 minutes on each side or until no longer pink. Remove from pan.
2. Add apples, brown sugar and mustard to the same pan; toss to combine. Cook, covered, over medium heat 3-4 minutes or until the apples are tender. Stir in chicken; heat through.

1 serving: 263 cal., 8g fat (4g sat. fat), 71mg chol., 519mg sod., 24g carb. (22g sugars, 1g fiber), 27g pro.

COUNTRY CHICKEN WITH GRAVY

🍎🍲 CHICKEN MERLOT WITH MUSHROOMS

A dear friend who liked cooking as much as I do shared this recipe with me, and I think of her every time I make it. Friends and family love it and request it often.
—*Shelli McWilliam, Salem, OR*

PREP: 15 min. • **COOK:** 5 hours
MAKES: 8 servings

- ¾ lb. sliced fresh mushrooms
- 1 large onion, chopped
- 2 garlic cloves, minced
- 3 lbs. boneless skinless chicken thighs
- 1 can (6 oz.) tomato paste
- ¾ cup chicken broth
- ¼ cup merlot or additional chicken broth
- 2 Tbsp. quick-cooking tapioca
- 2 tsp. sugar
- 1½ tsp. dried basil
- ½ tsp. salt
- ¼ tsp. pepper
- 2 Tbsp. grated Parmesan cheese
  Hot cooked pasta, optional

1. Place the mushrooms, onion and garlic in a 5-qt. slow cooker. Top with chicken thighs.
2. In a small bowl, combine the tomato paste, broth, wine, tapioca, sugar, basil, salt and pepper. Pour over chicken. Cover and cook on low for 5-6 hours or until chicken is tender.
3. Sprinkle with cheese. Serve with pasta if desired.
Freeze option: Freeze cooled chicken mixture in freezer containers. To use, partially thaw in refrigerator overnight. Heat through in a saucepan, stirring occasionally; add broth or water if necessary.
5 oz. cooked chicken with ½ cup sauce: 310 cal., 13g fat (4g sat. fat), 115mg chol., 373mg sod., 11g carb. (5g sugars, 1g fiber), 35g pro. **Diabetic exchanges:** 5 lean meat, ½ starch.

CHICKEN MERLOT WITH MUSHROOMS

⏱ 🍎 SNAPPY CHICKEN STIR-FRY

Don't just reheat leftover chicken—stir-fry it up with some frozen veggies (the ones you have hiding in your freezer). In no time, you have a great weeknight meal. We don't call this recipe snappy for nothing.
—Taste of Home *Test Kitchen*

- -

TAKES: 30 min. • **MAKES:** 4 servings

- 3 Tbsp. cornstarch
- 1½ cups reduced-sodium chicken broth
- 3 Tbsp. reduced-sodium soy sauce
- ¾ tsp. garlic powder
- ¾ tsp. ground ginger
- ¼ tsp. crushed red pepper flakes
- 1 pkg. (16 oz.) frozen sugar snap stir-fry vegetable blend
- 1 Tbsp. sesame or canola oil
- 2 cups cubed cooked chicken breast
- 2 cups hot cooked brown rice
- ¼ cup sliced almonds, toasted

1. In a small bowl, combine the cornstarch, broth, soy sauce, garlic powder, ginger and pepper flakes; set aside.
2. In a large skillet or wok, stir-fry vegetable blend in oil for 5-7 minutes or until vegetables are tender.
3. Stir cornstarch mixture and add to the pan. Bring to a boil; cook and stir for 2 minutes or until thickened. Add chicken; heat through. Serve with rice; sprinkle with almonds.

1 cup chicken mixture with ½ cup rice and 1 Tbsp. almonds: 382 cal., 10g fat (2g sat. fat), 54mg chol., 723mg sod., 43g carb. (6g sugars, 5g fiber), 28g pro. **Diabetic exchanges:** 3 lean meat, 2½ starch, 1 fat.

**SWEET CHILI &
ORANGE CHICKEN**

⏱ SWEET CHILI & ORANGE CHICKEN

My husband loves this simple chicken dish so much he often requests it when he comes home from deployment. The sweet chili sauce adds just the right amount of heat to the bright citrusy sauce.
—*Jessica Eastman, Bremerton, WA*

- -

TAKES: 20 min. • **MAKES:** 4 servings

- 1 lb. boneless skinless chicken breasts, cut into 1-in. pieces
- ¼ tsp. salt
- ¼ tsp. pepper
- 2 Tbsp. butter
- ¾ cup sweet chili sauce
- ⅓ cup thawed orange juice concentrate
  Hot cooked jasmine or other rice
  Minced fresh basil

1. Toss chicken with salt and pepper. In a large skillet, heat butter over medium-high heat; stir-fry the chicken until no longer pink, 5-7 minutes. Remove from pan; keep warm.
2. Add chili sauce and juice concentrate to the skillet; cook and stir until heated through. Stir in chicken. Serve with rice; sprinkle with basil.

½ cup chicken mixture: 309 cal., 9g fat (4g sat. fat), 78mg chol., 1014mg sod., 33g carb. (31g sugars, 1g fiber), 24g pro.

WHY YOU'LL LOVE IT...

"Great recipe! So easy and tasty! Will add in some broccoli or snow peas next time."
—CROMYAK, TASTEOFHOME.COM

CHICKEN
CHILES RELLENOS
ALFREDO

🕐 CHICKEN CHILES RELLENOS ALFREDO

This recipe combines my daughter's love of chiles rellenos and my love of chicken Alfredo! To cut down on the spice level you could substitute Monterey Jack cheese for the pepper jack.
—*Jennifer Stowell, Deep River, IA*

TAKES: 30 min. • **MAKES:** 8 servings

- 1 pkg. (16 oz.) angel hair pasta
- 1½ to 2 lbs. boneless skinless chicken breasts, cubed
- 1 Tbsp. garlic powder
- 1 Tbsp. dried cilantro
- 1 tsp. ground cumin
- ½ cup butter
- 2 cups heavy whipping cream
- ½ cup cream cheese, softened
- 1½ tsp. grated lime zest
- ½ cup pepper jack cheese
- 2 cans (4 oz. each) chopped green chiles
- 2 Tbsp. lime juice

1. Cook angel hair according to package directions. Drain.
2. Meanwhile, sprinkle chicken with garlic powder, cilantro and cumin. In a large nonstick skillet, cook and stir chicken over medium heat until no longer pink, 6-8 minutes. Remove.
3. In same skillet, melt butter. Stir in heavy cream, cream cheese and lime zest until combined, 4-6 minutes. Stir in pepper jack until melted. Add chiles and lime juice. Return chicken to skillet; heat through. Toss chicken mixture with pasta.
1 cup: 698 cal., 43g fat (26g sat. fat), 167mg chol., 354mg sod., 48g carb. (4g sugars, 3g fiber), 30g pro.

LEMON & ROSEMARY CHICKEN

🕐 LEMON & ROSEMARY CHICKEN

This baked chicken with a tangy lemon and rosemary sauce is my husband's favorite, and my sister always wants it for her birthday dinner.
—*Laurel Dalzell, Manteca, CA*

TAKES: 30 min. • **MAKES:** 4 servings

- 4 boneless skinless chicken breast halves (4 oz. each)
- ¼ tsp. salt
- ¼ tsp. pepper
- 2 tsp. canola oil
- 1 shallot, finely chopped
- 1 Tbsp. minced fresh rosemary or 1 tsp. dried rosemary, crushed
- ½ cup reduced-sodium chicken broth
- 2 tsp. grated lemon zest
- 4½ tsp. lemon juice
- ¼ cup cold butter

1. Preheat oven to 400°. Sprinkle the chicken with salt and pepper. In a large cast-iron or other heavy skillet, heat oil over medium heat; brown chicken on both sides. Transfer chicken to a 15x10x1-in. baking pan; reserve the drippings. Bake chicken, uncovered, until a thermometer reads 165°, 8-10 minutes.
2. Meanwhile, in same skillet, cook and stir shallot and rosemary in drippings until tender. Stir in broth. Bring to a boil; cook until the liquid is reduced by half. Reduce heat to low; stir in lemon zest and juice. Whisk in butter, 1 Tbsp. at a time, until creamy. Serve with chicken.
1 chicken breast half with 1 Tbsp. sauce: 252 cal., 16g fat (8g sat. fat), 93mg chol., 355mg sod., 2g carb. (0 sugars, 0 fiber), 24g pro.

🕐 QUICK SESAME CHICKEN NOODLES

I love playing around with different ingredients and spices in my stir-fry recipes. As my children get older, I have more evenings when I need to whip up dinner quickly, and this easy dish with chicken strips and ramen is perfect.
—*Heather Chambers, Largo, FL*

TAKES: 25 min. • **MAKES:** 4 servings

- 1 Tbsp. sesame oil
- 1 pkg. (22 oz.) frozen grilled chicken breast strips
- 1 medium yellow summer squash, thinly sliced
- 1 cup julienned carrots
- ⅓ cup halved fresh snow peas
- 3 garlic cloves, minced
- 2 pkg. (3 oz. each) chicken ramen noodles, broken into small pieces
- 1⅓ cups water
- ⅓ cup white wine or chicken broth
- 3 Tbsp. reduced-sodium teriyaki sauce
- 4 green onions, sliced

1. In a large skillet, heat oil over medium-high heat; saute chicken, squash and carrots until chicken is heated through, 6-8 minutes. Add snow peas; cook until vegetables are crisp-tender, 3-4 minutes. Add garlic and contents of 1 ramen seasoning packet (discard or save second packet for another use); cook and stir 1 minute.
2. Add noodles, water, wine and teriyaki sauce. Bring to a boil; cook, uncovered, until noodles are tender, 3-4 minutes, stirring occasionally.
3. Remove from heat; stir in green onions. Serve immediately.
1½ cups: 460 cal., 15g fat (5g sat. fat), 93mg chol., 1626mg sod., 37g carb. (6g sugars, 3g fiber), 45g pro.

MEXICAN CHICKEN FAJITA PIZZA

🕐 🍎 MEXICAN CHICKEN FAJITA PIZZA

Chicken fajita pizza has always been a hit with my children. And it's such a great way to sneak in some extra vegetables.
—*Carrie Shaub, Mount Joy, PA*

TAKES: 30 min. • **MAKES:** 6 servings

- 1 pkg. (13.8 oz.) refrigerated pizza crust
- 8 oz. boneless skinless chicken breasts, cut into thin strips
- 1 tsp. canola oil, divided
- 1 medium onion, sliced
- 1 medium sweet red pepper, sliced
- 1 medium green pepper, sliced
- 1 tsp. chili powder
- ½ tsp. ground cumin
- 1 garlic clove, minced
- ¼ cup chunky salsa
- 2 cups shredded reduced-fat Mexican cheese blend
- 1 Tbsp. minced fresh cilantro Optional: Sour cream and additional salsa

1. Unroll dough in a 15x10x1-in. baking pan coated with cooking spray; flatten dough and build up edges slightly. Bake at 425° for 8-10 minutes or until edges are lightly browned.
2. Meanwhile, in a large skillet coated with cooking spray, cook the chicken strips over medium heat in ½ tsp. oil for 4-6 minutes or until no longer pink; remove and keep warm.
3. In the same pan, saute the onion, peppers, chili powder and cumin in remaining oil until crisp-tender. Add garlic; cook 1 minute longer. Stir in salsa and chicken.
4. Sprinkle half of the cheese over a prepared crust; top with the chicken mixture and remaining cheese. Bake for 8-10 minutes or until crust is golden brown and cheese is melted. Sprinkle with cilantro. Serve with sour cream and additional salsa if desired.

1 piece: 351 cal., 12g fat (4g sat. fat), 48mg chol., 767mg sod., 38g carb. (7g sugars, 2g fiber), 25g pro. **Diabetic exchanges:** 3 lean meat, 2 starch, 1 vegetable, ½ fat.

🕐 🍎 BALSAMIC CHICKEN FETTUCCINE

Skip the marinara and serve noodles an elegant new way. Not only is our easy balsamic-infused entree a meal in itself, it's a tasty twist on an Italian classic.
—Taste of Home *Test Kitchen*

TAKES: 25 min. • **MAKES:** 5 servings

- 8 oz. uncooked fettuccine
- 1½ lbs. boneless skinless chicken breasts, cut into strips
- 2 Tbsp. plus ½ cup balsamic vinaigrette, divided
- ½ lb. sliced fresh mushrooms
- 1 medium red onion, chopped
- 2 cans (14½ oz. each) diced tomatoes, undrained
- 2 cups frozen broccoli florets
- ½ tsp. Italian seasoning

1. Cook fettuccine according to package directions. Meanwhile, in a large skillet, saute chicken in 1 Tbsp. vinaigrette until no longer pink. Remove and keep warm.
2. In the same skillet, saute mushrooms and onion in 1 Tbsp. vinaigrette until tender. Add the tomatoes, broccoli, Italian seasoning and the remaining vinaigrette; cook 5-6 minutes longer or until heated through.
3. Drain fettuccine. Add fettuccine and chicken to skillet and toss to coat.

1½ cups: 427 cal., 9g fat (2g sat. fat), 75mg chol., 705mg sod., 47g carb. (11g sugars, 6g fiber), 37g pro.

🕐 🍎 CREAMY DIJON CHICKEN

You'll save both time and money with this chicken dish. It makes a nice sauce that works well over brown rice or wide noodles. If you want extra sauce for leftovers, double the recipe.
—*Irene Boffo, Fountain Hills, AZ*

- -

TAKES: 25 min. • **MAKES:** 4 servings

- ½ cup half-and-half cream
- ¼ cup Dijon mustard
- 1 Tbsp. brown sugar
- 4 boneless skinless chicken breast halves (6 oz. each)
- ¼ tsp. salt
- ¼ tsp. pepper
- 2 tsp. olive oil
- 2 tsp. butter
- 1 small onion, halved and very thinly sliced
  Minced fresh parsley

1. Whisk together cream, mustard and brown sugar. Pound chicken breasts with a meat mallet to even thickness; sprinkle with salt and pepper.
2. In a large skillet, heat oil and butter over medium-high heat; brown chicken on both sides. Reduce heat to medium. Add onion and cream mixture; bring to a boil. Reduce heat; simmer, covered, until a thermometer inserted in chicken reads 165°, 10-12 minutes. Sprinkle with parsley.
1 chicken breast half with 3 Tbsp. sauce: 295 cal., 11g fat (5g sat. fat), 114mg chol., 621mg sod., 6g carb. (5g sugars, 0 fiber), 36g pro. **Diabetic exchanges:** 5 lean meat, 1 fat, ½ starch.

WHY YOU'LL LOVE IT...

"Delicious! I followed the recipe exactly as written, except I used a bit more onion. There was plenty of sauce, but it was so good I will double it next time."
—ELAINE, TASTEOFHOME.COM

BARBECUE CHICKEN TOSTADAS

🕐 BARBECUE CHICKEN TOSTADAS

Lots of my recipes (just like this one!) start out as fun ways to use leftovers. My kids love tostadas, so this day-after-cookout dinner was a big hit.
—*Lauren Wyler, Dripping Springs, TX*

- -

TAKES: 30 min. • **MAKES:** 4 servings

- 2 Tbsp. lemon juice
- 2 Tbsp. mayonnaise
- 1 Tbsp. light brown sugar
- ⅛ tsp. pepper
- 2 cups coleslaw mix
- 2 green onions, thinly sliced
- 1 cup baked beans
- 2⅔ cups shredded cooked chicken
- ⅔ cup barbecue sauce
- 8 tostada shells
- 1 cup shredded smoked cheddar cheese

1. Preheat broiler. Mix first 4 ingredients and toss with coleslaw mix and green onions. Refrigerate until serving.
2. Place beans in a small saucepan; mash with a potato masher until smooth. Cook over low heat until heated through, about 10 minutes, stirring frequently.
3. Meanwhile, in another saucepan, mix chicken and barbecue sauce; cook over medium-low heat until heated through, about 10 minutes, stirring occasionally.
4. To assemble, place tostada shells on ungreased baking sheets. Spread with beans; top with chicken mixture and cheese. Broil 3-4 in. from heat until tostada shells are lightly browned and cheese is melted, 1-2 minutes. Top with slaw. Serve immediately.
2 tostadas: 612 cal., 29g fat (10g sat. fat), 116mg chol., 1113mg sod., 51g carb. (21g sugars, 6g fiber), 39g pro.

SUE'S SPICY TOMATO BASIL TORTELLINI

A friend remarked about a baked tortellini dish at a restaurant, so I tried making it for her. My version makes it weeknight easy.
—*Cyndy Gerken, Naples, FL*

TAKES: 30 min. • **MAKES:** 8 servings

- 1 pkg. (19 oz.) frozen cheese tortellini
- 2 Tbsp. olive oil, divided
- 1 lb. boneless skinless chicken breasts, cut into 1-in. cubes
- 2 tsp. Italian seasoning, divided
- ½ tsp. salt
- ¼ tsp. pepper
- 1 large onion, chopped
- 1 habanero pepper, seeded and finely chopped
- 3 garlic cloves, minced
- 1 can (14½ oz.) fire-roasted diced tomatoes, drained
- 2 cups heavy whipping cream
- ½ cup shredded Italian cheese blend
- ⅓ cup chopped fresh basil

1. Cook pasta according to package directions; drain.

2. Meanwhile, heat 1 Tbsp. oil in a Dutch oven over medium-high heat. Add chicken, 1 tsp. Italian seasoning, salt and pepper; saute until meat is no longer pink, about 5 minutes. Remove from pan.

3. In the same pan, add onion, habanero pepper, garlic and the remaining Italian seasoning and oil; reduce the heat to medium. Cook and stir until onion is tender, about 5 minutes. Add tomatoes; cook and stir until slightly thickened, about 2 minutes. Stir in cream; bring to a boil. Add tortellini, chicken and cheese; heat through. Top with basil to serve.

Note: Wear disposable gloves when cutting hot peppers; the oils can burn skin. Avoid touching your face.

1¼ cups: 488 cal., 31g fat (17g sat. fat), 126mg chol., 575mg sod., 30g carb. (5g sugars, 2g fiber), 22g pro.

EASY CHICKEN & WAFFLES

My first experience with chicken and waffles sent my taste buds into orbit. I first made the dish as appetizers, but we all love it as a main course, too.
—*Lisa Renshaw, Kansas City, MO*

TAKES: 25 min. • **MAKES:** 4 servings

- 12 frozen crispy chicken strips (about 18 oz.)
- ½ cup honey
- 2 tsp. hot pepper sauce
- 8 frozen waffles, toasted

1. Bake chicken strips according to package directions. Meanwhile, in a small bowl, mix honey and pepper sauce.

2. Cut chicken into bite-sized pieces; serve on waffles. Drizzle with the honey mixture.

1 serving: 643 cal., 22g fat (3g sat. fat), 32mg chol., 958mg sod., 93g carb. (39g sugars, 6g fiber), 21g pro.

SUE'S SPICY TOMATO BASIL TORTELLINI

STARTERS
& SNACKS

STICKY HONEY CHICKEN
WINGS, PAGE 63

⏱ BUFFALO CHICKEN DIP

Buffalo wing sauce, cream cheese and ranch or blue cheese dressing make a lively party dip. Everywhere I take it, people want the recipe.
—*Belinda J. Gibson, Dry Ridge, KY*

- -

TAKES: 30 min. • **MAKES:** about 2 cups

- 1 pkg. (8 oz.) cream cheese, softened
- 1 cup chopped cooked chicken breast
- ½ cup Buffalo wing sauce
- ½ cup ranch or blue cheese salad dressing
- 2 cups shredded Colby-Monterey Jack cheese
   French bread baguette slices, celery ribs or tortilla chips

1. Preheat oven to 350°. Spread cream cheese into an ungreased shallow 1-qt. baking dish. Layer with chicken, wing sauce and salad dressing. Sprinkle with cheese.

2. Bake, uncovered, until cheese is melted, 20-25 minutes. Serve with baguette slices.

2 Tbsp.: 152 cal., 13g fat (7g sat. fat), 36mg chol., 409mg sod., 2g carb. (1g sugars, 0 fiber), 7g pro.

WHY YOU'LL LOVE IT...

"This recipe is so easy to make and so delicious to eat. During football season, this is the ultimate recipe to share with friends and family. It's a keeper for sure."
—HANNAH658, TASTEOFHOME.COM

FOLLOW OUR LEAD WHEN MAKING THIS DIP
Just hover your camera here.

BUFFALO CHICKEN DIP

FRUITY CHICKEN SALAD MINI SANDWICHES

🕐 FRUITY CHICKEN SALAD MINI SANDWICHES

Chicken salad ranks among the classics, and this version is great for parties of all kinds. Feel free to substitute green grapes for the red, or toss in extra strawberries when they're in season. The filling can also be served on a bed of salad greens.
—*Marcy Kamery, Blasdell, NY*

- -

TAKES: 25 min. • **MAKES:** 12 servings

- 6   cups chopped cooked chicken
- ¾   cup sliced fresh strawberries
- ½   cup halved seedless red grapes
- 2   celery ribs, finely chopped
- ⅓   cup chopped pecans, toasted
- ¾   cup sour cream
- ¾   cup mayonnaise
- ⅓   cup chopped fresh basil
- 2   tsp. lemon juice
- ¾   tsp. salt
- ¼   tsp. garlic powder
- ¼   tsp. pepper
- 24   potato dinner rolls or Hawaiian sweet rolls, split

1. Place first 5 ingredients in a large bowl. In a small bowl, mix sour cream, mayonnaise, basil, lemon juice and seasonings; stir into chicken mixture. Refrigerate, covered, until serving.

2. To serve, fill each roll with ⅓ cup chicken mixture.

Note: To toast nuts, bake in a shallow pan in a 350 oven for 5-10 minutes or cook in a skillet over low heat until lightly browned, stirring occasionally.

2 sandwiches: 524 cal., 23g fat (5g sat. fat), 67mg chol., 669mg sod., 49g carb. (8g sugars, 3g fiber), 29g pro.

BUFFALO CHICKEN DEVILED EGGS

My daughter Sara loves spicy Buffalo chicken and deviled eggs, so I combined the two. Make and chill a day ahead so the flavors mingle.
—*Robin Spires, Tampa, FL*

PREP: 25 min. + chilling • **MAKES:** 2 dozen

12 hard-boiled large eggs
½ cup crumbled blue cheese, divided
2 celery ribs, finely chopped
½ cup mayonnaise
¼ cup finely chopped cooked chicken breast
3 Tbsp. minced fresh parsley
1 Tbsp. Buffalo wing sauce or 1 tsp. hot pepper sauce
⅛ tsp. pepper
Optional: Additional Buffalo wing or hot pepper sauce

1. Cut eggs lengthwise in half. Remove yolks, reserving whites. In a bowl, mash yolks and ¼ cup cheese. Stir in celery, mayonnaise, chicken, parsley, wing sauce and pepper.
2. Spoon into egg whites. Refrigerate, covered, at least 1 hour before serving. To serve, sprinkle tops with remaining cheese and, if desired, drizzle with additional wing sauce.
1 stuffed egg half: 85 cal., 7g fat (2g sat. fat), 98mg chol., 111mg sod., 1g carb. (0 sugars, 0 fiber), 4g pro.

LAYERED ASIAN DIP

🍎 LAYERED ASIAN DIP

Guests at gatherings we host are quick to dig into this delectable dip. With tender chunks of chicken and Asian seasoning, it's a nice switch from traditional taco dip.
—*Bonnie Mazur, Reedsburg, WI*

PREP: 20 min. + chilling
MAKES: 20 servings

1 cup chopped cooked chicken breast
½ cup shredded carrot
¼ cup chopped unsalted peanuts
3 Tbsp. chopped green onions
1 Tbsp. minced fresh parsley
1 tsp. toasted sesame seeds
3 Tbsp. reduced-sodium soy sauce, divided
1 garlic clove, minced
1½ tsp. cornstarch
½ cup water
2 Tbsp. brown sugar
2 Tbsp. ketchup
1½ tsp. Worcestershire sauce
½ tsp. cider vinegar
2 drops hot pepper sauce
1 pkg. (8 oz.) reduced-fat cream cheese
Assorted rice crackers

1. In a bowl, combine first 6 ingredients. Mix 2 Tbsp. soy sauce and garlic; toss with the chicken mixture. Refrigerate, covered, several hours.
2. For sauce, in a small saucepan, mix cornstarch and water until smooth; stir in brown sugar, ketchup, Worcestershire sauce, vinegar and pepper sauce. Bring to a boil; cook and stir until thickened, 1-2 minutes. Cool slightly. Refrigerate, covered, until cold.
3. To serve, mix cream cheese and remaining soy sauce until blended; transfer to a serving plate, spreading evenly. Top with the chicken mixture. Drizzle with sauce. Serve with crackers.
1 serving: 61 cal., 4g fat (2g sat. fat), 13mg chol., 165mg sod., 3g carb. (2g sugars, 0 fiber), 4g pro. **Diabetic exchanges:** 1 fat.

MARGARITA CHICKEN QUESADILLAS

Quesadillas have never tasted so good as when they are filled with slightly sweet onions and peppers and topped with lime butter and salt, the perfect balance of sweet and savory.
—*Stephanie Bright, Simpsonville, SC*

PREP: 35 min. + marinating • **BAKE:** 10 min.
MAKES: 16 wedges

- 4   boneless skinless chicken breast halves (5 oz. each)
- ¾   cup thawed frozen limeade concentrate
- 1   large onion, sliced
- 1   medium sweet orange pepper, julienned
- 1   medium sweet yellow pepper, julienned
- 1   Tbsp. canola oil
- ¼   tsp. salt
- ¼   tsp. pepper
- 4   flour tortillas (10 in.)
- 1   cup shredded Monterey Jack cheese
- 1   cup shredded cheddar cheese
- 2   Tbsp. butter, melted
- 1   Tbsp. lime juice
- 1   Tbsp. chopped fresh cilantro
  Lime wedges, optional

1. Place chicken in a large bowl. Add limeade concentrate and turn to coat. Cover bowl; refrigerate for 6 hours or overnight.
2. In a large nonstick skillet, saute the onion and sweet peppers in oil until tender; season with salt and pepper. Remove and set aside; wipe out skillet. Drain chicken, discarding marinade.
3. Grill chicken, covered, on a greased rack over medium heat or broil 4 in. from the heat for 5-8 minutes on each side or until a thermometer reads 165°. Cut chicken into ¼-in. strips; set aside. On half of each tortilla, layer the Monterey Jack cheese, chicken, pepper mixture and cheddar cheese; fold over. Combine butter and lime juice; brush over tortillas.
4. In the same skillet used to cook vegetables, cook quesadillas over medium heat until cheese is melted, 2-3 minutes per side. Keep warm in the oven while cooking remaining quesadillas. Cut each quesadilla into 4 wedges. Sprinkle with cilantro; serve with lime wedges if desired.
1 wedge: 204 cal., 9g fat (4g sat. fat), 37mg chol., 288mg sod., 18g carb. (8g sugars, 1g fiber), 12g pro.

SMOKY CHICKEN NACHOS

Nachos are always a hit with a crowd. This recipe combines layers of crunchy tortilla chips and some black beans with a creamy, smoky chicken mixture that takes it from a simple snack to a can't-stop-munching treat. Whenever we entertain on game day, this pan is gone by halftime!
—*Whitney Smith, Winter Haven, FL*

PREP: 20 min. • **BAKE:** 15 min.
MAKES: 12 servings

- 1   lb. ground chicken
- ⅔   cup water
- 1   envelope taco seasoning
- ¼   cup cream cheese, softened
- 3   Tbsp. minced fresh chives
- 2   Tbsp. plus 1½ tsp. 2% milk
- 2   Tbsp. dry bread crumbs
- 1   tsp. prepared mustard
- ½   tsp. paprika
- ¾   tsp. liquid smoke, optional
- 6   cups tortilla chips
- 1   can (15 oz.) black beans, rinsed and drained
- 1   cup shredded cheddar-Monterey Jack cheese
  Optional toppings: Chopped tomatoes and sliced ripe olives

1. In a large skillet over medium heat, cook chicken until no longer pink, breaking it into crumbles; drain. Add water and taco seasoning; bring to a boil. Reduce heat and simmer for 5 minutes. Combine the cream cheese, chives, milk, bread crumbs, mustard, paprika and, if desired, liquid smoke; stir into chicken mixture until blended.
2. In an ungreased 13x9-in. baking dish, layer half the chips, chicken mixture, beans and cheese. Repeat layers.
3. Bake at 350° for 15-20 minutes or until cheese is melted. Serve with tomatoes and olives if desired.
1 serving: 195 cal., 10g fat (5g sat. fat), 41mg chol., 224mg sod., 14g carb. (1g sugars, 2g fiber), 11g pro.

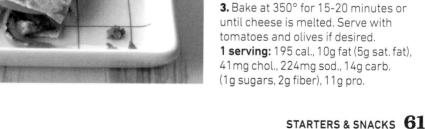

• *MARGARITA CHICKEN QUESADILLAS*

CHICKEN HOT POPPERS

The taste of Buffalo wings and pepper poppers pair up in this appealing appetizer. It will disappear fast—so make a double batch, and have copies of the recipe handy
—*Barbara Nowakowski, Mesa, AZ*

PREP: 20 min. • **BAKE:** 20 min.
MAKES: 40 appetizers

- 20 jalapeno peppers
- 1 pkg. (8 oz.) cream cheese, softened
- 1½ cups shredded part-skim mozzarella cheese
- 1 cup diced cooked chicken
- ½ cup blue cheese salad dressing
- ½ cup Buffalo wing sauce

1. Preheat oven to 325°. Cut peppers in half lengthwise, leaving stems intact; discard seeds. In a small bowl, combine the remaining ingredients. Pipe or stuff into pepper halves.

2. Place in a greased 15x10x1-in. baking pan. Bake, uncovered, for 20 minutes for spicy flavor, 30 minutes for medium and 40 minutes for mild.

Note: Wear disposable gloves when cutting hot peppers; the oils can burn skin. Avoid touching your face.

1 popper: 57 cal., 5g fat (2g sat. fat), 12mg chol., 159mg sod., 1g carb. 1(1g sugars, 0 fiber), 2g pro.

TEST KITCHEN TIP

For a milder pepper, be careful to remove as much membrane as possible, in addition to the seeds. The longer you bake the hot peppers, the milder in taste they become. Or go extra mild (and colorful) by stuffing mini rainbow sweet peppers.

CHICKEN
HOT POPPERS

STICKY HONEY
CHICKEN WINGS

CHECK OUT MORE WING RECIPES

Just hover your camera here.

STICKY HONEY CHICKEN WINGS

This tasty honey chicken wings recipe was given to me by a special lady who was like a grandmother to me.
—*Marisa Raponi, Vaughan, ON*

PREP: 15 min. + marinating • **BAKE:** 30 min.
MAKES: 3 dozen

- ½ cup orange blossom honey
- ⅓ cup white vinegar
- 2 Tbsp. paprika
- 2 tsp. salt
- 1 tsp. pepper
- 4 lbs. chicken wings

1. Combine honey, vinegar, paprika, salt and pepper in a small bowl.
2. Cut through the 2 wing joints with a sharp knife, discarding wing tips. Add remaining wing pieces and honey mixture to a large bowl; stir to coat. Cover and refrigerate for 4 hours or overnight.
3. Preheat oven to 375°. Remove wings; reserve honey mixture. Place wings on greased 15x10x1-in. baking pans. Bake until juices run clear, about 30 minutes, turning halfway through.
4. Meanwhile, place reserved honey mixture in a small saucepan. Bring to a boil; cook 1 minute.
5. Remove wings from oven; preheat broiler. Place wings on a greased rack in a broiler pan; brush with honey mixture. Broil 4-5 in. from heat until crispy, 3-5 minutes. Serve with remaining honey mixture.

1 piece: 71 cal., 4g fat (1g sat. fat), 16mg chol., 147mg sod., 4g carb. (4g sugars, 0 fiber), 5g pro.

HOW-TO

Cut Your Own Chicken Wings

- Place chicken wing on a cutting board. With a sharp knife, cut through the joint at the tip end.
- Cut through remaining wing joint, creating a wingette and drumette. Repeat with remaining wings.
- Discard the wing tips or save them for making broth.

CHICKEN PICCATA MEATBALLS

CHICKEN PICCATA MEATBALLS

The classic chicken piccata entree is my favorite dish, but I wanted another way to have all the same flavors. These chicken piccata meatballs are the perfect solution, whether served alone or with a sauce like marinara or Buffalo! Serve them over buttered noodles or stick toothpicks in them for appetizers.
—Dawn Collins, Rowley, MA

- -

PREP: 20 min. • **COOK:** 25 min.
MAKES: 2 dozen

½ cup dry bread crumbs
⅓ cup grated Parmesan cheese
1 large egg, lightly beaten
1 tsp. garlic powder
¼ tsp. salt
⅛ tsp. pepper
1 lb. ground chicken
2 Tbsp. canola oil, divided
2 garlic cloves, minced
⅓ cup chicken broth
¼ cup white wine
1 jar (3½ oz.) capers, drained
1 Tbsp. lemon juice
2 Tbsp. butter
   Shredded Parmesan cheese
   and lemon wedges

1. In a large bowl, combine the first 6 ingredients. Add chicken; mix lightly but thoroughly. With wet hands, shape into 1-in. balls.
2. In a large skillet, heat 1 Tbsp. oil over medium heat. Brown meatballs in batches; drain. Remove and keep warm. In the same skillet, heat the remaining 1 Tbsp. oil over medium heat. Add garlic; cook 1 minute.
3. Add broth and wine to pan; increase heat to medium-high. Cook 1 minute, stirring to loosen browned bits from pan. Add capers and lemon juice; bring to a boil. Add meatballs. Reduce heat; simmer, uncovered, until meatballs are cooked through, 5-7 minutes, stirring occasionally. Remove from heat; stir in

butter until melted. Sprinkle with Parmesan cheese and serve with lemon wedges.
1 meatball: 63 cal., 4g fat (1g sat. fat), 24mg chol., 193mg sod., 2g carb. (0 sugars, 0 fiber), 4g pro.

CHICKEN SALAD IN BASKETS

When I first made these cute little cups, they were a big hit. They make a yummy appetizer for an Easter gathering.
—Gwendolyn Fae Trapp, Strongsville, OH

- -

PREP: 15 min. • **BAKE:** 15 min. + chilling
MAKES: 20 appetizers

1 cup diced cooked chicken
3 bacon strips, cooked and crumbled
⅓ cup chopped mushrooms
2 Tbsp. chopped pecans
2 Tbsp. diced peeled apple
¼ cup mayonnaise
⅛ tsp. salt
   Dash pepper
20 slices bread
6 Tbsp. butter, melted
2 Tbsp. minced fresh parsley

1. In a small bowl, combine the first 5 ingredients. Combine the mayonnaise, salt and pepper; add to chicken mixture and stir to coat. Cover and refrigerate until serving.
2. Preheat oven to 350°. Cut each slice of bread with a 3-in. round cookie cutter; brush both sides with butter. Press into ungreased mini muffin cups. Bake 11-13 minutes or until golden brown and crisp.
3. Cool 3 minutes before removing from pans to wire racks to cool completely. Spoon 1 Tbsp. of chicken salad into each bread basket. Cover and refrigerate up to 2 hours. Just before serving, sprinkle with parsley.
1 basket: 140 cal., 8g fat (3g sat. fat), 17mg chol., 223mg sod., 12g carb. (2g sugars, 1g fiber), 5g pro.

⏱ BARBECUE CHICKEN BITS

Folks who enjoy the taste of barbecue will gobble up these tender chunks of chicken coated in crushed barbecue potato chips. They're a hit at home and at parties.
—Celena Cantrell-Richardson, Eau Claire, MI

- -

TAKES: 25 min. • **MAKES:** 4 servings

1 large egg
2 Tbsp. 2% milk
4 cups barbecue potato chips, crushed
½ lb. boneless skinless chicken
   breasts, cut into 1½-in. cubes
   Barbecue sauce

Preheat oven to 400°. In a shallow bowl, whisk egg and milk. Place potato chips in another shallow bowl. Dip chicken in egg mixture, then roll in chips. Place in a single layer on a greased baking sheet. Bake for 10-15 minutes or until meat is no longer pink. Serve with the barbecue sauce.
2 oz. cooked chicken: 383 cal., 22g fat (7g sat. fat), 85mg chol., 380mg sod., 30g carb. (1g sugars, 3g fiber), 17g pro.

🍲 BUTTER CHICKEN MEATBALLS

My husband and I love meatballs, and we love butter chicken. Before an appetizer party, we had the idea to combine the two, and these got rave reviews! Want them as a main dish? Just serve with basmati rice.
—*Shannon Dobos, Calgary, AB*

PREP: 30 min. • **COOK:** 3 hours
MAKES: about 3 dozen

- 1½ lbs. ground chicken or turkey
- 1   large egg, lightly beaten
- ½   cup soft bread crumbs
- 1   tsp. garam masala
- ½   tsp. tandoori masala seasoning
- ½   tsp. salt
- ¼   tsp. cayenne pepper
- 3   Tbsp. minced fresh cilantro, divided
- 1   jar (14.1 oz.) butter chicken sauce

1. Combine the first 7 ingredients plus 2 Tbsp. cilantro; mix lightly but thoroughly. With wet hands, shape into 1-in. balls. Place the meatballs in a 3-qt. slow cooker coated with cooking spray. Pour butter sauce over meatballs.
2. Cook, covered, on low until meatballs are cooked through, 3-4 hours. Top with remaining cilantro.

Freeze option: Omitting remaining cilantro, freeze cooled meatball mixture in freezer containers. To use, partially thaw in refrigerator overnight. Microwave, covered, on high in a microwave-safe dish until heated through, stirring occasionally; add water if necessary. To serve, sprinkle with remaining cilantro.

Note: To make soft bread crumbs, tear bread into pieces and place in a food processor or blender. Cover and pulse until crumbs form. One slice of bread yields ½-¾ cup crumbs. Look for butter chicken sauce in the Indian foods section.

1 meatball: 40 cal., 2g fat (1g sat. fat), 18mg chol., 87mg sod., 1g carb. (1g sugars, 0 fiber), 3g pro.

BUTTER CHICKEN MEATBALLS

**BACON BUFFALO
CHICKEN DIP**

BACON BUFFALO CHICKEN DIP

This Buffalo dip is must-have dish at our annual Fourth of July backyard barbecue. It celebrates America's love for Buffalo chicken dipped in heaps of creamy, tangy blue cheese dressing. And the bacon? That's just a bonus! My kids aren't big fans of blue cheese, but its strong flavor can be mellowed out by adding more mild cheddar in its place.

—*Katie O'Keeffe, Derry, NH*

PREP: 15 min. • **BAKE:** 25 min.
MAKES: 6 cups

- 1 lb. ground chicken
- 2 cups sour cream
- 2 cups shredded mild cheddar cheese, divided
- 2 cups crumbled blue cheese, divided
- ¼ cup Buffalo wing sauce
- 2 Tbsp. butter
- ¼ tsp. pepper
- 1½ cups crushed tortilla chips
- 4 green onions, chopped
- 8 thick-sliced peppered bacon strips, cooked and chopped
  Celery sticks
  Tortilla chips

1. Preheat oven to 350°. In a large skillet, cook chicken over medium heat until no longer pink, 5-7 minutes, breaking into crumbles; drain. Transfer chicken to a large bowl; stir in sour cream, 1 cup cheddar cheese, 1 cup blue cheese, wing sauce, butter and pepper.
2. Transfer chicken mixture to a greased 8-in. square baking dish. Top with remaining cheeses and crushed chips. Bake 10-12 minutes, or until cheese is melted, . Top with green onions and bacon. Serve with celery sticks and tortilla chips.
½ cup: 381 cal., 31g fat (16g sat. fat), 82mg chol., 779mg sod., 8g carb. (2g sugars, 0 fiber), 20g pro.

🕐 THAI CHICKEN PIZZA

I came up with this recipe after trying a similar appetizer pizza at a restaurant. It's a great way to use up leftover grilled or baked chicken. And it's a breeze to vary based on everyone's tastes.
—*Cheryl Taylor, Ortonville, MI*

- -

TAKES: 25 min. • **MAKES:** 8 servings

- 1   prebaked 12-in. pizza crust
- 1   Tbsp. olive oil
- 4   oz. ready-to-serve roasted chicken breast strips
- 2   to 3 large fresh mushrooms, thinly sliced
- ¼   cup plus 2 Tbsp. Thai peanut sauce, divided
- 2   cups shredded part-skim mozzarella cheese, divided
- ¼   cup thinly sliced red onion
- ½   cup fresh snow peas, halved
- ¼   cup chopped sweet red pepper
- ¼   cup julienned carrot
- 2   green onions, sliced
- ½   cup salted peanuts

1. Preheat oven to 450°. Place crust on an ungreased 12-in. pizza pan; brush with oil. In a small bowl, combine the chicken, mushrooms and ¼ cup peanut sauce; spread over crust. Sprinkle with 1 cup cheese.

2. Layer with the red onion, snow peas, red pepper and carrot. Sprinkle with remaining cheese. Top with green onions and peanuts. Drizzle with remaining peanut sauce.

3. Bake until cheese is melted, 10-12 minutes.

1 piece: 352 cal., 18g fat (5g sat. fat), 27mg chol., 660mg sod., 30g carb. (6g sugars, 2g fiber), 20g pro.

THAI CHICKEN PIZZA

SWEET POTATO-CRUSTED CHICKEN NUGGETS

I was looking for new ways to spice up traditional chicken nuggets and came up with this recipe. The chips add a crunchy texture and flavor, and the meat is tender on the inside.
—*Kristina Segarra, Yonkers, NY*

- -

TAKES: 30 min. • **MAKES:** 4 servings

   Oil for deep-fat frying
1 cup sweet potato chips
¼ cup all-purpose flour
1 tsp. salt, divided
½ tsp. coarsely ground pepper
¼ tsp. baking powder
1 Tbsp. cornstarch
1 lb. chicken tenderloins, cut into
   1½-in. pieces

1. In an electric skillet or deep fryer, heat oil to 350°. Place chips, flour, ½ tsp. salt, pepper and baking powder in a food processor; pulse until ground. Transfer to a shallow dish.
2. Mix cornstarch and remaining salt; toss with chicken. Toss with potato chip mixture, pressing gently to coat.
3. Fry nuggets, a few at a time, until golden brown, 2-3 minutes. Drain on paper towels.
3 ounces cooked chicken: 308 cal., 17g fat (1g sat. fat), 56mg chol., 690mg sod., 12g carb. (1g sugars, 1g fiber), 28g pro.

EASY BUFFALO CHICKEN LETTUCE WRAPS

Once when making sloppy joes, I wanted mine spicy, so I doused it in hot sauce. After that, my mind went wild and I created a Buffalo chicken-style with ground chicken, diced celery and blue cheese crumbles. I've been making it this way ever since.
—*Jennifer Nielson, Spanish Fork, UT*

- -

TAKES: 25 min. • **MAKES:** 6 servings

1½ lbs. lean ground chicken
1 celery rib, diced
¼ tsp. pepper
⅓ cup ketchup
¼ cup Louisiana-style hot sauce
3 Tbsp. brown sugar
1 Tbsp. cider vinegar
2 tsp. yellow mustard
12 Bibb or Boston lettuce leaves
   Crumbled blue cheese, optional

1. In a large cast-iron or other heavy skillet, cook and crumble chicken over medium-high heat 3 minutes. Stir in celery and pepper; cook and stir until chicken is no longer pink and celery is crisp-tender, 2-3 minutes.
2. Stir in ketchup, hot sauce, brown sugar, vinegar and mustard; bring to a boil. Reduce heat; simmer, covered, until flavors are blended, about 5 minutes, stirring occasionally. Serve in lettuce leaves. If desired, top with cheese.
Freeze option: Freeze cooled chicken mixture in freezer containers. To use, partially thaw in refrigerator overnight. Heat through in a saucepan, stirring occasionally; add broth or water if necessary.
2 lettuce wraps: 198 cal., 6g fat (2g sat. fat), 81mg chol., 612mg sod., 11g carb. (11g sugars, 1g fiber), 24g pro. **Diabetic exchanges:** 3 lean meat, 1 starch.

EASY BUFFALO CHICKEN LETTUCE WRAPS

🍲 CHEESY CHICKEN TACO DIP

We're huge college football fans (go Irish!), and my chicken taco dip hasn't missed a season opener in many years. A slow cooker keeps the dip warm for the whole game—if it lasts that long!
—*Deanna Garretson, Yucaipa, CA*

PREP: 15 min. • **COOK:** 4 hours 10 min.
MAKES: 8 cups

- 1 jar (16 oz.) salsa
- 1 can (30 oz.) refried beans
- 1½ lbs. boneless skinless chicken breasts
- 1 Tbsp. taco seasoning
- 2 cups shredded cheddar cheese
- 3 green onions, chopped
- 1 medium tomato, chopped
- ¼ cup chopped fresh cilantro
  Tortilla chips

1. In a greased 3- or 4-qt. slow cooker, mix salsa and beans. Top with chicken; sprinkle with the taco seasoning. Cook, covered, on low until chicken is tender, 4-5 hours.
2. Remove chicken; shred finely using 2 forks. Return to slow cooker; stir in cheese. Cook, covered, on low until cheese is melted, 10-15 minutes, stirring occasionally.
3. To serve, top with green onions, tomato and cilantro. Serve with chips.
¼ cup dip: 82 cal., 3g fat (2g sat. fat), 19mg chol., 238mg sod., 5g carb. (1g sugars, 1g fiber), 7g pro.

TEST KITCHEN TIP

Skip the chips and serve the dip with crunch celery sticks and carrots for a lighter bite.

FIVE-SPICE CHICKEN WINGS

FIVE-SPICE CHICKEN WINGS

These wings are baked to a perfect golden brown, and shine with mild Asian spices. Thanks to an overnight marinade, the chicken inside stays tender while the skin maintains that signature crunch.
—*Crystal Jo Bruns, Iliff, CO*

PREP: 20 min. + marinating • **BAKE:** 25 min.
MAKES: about 3 dozen

- 3½ lbs. chicken wings
- 3 green onions, chopped
- 2 Tbsp. sweet chili sauce
- 2 Tbsp. reduced-sodium soy sauce
- 2 Tbsp. fish sauce or additional soy sauce
- 4 garlic cloves, minced
- 1 Tbsp. sugar
- 1 Tbsp. Chinese five-spice powder
- 2 medium limes, cut into wedges

1. Cut chicken wings into 3 sections; discard wing tip sections. Combine the onions, chili sauce, soy sauce, fish sauce, garlic, sugar and five-spice powder in a large container. Add wings and toss to coat. Cover and refrigerate 8 hours or overnight.
2. Preheat oven to 425°. Drain the chicken, discarding the marinade. Place the chicken pieces in a greased 15x10x1-in. baking pan.
3. Bake for 25-30 minutes or until no longer pink, turning every 10 minutes. Serve with lime wedges for squeezing over wings.
1 piece: 52 cal., 3g fat (1g sat. fat), 14mg chol., 81mg sod., 1g carb. (0 sugars, 0 fiber), 5g pro.

🍲 BUFFALO CHICKEN SLIDERS

I came up with the idea for these sliders after my mom and dad made a similar recipe for a family get-together. To make it special, I sometimes use several different styles of Buffalo sauce and let guests mix and match their favorites.
—Christina Addison, Blanchester, OH

- -

PREP: 20 min. • **COOK:** 3 hours
MAKES: 6 servings

- 1 lb. boneless skinless chicken breasts
- 2 Tbsp. plus ⅓ cup Louisiana-style hot sauce, divided
- ¼ tsp. pepper
- ¼ cup butter, cubed
- ¼ cup honey
- 12 Hawaiian sweet rolls, warmed
  Optional: Lettuce leaves, sliced tomato, thinly sliced red onion and crumbled blue cheese

1. Place chicken in a 3-qt. slow cooker. Toss chicken with 2 Tbsp. hot sauce and pepper; cook, covered, on low 3-4 hours or until tender.
2. Remove chicken; discard cooking juices. In a small saucepan, combine butter, honey and remaining hot sauce; cook and stir over medium heat until blended. Shred chicken with 2 forks; stir into sauce and heat through. Serve on rolls with desired optional ingredients
Freeze option: Freeze cooled chicken mixture in freezer containers. To use, partially thaw in refrigerator overnight. Microwave, covered, on high in a microwave-safe dish until heated through, stirring occasionally; add water or broth if necessary.
2 sliders: 396 cal., 15g fat (8g sat. fat), 92mg chol., 873mg sod., 44g carb. (24g sugars, 2g fiber), 24g pro.

STUFFED BUFFALO CHICKEN & RANCH BUNS

The Buffalo-wing fans in my family were happy to do the taste testing as I was perfecting these zingy snacks. This version was the winner!
—Jasey McBurnett, Rock Springs, WY

- -

PREP: 25 min. • **BAKE:** 15 min.
MAKES: 2 dozen (2 cups dressing)

- 2 Tbsp. grated Parmesan cheese
- 1 envelope ranch salad dressing mix, divided
- 1 cup mayonnaise
- 1 cup 2% milk
- ¼ cup crumbled blue cheese, optional
- 1¼ cups finely chopped cooked chicken breast
- 1¼ cups shredded cheddar-Monterey Jack cheese
- ¼ cup Buffalo wing sauce
- 1 tube (13.8 oz.) refrigerated pizza crust
- 2 Tbsp. butter, melted

1. Preheat oven to 400°. In a small bowl, combine Parmesan cheese and 1 tsp. dressing mix. In another bowl, mix the mayonnaise, milk and remaining dressing mix. If desired, stir in blue cheese. Refrigerate until serving.
2. In a large bowl, mix chicken, cheddar-Monterey Jack cheese and wing sauce. On a lightly floured surface, unroll pizza crust dough and pat into a 14x12-in. rectangle. Cut into 24 squares.
3. Place 1 rounded Tbsp. chicken mixture on the center of each square. Pull corners together to enclose filling; pinch to seal. Place 1 in. apart on greased baking sheets, seam side down. Brush tops with butter; sprinkle with Parmesan cheese mixture.
4. Bake 15-17 minutes or until golden brown. Serve with dressing.
1 appetizer: 165 cal., 12g fat (3g sat. fat), 18mg chol., 374mg sod., 9g carb. (1g sugars, 0 fiber), 5g pro.

BUFFALO CHICKEN SLIDERS

SALADS & SANDWICHES

GINGER-CASHEW
CHICKEN SALAD, PAGE 76

SESAME CHICKEN VEGGIE WRAPS

TOMATO-MELON CHICKEN SALAD

Nothing says it's summer like picking watermelon, tomatoes and raspberries, then tossing them together in a salad. The addition of grilled chicken makes it a satisfying, yet still summery, meal.
—*Betsy Hite, Wilton, CA*

TAKES: 15 min. • **MAKES:** 6 servings

- 4 medium tomatoes, cut into wedges
- 2 cups cubed seedless watermelon
- 1 cup fresh raspberries
- ¼ cup minced fresh basil
- ¼ cup olive oil
- 2 Tbsp. balsamic vinegar
- ¼ tsp. salt
- ¼ tsp. pepper
- 9 cups torn mixed salad greens
- 4 grilled chicken breasts (4 oz. each), sliced

In a large bowl, combine the tomatoes, watermelon and raspberries. In a small bowl, whisk the basil, oil, vinegar, salt and pepper. Drizzle over the tomato mixture; toss to coat. Divide salad greens among 6 serving plates; top with tomato mixture and chicken.
1 serving: 266 cal., 13g fat (2g sat. fat), 64mg chol., 215mg sod., 15g carb. (9g sugars, 4g fiber), 26g pro. **Diabetic exchanges:** 3 lean meat, 2 vegetable, 2 fat.

WHY YOU'LL LOVE IT...

"I had to try this salad since I found the ingredients so intriguing. It is very good and refreshing. I used dried basil since I did not have any fresh. This would be especially good with garden-fresh tomatoes, too. Very nice summer dish!"
—ANNMOMOF4, TASTEOFHOME.COM

SESAME CHICKEN VEGGIE WRAPS

I'm always on the lookout for fast, nutritious recipes that appeal to my three little kids. They happen to love edamame, so this is a smart choice for those on-the-go days.
—*Elisabeth Larsen, Pleasant Grove, UT*

TAKES: 30 min. • **MAKES:** 8 servings

- 1 cup frozen shelled edamame
- **DRESSING**
- 2 Tbsp. orange juice
- 2 Tbsp. olive oil
- 1 tsp. sesame oil
- ½ tsp. ground ginger
- ¼ tsp. salt
- ⅛ tsp. pepper
- **WRAPS**
- 2 cups fresh baby spinach
- 1 cup thinly sliced cucumber
- 1 cup fresh sugar snap peas, chopped
- ½ cup shredded carrots
- ½ cup thinly sliced sweet red pepper
- 1 cup chopped cooked chicken breast
- 8 whole wheat tortillas (8 in.), room temperature

1. Cook edamame according to package directions. Drain; rinse with cold water and drain well. Whisk together the dressing ingredients.
2. In a large bowl, combine remaining vegetables, chicken and edamame; toss with dressing. Place about ½ cup mixture on each tortilla. Fold bottom and sides of tortilla over filling and roll up.
1 wrap: 214 cal., 7g fat (1g sat. fat), 13mg chol., 229mg sod., 28g carb. (2g sugars, 5g fiber), 12g pro. **Diabetic exchanges:** 2 starch, 1 lean meat, 1 fat.

**TOMATO-MELON
CHICKEN SALAD**

🍎 GINGER-CASHEW CHICKEN SALAD

I revamped an Asian-style chicken salad recipe to create this gingery, crunchy salad. Now it's a huge success when I serve it at ladies luncheons.
—*Shelly Gramer, Long Beach, CA*

- -

PREP: 20 min. + marinating • **BROIL:** 10 min.
MAKES: 8 servings

- ½ cup cider vinegar
- ½ cup molasses
- ⅓ cup canola oil
- 2 Tbsp. minced fresh gingerroot
- 2 tsp. reduced-sodium soy sauce
- 1 tsp. salt
- ⅛ tsp. cayenne pepper
- 4 boneless skinless chicken breast halves (6 oz. each)

SALAD
- 8 oz. fresh baby spinach (about 10 cups)
- 1 can (11 oz.) mandarin oranges, drained
- 1 cup shredded red cabbage
- 2 medium carrots, shredded
- 3 green onions, thinly sliced
- 2 cups chow mein noodles
- ¾ cup salted cashews, toasted
- 2 Tbsp. sesame seeds, toasted

GINGER-CASHEW CHICKEN SALAD

1. In a small bowl, whisk the first 7 ingredients until blended. Pour ¾ cup marinade into a large shallow dish. Add chicken; turn to coat. Cover and refrigerate at least 3 hours. Cover and refrigerate remaining marinade.

2. Preheat broiler. Drain chicken, discarding marinade in dish. Place chicken in a 15x10x1-in. baking pan. Broil 4-6 in. from heat 4-6 minutes on each side or until a thermometer reads 165°. Cut chicken into strips.

3. Place spinach on a serving platter. Arrange chicken, oranges, cabbage, carrots and green onions on top. Sprinkle with chow mein noodles, cashews and sesame seeds. Stir reserved molasses mixture; drizzle over salad. Serve immediately.

Note: To toast nuts, bake in a shallow pan in a 350° oven for 5-10 minutes or cook in a skillet over low heat until lightly browned, stirring occasionally.

1½ cups: 379 cal., 18g fat (3g sat. fat), 47mg chol., 533mg sod., 33g carb. (16g sugars, 3g fiber), 23g pro. **Diabetic exchanges:** 2½ fat, 2 lean meat, 1½ starch, 1 vegetable.

CHICKEN CORDON BLEU STROMBOLI

🕐 CHICKEN CORDON BLEU STROMBOLI

If chicken cordon bleu and stromboli had a baby, this would be it. Serve with jarred or homemade Alfredo sauce, or classic Mornay sauce on the side if desired.
—*Cyndy Gerken, Naples, FL*

TAKES: 30 min. • **MAKES:** 6 servings

- 1 tube (13.8 oz.) refrigerated pizza crust
- 4 thin slices deli ham
- 1½ cups shredded cooked chicken
- 6 slices Swiss cheese
- 1 Tbsp. butter, melted
  Roasted garlic Alfredo sauce, optional

1. Preheat oven to 400°. Unroll dough onto a baking sheet. Layer with ham, chicken and cheese to within ½ in. of edges. Roll up jelly-roll style, starting with a long side; pinch seam to seal and tuck ends under. Brush with butter

2. Bake until crust is dark golden brown, 18-22 minutes. Let stand 5 minutes before slicing. If desired, serve with Alfredo sauce for dipping.

1 slice: 298 cal., 10g fat (4g sat. fat), 53mg chol., 580mg sod., 32g carb. (4g sugars, 1g fiber), 21g pro.

TEST KITCHEN TIP

Don't let this stand too long before slicing and eating, or the underside of the crust will get soft.

SLOW-COOKER BUFFALO CHICKEN SALAD

My husband and sons love Buffalo chicken with blue cheese, so I created this salad. You can even make the chicken the day before and reheat it when ready to serve.
—*Shauna Havey, Roy, UT*

PREP: 20 min. • **COOK:** 2½ hours
MAKES: 6 servings

- 1½ lbs. boneless skinless chicken breast halves
- ¾ cup Buffalo wing sauce
- 3 Tbsp. butter
- 1 envelope ranch salad dressing mix
- 1 pkg. (10 oz.) hearts of romaine salad mix
- 1 cup julienned carrot
- 1 medium ripe avocado, peeled and cubed
- ½ cup crumbled blue cheese
- ½ cup blue cheese salad dressing

1. Place chicken in a 1½- or 3-qt. slow cooker. Top with wing sauce, butter and ranch dressing mix. Cook, covered, on low until thermometer inserted in chicken reads 165°, 2½-3 hours.

2. Remove chicken; shred with 2 forks. Reserve ⅓ cup cooking juices; discard remaining juices. Return chicken and reserved juices to slow cooker; heat through.

3. Place romaine salad mix in a serving dish. Top with the shredded chicken, carrots, avocado and blue cheese; drizzle with blue cheese dressing. Serve immediately.

1 salad: 385 cal., 26g fat (9g sat. fat), 93mg chol., 1693mg sod., 12g carb. (2g sugars, 4g fiber), 28g pro.

SLOW-COOKER
BUFFALO
CHICKEN SALAD

OPEN-FACED CHICKEN AVOCADO BURGERS

OPEN-FACED CHICKEN AVOCADO BURGERS

A creamy avocado spread and thick slices of fresh mozzarella and tomato dress up these chicken patties.
—*Lisa Kennedy, Aberdeen, NC*

PREP: 30 min. • **COOK:** 15 min.
MAKES: 4 servings plus ¼ cup leftover spread

- 1 Tbsp. lemon juice
- ¼ tsp. Worcestershire sauce
- ½ medium ripe avocado, peeled
- ½ cup mayonnaise
- ¼ cup sour cream
- 4 green onions, coarsely chopped
- ½ tsp. salt
- ½ tsp. cayenne pepper

BURGERS
- ¼ cup shredded Parmesan cheese
- 2 Tbsp. prepared pesto
- 3 garlic cloves, minced
- ¼ tsp. salt
- 1 lb. ground chicken
- 4 Tbsp. olive oil, divided
- ½ lb. fresh mozzarella cheese, cut into 4 slices
- 4 slices Italian bread (¾ in. thick)
- 2 cups fresh arugula or baby spinach
- 8 slices tomato
- ¼ tsp. dried basil
- ¼ tsp. pepper

1. In a blender, combine the first 8 ingredients; cover and process until smooth. Chill until serving. For burgers, in a small bowl, combine the Parmesan cheese, pesto, garlic and salt. Crumble chicken over mixture and mix lightly but thoroughly. Shape into 4 patties.

2. In a large skillet over medium heat, cook burgers in 2 Tbsp. oil until a thermometer reads 165° and juices run clear, 5-7 minutes on each side. Top with cheese; cover and cook 1 minute longer.

3. Meanwhile, brush Italian bread with remaining oil; place on a baking sheet. Broil 3-4 in. from the heat until toasted, 1-2 minutes on each side.

4. Spread each slice of toast with 2 Tbsp. avocado spread (refrigerate remaining spread for another use). Top with arugula, a burger and sliced tomato. Sprinkle with basil and pepper.

1 burger: 723 cal., 55g fat (17g sat. fat), 136mg chol., 849mg sod., 22g carb. (3g sugars, 3g fiber), 35g pro.

🍎 CHICKEN FAJITA SALAD

This recipe came from Texas, which is famous for its Tex-Mex food. I love to cook, even though it's just for me and my husband now. I invite our grown kids over a lot, and they just love this recipe. I'm happy to share it!
—Lois Proudfit, Eugene, OR

TAKES: 30 min. + marinating
MAKES: 6 servings

4 Tbsp. canola oil, divided
½ cup lime juice
2 garlic cloves, minced
1 tsp. ground cumin
1 tsp. dried oregano
1 lb. boneless skinless chicken breasts, cut into thin strips
1 medium onion, cut into thin wedges
1 medium sweet red pepper, cut into thin strips
2 cans (4 oz. each) chopped green chiles
1 cup unblanched almonds, toasted
3 cups shredded lettuce
3 medium tomatoes, cut into wedges
1 medium ripe avocado, peeled and sliced

1. In a small bowl, combine 2 Tbsp. oil, lime juice, garlic, cumin and oregano. Pour half in a large bowl or dish; add chicken and turn to coat. Marinate for at least 30 minutes. Cover and refrigerate remaining marinade.
2. In a large skillet, heat remaining oil on medium-high. Saute onion for 2-3 minutes or until crisp-tender.
3. Drain chicken, discarding marinade. Add chicken to skillet; stir-fry until meat is no longer pink. Add the red pepper, chiles and reserved marinade; cook 2 minutes or until heated through. Stir in almonds. Serve immediately over shredded lettuce; top with tomatoes and avocado.

1½ cups: 372 cal., 26g fat (3g sat. fat), 42mg chol., 203mg sod., 16g carb. (5g sugars, 6g fiber), 22g pro.

TEST KITCHEN TIP
Avocados are high in monounsaturated fat, a so-called "good fat" that can lower your blood cholesterol along with the risk of stroke and heart disease.

CHICKEN FAJITA SALAD

*CAROLINA-STYLE
VINEGAR BBQ CHICKEN*

**SHREDDED
CHICKEN
TIPS &
TRICKS**
Just hover your
camera here.

🍎 🍲 CAROLINA-STYLE VINEGAR BBQ CHICKEN

I live in Georgia but I appreciate the tangy, sweet and slightly spicy taste of Carolina vinegar chicken. I make my version in the slow cooker. With the tempting aroma filling the house, your family is sure to be at the dinner table on time!
—*Ramona Parris, Canton, GA*

PREP: 10 min. • **COOK:** 4 hours
MAKES: 6 servings

- 2   cups water
- 1   cup white vinegar
- ¼   cup sugar
- 1   Tbsp. reduced-sodium chicken base
- 1   tsp. crushed red pepper flakes
- ¾   tsp. salt
- 1½   lbs. boneless skinless chicken breasts
- 6   whole wheat hamburger buns, split, optional

1. In a small bowl, mix the first 6 ingredients. Place chicken in a 3-qt. slow cooker; add the vinegar mixture. Cook, covered, on low 4-5 hours or until chicken is tender.
2. Remove chicken; cool slightly. Reserve 1 cup cooking juices; discard remaining juices. Shred chicken with 2 forks. Return meat and reserved cooking juices to slow cooker; heat through. If desired, serve chicken mixture on buns.
Note: Look for chicken base near the broth and bouillon.
½ cup: 134 cal., 3g fat (1g sat. fat), 63mg chol., 228mg sod., 3g carb. (3g sugars, 0 fiber), 23g pro. **Diabetic exchanges:** 3 lean meat.

HOW-TO

3 Fast Ways to Shred Chicken

- Cut cooked chicken into chunks and add it to a stand mixer with the paddle attachment. A few seconds on medium-low speed is just enough to shred it.
- Use 2 large forks to pull cooked chicken in opposite directions.
- Once chicken has cooled, pull it into shreds with your hands.

GRILLED CHICKEN SALAD WITH BLUEBERRY VINAIGRETTE

GRILLED CHICKEN SALAD WITH BLUEBERRY VINAIGRETTE

We love adding some grilled chicken to our salads during the summer, but the real star here is a vinaigrette made with blueberry preserves and maple syrup.
—*Susan Gauthier, Falmouth, ME*

PREP: 20 min. + marinating • **GRILL:** 10 min.
MAKES: 4 servings

- 2 boneless skinless chicken breast halves (6 oz. each)
- 1 Tbsp. olive oil
- 1 garlic clove, minced
- ¼ tsp. salt
- ¼ tsp. pepper
- VINAIGRETTE
- ¼ cup olive oil
- ¼ cup blueberry preserves
- 2 Tbsp. balsamic vinegar
- 2 Tbsp. maple syrup
- ¼ tsp. ground mustard
- ⅛ tsp. salt
- Dash pepper
- SALADS
- 1 pkg. (10 oz.) ready-to-serve salad greens
- 1 cup fresh blueberries
- ½ cup canned mandarin oranges
- 1 cup crumbled goat cheese

1. Toss chicken with oil, garlic, salt and pepper; refrigerate, covered, 30 minutes. In a small bowl, whisk together vinaigrette ingredients; refrigerate, covered, until serving.
2. Grill chicken, covered, over medium heat until a thermometer reads 165°, 5-7 minutes per side. Let stand 5 minutes before slicing.
3. Place greens on a serving plate; top with chicken, blueberries and mandarin oranges. Whisk vinaigrette again; drizzle over salad. Top with cheese.
1 serving: 455 cal., 26g fat (7g sat. fat), 82mg chol., 460mg sod., 36g carb. (27g sugars, 4g fiber), 24g pro.

CRESCENT CHICKEN BUNDLES

CRESCENT CHICKEN BUNDLES

When I was expecting our third child, this was one of the meals I put in the freezer ahead of time. We now have four kids and they all like these rich chicken pockets. You can substitute ham or turkey for chicken.
—*Jo Groth, Plainfield, IA*

PREP: 15 min. • **BAKE:** 20 min.
MAKES: 8 servings

- 6 oz. cream cheese, softened
- 4 Tbsp. butter, melted, divided
- 2 Tbsp. minced chives
- 2 Tbsp. 2% milk
- ½ tsp. salt
- ¼ tsp. pepper
- 4 cups cubed cooked chicken
- 2 tubes (8 oz. each) refrigerated crescent rolls
- 1 cup crushed seasoned stuffing

1. Preheat oven to 350°. In a bowl, beat cream cheese, 2 Tbsp. butter, chives, milk, salt and pepper until blended. Stir in chicken.
2. Unroll crescent roll dough and separate into 8 rectangles; press perforations together. Spoon about ½ cup chicken mixture in the center of each rectangle. Bring edges up to the center and pinch to seal. Brush with remaining butter. Sprinkle with crushed stuffing, lightly pressing down.
3. Transfer to ungreased baking sheets. Bake until golden brown, 20-25 minutes.
Freeze option: Freeze unbaked bundles on baking sheets until firm; transfer to a freezer container. May be frozen up to 2 months. To use, thaw in refrigerator. Bake as directed, increasing time as necessary to heat through.
1 bundle: 363 cal., 21g fat (9g sat. fat), 90mg chol., 622mg sod., 17g carb. (3g sugars, 1g fiber), 24g pro.

BBQ CHICKEN SANDWICHES

These great sandwiches are a cinch to make. For a spicier taste, eliminate the ketchup and increase the salsa to 1 cup.
—*Leticia Lewis, Kennewick, WA*

PREP: 20 min. • **COOK:** 15 min.
MAKES: 6 servings

- ½ cup chopped onion
- ½ cup diced celery
- 1 garlic clove, minced
- 1 Tbsp. butter
- ½ cup salsa
- ½ cup ketchup
- 2 Tbsp. brown sugar
- 2 Tbsp. cider vinegar
- 1 Tbsp. Worcestershire sauce
- ½ tsp. chili powder
- ¼ tsp. salt
- ⅛ tsp. pepper
- 2 cups shredded cooked chicken
- 6 hamburger buns, split and toasted

1. In a large saucepan, sauté the onion, celery and garlic in butter until tender. Stir in the salsa, ketchup, brown sugar, vinegar, Worcestershire sauce, chili powder, salt and pepper.

2. Stir in chicken. Bring to a boil. Reduce heat; cover and simmer for 15 minutes. Serve about ⅓ cup chicken mixture on each bun.

Freeze option: Freeze cooled meat mixture in freezer containers. To use, partially thaw in refrigerator overnight. Heat through in a saucepan, stirring occasionally; add water if necessary. Serve in buns.

1 sandwich: 284 cal., 8g fat (3g sat. fat), 47mg chol., 770mg sod., 35g carb. (12g sugars, 3g fiber), 18g pro. **Diabetic exchanges:** 2 starch, 2 lean meat.

BBQ CHICKEN SANDWICHES

RAMEN-VEGGIE CHICKEN SALAD

RAMEN-VEGGIE CHICKEN SALAD

Like a salad with plenty of crunch? Then this refreshing recipe is sure to please. Toasted ramen noodles, almonds and sesame seeds provide the crunch.
—*Linda Gearhart, Greensboro, NC*

- -

PREP: 30 min. • **GRILL:** 10 min.
MAKES: 2 servings

¼ cup sugar
¼ cup canola oil
2 Tbsp. cider vinegar
1 Tbsp. reduced-sodium soy sauce
1 pkg. (3 oz.) ramen noodles
1 Tbsp. butter
⅓ cup sliced almonds
1 Tbsp. sesame seeds
1 boneless skinless chicken breast half (6 oz.)
4 cups shredded Chinese or napa cabbage
½ large sweet red pepper, thinly sliced
3 green onions, thinly sliced
1 medium carrot, julienned

1. In a small saucepan, combine the sugar, oil, vinegar and soy sauce. Bring to a boil, cook and stir until sugar is dissolved, about 1 minute; set aside to cool.
2. Meanwhile, break noodles into small pieces (save the seasoning packet for another use). In a small skillet, melt the butter over medium heat. Add the noodles, almonds and sesame seeds; cook and stir until lightly toasted, 1-2 minutes.
3. Grill chicken, covered, over medium heat until a thermometer reads 165°, 4-6 minutes on each side.
4. Meanwhile, arrange the cabbage, red pepper, onions and carrot on 2 serving plates. Slice the chicken; place on salad. Top with noodle mixture and drizzle with dressing.
1 serving: 865 cal., 53g fat (11g sat. fat), 62mg chol., 574mg sod., 68g carb. (32g sugars, 7g fiber), 29g pro.

⏱ 🍎 SOUTH-OF-THE-BORDER CHICKEN SALAD WITH TEQUILA LIME DRESSING

Add a burst of color to your table with this main-dish salad that tastes like a fiesta. For a simple garnish, sprinkle salad with lightly crushed tortilla chips.

—*Annette Hottenstein, Sparks Glenco, MD*

TAKES: 30 min. • **MAKES:** 4 servings

- 2 romaine hearts, cut into ½-in. strips
- 2 cups shredded cooked chicken breast
- 3 plum tomatoes, seeded and chopped
- 1 medium ripe avocado, peeled and cubed
- ½ cup frozen corn, thawed
- ½ cup black beans, rinsed and drained
- ¼ cup crumbled queso fresco
- ¼ cup minced fresh cilantro
- 3 green onions, thinly sliced

DRESSING
- 3 Tbsp. olive oil
- 3 Tbsp. lime juice
- 2 Tbsp. tequila
- 4½ tsp. honey
- 1 garlic clove, minced
- ¼ tsp. salt
- ¼ tsp. coarsely ground pepper

Add romaine to a large salad bowl. Top with remaining salad ingredients. In a small bowl, whisk dressing ingredients. Pour over salad; toss to coat.

2 cups: 404 cal., 21g fat (4g sat. fat), 59mg chol., 258mg sod., 27g carb. (10g sugars, 7g fiber), 27g pro. **Diabetic exchanges:** 3 lean meat, 3 fat, 2 vegetable, 1½ starch.

SOUTH-OF-THE-BORDER CHICKEN SALAD WITH TEQUILA LIME DRESSING

⏱ CRISPY BUFFALO CHICKEN WRAPS

I'm big on wraps, even when I go out to eat. As a busy stay-at-home mom, I make this favorite a lot. It's great with chips and salsa.
—*Christina Addison, Blanchester, OH*

TAKES: 30 min. • **MAKES:** 4 servings

- 1 pkg. (12 oz.) frozen popcorn chicken
- 1 pkg. (8 oz.) shredded lettuce
- 2 medium tomatoes, finely chopped
- 1 cup shredded cheddar cheese
- ⅓ cup Buffalo wing sauce
- 4 flour tortillas (10 in.), warmed
  Optional: Ranch or chipotle ranch salad dressing

1. Cook chicken according to package directions; coarsely chop chicken. In a large bowl, mix chicken, lettuce, tomatoes and cheese. Drizzle with wing sauce; toss to coat.
2. Spoon 1½ cups chicken mixture down the center of each tortilla. Fold bottom of tortilla over filling; fold both sides to close. Serve immediately with salad dressing if desired.
1 wrap: 570 cal., 26g fat (9g sat. fat), 55mg chol., 1895mg sod., 62g carb. (7g sugars, 4g fiber), 23g pro.

DID YOU KNOW?

Many people agree that Teressa Bellissimo first tossed chicken wings in a mixture of cayenne pepper, hot sauce and butter at her family's Anchor Bar in Buffalo, New York, in 1964. Others say John Young created the combo, called "mambo sauce," at his restaurant, Wings 'n Things. Either way, the sauce is definitely from Buffalo.

SPECIAL SESAME CHICKEN SALAD

With its delicious mix of crunchy peanuts, tangy dried cranberries and mandarin oranges, this colorful pasta salad is a definite crowd-pleaser. Water chestnuts and a teriyaki dressing give this main dish its Asian flare.
—*Carolee Ewell, Santaquin, UT*

PREP: 30 min. + chilling
MAKES: 22 servings

- 1 pkg. (16 oz.) bow tie pasta
- 1 cup canola oil
- ⅔ cup white wine vinegar
- ⅔ cup teriyaki sauce
- ⅓ cup sugar
- ½ tsp. pepper
- 3 cans (11 oz. each) mandarin oranges, drained
- 2 cans (8 oz. each) sliced water chestnuts, drained
- 2 cups cubed cooked chicken
- 1⅓ cups honey-roasted peanuts
- 1 pkg. (9 oz.) fresh spinach, torn
- 1 pkg. (5 oz.) dried cranberries
- 6 green onions, chopped
- ½ cup minced fresh parsley
- ¼ cup sesame seeds, toasted

1. Cook pasta according to package directions; drain and place in a very large bowl.
2. In a small bowl, combine the oil, vinegar, teriyaki sauce, sugar and pepper. Pour over pasta and toss to coat. Cover and refrigerate for 2 hours.
3. Just before serving, add remaining ingredients and gently toss to coat.
1 cup: 302 cal., 16g fat (2g sat. fat), 11mg chol., 358mg sod., 32g carb. (13g sugars, 3g fiber), 10g pro.

⏱ CASHEW CHICKEN SALAD SANDWICHES

I think this is the best chicken salad recipe around! It's good for you and quick to make, and it has a wonderful flavor.
—*Peggi Kelly, Fairbury, NE*

TAKES: 15 min. • **MAKES:** 6 servings

- 2 cups diced cooked chicken
- ½ cup chopped salted cashews
- ½ cup chopped red apple
- ½ cup chopped peeled cucumber
- ½ cup mayonnaise
- ½ tsp. sugar
- ½ tsp. salt
  Dash pepper
- 6 kaiser rolls or croissants, split
- 6 lettuce leaves, optional

In a large bowl, combine the chicken, cashews, apple and cucumber. Combine mayonnaise, sugar, salt and pepper. Stir into chicken mixture. Serve on rolls, with lettuce if desired.
1 sandwich: 463 cal., 26g fat (4g sat. fat), 48mg chol., 720mg sod., 36g carb. (3g sugars, 2g fiber), 21g pro.
Peanut Chicken Salad Sandwiches: Substitute ½ chopped salted peanuts for the cashews.

*MANGO &
GRILLED
CHICKEN SALAD*

ALMOND-APRICOT CHICKEN SALAD

Here's a one-of-a-kind pasta salad that combines tender chicken, sweet apricots and crunchy vegetables. Plus, the lemony dressing can't be beat.
—*Susan Voigt, Plymouth, MN*

- -

PREP: 20 min. + chilling
MAKES: 10 servings

- 1 pkg. (8 oz.) spiral pasta
- 1 pkg. (6 oz.) dried apricots, thinly sliced
- 3 cups coarsely chopped fresh broccoli
- 2½ cups diced cooked chicken
- ½ cup chopped green onions
- ½ cup chopped celery
- 1 cup sour cream
- ¾ cup mayonnaise
- 1 Tbsp. lemon juice
- 2 tsp. grated lemon zest
- 2 tsp. Dijon mustard
- 1½ tsp. salt
- ¾ tsp. dried savory
- ½ tsp. pepper
- ¾ cup sliced almonds, toasted

1. Cook pasta according to package directions, adding apricots during the last 4 minutes. Drain and rinse with cold water; place in a large bowl. Add broccoli, chicken, onions and celery.
2. In a small bowl, combine the next 8 ingredients. Pour over salad and toss to coat. Cover and chill until serving; fold in almonds.
1 serving: 411 cal., 24g fat (6g sat. fat), 52mg chol., 524mg sod., 31g carb. (10g sugars, 4g fiber), 17g pro.

🕐 🍎 MANGO & GRILLED CHICKEN SALAD

We live in the hot South, and this awesome cool, fruity chicken salad is a weeknight standout. I buy salad greens and add veggies for color and crunch.
—*Sherry Little, Cabot, AR*

- -

TAKES: 25 min. • **MAKES:** 4 servings

- 1 lb. chicken tenderloins
- ½ tsp. salt
- ¼ tsp. pepper
SALAD
- 6 cups torn mixed salad greens
- ¼ cup raspberry or balsamic vinaigrette
- 1 medium mango, peeled and cubed
- 1 cup fresh sugar snap peas, halved lengthwise

1. Toss chicken with salt and pepper. On a lightly oiled rack, grill chicken, covered, over medium heat or broil 4 in. from heat on each side until no longer pink, 3-4 minutes. Cut the chicken into 1-in. pieces.
2. Divide greens among 4 plates; drizzle with vinaigrette. Top with chicken, mango and peas; serve immediately.
1 serving: 210 cal., 2g fat (0 sat. fat), 56mg chol., 447mg sod., 22g carb. (16g sugars, 4g fiber), 30g pro. **Diabetic exchanges:** 3 lean meat, 2 vegetable, ½ starch, ½ fat.

TEST KITCHEN TIP

Choose plump mangoes with a sweet, fruity fragrance. Avoid those that are bruised or very soft.

⏱ THAI CHICKEN WRAPS

Thanks to the quick-cooking chicken, convenient broccoli slaw mix, and an easy peanut sauce, you can wrap up this dinner in 25 minutes.
—*Trudy Williams, Shannonville, ON*

TAKES: 25 min. • **MAKES:** 6 servings

- ¼ cup sugar
- ¼ cup creamy peanut butter
- 3 Tbsp. soy sauce
- 2 to 3 Tbsp. water
- 2 garlic cloves, minced
- ¾ lb. boneless skinless chicken breasts, cut into thin strips
- ½ tsp. garlic salt
- ¼ tsp. pepper
- 2 Tbsp. canola oil, divided
- 4 cups broccoli coleslaw mix
- 1 medium red onion, halved and thinly sliced
- 1 tsp. minced fresh gingerroot
- 6 flour tortillas (8 in.), warmed

1. Whisk the first 5 ingredients until blended. Toss the chicken with garlic salt and pepper.
2. In a large cast-iron or other heavy skillet, heat 1 Tbsp. oil over medium-high heat; stir-fry chicken until no longer pink, 3-4 minutes. Remove from pan; keep warm.
3. In same pan, heat remaining oil over medium-high heat; stir-fry coleslaw mix, onion and ginger until broccoli is crisp-tender, 2-3 minutes. Stir in peanut butter mixture. Serve the chicken and vegetable mixture in tortillas.
1 wrap: 389 cal., 15g fat (3g sat. fat), 31mg chol., 935mg sod., 44g carb. (12g sugars, 4g fiber), 21g pro.

THAI CHICKEN WRAPS

⏱ 🍎 RASPBERRY PECAN CHICKEN SALAD

I gave this sweet-savory chicken salad a little zip with Chinese five-spice powder, which tastes a bit like pumpkin pie spice. Sprinkle some on roasted carrots for an awesome meal.
—*Lisa Renshaw, Kansas City, MO*

TAKES: 15 min. • **MAKES:** 6 sandwiches

- 1   carton (6 oz.) orange yogurt
- ½   cup mayonnaise
- ¼   tsp. Chinese five-spice powder
- 3   cups cubed cooked chicken
- 2   green onions, chopped
- ¼   cup sliced celery
- ¼   cup chopped pecans, toasted
- 1   cup fresh raspberries
- 12 slices multigrain bread

In a large bowl, mix yogurt, mayonnaise and five-spice powder. Stir in chicken, green onions, celery and pecans. Gently stir in raspberries. Serve on bread.

1 sandwich: 463 cal., 24g fat (4g sat. fat), 65mg chol., 371mg sod., 31g carb. (10g sugars, 6g fiber), 29g pro.

GET MORE POACHING KNOW-HOW
Just hover your camera here.

RASPBERRY PECAN CHICKEN SALAD

HOW-TO
Poach Chicken

- Choose a pan that's big enough to fit your chicken without overcrowding, but small enough that it won't require a lot of water. Place chicken breasts in a single layer in the pan without overlapping them.
- Add ½ cup white wine or beer and, if desired, aromatics. (We like 1 bay leaf, 1 smashed garlic clove, 3 fresh thyme sprigs and 6 whole peppercorns.) Add enough water to cover chicken by 1 in.
- Cook at a bare simmer 15-20 minutes, until a thermometer reads 165°.

🕐 HERBED CHICKEN CAESAR SALAD

This main-dish salad may sound fancy, but in reality it couldn't be easier to make.
—*Kay Andersen, Bear, DE*

TAKES: 25 min. • **MAKES:** 2 servings

- 2 boneless skinless chicken breast halves (½ lb.)
- 2 tsp. olive oil
- ⅛ tsp. dried basil
- ⅛ tsp. dried oregano
- ¼ tsp. garlic salt, optional
- ¼ tsp. pepper
- ¼ tsp. paprika
- 4 cups torn romaine
- 1 small tomato, thinly sliced
  Creamy Caesar salad dressing
  Caesar salad croutons, optional

1. Brush chicken with oil. Combine basil, oregano, garlic salt if desired, pepper and paprika; sprinkle over chicken. Grill, uncovered, over medium-low heat for 12-15 minutes or until a thermometer reads 165°, turning several times.

2. Arrange romaine and tomato on plates. Cut chicken into strips; arrange over salads. Drizzle with dressing. Sprinkle with croutons if desired.

1 serving: 219 cal., 8g fat (0 sat. fat), 73mg chol., 467mg sod., 6g carb. (0 sugars, 0 fiber), 29g pro. **Diabetic exchanges:** 3 lean meat, 1 vegetable, 1 fat.

HERBED CHICKEN CAESAR SALAD

🕐 🍎 STRAWBERRY TARRAGON CHICKEN SALAD

After thinking about creating this salad for some time, this past spring I used my homegrown strawberries and fresh tarragon to do a little experimenting. It didn't take me very long to come up with a winner! My husband enjoyed my creation as much as I did, and we can't until it's strawberry season again!
—*Sue Gronholz, Beaver Dam, WI*

TAKES: 30 min. • **MAKES:** 5 servings

- ½ cup mayonnaise
- 2 tsp. sugar
- 2 tsp. minced fresh tarragon or 1 tsp. dried tarragon
- ¼ tsp. salt
- ⅛ tsp. pepper
- 2½ cups cubed cooked chicken breast
- 2 cups quartered fresh strawberries
- 1 cup fresh shelled peas or frozen peas, thawed
- ½ cup chopped celery
- 2 Tbsp. chopped sweet onion
  Torn mixed salad greens
- ½ cup chopped pecans, toasted

1. In a large bowl, whisk the first 5 ingredients until blended. Stir in the chicken, strawberries, peas, celery and onion. Serve over salad greens; sprinkle with pecans.

1 cup: 378 cal., 26g fat (4g sat. fat), 56mg chol., 285mg sod., 13g carb. (7g sugars, 4g fiber), 23g pro.

TEST KITCHEN TIP

This salad is better when made ahead of time so the flavors can blend. But don't add the strawberries until you're ready to serve, as they tend to turn the salad pink when they sit!

STRAWBERRY TARRAGON CHICKEN SALAD

CHICKEN
SAUSAGE
PITA POCKETS

🕐 🍎 CHICKEN SAUSAGE PITA POCKETS

Chicken sausage comes in many flavors, so I try different ones when I make these pitas. With fresh basil and veggies, they are inspired by the Greek gyro.
—*Christina Price, Colorado Springs, CO*

TAKES: 25 min. • **MAKES:** 4 servings

6 tsp. olive oil, divided
1 pkg. (12 oz.) fully cooked roasted garlic chicken sausage links, or flavor of your choice, sliced
1 cup sliced fresh mushrooms
1 small onion, halved and sliced
1 medium zucchini, halved lengthwise and sliced
1 medium yellow summer squash, halved lengthwise and sliced
3 Tbsp. chopped fresh basil
8 whole wheat pita pocket halves, warmed
   Optional: Sliced tomato and plain Greek yogurt

1. In a large nonstick skillet, heat 2 tsp. oil over medium-high heat. Add the sausage; cook and stir 4-6 minutes or until slices are lightly browned. Remove from pan.
2. In same skillet, heat 2 tsp. oil over medium-high heat. Add mushrooms and onion; cook and stir 4-6 minutes or until tender. Remove from pan.
3. Add remaining oil to pan. Add the zucchini and yellow squash; cook and stir 3-5 minutes or until tender. Stir in basil, sausage and mushroom mixture; heat through. Serve in pitas. If desired, add tomato and yogurt.
2 filled pita halves: 376 cal., 16g fat (3g sat. fat), 70mg chol., 736mg sod., 39g carb. (5g sugars, 6g fiber), 22g pro.
Diabetic exchanges: 3 lean meat, 2 starch, 1½ fat, 1 vegetable.

MEXICAN-INSPIRED
CHICKEN SOUP, PAGE 113

SOUPS, STEWS, CHILI & MORE

CREAMY WHITE CHILI

I received this wonderful recipe from my sister-in-law, who made a big batch and served a crowd one night. It was a hit. Plus, it's easy and quick, which is helpful since I'm a college student. In all my years of 4-H cooking, I've never had another dish get so many compliments.
—*Laura Brewer, Lafayette, IN*

PREP: 10 min. • **COOK:** 40 min.
MAKES: 7 servings

- 1   lb. boneless skinless chicken breasts, cut into ½-in. cubes
- 1   medium onion, chopped
- 1½ tsp. garlic powder
- 1   Tbsp. canola oil
- 2   cans (15½ oz. each) great northern beans, rinsed and drained
- 1   can (14½ oz.) chicken broth
- 2   cans (4 oz. each) chopped green chiles
- 1   tsp. salt
- 1   tsp. ground cumin
- 1   tsp. dried oregano
- ½   tsp. pepper
- ¼   tsp. cayenne pepper
- 1   cup sour cream
- ½   cup heavy whipping cream
      Optional: Tortilla chips, shredded cheddar cheese, sliced seeded jalapeno pepper

1. In a large saucepan, saute chicken, onion and garlic powder in oil until the chicken is no longer pink. Add the beans, broth, chiles and seasonings. Bring to a boil. Reduce heat; simmer, uncovered, for 30 minutes.
2. Remove from the heat; stir in sour cream and heavy cream. If desired, top with tortilla chips, cheese and jalapenos.
1 cup: 334 cal., 16g fat (8g sat. fat), 81mg chol., 1045mg sod., 24g carb. (3g sugars, 7g fiber), 22g pro.

LENTIL & CHICKEN SAUSAGE STEW

🍎 🍲 LENTIL & CHICKEN SAUSAGE STEW

This hearty and healthy stew will warm your family right down to their toes! Serve with cornbread or rolls to soak up every last drop.
—*Jan Valdez, Chicago, IL*

PREP: 15 min. • **COOK:** 8 hours
MAKES: 6 servings (2¼ qt.)

- 1   carton (32 oz.) reduced-sodium chicken broth
- 1   can (28 oz.) diced tomatoes, undrained
- 3   fully cooked spicy chicken sausage links (3 oz. each), cut into ½-in. slices
- 1   cup dried lentils, rinsed
- 1   medium onion, chopped
- 1   medium carrot, chopped
- 1   celery rib, chopped
- 2   garlic cloves, minced
- ½   tsp. dried thyme

In a 4- or 5-qt. slow cooker, combine all ingredients. Cover and cook on low for 8-10 hours or until lentils are tender.
1½ cups: 231 cal., 4g fat (1g sat. fat), 33mg chol., 803mg sod., 31g carb. (8g sugars, 13g fiber), 19g pro. **Diabetic exchanges:** 2 vegetable, 2 lean meat, 1 starch.

CHICKEN POTPIE SOUP

My grandmother hand-wrote a cookbook. She included her amazing pie crust, and I added the delicious soup for it.
—*Karen LeMay, Seabrook, TX*

PREP: 20 min. + chilling • **COOK:** 20 min.
MAKES: 6 servings (2¼ qt.)

- 2 cups all-purpose flour
- 1¼ tsp. salt
- ⅔ cup shortening
- 5 to 6 Tbsp. 2% milk

SOUP

- 2 Tbsp. butter
- 1 cup cubed peeled potatoes
- 1 cup chopped sweet onion
- 2 celery ribs, chopped
- 2 medium carrots, chopped
- ½ cup all-purpose flour
- ½ tsp. salt
- ¼ tsp. pepper
- 3 cans (14½ oz. each) chicken broth
- 2 cups shredded cooked chicken
- 1 cup frozen petite peas
- 1 cup frozen corn

1. In a large bowl, mix flour and salt; cut in shortening until crumbly. Gradually add milk, tossing with a fork until dough holds together when pressed. Shape into a disk, cover and refrigerate for 30 minutes or overnight.

2. Preheat oven to 425°. On a lightly floured surface, roll the dough to ⅛-in. thickness. Using a floured 2½-in. heart-shaped or round cutter, cut 18 shapes. Place 1 in. apart on ungreased baking sheets. Bake for 8-11 minutes or until golden brown. Cool on a wire rack.

3. For soup, heat butter in a Dutch oven over medium-high heat. Add potatoes, onion, celery and carrots; cook and stir for 5-7 minutes or until onion is tender.

4. Stir in the flour, salt and pepper until blended; gradually whisk in broth. Bring to a boil over medium-high heat, stirring occasionally. Reduce heat; simmer, uncovered, 8-10 minutes or until potatoes are tender. Stir in the remaining ingredients; heat through. Serve with pie crust toppers.

1½ cups soup with 3 toppers: 614 cal., 30g fat (9g sat. fat), 57mg chol., 1706mg sod., 60g carb. (7g sugars, 5g fiber), 23g pro.

CHICKEN POTPIE SOUP

COCONUT CHICKEN & SWEET POTATO STEW

🍲 COCONUT CHICKEN & SWEET POTATO STEW

This stew tastes as if you spent hours in the kitchen. The flavors of coconut milk, sweet potato and coriander nicely complement the chicken. A garnish of cilantro and some toasted coconut adds a bit of sophistication.
—*Nicole Filizetti, Stevens Point, WI*

PREP: 20 min. • **COOK:** 6 hours
MAKES: 8 servings (2½ qt.)

- 1½ lbs. boneless skinless chicken breasts, cubed
- 2 lbs. sweet potatoes (about 3 medium), peeled and cubed
- 3 cups canned coconut milk, divided
- 1 can (8 oz.) unsweetened pineapple tidbits, drained
- 1 small onion, chopped
- 1 tsp. ground coriander
- ½ tsp. salt
- ½ tsp. crushed red pepper flakes
- ¼ tsp. pepper
  Optional: Hot cooked basmati rice, toasted unsweetened shredded coconut, minced fresh cilantro and lime wedges

1. Combine chicken, sweet potatoes, 2 cups coconut milk, pineapple, onion and seasonings in a 4- or 5-qt. slow cooker. Cook, covered, on low until chicken and sweet potatoes are tender, 6-8 hours.
2. Stir in remaining 1 cup coconut milk. If desired, serve stew with the optional ingredients.
1¼ cups: 365 cal., 16g fat (14g sat. fat), 47mg chol., 223mg sod., 34g carb. (17g sugars, 4g fiber), 21g pro.

SPICY PEANUT CHICKEN CHILI

While spending time in the Southwest, I discovered Mexican peanut chicken and thought it would be fun to make it into a chili. Chipotle peppers give it a nice spice that's extra warming on a cold day.
—*Crystal Schlueter, Northglenn, CO*

- -

TAKES: 30 min. • **MAKES:** 6 servings (2 qt.)

1 can (15 oz.) pinto beans, rinsed and drained
1 can (14½ oz.) Mexican diced tomatoes, undrained
1 can (14½ oz.) no-salt-added diced tomatoes, undrained
1 can (14½ oz.) reduced-sodium chicken broth
1 pkg. (12 oz.) frozen Southwestern corn
3 Tbsp. creamy peanut butter
1 to 2 Tbsp. minced chipotle peppers in adobo sauce
2 tsp. chili powder
½ tsp. ground cinnamon
3 cups coarsely shredded rotisserie chicken
6 Tbsp. reduced-fat sour cream
Minced fresh cilantro, optional

1. Place the first 9 ingredients in a 6-qt. stockpot; bring to a boil. Reduce heat; simmer, covered, until flavors are blended, about 15 minutes.
2. Stir in chicken; heat through. Serve with sour cream and, if desired, cilantro.
Freeze option: Freeze the cooled chili in freezer containers. To use, partially thaw in refrigerator overnight. Heat through in a saucepan, stirring occasionally; add broth if necessary.
1⅓ cups chili with 1 Tbsp. sour cream: 368 cal., 13g fat (3g sat. fat), 67mg chol., 797mg sod., 33g carb. (11g sugars, 6g fiber), 30g pro.

WEST AFRICAN CHICKEN STEW

I really love authentic African flavors, but they can be hard to come by in the U.S. This recipe features a delicious combination of African ingredients like peanut butter, sweet potatoes and black-eyed peas, all of which are readily available.
—*Michael Cohen, Los Angeles, CA*

- -

PREP: 20 min. • **COOK:** 30 min.
MAKES: 8 servings (2½ qt.)

1 lb. boneless skinless chicken breasts, cut into 1-in. cubes
½ tsp. salt
¼ tsp. pepper
3 tsp. canola oil, divided
1 medium onion, thinly sliced
6 garlic cloves, minced
2 Tbsp. minced fresh gingerroot
2 cans (15½ oz. each) black-eyed peas, rinsed and drained
1 can (28 oz.) crushed tomatoes
1 large sweet potato, peeled and cut into 1-in. cubes
1 cup reduced-sodium chicken broth
¼ cup creamy peanut butter
1½ tsp. minced fresh thyme or ½ tsp. dried thyme, divided
¼ tsp. cayenne pepper
Hot cooked brown rice, optional

1. Sprinkle the chicken with salt and pepper. In a Dutch oven, cook chicken over medium heat in 2 tsp. oil for 4-6 minutes or until no longer pink; remove and set aside.
2. In the same pan, saute the onion in remaining oil until tender. Add garlic and ginger; cook 1 minute longer.
3. Stir in peas, tomatoes, sweet potato, broth, peanut butter, 1¼ tsp. thyme and cayenne. Bring to a boil. Reduce heat; cover and simmer 15-20 minutes or until potato is tender.
4. Add chicken and heat through. Serve stew with rice if desired. Sprinkle with remaining thyme.
1¼ cups: 275 cal., 7g fat (1g sat. fat), 31mg chol., 636mg sod., 32g carb. (5g sugars, 6g fiber), 22g pro. **Diabetic exchanges:** 3 lean meat, 2 vegetable, 1 starch, 1 fat.

WEST AFRICAN CHICKEN STEW

CHICKEN & DUMPLINGS

⏱ CHICKEN & DUMPLINGS

Perfect for fall nights, my simple version of comforting chicken and dumplings is speedy, low in fat and a delicious, easy one-dish meal.
—*Nancy Tuck, Elk Falls, KS*

- -

TAKES: 30 min. • **MAKES:** 6 servings

- 3 celery ribs, chopped
- 2 medium carrots, sliced
- 3 cans (14½ oz. each) reduced-sodium chicken broth
- 3 cups cubed cooked chicken breast
- ½ tsp. poultry seasoning
- ⅛ tsp. pepper
- 1⅔ cups reduced-fat biscuit/baking mix
- ⅔ cup fat-free milk

1. In a Dutch oven coated with cooking spray, cook and stir celery and carrots over medium heat until tender, about 5 minutes. Stir in broth, chicken and seasonings. Bring to a boil; reduce the heat to a gentle simmer.
2. For dumplings, mix biscuit mix and milk until a soft dough forms. Drop by tablespoonfuls on top of the simmering liquid. Reduce the heat to low; cover and cook until a toothpick inserted in dumplings comes out clean (do not lift cover during the first 10 minutes), 10-15 minutes.
1 cup: 260 cal., 4g fat (1g sat. fat), 54mg chol., 964mg sod., 28g carb. (6g sugars, 2g fiber), 27g pro.

WHY YOU'LL LOVE IT...

"This was very good and my kids loved it. The only thing I changed was I used Italian seasoning instead of poultry seasoning because I don't like sage."
—TABITHABEEMAN, TASTEOFHOME.COM

CHECK OUT HOW EASY THIS IS
Just hover your camera here.

SAUSAGE &
CHICKEN GUMBO

MEXICAN CHICKEN CORN CHOWDER

I like to make this smooth, creamy soup when company comes to visit. Its zippy flavor is full of southwestern flair. Sometimes I top it with toasted strips of cut-up tortillas.
—*Susan Garoutte, Georgetown, TX*

- -

TAKES: 30 min. • **MAKES:** 8 servings (2 qt.)

1½ lbs. boneless skinless chicken breasts, cut into 1-in. pieces
½ cup chopped onion
3 Tbsp. butter
1 to 2 garlic cloves, minced
1 cup hot water
2 tsp. chicken bouillon granules
½ to 1 tsp. ground cumin
2 cups half-and-half cream
2 cups shredded Monterey Jack cheese
1 can (14¾ oz.) cream-style corn
1 can (4 oz.) chopped green chiles, undrained
¼ to 1 tsp. hot pepper sauce
1 medium tomato, chopped
   Optional: Minced fresh cilantro and fried tortilla strips

1. In a Dutch oven, brown chicken and onion in butter until chicken is no longer pink. Add garlic; cook 1 minute longer. Add water, bouillon and cumin; bring to a boil. Reduce heat; cover and simmer for 5 minutes.
2. Stir in the cream, cheese, corn, chiles and hot pepper sauce. Cook and stir over low heat until cheese is melted; add tomato. If desired, top with cilantro and tortilla strips.
1 cup: 368 cal., 21g fat (13g sat. fat), 114mg chol., 753mg sod., 14g carb. (5g sugars, 1g fiber), 28g pro.

SAUSAGE & CHICKEN GUMBO

This recipe for the classic southern comfort food was the first thing I ever cooked for my girlfriend. It was simple to make, but tasted gourmet. Lucky for me, it turned out to be love at first bite.
—*Kael Harvey, Brooklyn, NY*

- -

PREP: 35 min. • **COOK:** 6 hours
MAKES: 6 servings

¼ cup all-purpose flour
¼ cup canola oil
4 cups chicken broth, divided
1 pkg. (14 oz.) smoked sausage, cut into ½-in. slices
1 cup frozen sliced okra, thawed
1 small green pepper, chopped
1 medium onion, chopped
1 celery rib, chopped
3 garlic cloves, minced
½ tsp. pepper
¼ tsp. salt
¼ tsp. cayenne pepper
2 cups coarsely shredded cooked chicken
   Hot cooked rice

1. In a heavy saucepan, mix flour and oil until smooth; cook and stir over medium heat until light brown, about 4 minutes. Reduce heat to medium-low; cook and stir until dark reddish brown, about 15 minutes (do not burn). Gradually stir in 3 cups broth; transfer mixture to a 4- or 5-qt. slow cooker.
2. Stir in sausage, vegetables, garlic and seasonings. Cook, covered, on low until flavors are blended, 6-8 hours. Stir in chicken and remaining broth; heat through. Serve with rice.
Freeze option: Freeze the cooled soup in freezer containers. To use, partially thaw in refrigerator overnight. Heat through in a saucepan, stirring occasionally; add broth if necessary.
1 cup: 427 cal., 31g fat (9g sat. fat), 89mg chol., 1548mg sod., 11g carb. (4g sugars, 1g fiber), 25g pro.

**MEXICAN CHICKEN
CORN CHOWDER**

🍲 CHICKEN VEGGIE SOUP

This satisfying veggie soup hits the spot at lunch or dinner. Add a side salad and some whole grain bread for a filling and nutritious meal.
—*Amy Cheatham, Sandusky, OH*

- -

PREP: 25 min. • **COOK:** 5 hours
MAKES: 7 servings (about 2¾ qt.)

- 1 large sweet onion, chopped
- 1 cup sliced baby portobello mushrooms
- ½ cup chopped green pepper
- ½ cup chopped sweet red pepper
- 1 Tbsp. butter
- 1 Tbsp. olive oil
- 5 garlic cloves, minced
- ¾ lb. boneless skinless chicken breasts, cut into ½-in. cubes
- 1 can (49½ oz.) chicken broth
- 1 can (28 oz.) crushed tomatoes, undrained
- 2 medium carrots, cut into ¼-in. slices
- ½ cup medium pearl barley
- 1¾ tsp. Italian seasoning
- 1½ tsp. pepper
- ½ tsp. salt

1. In a large skillet, saute the onion, mushrooms and peppers in butter and oil until tender. Add garlic; cook 1 minute longer.

2. Transfer to a 5-qt. slow cooker. Add the remaining ingredients. Cover and cook on low until chicken and barley are tender, 5-6 hours.

Freeze option: Freeze cooled soup in freezer containers. To use, partially thaw in refrigerator overnight. Heat through in a saucepan, stirring occasionally; add broth if necessary.

1½ cups: 212 cal., 6g fat (2g sat. fat), 36mg chol., 1236mg sod., 27g carb. (4g sugars, 6g fiber), 15g pro.

CHICKEN VEGGIE SOUP

🍲 SQUASH & CHICKEN STEW

We put together a satisfying stew that's nutritious, family-friendly and loaded with flavor. Chicken thighs are slowly simmered with stewed tomatoes, butternut squash, green peppers and onion for delicious meal-in-one convenience.
—Taste of Home *Test Kitchen*

PREP: 15 min. • **COOK:** 6 hours
MAKES: 5 servings

- 2 lbs. boneless skinless chicken thighs, cut into ½-in. pieces
- 1 can (28 oz.) stewed tomatoes, cut up
- 3 cups cubed peeled butternut squash
- 2 medium green peppers, cut into ½-in. pieces
- 1 small onion, sliced and separated into rings
- 1 cup water
- 1 tsp. salt
- 1 tsp. ground cumin
- ½ tsp. ground coriander
- ½ tsp. pepper
- 2 Tbsp. minced fresh parsley
  Hot cooked couscous, optional

In a 5-qt. slow cooker, combine the first 10 ingredients. Cover and cook on low for 6-7 hours or until the chicken is no longer pink. Sprinkle with the parsley. Serve with couscous if desired.

1½ cups: 384 cal., 14g fat (4g sat. fat), 121mg chol., 867mg sod., 31g carb. (13g sugars, 7g fiber), 37g pro.

SQUASH & CHICKEN STEW

🍎 WHITE CHICKEN CHILI

Folks will enjoy a change from the traditional when they spoon into this flavorful blend of tender chicken, white beans and just enough zip.
—Taste of Home *Test Kitchen*

PREP: 15 min. • **COOK:** 25 min.
MAKES: 10 servings (2½ qt.)

- 1 lb. boneless skinless chicken breasts, chopped
- 1 medium onion, chopped
- 1 Tbsp. olive oil
- 2 garlic cloves, minced
- 2 cans (14 oz. each) chicken broth
- 1 can (4 oz.) chopped green chiles
- 2 tsp. ground cumin
- 2 tsp. dried oregano
- 1½ tsp. cayenne pepper
- 3 cans (14½ oz. each) great northern beans, drained, divided
- 1 cup shredded Monterey Jack cheese
  Sliced jalapeno pepper, optional

1. In a Dutch oven over medium heat, cook chicken and onion in oil until lightly browned. Add the garlic; cook 1 minute longer. Stir in the broth, chiles, cumin, oregano and cayenne; bring to a boil.
2. Reduce heat to low. With a potato masher, mash one can of beans until smooth. Add to the saucepan. Add the remaining beans to saucepan. Simmer for 20-30 minutes or until chicken is no longer pink and onion is tender.
3. Top each serving with cheese and, if desired, jalapeno pepper.
Freeze option: Freeze cooled chili in freezer containers. To use, partially thaw in refrigerator overnight. Heat through in a saucepan, stirring occasionally; add broth or water if necessary.
1 cup: 219 cal., 7g fat (3g sat. fat), 37mg chol., 644mg sod., 21g carb. (1g sugars, 7g fiber), 19g pro. **Diabetic exchanges:** 2 lean meat, 1½ starch, 1 fat.

🕐 ITALIAN CHICKEN STEW

My husband enjoys preparing this satisfying stew because it's so easy to make. With warm Italian bread, it's a winner on a cold day.
—*Jo Calizzi, Vandergrift, PA*

TAKES: 20 min. • **MAKES:** 4 servings

- 1 lb. boneless skinless chicken breasts, cubed
- 4 medium potatoes, peeled and cut into ¼-in. cubes
- 1 medium sweet red pepper, chopped
- 2 garlic cloves, minced
- 1 to 2 Tbsp. olive oil
- 1 jar (26 oz.) meatless spaghetti sauce
- 1¾ cups frozen cut green beans
- 1 tsp. dried basil
- ¼ to ½ tsp. salt
- ¼ tsp. crushed red pepper flakes
  Pepper to taste

In a Dutch oven, cook the chicken, potatoes, red pepper and garlic in oil until the chicken is no longer pink and vegetables are tender. Stir in the remaining ingredients; heat through.

1½ cups: 475 cal., 13g fat (3g sat. fat), 63mg chol., 995mg sod., 62g carb. (0 sugars, 11g fiber), 31g pro. **Diabetic exchanges:** 4 starch, 3 lean meat, 1 fat.

GRANDMA'S CHICKEN & DUMPLING SOUP

GRANDMA'S CHICKEN & DUMPLING SOUP

I've enjoyed making this rich soup for over 40 years. Every time I serve it, I remember my grandma, who was very special to me and was known as a great cook.
—*Paulette Balda, Prophetstown, IL*

- -

PREP: 20 min. + cooling • **COOK:** 2½ hours
MAKES: 12 servings (3 qt.)

- 1 broiler/fryer chicken (3½ to 4 lbs.), cut up
- 2¼ qt. cold water
- 5 chicken bouillon cubes
- 6 whole peppercorns
- 3 whole cloves
- 1 can (10¾ oz.) condensed cream of chicken soup, undiluted
- 1 can (10¾ oz.) condensed cream of mushroom soup, undiluted
- 1½ cups chopped carrots
- 1 cup fresh or frozen peas
- 1 cup chopped celery
- 1 cup chopped peeled potatoes
- ¼ cup chopped onion
- 1½ tsp. seasoned salt
- ¼ tsp. pepper
- 1 bay leaf

DUMPLINGS

- 2 cups all-purpose flour
- 4 tsp. baking powder
- 1 tsp. salt
- ¼ tsp. pepper
- 1 large egg, beaten
- 2 Tbsp. butter, melted
- ¾ to 1 cup 2% milk
- Snipped fresh parsley, optional

1. Place the chicken, water, bouillon, peppercorns and cloves in a stockpot. Cover and bring to a boil; skim foam. Reduce heat and cover and simmer until chicken is tender; 45-60 minutes. Strain broth; return to the stockpot.
2. Remove chicken and set aside until cool enough to handle. Remove meat from bones; discard bones and skin. Cut chicken into chunks. Cool broth and skim off fat.
3. Return chicken to stockpot with soups, vegetables and seasonings; bring to a boil. Reduce heat; cover and simmer for 1 hour. Uncover; increase heat to a gentle boil. Discard bay leaf.
4. For the dumplings, combine dry ingredients in a medium bowl. Stir in egg, butter and enough milk to make a moist, stiff batter. Drop by teaspoonfuls into soup. Cover and cook without lifting the lid for 18-20 minutes. Sprinkle with parsley if desired.

1 cup: 333 cal., 14g fat (5g sat. fat), 79mg chol., 1447mg sod., 28g carb. (4g sugars, 3g fiber), 22g pro.

HOW-TO

Mix Dumpling Dough

Combine flour, baking powder and seasonings. Make a well in the flour mixture; add the egg, butter and ½ cup milk. Gradually stir in more milk, incorporating flour mixture from the sides as you go. Stir just until a stiff dough comes together.

⏲ 🍎 SPICY CHICKEN STEW

When you're craving cozy Mexican flavors, try this slightly spicy stew that couldn't be easier to make. Round out the meal with a fresh tossed salad.
—Taste of Home *Test Kitchen*

TAKES: 30 min. • **MAKES:** 6 servings

- 2 lbs. boneless skinless chicken thighs, cut into ½-in. pieces
- 2 tsp. minced garlic
- 2 Tbsp. olive oil
- 1 can (15 oz.) garbanzo beans or chickpeas, rinsed and drained
- 1 can (14½ oz.) diced tomatoes with onions, undrained
- 1 cup lime-garlic salsa
- 1 tsp. ground cumin
- ⅓ cup minced fresh cilantro
  Sour cream, optional

In a Dutch oven, cook chicken and garlic in oil for 5 minutes. Stir in the beans, tomatoes, salsa and cumin. Cover and simmer until chicken is no longer pink, about 15 minutes. Stir in cilantro. Top with sour cream if desired.

1½ cups: 359 cal., 17g fat (4g sat. fat), 101mg chol., 622mg sod., 18g carb. (5g sugars, 4g fiber), 31g pro.

LEARN HOW TO MAKE IT
Just hover your camera here.

THE ULTIMATE CHICKEN NOODLE SOUP

THE ULTIMATE CHICKEN NOODLE SOUP

My first Wisconsin winter was so cold, all I wanted to eat was soup. This recipe is in heavy rotation at our house from November to April.
—Gina Nistico, Denver, CO

- -

PREP: 15 min. • **COOK:** 45 min. + standing
MAKES: 10 servings (about 3½ qt.)

2½ lbs. bone-in chicken thighs
½   tsp. salt
½   tsp. pepper
1   Tbsp. canola oil
1   large onion, chopped
1   garlic clove, minced
10 cups chicken broth
4   celery ribs, chopped
4   medium carrots, chopped
2   bay leaves
1   tsp. minced fresh thyme
    or ¼ tsp. dried thyme
3   cups uncooked kluski or other
    egg noodles (about 8 oz.)
1   Tbsp. chopped fresh parsley
1   Tbsp. lemon juice
    Optional: Additional salt and pepper

1. Pat chicken dry with paper towels; sprinkle with salt and pepper. In a 6-qt. stockpot, heat oil over medium-high heat. Add the chicken in batches, skin side down; cook until dark golden brown, 3-4 minutes. Remove chicken from pan; remove and discard skin. Discard drippings, reserving 2 Tbsp.
2. Add onion to drippings; cook and stir over medium-high heat until tender, 4-5 minutes. Add garlic; cook 1 minute longer. Add broth, stirring to loosen browned bits from pan. Bring to a boil. Return chicken to pan. Add the celery, carrots, bay leaves and thyme. Reduce heat; simmer, covered, until chicken is tender, 25-30 minutes.
3. Transfer chicken to a plate. Remove soup from heat. Add noodles; let stand, covered, until the noodles are tender, 20-22 minutes.
4. Meanwhile, when chicken is cool enough to handle, remove meat from bones; discard bones. Shred meat into bite-sized pieces. Return the meat to stockpot. Stir in parsley and lemon juice. If desired, adjust the seasoning with additional salt and pepper. Discard the bay leaves.
1⅓ cups: 239 cal., 12g fat (3g sat. fat), 68mg chol., 1176mg sod., 14g carb. (3g sugars, 2g fiber), 18g pro.

HOW-TO

Fix the Biggest Chicken Soup Problems

- **Mushy noodles.**
  To prevent soggy noodles, let the uncooked egg noodles stand in the hot soup, covered, for 20 minutes before serving. Cooking the noodles off-heat ensures they plump gently; doing so in the soup means they absorb the delicious broth instead of boring ol' water.

- **Dry, tasteless chicken.**
  Say buh-bye to blah chicken by opting for bone-in thighs instead. They stay juicy and moist, with a richer and more robust flavor than boneless skinless chicken breasts.

- **Bland broth.**
  The thighs are key here, too. Give a homey boost to store-bought broth by searing meaty, skin-on chicken thighs first. This builds those irresistible brown bits on the bottom of the pan before you add the broth (see image below left). A little spritz of lemon juice is the finishing touch. The subtle contrast brightens and balances the herby, savory broth.

INGREDIENT CLOSE-UP

Kluski Noodles

Kluski is a generic name for thin Polish egg noodles. They combine the best of Old and New Worlds: the tender texture of a handmade noodle in a go-to pantry item.

CURRY
CHICKEN
STEW

CREAMY CHICKEN GNOCCHI SOUP

I tasted a similar soup at Olive Garden and wanted to try and make it myself. Here's the delicious result! It's wonderful on a chilly evening.
—*Jaclynn Robinson, Shingletown, CA*

PREP: 25 min. • **COOK:** 15 min.
MAKES: 8 servings (2 qt.)

- 1 lb. boneless skinless chicken breasts, cut into ½-in. pieces
- ⅓ cup butter, divided
- 1 small onion, chopped
- 1 medium carrot, shredded
- 1 celery rib, chopped
- 2 garlic cloves, minced
- ⅓ cup all-purpose flour
- 3½ cups 2% milk
- 1½ cups heavy whipping cream
- 1 Tbsp. reduced-sodium chicken bouillon granules
- ¼ tsp. coarsely ground pepper
- 1 pkg. (16 oz.) potato gnocchi
- ½ cup chopped fresh spinach

1. In a Dutch oven, brown chicken in 2 Tbsp. butter. Remove and keep warm. In the same pan, saute the onion, carrot, celery and garlic in remaining butter until tender.
2. Whisk in the flour until blended; gradually stir in the milk, cream, bouillon and pepper. Bring to a boil. Reduce heat; cook and stir until thickened, about 2 minutes.
3. Add the gnocchi and spinach; cook until spinach is wilted, 3-4 minutes. Add the chicken. Cover and simmer until heated through (do not boil), about 10 minutes.
Note: Look for potato gnocchi in the pasta or frozen foods section.
1 cup: 482 cal., 28g fat (17g sat. fat), 125mg chol., 527mg sod., 36g carb. (10g sugars, 2g fiber), 21g pro.

🍲 CURRY CHICKEN STEW

My Grandma Inky grew up in India and passed down this recipe to my mother, who then passed it down to me. I tweaked the ingredients a bit to fit my toddler's taste buds, but it's just as scrumptious as the original. This recipe brings back fond memories of my family gathered around the table.
—*Teresa Flowers, Sacramento, CA*

PREP: 15 min. • **COOK:** 4 hours
MAKES: 6 servings (about 2½ qt.)

- 2 cans (14½ oz. each) chicken broth
- 1 can (10¾ oz.) condensed cream of chicken soup, undiluted
- 1 tub Knorr concentrated chicken stock (4.66 oz.)
- 4 garlic cloves, minced
- 1 Tbsp. curry powder
- ¼ tsp. salt
- ¼ tsp. cayenne pepper
- ¼ tsp. pepper
- 6 boneless skinless chicken breasts (6 oz. each)
- 1 medium green pepper, cut into thin strips
- 1 medium onion, thinly sliced
  Hot cooked rice
  Optional: Chopped fresh cilantro and chutney

1. In a large bowl, combine the first 8 ingredients. Place chicken, green pepper and onion in a 5- or 6-qt. slow cooker; pour broth mixture over top. Cook, covered, on low until chicken and vegetables are tender, 4-5 hours.
2. Remove chicken and cool slightly. Cut or shred meat into bite-sized pieces and return to slow cooker; heat through. Serve with rice. If desired, top with cilantro and chutney.
1¾ cups: 266 cal., 8g fat (2g sat. fat), 101mg chol., 1604mg sod., 9g carb. (2g sugars, 2g fiber), 36g pro.

CREAMY CHICKEN
GNOCCHI SOUP

CREAMY CHICKEN & BROCCOLI STEW

This recipe is so easy to make, but no one would ever guess. My husband, who doesn't like many chicken dishes, requests it regularly.
—*Mary Watkins, Little Elm, TX*

- -

PREP: 15 min. • **COOK:** 6 hours
MAKES: 8 servings

8   bone-in chicken thighs,
     skinned (about 3 lbs.)

1   cup Italian salad dressing
½   cup white wine or chicken broth
6   Tbsp. butter, melted, divided
1   Tbsp. dried minced onion
1   Tbsp. garlic powder
1   Tbsp. Italian seasoning
¾   tsp. salt, divided
¾   tsp. pepper, divided
1   can (10¾ oz.) condensed cream of
     mushroom soup, undiluted
1   pkg. (8 oz.) cream cheese, softened
2   cups frozen broccoli florets, thawed
2   lbs. red potatoes, quartered

1. Place chicken in a 4-qt. slow cooker. Combine the salad dressing, wine, 4 Tbsp. butter, onion, garlic powder, Italian seasoning, ½ tsp. salt and ½ tsp. pepper in a small bowl; pour over chicken.

2. Cover and cook on low for 5 hours. Skim fat. Remove the chicken from the slow cooker with a slotted spoon; shred the chicken with 2 forks and return to slow cooker. Combine the soup, cream cheese and 2 cups of liquid from slow cooker in a small bowl until blended; add to slow cooker. Cover and cook 45 minutes longer or until chicken is tender, adding the broccoli during the last 30 minutes of cooking.

3. Meanwhile, place potatoes in a large saucepan and cover with water. Bring to a boil. Reduce the heat; cover and simmer until tender, 15-20 minutes. Drain and return to pan. Mash the potatoes with the remaining butter, salt and pepper.

4. Serve chicken and broccoli mixture with potatoes.

⅔ cup chicken mixture with ½ cup potatoes: 572 cal., 36g fat (14g sat. fat), 142mg chol., 1126mg sod., 28g carb. (5g sugars, 3g fiber), 29g pro.

TEST KITCHEN TIP

If you don't have Italian seasoning, you can make your own with equal amounts of basil, thyme, rosemary and oregano. You can also add in parsley flakes, marjoram, sage, savory or garlic powder.

CREAMY CHICKEN & BROCCOLI STEW

MEXICAN-INSPIRED CHICKEN SOUP

This zesty soup is loaded with chicken, corn and black beans in a mildly spicy red broth. As a busy mom of three young children, I'm always looking for dinner recipes that can be prepared in the morning. The kids love the taco taste of this easy soup.
—*Marlene Kane, Lainesburg, MI*

- -

PREP: 10 min. • **COOK:** 3 hours
MAKES: 6 servings

- 1½ **lbs. boneless skinless chicken breasts, cubed**
- 2 **tsp. canola oil**
- ½ **cup water**
- 1 **envelope reduced-sodium taco seasoning**
- 1 **can (32 oz.) V8 juice**
- 1 **jar (16 oz.) salsa**
- 1 **can (15 oz.) black beans, rinsed and drained**
- 1 **pkg. (10 oz.) frozen corn, thawed**
  Optional toppings: Shredded cheddar cheese, sour cream and chopped fresh cilantro

1. In a large nonstick skillet, saute chicken in oil until no longer pink. Add water and the taco seasoning; simmer, uncovered, until chicken is well coated.
2. Transfer to a 5-qt. slow cooker. Stir in the V8 juice, salsa, beans and corn. Cover and cook on low for 3-4 hours or until heated through. If desired, serve with optional toppings.
1½ cups: 304 cal., 5g fat (1g sat. fat), 63mg chol., 1199mg sod., 35g carb. (11g sugars, 5g fiber), 29g pro.

MEXICAN-INSPIRED CHICKEN SOUP

CHICKEN WILD RICE SOUP

This savory soup has a lot of substance, and we enjoy brimming bowls of it all winter long. The men in my family especially love it.

—*Virginia Montmarquet, Riverside, CA*

PREP: 20 min. • **COOK:** 40 min.
MAKES: 14 servings (3½ qt.)

- 2 qt. chicken broth
- ½ lb. fresh mushrooms, chopped
- 1 cup finely chopped celery
- 1 cup shredded carrots
- ½ cup finely chopped onion
- 1 tsp. chicken bouillon granules
- 1 tsp. dried parsley flakes
- ¼ tsp. garlic powder
- ¼ tsp. dried thyme
- ¼ cup butter, cubed
- ¼ cup all-purpose flour
- 1 can (10¾ oz.) condensed cream of mushroom soup, undiluted
- ½ cup dry white wine or additional chicken broth
- 3 cups cooked wild rice
- 2 cups cubed cooked chicken

1. In a large saucepan, combine the first 9 ingredients. Bring to a boil. Reduce the heat; cover and simmer for 30 minutes.
2. In Dutch oven, melt butter; stir in flour until smooth. Gradually whisk in broth mixture. Bring to a boil; cook and stir for 2 minutes or until thickened. Whisk in soup and wine. Add rice and chicken; heat through.
1 cup: 154 cal., 6g fat (3g sat. fat), 27mg chol., 807mg sod., 14g carb. (2g sugars, 2g fiber), 10g pro.

WHITE BEAN CHICKEN CHILI

My sister shared this white bean chili recipe with me. I usually double it and add one extra can of beans, then serve it with cheddar biscuits or warmed tortillas. The jalapeno adds just enough heat to notice but not too much for my children.
—*Kristine Bowles, Rio Rancho, NM*

- -

PREP: 25 min. • **COOK:** 3 hours
MAKES: 6 servings

- ¾ lb. boneless skinless chicken breasts, cut into 1¼-in. pieces
- ¼ tsp. salt
- ¼ tsp. pepper
- 2 Tbsp. olive oil, divided
- 1 medium onion, chopped
- 1 jalapeno pepper, seeded and chopped
- 4 garlic cloves, minced
- 2 tsp. dried oregano
- 1 tsp. ground cumin
- 2 cans (15 oz. each) cannellini beans, rinsed and drained, divided
- 2½ cups chicken broth, divided
- 1½ cups shredded cheddar cheese
  Optional toppings: Sliced avocado, quartered cherry tomatoes and chopped cilantro

1. Toss chicken with salt and pepper. In a large skillet, heat 1 Tbsp. oil over medium-high heat; saute the chicken until browned. Transfer chicken to a 3-qt. slow cooker.

2. In same skillet, heat remaining oil over medium heat; saute onion until tender. Add jalapeno, garlic, oregano and cumin; cook and stir 2 minutes. Add to slow cooker.

3. In a bowl, mash 1 cup beans; stir in ½ cup broth. Stir bean mixture and the remaining whole beans and broth into chicken mixture.

4. Cook, covered, on low until chicken is tender, 3-3½ hours. Stir before serving. Sprinkle with the cheese; add toppings if desired.

Freeze option: Freeze cooled chili in freezer containers. To use, partially thaw in refrigerator overnight. Heat through in a saucepan, stirring occasionally; add broth or water if necessary.

Note: Wear disposable gloves when cutting hot peppers; the oils can burn skin. Avoid touching your face.

1 cup: 344 cal., 16g fat (6g sat. fat), 62mg chol., 894mg sod., 23g carb. (1g sugars, 6g fiber), 25g pro.

TEST KITCHEN TIP

Want a slimmer chili? Leave off the cheese and this winter warmer is just 230 calories and 7grams of fat per serving. Garnish it with flavorful (and almost calorie-free) cilantro instead!

WHITE BEAN CHICKEN CHILI

SEE HOW WE MADE IT
Just hover your camera here.

SAUSAGE & VEGETABLE
SKILLET DINNER, PAGE 123

STOVETOP
SPECIALTIES

CHICKEN TACOS WITH AVOCADO SALSA

⏱ 🍎 ONE-PAN CHICKEN RICE CURRY

I've been loving the subtle spice from curry lately, so I incorporated it into this saucy chicken and rice dish. It's a one-pan meal that's become a go-to dinnertime favorite.
—*Mary Lou Timpson, Colorado City, AZ*

TAKES: 30 min. • **MAKES:** 4 servings

- 2 Tbsp. butter, divided
- 1 medium onion, halved and thinly sliced
- 2 Tbsp. all-purpose flour
- 3 tsp. curry powder
- ½ tsp. salt
- ½ tsp. pepper
- 1 lb. boneless skinless chicken breasts, cut into 1-in. pieces
- 1 can (14½ oz.) reduced-sodium chicken broth
- 1 cup uncooked instant rice Chopped fresh cilantro leaves, optional

⏱ 🍎 CHICKEN TACOS WITH AVOCADO SALSA

A few people in my family have special dietary needs, but luckily, these chicken tacos work for all of us. I toss up a simple green salad and have a meal we can all enjoy together.
—*Christine Schenher, Exeter, CA*

TAKES: 30 min. • **MAKES:** 4 servings

- 1 lb. boneless skinless chicken breasts, cut into ½-in. strips
- ⅓ cup water
- 1 tsp. sugar
- 1 Tbsp. chili powder
- 1 tsp. onion powder
- 1 tsp. dried oregano
- 1 tsp. ground cumin
- 1 tsp. paprika
- ½ tsp. salt
- ½ tsp. garlic powder
- 1 medium ripe avocado, peeled and cubed
- 1 cup fresh or frozen corn, thawed
- 1 cup cherry tomatoes, quartered
- 2 tsp. lime juice
- 8 taco shells, warmed

1. Place a large skillet coated with cooking spray over medium-high heat. Brown chicken. Add the water, sugar and seasonings. Cook chicken 4-5 minutes or until it is no longer pink, stirring occasionally.
2. Meanwhile, in a small bowl, gently mix avocado, corn, tomatoes and lime juice. Spoon chicken mixture into taco shells; top with avocado salsa.
Freeze option: Freeze cooled meat mixture in freezer containers. To use, partially thaw in refrigerator overnight. Heat through in a saucepan, stirring occasionally; add water if necessary.
2 tacos: 354 cal., 15g fat (3g sat. fat), 63mg chol., 474mg sod., 30g carb. (4g sugars, 6g fiber), 27g pro. **Diabetic exchanges:** 3 lean meat, 2 starch, 1 fat.

1. In a large nonstick skillet, heat 1 Tbsp. butter over medium-high heat; saute onion until tender and lightly browned, 3-5 minutes. Remove from pan.
2. In a bowl, mix flour and seasonings; toss with chicken. In the same skillet, heat remaining butter over medium-high heat. Add the chicken; cook just until no longer pink, 4-6 minutes, turning occasionally.
3. Stir in broth and onion; bring to a boil. Stir in rice. Remove from heat; let stand, covered, 5 minutes (the mixture will be saucy). If desired, sprinkle with cilantro.
1 cup: 300 cal., 9g fat (4g sat. fat), 78mg chol., 658mg sod., 27g carb. (2g sugars, 2g fiber), 27g pro. **Diabetic exchanges:** 3 lean meat, 2 starch, 1½ fat.

ONE-PAN
CHICKEN RICE CURRY

⏱ GNOCCHI WITH SPINACH & CHICKEN SAUSAGE

Dinner's easy when I can use ingredients typically found in my fridge and pantry.
—*Laura Miller, Lake Ann, MI*

TAKES: 25 min. • **MAKES:** 4 servings

- 1 pkg. (16 oz.) potato gnocchi
- 2 Tbsp. olive oil
- 1 pkg. (12 oz.) fully cooked Italian chicken sausage links, halved and sliced
- 2 shallots, finely chopped
- 2 garlic cloves, minced
- 1 cup white wine or chicken broth
- 1 Tbsp. cornstarch
- ½ cup reduced-sodium chicken broth
- 3 cups fresh baby spinach
- ½ cup heavy whipping cream
- ¼ cup shredded Parmesan cheese

1. Cook gnocchi according to package directions. Meanwhile, in a large skillet, heat oil over medium-high heat; cook sausage and shallots until sausage is browned and shallots are tender. Add garlic; cook 1 minute longer.

2. Stir in wine. Bring to a boil; cook until liquid is reduced by half, 3-4 minutes. In a small bowl, mix cornstarch and broth until smooth; stir into sausage mixture. Return to a boil, stirring constantly; cook and stir until thickened, 1-2 minutes. Add spinach and cream; cook and stir until spinach is wilted.

3. Drain gnocchi; add to pan and heat through. Sprinkle with cheese.

Note: Look for potato gnocchi in the pasta or frozen foods section.

1 cup: 604 cal., 28g fat (12g sat. fat), 119mg chol., 1226mg sod., 58g carb. (3g sugars, 4g fiber), 27g pro.

GNOCCHI WITH SPINACH & CHICKEN SAUSAGE

SIMPLE
SESAME CHICKEN
WITH COUSCOUS

🕐 🍎 SIMPLE SESAME CHICKEN WITH COUSCOUS

I created this dish after my three kids tried Chinese takeout and asked for more. To make things easy for myself, I typically use a rotisserie chicken from the deli.
—Naylet LaRochelle, Miami, FL

- -

TAKES: 25 min. • **MAKES:** 4 servings

1½ **cups water**
1 **cup uncooked whole wheat couscous**
1 **Tbsp. olive oil**
2 **cups coleslaw mix**
4 **green onions, sliced**
2 **Tbsp. plus ½ cup reduced-fat Asian toasted sesame salad dressing, divided**
2 **cups shredded cooked chicken breast**
2 **Tbsp. minced fresh cilantro Chopped peanuts, optional**

1. In a small saucepan, bring water to a boil. Stir in couscous. Remove from heat; let stand, covered, 5-10 minutes or until water is absorbed. Fluff with a fork.

2. In a large nonstick skillet, heat oil over medium heat. Add coleslaw mix; cook and stir 3-4 minutes or just until tender. Add green onions, 2 Tbsp. dressing and couscous; heat through. Remove couscous from pan; keep warm.

3. In same skillet, add chicken and remaining dressing; cook and stir over medium heat until heated through. Serve over couscous; top with cilantro and, if desired, peanuts.

1 cup couscous with ½ cup chicken mixture: 320 cal., 9g fat (1g sat. fat), 54mg chol., 442mg sod., 35g carb. (9g sugars, 5g fiber), 26g pro. **Diabetic exchanges:** 3 lean meat, 2 starch, 1 fat.

CHICKEN PESTO MEATBALLS

These tender, pesto-stuffed meatballs get gobbled up in our house. They're short on ingredients, but packed with flavor. I always make a double batch, freezing the other half for a busy night.
—Ally Billhorn, Wilton, IA

TAKES: 30 min. • **MAKES:** 4 servings

- 6 oz. uncooked whole grain spaghetti
- ¼ cup dry bread crumbs
- 2 Tbsp. prepared pesto
- 2 Tbsp. grated Parmesan cheese
- 1 tsp. garlic powder
- 1 lb. lean ground chicken
- 1½ cups marinara sauce
- ¼ cup water

Optional: Torn fresh basil and additional Parmesan cheese

1. Cook spaghetti according to the package directions; drain.

2. In a large bowl, combine the bread crumbs, pesto, cheese and garlic powder. Add the chicken; mix lightly but thoroughly. Shape into 1-in. balls. In a large skillet, brown meatballs over medium heat, turning occasionally. Add sauce and water; bring to a boil. Reduce heat; simmer, covered, until meatballs are cooked through, about 5 minutes. Serve with spaghetti. If desired, top with basil and additional cheese.

Freeze option: Freeze cooled meatball mixture in freezer containers. To use, partially thaw in refrigerator overnight. Heat through in a covered saucepan over low heat, stirring gently; add water if necessary.

¾ cup meatball mixture with 1 cup spaghetti: 422 cal., 12g fat (3g sat. fat), 85mg chol., 706mg sod., 45g carb. (7g sugars, 7g fiber), 32g pro. **Diabetic exchanges:** 3 starch, 3 lean meat, 1½ fat.

TEST KITCHEN TIP

If you don't have dry bread crumbs, you can substitute ¼ cup of unsalted cracker crumbs or uncooked oats, or ¾ cup of soft bread crumbs.

CHICKEN PESTO MEATBALLS

⏱ RAVIOLI WITH APPLE CHICKEN SAUSAGE

I love butternut squash ravioli but was never quite sure what flavors would best complement the squash. Turns out that creamy spinach, chicken sausage and a hint of sweet spice are perfect.
—*Mary Brodeur, Millbury, MA*

TAKES: 30 min. • **MAKES:** 4 servings

- 1 pkg. (18 oz.) frozen butternut squash ravioli
- 2 pkg. (10 oz. each) frozen creamed spinach
- 1 Tbsp. olive oil
- 1 pkg. (12 oz.) fully cooked apple chicken sausage links or flavor of your choice, cut into ½-in. slices
- 1 tsp. maple syrup
- ¼ tsp. pumpkin pie spice

1. Cook ravioli according to package directions. Prepare spinach according to package directions. Meanwhile, in a large skillet, heat oil over medium heat. Add sausage; cook and stir until browned, 2-4 minutes.
2. Drain ravioli. Add ravioli, spinach, maple syrup and pie spice to sausage; heat through.

1½ cups: 531 cal., 16g fat (4g sat. fat), 64mg chol., 1409mg sod., 69g carb. (19g sugars, 4g fiber), 26g pro.

SAUSAGE & VEGETABLE SKILLET DINNER

⏱ 🍎 SAUSAGE & VEGETABLE SKILLET DINNER

I threw this together one night to use up produce before going out of town. Who knew it was going to be such a hit? Now it's a recipe I turn to whenever time is tight.
—*Elizabeth Kelley, Chicago, IL*

TAKES: 30 min. • **MAKES:** 4 servings

- 1 Tbsp. olive oil
- 1 pkg. (12 oz.) fully cooked Italian chicken sausage links, cut into 1-in. pieces
- 1 large onion, chopped
- 3 garlic cloves, minced
- ¼ tsp. crushed red pepper flakes
- 1½ lbs. red potatoes (about 5 medium), thinly sliced
- 1 pkg. (10 oz.) frozen corn
- ¼ tsp. pepper
- 1¼ cups vegetable broth
- 2 cups fresh baby spinach

1. In a 12-in. skillet, heat oil over medium-high heat; saute sausage and onion until onion is tender. Add garlic and pepper flakes; cook and stir 1 minute.
2. Add potatoes, corn, pepper and broth; bring to a boil. Reduce heat to medium; cook, covered, until potatoes are tender, 15-20 minutes. Stir in spinach until leaves are wilted.

1½ cups: 371 cal., 11g fat (3g sat. fat), 65mg chol., 715mg sod., 48g carb. (6g sugars, 5g fiber), 22g pro. **Diabetic exchanges:** 3 starch, 3 lean meat, 1 fat.

TEST KITCHEN TIP

Italian chicken sausage has less than half the fat of regular (pork) Italian sausage. It's lean, but it packs a lot of flavor.

🕐 MONTEREY BARBECUED CHICKEN

It's easy to turn regular chicken into a dish to savor, with barbecue sauce, crisp bacon and melted cheese. It gets even better with a sprinkling of fresh tomato and green onion.
—*Linda Coleman, Cedar Rapids, IA*

- -

TAKES: 25 min. • **MAKES:** 4 servings

- 4 bacon strips
- 4 boneless skinless chicken breast halves (4 oz. each)
- 1 Tbsp. butter
- ½ cup barbecue sauce
- 3 green onions, chopped
- 1 medium tomato, chopped
- 1 cup shredded cheddar cheese

1. Cut bacon strips in half widthwise. In a large skillet, cook bacon over medium heat until cooked but not crisp. Remove to paper towels to drain.

2. Drain drippings from skillet; cook chicken in butter over medium heat for 5-6 minutes on each side or until a thermometer reads 170°.

3. Top each chicken breast with the barbecue sauce, green onions, tomato and 2 reserved bacon pieces; sprinkle with the cheese. Cover and cook for 5 minutes or until cheese is melted.

1 serving: 318 cal., 17g fat (10g sat. fat), 107mg chol., 680mg sod., 8g carb. (5g sugars, 1g fiber), 32g pro.

WHY YOU'LL LOVE IT...

"So tasty and quick! A picky eater's dream!"
—BARBIEGOULD, TASTEOFHOME.COM

CASHEW CHICKEN WITH NOODLES

⏱ CASHEW CHICKEN WITH NOODLES

I tried this recipe with some friends one night when we were doing freezer meals. I was smitten! It's quick, easy and so delicious!
—*Anita Beachy, Bealeton, VA*

TAKES: 20 min. • **MAKES:** 4 servings

- 8 oz. uncooked thick rice noodles
- ¼ cup reduced-sodium soy sauce
- 2 Tbsp. cornstarch
- 3 garlic cloves, minced
- 1 lb. boneless skinless chicken breasts, cubed
- 1 Tbsp. peanut oil
- 1 Tbsp. sesame oil
- 6 green onions, cut into 2-in. pieces
- 1 cup unsalted cashews
- 2 Tbsp. sweet chili sauce
  Toasted sesame seeds, optional

1. Cook the rice noodles according to package directions.
2. Meanwhile, in a small bowl, combine the soy sauce, cornstarch and garlic. Add chicken. In a large cast-iron or other heavy skillet, saute chicken mixture in peanut and sesame oils until no longer pink. Add onions; cook 1 minute longer.
3. Drain noodles; stir into skillet. Add cashews and chili sauce and heat through. If desired, top with toasted sesame seeds.
1½ cups: 638 cal., 26g fat (5g sat. fat), 63mg chol., 870mg sod., 68g carb. (6g sugars, 3g fiber), 33g pro.

⏱ CHICKEN CORDON BLEU SKILLET

Here's a good and hearty supper. If I have fresh mushrooms on hand, I slice them and toss them in the skillet. You could add cooked veggies such as broccoli or cauliflower, too.
—*Sandy Harz, Spring Lake, MI*

TAKES: 25 min. • **MAKES:** 4 servings

- 8 oz. uncooked medium egg noodles (about 5 cups)
- 1 lb. boneless skinless chicken breasts, cut in 1-in. pieces
- ½ tsp. pepper
- 1 Tbsp. butter
- 1 can (10¾ oz.) condensed cream of chicken soup, undiluted
- ½ cup shredded Swiss cheese
- ½ cup cubed fully cooked ham
- ¼ cup water
  Minced fresh parsley

1. Cook the noodles according to package directions; drain.
2. Meanwhile, sprinkle chicken with pepper. In a large cast-iron or other heavy skillet, heat butter over medium-high heat; saute the chicken just until browned, 3-5 minutes. Stir in soup, cheese, ham and water; cook, covered, over medium heat until cheese is melted and chicken is no longer pink, 6-8 minutes, stirring occasionally. Stir in noodles. Sprinkle with parsley.
1½ cups: 516 cal., 18g fat (8g sat. fat), 147mg chol., 878mg sod., 47g carb. (2g sugars, 3g fiber), 40g pro.

Care for Cast Iron

Home cooks love their cast-iron skillets and find themselves using the cookware for all sorts of recipes. If you're on the fence about buying cast iron due to the care involved, don't be! Just follow these do's and don'ts.

- **DO cool it.** Always wait until the pan is cool to the touch before washing it in the sink. Submerging hot cast iron in cold water can cause it to crack.
- **DO clean immediately (once the pan has cooled).**
- **DO soap it up.** Use hot water and soap if you like. It's a common misconception that soap will strip the seasoning from cast iron.
- **DON'T soak it.** Remember that cast iron + extended exposure to water = rust. Yuck!

SPINACH-FETA
CHICKEN PENNE

SPINACH-FETA CHICKEN PENNE

I wanted a light sauce for pasta, so I cooked tomatoes with garlic, wine and olive oil. It's a blockbuster combo for seafood, too.
—*Lyn Sipos, Blandon, PA*

- -

TAKES: 30 min. • **MAKES:** 6 servings

- 1 pkg. (12 oz.) whole wheat penne pasta
- 1½ lbs. boneless skinless chicken breasts, cut into ¼-in.-thick strips
- 3 Tbsp. olive oil, divided
- ¾ tsp. salt, divided
- ¼ tsp. pepper
- 3 garlic cloves, minced
- ½ cup reduced-sodium chicken broth
- ½ cup dry white wine or additional broth
- 6 plum tomatoes, chopped
- 2 cups fresh baby spinach
- ¾ cup crumbled feta cheese

1. In a 6-qt. stockpot, cook the pasta according to package directions. Drain; return to pot.
2. Meanwhile, toss the chicken with 2 Tbsp. oil, ½ tsp. salt and pepper. In a large skillet, cook and stir chicken, half at a time, over medium-high heat 3-5 minutes or until no longer pink; remove from pan.
3. In same skillet, heat remaining oil over medium heat. Add garlic; cook and stir 1-2 minutes or until tender. Add broth and wine. Bring to a boil, stirring to loosen browned bits from pan; cook 2 minutes. Stir in tomatoes and remaining salt; cook until tomatoes are softened. Stir in spinach until wilted.
4. Add chicken and tomato mixture to pasta; heat through, tossing to combine. Serve with cheese.
1½ cups: 455 cal., 13g fat (3g sat. fat), 70mg chol., 552mg sod., 46g carb. (3g sugars, 8g fiber), 36g pro. **Diabetic exchanges:** 3 lean meat, 2½ starch, 2 fat, 1 vegetable.

SUNSHINE CHICKEN

SUNSHINE CHICKEN

Since it can be easily doubled and takes little time or effort to prepare, this recipe is ideal to serve for large groups. Even my husband, who usually doesn't enjoy cooking, likes to make this dish.
—*Karen Gardiner, Eutaw, AL*

- -

PREP: 15 min. • **COOK:** 20 min.
MAKES: 6 servings

- 2 to 3 tsp. curry powder
- 1¼ tsp. salt, divided
- ¼ tsp. pepper
- 6 boneless skinless chicken breast halves (5 oz. each)
- 1½ cups orange juice
- 1 cup uncooked long grain rice
- ¾ cup water
- 1 Tbsp. brown sugar
- 1 tsp. ground mustard
   Chopped fresh parsley

1. Combine curry powder, ½ tsp. salt and the pepper; rub over both sides of chicken. In a skillet, combine orange juice, rice, water, brown sugar, mustard and remaining salt. Add chicken pieces; bring to a boil. Reduce heat; cover and simmer until chicken juices run clear, 20-25 minutes.
2. Remove from the heat and let stand, covered, until all the liquid is absorbed, about 5 minutes. Sprinkle with parsley.
1 serving: 317 cal., 4g fat (1g sat. fat), 78mg chol., 562mg sod., 36g carb. (8g sugars, 1g fiber), 32g pro. **Diabetic exchanges:** 4 lean meat, 2 starch.

TEST KITCHEN TIP

This one-pan dinner is easy to make and tastes special enough for company. Plus, it's free from gluten, egg and dairy, so it's allergy-sensitive, too!

CHICKEN & VEGETABLE FETTUCCINE

CHICKEN & VEGETABLE FETTUCCINE

When you've cooked a whole chicken and have leftovers, this is a go-to recipe. My boys have always loved this comfort food. It's nice with a side salad and breadsticks.
—*Andrea Bergen, Altona, MB*

PREP: 10 min. • **COOK:** 30 min.
MAKES: 6 servings

1	pkg. (12 oz.) fettuccine
5	Tbsp. butter, divided
1	small onion, chopped
3	Tbsp. all-purpose flour
1	can (14½ oz.) chicken broth
1	cup heavy whipping cream
1¼	tsp. salt
¼	tsp. pepper
1	pkg. (12 oz.) frozen mixed vegetables
2	cups cubed cooked chicken

1. Cook fettuccine according to package directions. Drain fettuccine; toss with 3 Tbsp. butter.

2. Meanwhile, in a large saucepan, heat remaining butter over medium heat. Add onion; cook and stir 2-3 minutes or until tender. Stir in flour until blended; gradually whisk in the broth, cream, salt and pepper. Bring to a boil, stirring constantly; cook 8-10 minutes or until thickened, stirring occasionally.

3. Stir in the vegetables; return just to a boil. Stir in chicken; heat through. Serve with fettuccine.

Freeze option: Do not cook fettuccine. Freeze cooled chicken mixture in freezer containers. To use, partially thaw chicken in refrigerator overnight. Prepare the fettuccine as directed. Place chicken mixture in a saucepan or skillet; cook over medium-low heat until heated through, stirring occasionally. (Sauce may appear curdled initially, but will become smooth upon heating.) Serve with buttered fettuccine.

¾ cup pasta with ¾ cup chicken mixture: 565 cal., 29g fat (17g sat. fat), 114mg chol., 954mg sod., 52g carb. (6g sugars, 5g fiber), 25g pro.

WATCH HOW SIMPLE THIS IS
Just hover your camera here.

CHICKEN BURRITO SKILLET

🍎 CHICKEN BURRITO SKILLET

We love Mexican night at our house, and this burrito-inspired dish is ready for the table in almost no time!
—*Krista Marshall, Fort Wayne, IN*

PREP: 15 min. • **COOK:** 30 min.
MAKES: 6 servings

1	lb. boneless skinless chicken breasts, cut into 1½-in. pieces
⅛	tsp. salt
⅛	tsp. pepper
2	Tbsp. olive oil, divided
1	cup uncooked long grain rice
1	can (15 oz.) black beans, rinsed and drained
1	can (14½ oz.) diced tomatoes, drained
1	tsp. ground cumin
½	tsp. onion powder
½	tsp. garlic powder
½	tsp. chili powder
2½	cups reduced-sodium chicken broth
1	cup shredded Mexican cheese blend
1	medium tomato, chopped
3	green onions, chopped

1. Toss chicken with salt and pepper. In a large cast-iron or other heavy skillet, heat 1 Tbsp. oil over medium-high heat; saute chicken until browned, about 2 minutes. Remove from pan.
2. In same pan, heat remaining oil over medium-high heat; saute rice until lightly browned, 1-2 minutes. Stir in beans, canned tomatoes, seasonings and broth; bring to a boil. Place chicken on top (do not stir into the rice). Simmer, covered, until rice is tender and chicken is no longer pink, 20-25 minutes.
3. Remove from the heat; sprinkle with cheese. Let stand, covered, until the cheese is melted. Top with tomato and green onions.

1⅓ cups: 403 cal., 13g fat (4g sat. fat), 58mg chol., 690mg sod., 43g carb. (4g sugars, 5g fiber), 27g pro. **Diabetic exchanges:** 3 starch, 3 lean meat, 1½ fat.

⏱ ASIAN CHICKEN SKILLET

This scrumptious recipe is a meal in itself. It uses a convenient Rice-A-Roni mix and only one pan. So cleanup is as short as the prep time!

—*Terri Christensen, Montague, MI*

TAKES: 30 min. • **MAKES:** 4 servings

- 1 pkg. (5.9 oz.) chicken and garlic-flavored rice and vermicelli mix
- 2 Tbsp. butter
- 1 lb. boneless skinless chicken breasts, cut into strips
- 2¼ cups water
- ¼ cup reduced-sodium teriyaki sauce
- ½ tsp. ground ginger
- 1 pkg. (16 oz.) frozen stir-fry vegetable blend, thawed

1. In a large skillet, saute rice mix in butter until golden brown. Stir in the chicken, water, teriyaki sauce, ginger and contents of rice seasoning packet. Bring to a boil. Reduce heat; cover and simmer for 10 minutes.

2. Stir in vegetable blend. Cover and cook 5-8 minutes longer or until rice is tender and chicken is no longer pink.

1½ cups: 397 cal., 9g fat (4g sat. fat), 78mg chol., 955mg sod., 49g carb. (6g sugars, 6g fiber), 31g pro.

SKILLET CHICKEN WITH OLIVES

⏱🍎 SKILLET CHICKEN WITH OLIVES

While I was visiting my cousin Lilliana in Italy, she made this heavenly chicken for lunch. Now it's a family favorite stateside, too.

—*Rosemarie Pisano, Revere, MA*

TAKES: 20 min. • **MAKES:** 4 servings

- 4 boneless skinless chicken thighs (about 1 lb.)
- 1 tsp. dried rosemary, crushed
- ½ tsp. pepper
- ¼ tsp. salt
- 1 Tbsp. olive oil
- ½ cup pimiento-stuffed olives, coarsely chopped
- ¼ cup white wine or chicken broth
- 1 Tbsp. drained capers, optional

1. Sprinkle chicken with rosemary, pepper and salt. In a large skillet, heat oil over medium-high heat. Brown chicken on both sides.

2. Add the olives, wine and, if desired, capers. Reduce heat; simmer, covered, 2-3 minutes or until a thermometer inserted in chicken reads 170°.

1 serving: 237 cal., 15g fat (3g sat. fat), 76mg chol., 571mg sod., 2g carb. (0 sugars, 0 fiber), 21g pro. **Diabetic exchanges:** 3 lean meat, 2 fat.

ARROZ CON POLLO

This authentic specialty gets its wonderful flavor from a robust blend of seasonings, including garlic, Mexican oregano and chili powder.

—Taste of Home *Test Kitchen*

PREP: 10 min. • **COOK:** 50 min.
MAKES: 5-6 servings

1	can (14½ oz.) diced tomatoes, drained
½	cup chopped onion
4	garlic cloves, peeled
1	tsp. salt, divided
½	tsp. dried Mexican oregano
½	tsp. chili powder
½	tsp. pepper, divided
1	broiler/fryer chicken (3 to 4 lbs.), cut up
3	Tbsp. canola oil, divided
1½	cups uncooked long grain rice
3	cups chicken broth
1	cup frozen peas

1. In a blender, combine the tomatoes, onion, garlic, ½ tsp. salt, oregano, chili powder and ¼ tsp. pepper; cover and process until smooth. Set aside.
2. Sprinkle chicken with the remaining salt and pepper. In a large skillet over medium heat, cook chicken in batches in 2 Tbsp. oil for 10 minutes or until lightly browned. Remove and keep warm. In the same skillet, saute the rice for 2 minutes or until chicken is lightly browned. Stir in broth.
3. In a Dutch oven, heat the remaining oil; add tomato mixture. Bring to a boil; cook and stir for 4 minutes. Stir in rice mixture; bring to a boil.
4. Arrange chicken in pan. Reduce heat to medium; cover and cook for 25-30 minutes or until rice is tender and chicken juices run clear. Stir in peas; cover and let stand for 4 minutes or until peas are heated through.
1 serving: 526 cal., 22g fat (5g sat. fat), 90mg chol., 1078mg sod., 46g carb. (5g sugars, 3g fiber), 34g pro.

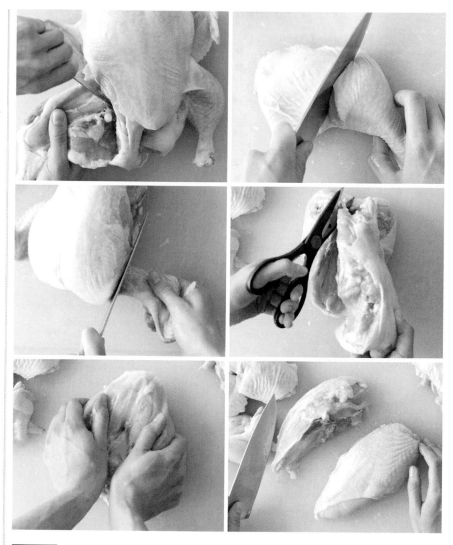

HOW-TO
Cut Up a Whole Chicken
1. **Pull a leg away from the body.** With a small sharp knife, cut through the skin to expose the joint. Cut through joint, then skin, to free the leg. Repeat with other leg.
2. **Separate drumstick from thigh by cutting skin at the joint.** Bend drumstick to expose joint; cut through joint and skin.
3. **Pull wing away from the body.** Cut through skin to expose joint. Cut through joint and skin to separate wing from body. Repeat on other side.
4. **With kitchen shears, cut through the ribs along each side of the backbone; remove backbone.**
5. **Hold chicken breast in both hands (skin side down) and bend it downward to snap breastbone.** Turn over.
6. **With a knife, cut in half along breastbone.** Breastbone will remain attached to one of the halves.

⏱ JEZEBEL CHICKEN THIGHS

On busy weeknights, this sweet and spicy chicken is our standby.
—*Judy Armstrong, Prairieville, LA*

TAKES: 25 min. • **MAKES:** 4 servings

- 4　bone-in chicken thighs
- ½　tsp. salt
- ½　tsp. paprika
- ¼　tsp. pepper
- 1　Tbsp. olive oil
- 1　shallot, finely chopped
- 2　garlic cloves, minced
- ½　cup apricot preserves
- ¼　cup chicken broth
- 1　to 2 Tbsp. horseradish sauce
- 4　green onions, sliced, divided

1. Sprinkle chicken with seasonings. In a large nonstick skillet, heat oil over medium-high heat; brown chicken on both sides, beginning skin side down. Remove from pan, reserving drippings.
2. In same pan, saute shallot and garlic in drippings over medium-high heat until tender, 1-2 minutes. Stir in the preserves, broth, horseradish sauce and half of the green onions. Add the chicken; cook, covered, over medium heat until a thermometer reads 170°-175°, 10-12 minutes.
3. To serve, spoon sauce over chicken; sprinkle with remaining green onions.
1 chicken thigh with 2 Tbsp. sauce: 380 cal., 19g fat (5g sat. fat), 82mg chol., 474mg sod., 30g carb. (19g sugars, 1g fiber), 23g pro.

JEZEBEL CHICKEN THIGHS

⏱ 🍎 THAI CHICKEN PASTA SKILLET

This gorgeous Bangkok-style pasta has been a faithful standby for many years and always gets loads of praise. For a potluck, we increase it and do it ahead.
—*Susan Ten Pas, Myrtle Creek, OR*

TAKES: 30 min. • **MAKES:** 6 servings

- 6　oz. uncooked whole wheat spaghetti
- 2　tsp. canola oil
- 1　pkg. (10 oz.) fresh sugar snap peas, trimmed and cut diagonally into thin strips
- 2　cups julienned carrots (about 8 oz.)
- 2　cups shredded cooked chicken
- 1　cup Thai peanut sauce
- 1　medium cucumber, halved lengthwise, seeded and sliced diagonally
　　Chopped fresh cilantro, optional

1. Cook spaghetti according to package directions; drain.
2. Meanwhile, in a large skillet, heat oil over medium-high heat. Add snap peas and carrots; stir-fry 6-8 minutes or until crisp-tender. Add chicken, peanut sauce and spaghetti; heat the mixture through, tossing to combine.
3. Transfer to a serving plate. Top with the cucumber and, if desired, cilantro.
1⅓ cups: 403 cal., 15g fat (3g sat. fat), 42mg chol., 432mg sod., 43g carb. (15g sugars, 6g fiber), 25g pro. **Diabetic exchanges:** 3 lean meat, 2½ starch, 2 fat, 1 vegetable.

DID YOU KNOW?

The hearty texture and nutty taste of whole wheat pasta make it an ideal stand-in for buckwheat or soba noodles when you're preparing Asian recipes. Even if you don't like whole wheat pasta in your favorite Italian recipes, you might enjoy it in Asian ones!

🕐 🍎 HEALTHIER-THAN-EGG ROLLS

Frying anything at home can be a little intimidating for me, but I love egg rolls. With this recipe, I've figured out a way to get the best part without the mess. This can be used to stuff egg roll wrappers, but we love it on its own, too.
—*Sue Mitchell, Kerrville, TX*

TAKES: 25 min. • **MAKES:** 4 servings

1	lb. lean ground chicken
1½	cups sliced fresh mushrooms
1	medium onion, chopped
2	garlic cloves, minced
1	tsp. minced fresh gingerroot
2	Tbsp. reduced-sodium soy sauce
1	pkg. (14 oz.) coleslaw mix
1	Tbsp. sesame oil
3	cups hot cooked brown rice
½	cup sweet-and-sour sauce
	Wonton strips, optional

1. In a large cast-iron or other heavy skillet, cook and crumble chicken with mushrooms, onion, garlic and ginger over medium-high heat until chicken is no longer pink, 6-8 minutes; drain. Stir in soy sauce.
2. Add coleslaw mix; cook and stir until wilted, 3-4 minutes. Stir in sesame oil. Serve with rice and sweet-and-sour sauce. If desired, top with wonton strips.
1¼ cups chicken mixture with ¾ cup rice: 451 cal., 11g fat (3g sat. fat), 81mg chol., 591mg sod., 58g carb. (13g sugars, 6g fiber), 30g pro.

HEALTHIER-THAN-EGG ROLLS

**CONTEST-WINNING
PEANUT CHICKEN STIR-FRY**

SAUCY MEDITERRANEAN CHICKEN WITH RICE

The hints of Mediterranean flavor in this chicken dish make it a family favorite.
—Tabitha Alloway, Edna, KS

TAKES: 30 min. • **MAKES:** 4 servings

- ¾ cup water
- 3 Tbsp. tomato paste
- 2 Tbsp. lemon juice
- ¾ tsp. salt
- 1 tsp. chili powder
- ½ tsp. garlic powder
- ½ tsp. ground ginger
- ¼ tsp. ground fennel seed
- ¼ tsp. ground turmeric
- 1 tsp. ground coriander, optional
- 3 Tbsp. olive oil
- 1 medium onion, chopped
- 1 lb. boneless skinless chicken breasts, cut into 1-in. cubes
- 3 cups hot cooked rice
  Minced fresh parsley, optional

1. In a small bowl, mix the water, tomato paste, lemon juice, salt, chili powder, garlic powder, ginger, fennel, turmeric and, if desired, coriander until smooth.
2. In a large skillet, heat the oil over medium-high heat. Add onions; cook and stir until tender. Stir in chicken; brown 3-4 minutes. Pour the water mixture into pan.
3. Bring to a boil. Reduce heat; simmer, uncovered, until chicken is no longer pink, 8-10 minutes. Serve with rice. If desired, top with parsley.
¾ cup chicken mixture with ¾ cup rice: 394 cal., 13g fat (2g sat. fat), 63mg chol., 527mg sod., 40g carb. (3g sugars, 2g fiber), 27g pro. **Diabetic exchanges:** 3 lean meat, 2½ starch, 2 fat.

CONTEST-WINNING PEANUT CHICKEN STIR-FRY

Here's a colorful and comforting peanut chicken dish with just a touch of heat from the crushed red pepper. If you want even more color, add frozen stir-fry veggies.
—Lisa Erickson, Ripon, WI

TAKES: 30 min. • **MAKES:** 6 servings

- 8 oz. uncooked thick rice noodles
- ⅓ cup water
- ¼ cup reduced-sodium soy sauce
- ¼ cup peanut butter
- 4½ tsp. brown sugar
- 1 Tbsp. lemon juice
- 2 garlic cloves, minced
- ½ tsp. crushed red pepper flakes
- 2 Tbsp. canola oil, divided
- 1 lb. boneless skinless chicken breasts, cut into ½-in. strips
- 1 bunch broccoli, cut into florets
- ½ cup shredded carrot
  Sesame seeds, optional

1. Cook noodles according to package directions. Meanwhile, in a small bowl, combine the water, soy sauce, peanut butter, brown sugar, lemon juice, garlic and pepper flakes; set aside.
2. In a large skillet, heat 1 Tbsp. oil over medium-high heat. Add chicken; stir-fry until no longer pink, 3-4 minutes. Remove from pan.
3. Stir-fry broccoli and carrot in remaining oil until crisp-tender, 4-6 minutes. Add soy sauce mixture; bring to a boil. Cook and stir until sauce is thickened, 1-2 minutes. Return the chicken to pan; heat through. Drain noodles; toss with chicken mixture in pan. If desired, sprinkle with the sesame seeds.
1⅓ cups: 384 cal., 13g fat (2g sat. fat), 42mg chol., 575mg sod., 45g carb. (7g sugars, 4g fiber), 24g pro. **Diabetic exchanges:** 3 starch, 3 lean meat, 2 fat.

SAUCY MEDITERRANEAN
CHICKEN WITH RICE

🕐 CHICKEN WITH TARRAGON SAUCE

This is comfort food at its finest. I cook it at least once a week and usually serve it with homemade mashed potatoes and sauteed fresh green beans.
—*Cher Schwartz, Ellisville, MO*

TAKES: 30 min. • **MAKES:** 4 servings

- 4 boneless skinless chicken breast halves (5 oz. each)
- ¾ tsp. salt, divided
- ¼ tsp. pepper
- 1 Tbsp. butter
- 1 Tbsp. olive oil
- 1 shallot, chopped
- ¾ cup heavy whipping cream
- 3 tsp. minced fresh tarragon, divided
- 2 tsp. lemon juice

1. Pound chicken breasts with a meat mallet to ½-in. thickness. Sprinkle chicken with ½ tsp. salt and pepper.
2. In a large skillet, heat butter and oil over medium heat. Add chicken; cook 4-5 minutes on each side or until no longer pink. Remove chicken from pan; keep warm.
3. Add shallot to same pan; cook and stir over medium heat until tender. Add cream, stirring to loosen browned bits from pan. Increase heat to medium-high; cook until slightly thickened. Stir in 2 tsp. tarragon, lemon juice and remaining salt. Serve with chicken. Sprinkle with remaining tarragon.
1 chicken breast half with 2 Tbsp. sauce: 370 cal., 26g fat (14g sat. fat), 137mg chol., 547mg sod., 3g carb. (2g sugars, 0 fiber), 30g pro.

CHICKEN MARSALA BOW TIES

CHICKEN MARSALA BOW TIES

Back in 2008, I won first place in a state fair cooking contest with this recipe. I absolutely love mushrooms, and this dish is full of them! You can substitute Italian dressing mix for the ranch with equally delicious results.
—*Regina Farris, Mesquite, TX*

- -

PREP: 20 min. • **COOK:** 25 min.
MAKES: 8 servings

- 2 cups uncooked bow tie pasta
- ⅓ cup all-purpose flour
- ½ tsp. salt
- ½ tsp. garlic powder
- ½ tsp. dried thyme
- 1¾ lbs. boneless skinless chicken breasts, cut into ½-in. cubes
- 3 Tbsp. olive oil
- 6 Tbsp. butter, cubed
- ½ lb. sliced baby portobello mushrooms
- 3 shallots, finely chopped
- ½ cup Marsala wine or chicken broth
- 1 can (10¾ oz.) condensed golden mushroom soup, undiluted
- 1 pkg. (3 oz.) cream cheese, cubed
- ½ cup heavy whipping cream
- 1 envelope ranch salad dressing mix
- ⅓ cup grated Parmesan cheese
  Minced fresh parsley, optional

1. Cook pasta according to package directions. In a small bowl, combine flour and seasonings. Add the chicken, a few pieces at a time, tossing to coat.
2. In a Dutch oven, heat oil over medium heat. Add chicken in batches; cook and stir until no longer pink, 5-7 minutes. Remove from pan; set aside.
3. In same pan, heat butter over medium-high heat. Add mushrooms and shallots; cook and stir until tender, 2-3 minutes. Stir in wine; bring to a boil. Cook until the liquid is reduced by half. Stir in soup, cream cheese, cream and dressing mix; stir until cream cheese is melted.
4. Drain pasta. Add pasta and chicken to mushroom mixture; heat through, tossing to coat. Sprinkle with Parmesan cheese and parsley.
1 cup: 468 cal., 28g fat (13g sat. fat), 108mg chol., 870mg sod., 28g carb. (3g sugars, 2g fiber), 27g pro.

TEST KITCHEN TIP

Marsala is a fortified (higher in alcohol) wine from Sicily that's popular in Italian cooking. It's made in dry and sweet styles. Use dry Marsala or cooking Marsala in this recipe. You could also prepare the recipe with sherry.

⏱ 🍎 SUMMER GARDEN CHICKEN STIR-FRY

I tend to substitute vegetables in this dish depending on what is in season, so one summer version of this stir-fry might also include baby green beans.
—*Wendy Chiapparo, Mena, AR*

TAKES: 30 min. • **MAKES:** 4 servings

- 2 Tbsp. cornstarch
- 1⅓ cups chicken broth
- 3 Tbsp. cider vinegar
- 2 Tbsp. brown sugar
- 2 Tbsp. soy sauce
- ¼ tsp. crushed red pepper flakes
- 2 Tbsp. olive oil, divided
- 1 lb. boneless skinless chicken breasts, cut into ¾-in. cubes
- 2 medium carrots, thinly sliced diagonally
- 1 medium zucchini, halved lengthwise and sliced
- 1 medium yellow summer squash, halved lengthwise and sliced
- 1 medium sweet red pepper, julienned
- 2 garlic cloves, minced
- 1 tsp. minced fresh gingerroot
- 6 green onions, sliced diagonally
  Hot cooked rice

1. Mix the first 6 ingredients until blended. In a large skillet, heat 1 Tbsp. oil over medium-high heat; stir-fry the chicken until no longer pink, 4-5 minutes. Remove from pan.

2. In same pan, heat remaining oil over medium-high heat. Stir-fry the carrots, zucchini and yellow squash 2 minutes. Add pepper, garlic and ginger; stir-fry until the pepper is crisp-tender, 1-2 minutes.

3. Stir the cornstarch mixture into the vegetables. Bring to a boil; cook and stir until sauce is thickened, 2-3 minutes. Stir in green onions and chicken; heat through. Serve with rice.

1¼ cups: 284 cal., 10g fat (2g sat. fat), 64mg chol., 878mg sod., 21g carb. (12g sugars, 3g fiber), 27g pro. **Diabetic exchanges:** 3 lean meat, 2 fat, 1 starch, 1 vegetable.

SUMMER GARDEN CHICKEN STIR-FRY

DISCOVER A STIR-FRY SECRET
Just hover your camera here.

HOW-TO

Up Your Garnish Game

Cutting green onions thinly on the diagonal is an easy way to give them a delicate look, especially in Asian dishes.

⏰ CHICKEN FAJITA ALFREDO

Need a to-go box for those chicken fajitas? Yes—especially when you know you can fix a hearty recipe like this with the leftovers! Other types of homemade or restaurant fajitas would work equally well in this dish.
—Taste of Home *Test Kitchen*

- -

TAKES: 30 min. • **MAKES:** 5 servings

- 8 oz. cellentani or spiral pasta
- ½ lb. sliced fresh mushrooms
- 1 yellow summer squash, sliced
- 2 tsp. olive oil
- 2 garlic cloves, minced
- 1 serving leftover Chili's chicken fajitas, coarsely chopped
- 2 cans (14½ oz. each) diced tomatoes with basil, oregano and garlic, undrained
- ¾ cup Alfredo sauce
- ¾ tsp. dried oregano

1. Cook pasta according to package directions.
2. Meanwhile, in a Dutch oven, saute mushrooms and squash in oil until tender. Add garlic; saute 1 minute longer. Stir in the fajitas, tomatoes, Alfredo sauce and oregano. Bring to a boil. Reduce heat; simmer, uncovered, for 5-10 minutes, stirring occasionally. Drain pasta; add to fajita mixture and toss to coat.
1½ cups: 377 cal., 10g fat (4g sat. fat), 11mg chol., 1217mg sod., 55g carb. (11g sugars, 6g fiber), 21g pro.

JERK CHICKEN WITH TROPICAL COUSCOUS

⏰ 🍎 JERK CHICKEN WITH TROPICAL COUSCOUS

Caribbean cuisine always brightens up our weeknights thanks to its bold colors and flavors. Done in less than 30 minutes, this chicken is one of my go-to easy meals.
—*Jeanne Holt, St. Paul, MN*

- -

TAKES: 25 min. • **MAKES:** 4 servings

- 1 can (15.25 oz.) mixed tropical fruit
- 1 lb. boneless skinless chicken breasts, cut into 2½-in. strips
- 3 tsp. Caribbean jerk seasoning
- 1 Tbsp. olive oil
- ½ cup chopped sweet red pepper
- 1 Tbsp. finely chopped seeded jalapeno pepper
- ⅓ cup thinly sliced green onions (green portion only)
- 1½ cups reduced-sodium chicken broth
- 3 Tbsp. chopped fresh cilantro, divided
- 1 Tbsp. lime juice
- ¼ tsp. salt
- 1 cup uncooked whole wheat couscous Lime wedges

1. Drain the mixed fruit, reserving ¼ cup syrup. Chop the fruit.
2. Toss chicken with jerk seasoning. In a large cast-iron or other heavy skillet, heat oil over medium-high heat; saute chicken until no longer pink, 4-5 minutes. Remove from pan, reserving drippings.
3. In same pan, saute peppers and green onions in drippings 2 minutes. Add broth, 1 Tbsp. cilantro, lime juice, salt, reserved syrup and chopped fruit; bring to a boil. Stir in couscous; reduce heat to low. Place chicken on top; cook, covered, until liquid is absorbed and chicken is heated through, 3-4 minutes. Sprinkle with remaining cilantro. Serve with lime.
1½ cups: 411 cal., 7g fat (1g sat. fat), 63mg chol., 628mg sod., 57g carb. (19g sugars, 7g fiber), 31g pro.
Note: Wear disposable gloves when cutting hot peppers; the oils can burn skin. Avoid touching your face.

ROSEMARY-LEMON CHICKEN THIGHS

🕐 ROSEMARY-LEMON CHICKEN THIGHS

A cooking show inspired me to create this lemony chicken. Ask your butcher to remove the bones from chicken thighs but leave the skin intact.
—*Jenn Tidwell, Fair Oaks, CA*

TAKES: 30 min. • **MAKES:** 4 servings

- 2 bacon strips, chopped
- 1 tsp. minced fresh rosemary or ¼ tsp. dried rosemary, crushed
- 4 boneless, skin-on chicken thighs
- ⅛ tsp. pepper
   Dash salt
- ⅓ cup chicken broth
- 3 Tbsp. lemon juice

1. In a large skillet, cook the bacon and rosemary over medium heat until bacon is crisp, stirring occasionally. Using a slotted spoon, remove bacon to paper towels; reserve drippings in pan.
2. Sprinkle chicken with pepper and salt; brown in drippings on both sides. Cook, covered, skin side down, over medium heat 4-6 minutes or until a thermometer reads 170°. Remove from the pan; keep warm. Pour off drippings from the pan.
3. Add broth and lemon juice to same skillet. Bring to a boil, scraping to loosen browned bits from pan; cook until liquid is reduced by half. Spoon over chicken; sprinkle with bacon.
1 chicken thigh with 1 Tbsp. sauce and 2 tsp. cooked bacon: 286 cal., 20g fat (6g sat. fat), 91mg chol., 279mg sod., 1g carb. (1g sugars, 0 fiber), 24g pro.

🍎 GRECIAN PASTA & CHICKEN SKILLET

We love a homemade meal at the end of the day. But the prep involved? Not so much. My Greek-inspired pasta is lemony, herby and, thankfully, easy.
—*Roxanne Chan, Albany, CA*

PREP: 30 min. • **COOK:** 10 min.
MAKES: 4 servings

- 1 can (14½ oz.) reduced-sodium chicken broth
- 1 can (14½ oz.) no-salt-added diced tomatoes, undrained
- ¾ lb. boneless skinless chicken breasts, cut into 1-in. pieces
- ½ cup white wine or water
- 1 garlic clove, minced
- ½ tsp. dried oregano
- 4 oz. multigrain thin spaghetti
- 1 jar (7½ oz.) marinated quartered artichoke hearts, drained and coarsely chopped
- 2 cups fresh baby spinach
- ¼ cup roasted sweet red pepper strips
- ¼ cup sliced ripe olives
- 1 green onion, finely chopped
- 2 Tbsp. minced fresh parsley
- ½ tsp. grated lemon zest
- 2 Tbsp. lemon juice
- 1 Tbsp. olive oil
- ½ tsp. pepper
   Crumbled reduced-fat feta cheese, optional

1. In a large skillet, combine the first 6 ingredients; add spaghetti. Bring to a boil. Cook until chicken is no longer pink and spaghetti is tender, 5-7 minutes.
2. Add artichokes, spinach, red pepper, olives, green onion, parsley, lemon zest, lemon juice, oil and pepper. Cook and stir until spinach is wilted, 2-3 minutes. If desired, sprinkle with cheese.
1½ cups: 373 cal., 15g fat (3g sat. fat), 47mg chol., 658mg sod., 30g carb. (8g sugars, 4g fiber), 25g pro. **Diabetic exchanges:** 2 starch, 2 lean meat, 2 fat, 1 vegetable.

GRECIAN PASTA &
CHICKEN SKILLET

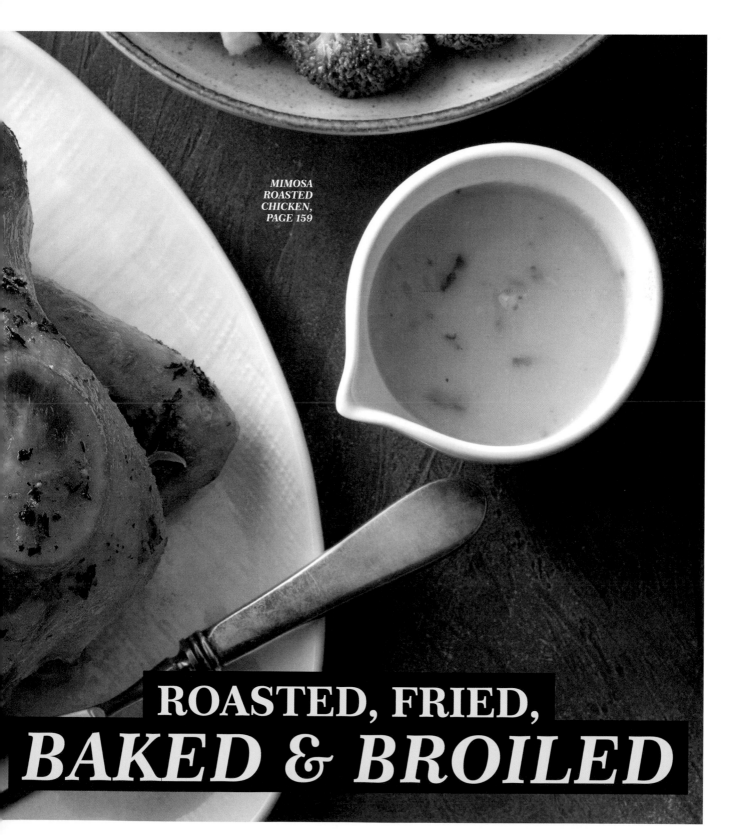

MIMOSA
ROASTED
CHICKEN,
PAGE 159

ROASTED, FRIED,
BAKED & BROILED

🍎 OVEN-FRIED CHICKEN DRUMSTICKS

This fabulous recipe uses Greek yogurt to create an amazing marinade that makes the chicken incredibly moist. No one will guess that it's been lightened up and not even fried!
—*Kimberly Wallace, Dennison, OH*

PREP: 20 min. + marinating • **BAKE:** 40 min.
MAKES: 4 servings

- 1 cup fat-free plain Greek yogurt
- 1 Tbsp. Dijon mustard
- 2 garlic cloves, minced
- 8 chicken drumsticks (4 oz. each), skin removed
- ½ cup whole wheat flour
- 1½ tsp. paprika
- 1 tsp. baking powder
- 1 tsp. salt
- 1 tsp. pepper
  Olive oil-flavored cooking spray

1. In a large bowl or dish, combine the yogurt, mustard and garlic. Add chicken and turn to coat. Cover and refrigerate 8 hours or overnight.

2. Preheat oven to 425°. In another bowl, mix flour, paprika, baking powder, salt and pepper. Remove the chicken from marinade and add, 1 piece at a time, to flour mixture; toss to coat. Place on a wire rack over a baking sheet; spritz with cooking spray. Bake chicken for 40-45 minutes or until a thermometer reads 170°-175°.

2 drumsticks: 227 cal., 7g fat (1g sat. fat), 81mg chol., 498mg sod., 9g carb. (2g sugars, 1g fiber), 31g pro. **Diabetic exchanges:** 4 lean meat, ½ starch.

OVEN-FRIED CHICKEN DRUMSTICKS

CITRUS-SPICED ROAST CHICKEN

● CITRUS-SPICED ROAST CHICKEN

I am the designated Thanksgiving host in my family because of my chipotle citrus roast turkey. Even finicky eaters love it. That's why I use the same recipe for chicken, so we can enjoy the delicious flavors year-round.
—*Robin Haas, Cranston, RI*

PREP: 20 min. • **BAKE:** 1 hour + standing
MAKES: 6 servings

- 3   Tbsp. orange marmalade
- 4½ tsp. chopped chipotle peppers in adobo sauce
- 3   garlic cloves, minced
- ¾   tsp. salt, divided
- ½   tsp. ground cumin
- 1   broiler/fryer chicken (4 lbs.)

1. Preheat oven to 350°. Mix marmalade, chipotle peppers, garlic, ½ tsp. salt and cumin. Using your fingers, carefully loosen the skin from the chicken; rub mixture under the skin.
2. Place chicken on a rack in a shallow roasting pan, breast side up. Tuck wings under chicken; tie drumsticks together. Rub skin with remaining salt. Roast 1-1¼ hours or until a thermometer inserted in thickest part of the thigh reads 170°-175°, covering the chicken with foil halfway through cooking to prevent overbrowning.
3. Remove chicken from oven; let stand, loosely covered, 15 minutes before carving. Remove and discard skin before serving.
4 oz. cooked chicken (skin removed): 239 cal., 8g fat (2g sat. fat), 98mg chol., 409mg sod., 8g carb. (6g sugars, 0 fiber), 32g pro. **Diabetic exchanges:** 4 lean meat.

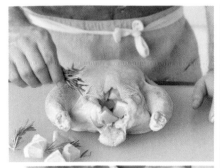

HOW-TO

Roast Chicken

- After patting the chicken skin dry, stuff the bird with herbs and/or citrus.
- Truss the chicken (see how, page 223), then place it on a rack in a shallow roasting pan, and brush lightly with oil. Combine seasonings in a small bowl. Liberally pat this mixture all over the chicken, making sure to get it up and down the sides.
- Bake the chicken, uncovered, in a 350° oven for 2¼-2¾ hours or until a thermometer reads 170°-175°. For accuracy, insert thermometer into the thickest part of the chicken thigh, being careful not to touch bone.

SUNDAY'S BEST CHICKEN

I am the busy mom of four and a nursing student, so weeknight dinners are often rushed. Sunday dinner is very important to our family, and everyone loves when I make this old-fashioned chicken recipe.
—*Amy Jenkins, Mesa, AZ*

PREP: 40 min. • **BAKE:** 2¼ hours + standing
MAKES: 6 servings

2	to 3 medium lemons
2	fresh rosemary sprigs
1	roasting chicken (6 to 7 lbs.)
1	Tbsp. olive oil
2	Tbsp. minced fresh rosemary
1	Tbsp. coarsely ground pepper
1½	tsp. salt

1. Finely grate enough zest from the lemons to measure 2 Tbsp.; set aside. Coarsely chop 2 lemons; place chopped lemons and rosemary sprigs in chicken cavity. Save the remaining lemon for another use.

2. Place chicken on a rack in a shallow roasting pan; brush with oil. Combine the minced rosemary, pepper, salt and lemon zest; rub over chicken.

3. Bake chicken, uncovered, at 350° for 2¼-2¾ hours or until a thermometer inserted in thickest part of thigh reads 170°-175°, basting occasionally with drippings. (Cover loosely with foil if chicken browns too quickly.)

4. Let stand 15 minutes before carving. Discard lemons and rosemary sprigs.

1 serving: 555 cal., 34g fat (9g sat. fat), 179mg chol., 801mg sod., 3g carb. (0 sugars, 1g fiber), 57g pro.

SUNDAY'S BEST CHICKEN

FIND ROASTING EXPERTISE
Just hover your camera here.

MISO BUTTER ROASTED CHICKEN

I love this recipe because most of the work is done in the beginning. Look for a prepared spatchcocked chicken in your grocery store or ask the butcher to prepare the bird. Once it's in the oven, there's ample time to set the table and talk.
—*Stefanie Schaldenbrand, Los Angeles, CA*

PREP: 25 min. • **BAKE:** 1½ hours + standing
MAKES: 6 servings

- 1   lb. medium fresh mushrooms
- 1   lb. baby red potatoes
- 1   lb. fresh Brussels sprouts, halved
- 6   garlic cloves, minced
- 1   Tbsp. olive oil
- 1½ tsp. minced fresh thyme or
     ½ tsp. dried thyme
- ½   tsp. salt
- ½   tsp. pepper
- 1   roasting chicken (5 to 6 lbs.)
- ¼   cup butter, softened
- ¼   cup white miso paste

1. Preheat oven to 425°. Mix the mushrooms, potatoes, Brussels sprouts and garlic; drizzle with oil. Sprinkle with the thyme, salt and pepper; toss to coat. Place in a shallow roasting pan.

2. Place chicken on a work surface, breast side down and tail end facing you. Using kitchen shears, cut along each side of the backbone; discard backbone. Turn chicken over so breast side is up; flatten by pressing down firmly on breastbone until it cracks. Place chicken on a rack over vegetables. Twist and tuck wings under to secure in place. Combine butter and miso paste; spread over skin (mixture will be thick).

3. Roast until a thermometer inserted in thickest part of thigh reads 170°-175°, 1½-1¾ hours, covering loosely with foil after 45 minutes of cooking. (The miso mixture on chicken will appear very dark while roasting.)

**MISO BUTTER
ROASTED
CHICKEN**

4. Remove chicken from oven; tent with foil. Let chicken stand 15 minutes before carving. If desired, skim fat and thicken pan drippings for gravy. Serve with the chicken. Top with additional fresh thyme if desired.

Note: See page 199 for a how-to on spatchcocking a chicken.

1 serving: 653 cal., 37g fat (13g sat. fat), 170mg chol., 912mg sod., 25g carb. (3g sugars, 4g fiber), 54g pro.

TEST KITCHEN TIPS

- Toss vegetables with grated Parmesan cheese and lemon zest once they are finished roasting.

- Mix Thai basil or ginger with the miso butter for additional flavor.

- For more spice, add red pepper flakes to the chicken or vegetables.

SHEET-PAN CORDON BLEU

The addition of bacon in this version of cordon bleu makes it one of my favorite comforting recipes. I've made it for both friends and family, and everyone's a fan.
—*Jim Wick, Orlando, FL*

- -

PREP: 15 min. • **BAKE:** 40 min.
MAKES: 4 servings

- 4 boneless skinless chicken breast halves (8 oz. each)
- 2 Tbsp. butter, softened
- 1 tsp. dried thyme
- 4 thin slices fully cooked ham
- 4 thin slices Swiss cheese
- 8 bacon strips
- 2 large eggs
- ½ cup 2% milk
- ½ cup all-purpose flour
- ¾ cup dry bread crumbs
- ½ tsp. garlic powder
- 1 tsp. dried oregano
- ¼ cup shredded Parmesan cheese

1. Preheat oven to at 350°. Flatten the chicken breasts to ⅛-in. thickness; spread butter on the insides. Sprinkle with thyme. Top with a slice of ham and cheese; roll up tightly. Wrap each with 2 bacon slices; secure with toothpicks.
2. In a small bowl, beat eggs and milk. Place flour in another bowl. Combine bread crumbs, garlic powder, oregano and cheese. Dip each chicken breast into egg mixture; dip into flour to coat. Dip each again into egg mixture, then coat with crumbs.
3. Place on a greased baking sheet. Bake, uncovered, for 40-45 minutes or until chicken juices run clear.
1 chicken breast half : 654 cal., 27g fat (11g sat. fat), 280mg chol., 961mg sod., 30g carb. (3g sugars, 2g fiber), 70g pro.

🕐 FRIED CHICKEN STRIPS

I recently made this recipe of Mom's for my in-laws, and they said it was the best fried chicken ever. Slicing the chicken into strips cuts down on cooking time and ensures each piece is crunchy and evenly coated.
—*Genny Monchamp, Redding, CA*

- -

TAKES: 20 min. • **MAKES:** 6 servings

- 2⅔ cups crushed saltines (about 80 crackers)
- 1 tsp. garlic salt
- ½ tsp. dried basil
- ½ tsp. paprika
- ⅛ tsp. pepper
- 1 large egg
- 1 cup 2% milk
- 1½ lbs. boneless skinless chicken breasts, cut into ½-in. strips
   Oil for frying

1. In a shallow bowl, combine the first 5 ingredients. In another shallow bowl, beat egg and milk. Dip chicken into egg mixture, then cracker mixture.
2. In an electric skillet or deep-fat fryer, heat oil to 375°. Fry the chicken, a few strips at a time, for 2-3 minutes on each side or until golden brown. Drain on paper towels.
4 oz. cooked chicken: 388 cal., 19g fat (3g sat. fat), 98mg chol., 704mg sod., 25g carb. (2g sugars, 1g fiber), 28g pro.

SHEET-PAN CORDON BLEU

ROASTED LIME CHICKEN

The hints of lime that infuse this moist, juicy chicken make it the most requested dish for our family dinners.
—*Kathy Lewis-Martinez, Spring Valley, CA*

- -

PREP: 20 min. + marinating
BAKE: 2 hours + standing
MAKES: 10 servings

- ½ cup Dijon mustard
- ¼ cup lime juice
- ¼ cup soy sauce
- 2 Tbsp. minced fresh parsley or 2 tsp. dried parsley flakes
- 2 Tbsp. minced fresh rosemary or 2 tsp. dried rosemary, crushed
- 2 Tbsp. minced fresh sage or 2 tsp. rubbed sage
- 2 Tbsp. minced fresh thyme or 2 tsp. dried thyme
- 1 tsp. white pepper
- 1 tsp. ground nutmeg
- 1 roasting chicken (6 to 7 lbs.)
- 4 medium limes, cut into wedges

1. Combine the first 9 ingredients in a small bowl. Cover and refrigerate ¼ cup marinade; pour remaining marinade into a large shallow dish. Add the chicken and turn to coat. Refrigerate for at least 4 hours.
2. Drain chicken, discarding marinade. Place lime wedges inside the cavity. Tuck wings under chicken; tie the drumsticks together. Place chicken breast-side up on a rack in a shallow roasting pan. Brush reserved marinade over chicken.
3. Bake at 350° for 2-2½ hours or until a thermometer inserted in thigh reads 170°-175°. Cover loosely with foil if chicken browns too quickly. Let stand 15 minutes before carving.
5 oz. cooked chicken: 341 cal., 19g fat (5g sat. fat), 108mg chol., 629mg sod., 4g carb. (1g sugars, 1g fiber), 35g pro.

ROASTED LIME CHICKEN

PAN-ROASTED CHICKEN & VEGETABLES

This one-dish meal tastes as if it took hours of work, but the simple ingredients can be prepped in minutes. The rosemary gives it a rich flavor, and the meat juices cook the veggies to perfection. Easy!
—*Sherri Melotik, Oak Creek, WI*

PREP: 15 min. • **BAKE:** 45 min.
MAKES: 6 servings

- 2 lbs. red potatoes (about 6 medium), cut into ¾-in. pieces
- 1 large onion, coarsely chopped
- 2 Tbsp. olive oil
- 3 garlic cloves, minced
- 1¼ tsp. salt, divided
- 1 tsp. dried rosemary, crushed, divided
- ¾ tsp. pepper, divided
- ½ tsp. paprika
- 6 bone-in chicken thighs (about 2¼ lbs.), skin removed
- 6 cups fresh baby spinach (about 6 oz.)

1. Preheat oven to 425°. In a large bowl, combine the potatoes, onion, oil, garlic, ¾ tsp. salt, ½ tsp. rosemary and ½ tsp. pepper; toss to coat. Transfer to a 15x10x1-in. baking pan coated with cooking spray.

2. In a small bowl, mix paprika and the remaining salt, rosemary and pepper. Sprinkle chicken with paprika mixture; arrange over vegetables. Roast until a thermometer inserted in chicken reads 170°-175° and vegetables are just tender, 35-40 minutes.

3. Remove chicken to a serving platter; keep warm. Top the vegetables with spinach. Roast until vegetables are tender and the spinach is wilted, 8-10 minutes longer. Stir vegetables to combine; serve with chicken.

1 chicken thigh with 1 cup vegetables: 357 cal., 14g fat (3g sat. fat), 87mg chol., 597mg sod., 28g carb. (3g sugars, 4g fiber), 28g pro. **Diabetic exchanges:** 4 lean meat, 1½ starch, 1 vegetable, 1 fat.

PAN-ROASTED CHICKEN & VEGETABLES

WATCH US PREPARE IT
Just hover your camera here.

🍎 BALSAMIC ROAST CHICKEN

When the aroma from this dish fills your house, your family will think you spent all day cooking. But this elegant Sunday-special entree, flavored with rosemary, wine and balsamic vinegar, is surprisingly simple to make.
—*Tracy Tylkowski, Omaha, NE*

PREP: 20 min. • **BAKE:** 2 hours + standing
MAKES: 12 servings (1½ cups onion sauce)

- 2 Tbsp. minced fresh rosemary or 2 tsp. dried rosemary, crushed
- 3 garlic cloves, minced
- 1 tsp. salt
- 1 tsp. pepper
- 2 medium red onions, chopped
- 1 roasting chicken (6 to 7 lbs.)
- ½ cup dry red wine or reduced-sodium chicken broth
- ½ cup balsamic vinegar

1. Preheat oven to 350°. Mix rosemary, garlic, salt and pepper. Place onions in a roasting pan; place chicken over onions, breast side up.
2. Pat chicken dry. With fingers, carefully loosen skin from chicken; rub rosemary mixture under the skin. Secure skin to underside of breast with toothpicks. Tuck wings under chicken; tie the drumsticks together.
3. Mix wine and vinegar; pour over chicken. Roast 2-2½ hours or until a thermometer inserted in thickest part of thigh reads 170°-175°. (Cover loosely with foil if chicken browns too quickly.)
4. Remove chicken from oven; tent with foil. Let stand 15 minutes before carving. Transfer onion and pan drippings to a small bowl; skim fat. Remove and discard skin from chicken before serving. Serve with onion sauce.
3 oz. cooked chicken (skin removed) with 2 Tbsp. sauce: 182 cal., 7g fat (2g sat. fat), 77mg chol., 275mg sod., 4g carb. (2g sugars, 0 fiber), 25g pro. **Diabetic exchanges:** 4 lean meat.

OVEN CHICKEN CORDON BLEU

⏱ 🍎 OVEN CHICKEN CORDON BLEU

My son loves Chicken cordon bleu, but I'm not a fan of store versions. My recipe has all the yummy flavors in a 30-minute meal. The leftovers freeze well, too.
—*Ronda Eagle, Goose Creek, SC*

TAKES: 30 min. • **MAKES:** 6 servings

- 6 boneless skinless chicken breast halves (4 oz. each)
- ¼ tsp. salt
- ¼ tsp. pepper
- 6 slices deli ham
- 3 slices aged Swiss cheese, halved
- 1 cup panko bread crumbs
  Cooking spray
SAUCE
- 2 Tbsp. all-purpose flour
- 1 cup 2% milk
- ½ cup dry white wine
- ⅓ cup finely shredded Swiss cheese
- ¼ tsp. salt
- ⅛ tsp. pepper

1. Preheat oven to 375°. Sprinkle the chicken with salt and pepper; arrange in a greased 13x9-in. baking dish.
2. Top each with 1 slice of ham and a half slice of cheese, folding ham in half and covering chicken as much as possible. Sprinkle with bread crumbs. Carefully spritz the bread crumbs with cooking spray, keeping crumbs in place. Bake 15-20 minutes or until golden brown and a thermometer inserted in the chicken reads 165°.
3. For sauce, in a small saucepan, whisk flour and milk until smooth. Bring to a boil, stirring constantly; cook and stir 1-2 minutes or until thickened.
4. Reduce to medium heat. Stir in wine and cheese; cook and stir 2-3 minutes or until cheese is melted and sauce is thickened and bubbly. Stir in salt and pepper. Keep warm over low heat until ready to serve. Serve with chicken.
1 chicken breast half with 3 Tbsp. sauce: 290 cal., 10g fat (4g sat. fat), 89mg chol., 498mg sod., 12g carb. (3g sugars, 0 fiber), 34g pro. **Diabetic exchanges:** 4 lean meat, 1 starch.

MOM'S ROAST CHICKEN

This is the best way to cook a whole chicken—it roasts up super juicy with crisp, golden skin. This chicken is simply seasoned, but packs in so much flavor.
—*James Schend, Pleasant Prairie, WI*

PREP: 15 min. + chilling
BAKE: 35 min. + standing
MAKES: 6 servings

1 broiler/fryer chicken (4 to 5 lbs.)
2 tsp. kosher salt
1 tsp. coarsely ground pepper
2 tsp. olive oil
  Optional: Minced fresh thyme or rosemary

1. Rub outside of chicken with salt and pepper. Transfer chicken to a rack on a rimmed baking sheet. Refrigerate, uncovered, overnight.
2. Preheat oven to 450°. Remove chicken from refrigerator while oven heats. Heat a 12-in. cast-iron or ovenproof skillet in the oven for 15 minutes.
3. Place chicken on a work surface, neck side down. Cut through skin where legs connect to body. Press thighs down so joints pop and legs lie flat.
4. Carefully place chicken, breast side up, into hot skillet; press legs down so they lie flat on bottom of pan. Brush with oil. Roast until a thermometer inserted in thickest part of thigh reads 170°-175°, 35-40 minutes. Remove chicken from oven; let stand 10 minutes before carving. If desired, top with herbs before serving.

5 oz. cooked chicken: 405 cal., 24g fat (6g sat. fat), 139mg chol., 760mg sod., 0 carb. (0 sugars, 0 fiber), 44g pro.

*CURRY-RUBBED
ROAST CHICKEN*

CURRY-RUBBED ROAST CHICKEN

There is just something so right about serving a roasted chicken to loved ones! This recipe is simple—yet it's full of spicy showoff flavors suitable for any special occasion.
—*Merry Graham, Newhall, CA*

- -

PREP: 20 min. • **COOK:** 1½ hours + standing
MAKES: 6 servings

- 4 Tbsp. coconut oil, divided
- 2½ tsp. salt, divided
- 2 tsp. Madras curry powder
- ½ tsp. granulated garlic
- 1 roasting chicken (5 to 6 lbs.)
- ¼ tsp. pepper
- 1 cup chopped leeks (white part only)
- 1 celery rib, coarsely chopped
- 3 green onions, chopped
- 1 medium lemon, quartered
- 1 cup reduced-sodium chicken broth

GRAVY
- 1 Tbsp. unsalted butter
- 1 Tbsp. all-purpose flour
- 1 cup reduced-sodium chicken broth
- ½ cup white wine
   Optional: Lemon slices, minced fresh parsley and minced chives

DID YOU KNOW?
Madras curry powder is spicier than regular curry powder. As a substitute, add ⅛ tsp. ground cayenne and a few dashes ground mustard to 1¾ tsp. curry powder.

1. Preheat oven to 350°. Mix 2 Tbsp. coconut oil and 2 tsp. salt with curry powder and garlic. With your fingers, carefully loosen skin from chicken breast and upper legs; rub coconut oil mixture under skin. Remove giblets from cavity and save for another use. Sprinkle the cavity with pepper and remaining salt; rub inside and outside of chicken with remaining coconut oil.
2. Combine leeks, celery, green onions and lemon and toss lightly; loosely stuff cavity. Tuck wings under the chicken; tie drumsticks together. Place breast side up on a rack in a shallow roasting pan.
3. Roast 45 minutes; add broth to pan. Continue roasting until a thermometer reads 165° when inserted in center of stuffing and at least 170° in the thigh, 45-60 minutes. (Cover loosely with foil if chicken browns too quickly.)
4. Pour juices from cavity into pan. Remove chicken to a serving platter; tent with foil. Let stand 15-20 minutes before removing stuffing and slicing.
5. For gravy, pour pan juices into a large saucepan; skim off fat. Bring juices to a boil over medium heat. Add the butter and flour; cook and stir until slightly thickened. Add broth and wine; cook and stir until thickened, 2-3 minutes. Serve with chicken and, if desired, lemon slices, parsley and chives.
1 serving: 580 cal., 38g fat (17g sat. fat), 154mg chol., 1328mg sod., 6g carb. (2g sugars, 1g fiber), 49g pro.

🕐 BROILED CHICKEN & ARTICHOKES

My wife and I first made this as newlyweds, and we have been hooked on it since. It's so simple and affordable, yet delicious and healthy. Can't beat that!
—*Chris Koon, Midlothian, VA*

TAKES: 15 min. • **MAKES:** 8 servings

- 8   boneless skinless chicken thighs (about 2 lbs.)
- 2   jars (7½ oz. each) marinated quartered artichoke hearts, drained
- 2   Tbsp. olive oil
- 1   tsp. salt
- ½   tsp. pepper
- ¼   cup shredded Parmesan cheese
- 2   Tbsp. minced fresh parsley

1. Preheat broiler. In a large bowl, toss chicken and artichokes with oil, salt and pepper. Transfer to a broiler pan.
2. Broil 3 in. from heat 8-10 minutes or until a thermometer inserted in chicken reads 170°, turning the chicken and artichokes halfway through cooking. Sprinkle with cheese. Broil 1-2 minutes longer or until cheese is melted. Sprinkle with parsley.
1 serving: 288 cal., 21g fat (5g sat. fat), 77mg chol., 584mg sod., 4g carb. (0 sugars, 0 fiber), 22g pro.

PICNIC FRIED CHICKEN

SEE US FRY PERFECT CHICKEN
Just hover your camera here.

PICNIC FRIED CHICKEN

For our family, it's not a picnic unless we have fried chicken! Chicken, deviled eggs and potato salad are all musts for a picnic as far as my husband is concerned. This is a golden oldie recipe for me—I've used it any number of times.

—Edna Hoffman, Hebron, IN

PREP: 30 min. + marinating • **COOK:** 40 min.
MAKES: 6 servings

  1 broiler/fryer chicken (3 lbs.), cut up
  ¾ to 1 cup buttermilk
COATING
  1½ to 2 cups all-purpose flour
  1½ tsp. salt
  ½ tsp. pepper
  ½ tsp. garlic powder
  ½ tsp. onion powder
  1 Tbsp. paprika
  ¼ tsp. ground sage
  ¼ tsp. ground thyme
  ⅛ tsp. baking powder
    Oil for frying

1. Pat chicken pieces with paper towels; place in large flat dish. Pour buttermilk over chicken; cover, and allow to soak at least 1 hour or overnight in refrigerator.
2. Combine coating ingredients in large shallow dish or resealable bag. Add chicken pieces, 1 at a time, and turn to coat well. Lay coated pieces on waxed paper for 15 minutes to allow coating to dry (it will cling better in frying).
3. In a Dutch oven or deep skillet, heat ½ in. oil over medium heat to 350°. Fry chicken, uncovered, until coating is dark golden brown and meat is no longer pink, turning occasionally, 7-8 minutes per side. Drain chicken on paper towels.
5 oz. cooked chicken: 623 cal., 40g fat (7g sat. fat), 106mg chol., 748mg sod., 26g carb. (2g sugars, 1g fiber), 38g pro.

HOW-TO
Pan-Fry Chicken

• Remove excess moisture from your chicken pieces by patting them dry with paper towels. Place them in a large flat dish with high sides. Pour buttermilk over chicken, then cover and refrigerate for at least an hour or overnight.

• In a large shallow dish or resealable bag, combine the coating ingredients. Dredge the chicken well, working one piece at a time. Place on a sheet of waxed paper.

• Let the chicken stand for about 15 minutes after coating. During this time, the moisture from the buttermilk will become evenly distributed, which will help the coating adhere.

• In a Dutch oven or deep skillet, heat ½ in. of oil over medium heat until it reaches 350°. Carefully add a few pieces of the chicken into the oil, making sure not to overcrowd the pan. Cook, uncovered, for 7-8 minutes per side. Turn occasionally until the coating turns dark golden brown and the meat is no longer pink. Remove to paper towels and keep warm.

⏱ 🍎 BAKED CHICKEN WITH BACON-TOMATO RELISH

We eat a lot of chicken for dinner, so I'm always trying to do something a little bit different with it. My children all love the crispness of this chicken and my husband and I love the flavorful relish—you can't go wrong with bacon!
—*Elisabeth Larsen, Pleasant Grove, UT*

- -

TAKES: 30 min. • **MAKES:** 4 servings

- 1   cup panko bread crumbs
- 2   Tbsp. plus 1 tsp. minced fresh thyme, divided
- ½   tsp. salt, divided
- ½   tsp. pepper, divided
- ⅓   cup all-purpose flour
- 1   large egg, beaten
- 1   lb. chicken tenderloins
- 4   bacon strips, cut into ½-in. pieces
- 1½ cups grape tomatoes, halved
- 1   Tbsp. red wine vinegar
- 1   Tbsp. brown sugar

1. Preheat oven to 425°. In a shallow bowl, mix bread crumbs, 2 Tbsp. thyme, and ¼ tsp. each salt and pepper. Place flour and egg in separate shallow bowls. Dip chicken in flour; shake off excess. Dip in egg, then in crumb mixture, patting to help coating adhere. Place the chicken on a greased rack in a 15x10x1-in. baking pan. Bake until a thermometer reads 165°, about 15 minutes.

2. Meanwhile, in a large skillet, cook bacon over medium heat until crisp, stirring occasionally, about 5 minutes. Remove with a slotted spoon; drain on paper towels. Reserve 2 Tbsp. drippings in pan; discard remaining drippings.

3. Add tomatoes, vinegar, sugar and remaining salt and pepper to drippings; cook and stir until tomatoes are tender, 2-3 minutes. Stir in the bacon and the remaining thyme. Serve with chicken.

2 chicken tenders with ¼ cup relish: 326 cal., 13g fat (4g sat. fat), 95mg chol., 602mg sod., 19g carb. (6g sugars, 2g fiber), 34g pro. **Diabetic exchanges:** 4 lean meat, 2 fat, 1 starch.

TEST KITCHEN TIPS
- Using chicken tenders instead of chicken breast halves speeds along the bake time to make this a quick dinner.
- Baking on a rack will help the coating on the underside of the chicken stay crunchy, but it isn't a must if you don't have a rack that fits into the pan.

BAKED CHICKEN WITH BACON-TOMATO RELISH

🍎 BROILED CHICKEN SLICES

This recipe is ideal for a quick supper or a special dinner with friends. The leftover slices stay flavorful reheated or tossed into a salad.
—*Christi Gillentine, Tulsa, OK*

PREP: 5 min. + marinating • **BAKE:** 10 min.
MAKES: 4 servings

- ½ cup cider or red wine vinegar
- ¼ cup soy sauce
- 4 garlic cloves, minced
- 1 lb. boneless skinless chicken breasts, cut into 1-in. slices
  Hot cooked rice, optional

1. In a resealable container, combine vinegar, soy sauce and garlic. Add the chicken; turn to coat. Seal; refrigerate for 15 minutes.
2. Broil 4 in. from heat for 10-12 minutes or until juices run clear; turn frequently. Serve over rice if desired.
3 oz. cooked chicken: 126 cal., 3g fat (1g sat. fat), 63mg chol., 349mg sod., 1g carb. (0 sugars, 0 fiber), 24g pro. **Diabetic exchanges:** 3 lean meat.

ROASTED HONEY MUSTARD CHICKEN

I love a good roasted chicken, and this one is easy and delicious. The marinade does its magic until it's time for roasting. It's fun to dress the dish up with whatever vegetables are fresh at the market.
—*Kara Brook, Owings Mills, MD*

PREP: 20 min. + marinating
BAKE: 1¾ hours + standing
MAKES: 6 servings

- ¾ cup honey
- ⅓ cup extra virgin olive oil
- ⅓ cup Dijon mustard
- ¼ cup lemon juice
- 3 Tbsp. chicken seasoning

ROASTED HONEY MUSTARD CHICKEN

- 7 garlic cloves, minced
- 1 broiler/fryer chicken (3 to 4 lbs.)
VEGETABLES
- 1½ lbs. baby red potatoes
- 1 lb. carrots, cut into 1-in. pieces
- 3 to 4 fresh rosemary sprigs
- 2 Tbsp. extra virgin olive oil
- 1 tsp. chicken seasoning
- ½ tsp. salt
- ¼ tsp. pepper
- 1 medium lemon, sliced

1. In a small bowl, whisk the first 6 ingredients until blended. Pour 1 cup marinade into a large bowl or shallow dish. Add chicken and turn to coat. Refrigerate at least 3 hours, turning occasionally. Cover and refrigerate remaining marinade for basting.
2. Drain chicken, discarding marinade left in bowl. Preheat oven to 450°. Place chicken on a rack in a shallow roasting pan, breast side up. Tuck wings under chicken; tie drumsticks together.

3. Roast 15 minutes. Meanwhile, in a large bowl, combine potatoes, carrots, rosemary, oil, chicken seasoning, salt and pepper. Add to roasting pan; reduce oven setting to 350°.
4. Roast until a thermometer inserted in thickest part of thigh reads 170°-175°, 1½-1¾ hours, adding the lemon slices during the last 15 minutes of roasting and brushing occasionally with reserved marinade. Cover loosely with foil if the chicken browns too quickly.
5. Remove chicken from oven; tent with foil. Let stand 15 minutes before carving; discard rosemary sprigs.
Note: This recipe was tested with McCormick Montreal Chicken Seasoning. Look for it in the spice aisle.
5 oz. cooked chicken with 1 cup vegetables: 654 cal., 31g fat (7g sat. fat), 104mg chol., 919mg sod., 58g carb. (32g sugars, 4g fiber), 36g pro.

SHEET-PAN CAESAR CHICKEN & POTATOES

In our area, we have an abundance of fresh lemons year-round. When I had a few extra on hand, I put together a quick marinade and created a really tasty meal with a burst of flavor. I baked it so I could add potatoes, but you can grill the chicken if you prefer.
—*Kallee Krong-McCreery, Escondido, CA*

- -

PREP: 15 min. + marinating • **BAKE:** 30 min.
MAKES: 4 servings

¼ cup lemon juice
¼ cup Caesar vinaigrette
4 bone-in chicken thighs
   (about 1½ lbs.)
3 medium red potatoes (about 1¼ lbs.),
   each cut into 8 wedges
½ lb. medium carrots, cut into
   1½-in. pieces
1 tsp. garlic salt
½ tsp. dill weed
¼ tsp. pepper

1. For marinade, in a large bowl, mix lemon juice and dressing; remove 2 Tbsp. mixture for potatoes. Add chicken to remaining marinade; turn to coat. Cover and refrigerate the chicken and reserved marinade 4 hours or overnight.
2. Preheat oven to 400°. Place the chicken on center of a foil-lined 15x10x1-in. baking pan; discard chicken marinade. Toss potatoes and carrots with reserved marinade and seasonings; arrange around chicken.
3. Roast until a thermometer inserted in chicken reads 170°-175° and potatoes are tender, 30-40 minutes.
1 chicken thigh with 1 cup vegetables:
348 cal., 18g fat (5g sat. fat), 80mg chol., 698mg sod., 20g carb. (4g sugars, 3g fiber), 25g pro.

SHEET-PAN CAESAR CHICKEN & POTATOES

MIMOSA ROASTED CHICKEN

MIMOSA ROASTED CHICKEN

This aromatic seasoned chicken with a rich and buttery champagne gravy will delight all who taste it.
—Taste of Home *Test Kitchen*

- -

PREP: 15 min. • **BAKE:** 2 hours + standing
MAKES: 6 servings

- 2   medium navel oranges
- 1   roasting chicken (6 to 7 lbs.)
- ¾   tsp. pepper, divided
- ¼   cup butter, softened
- 4   garlic cloves, minced
- 1   Tbsp. dried basil
- 1   tsp. salt
- ½   tsp. onion powder
- ½   tsp. dried marjoram
- 2   cups brut champagne
- 2   medium onions, cut into wedges
- ½   cup chicken broth
- ½   cup orange juice

GRAVY
-      Chicken broth or water
- 1   Tbsp. butter
- 2   Tbsp. all-purpose flour

1. Cut 1 orange into slices; cut second orange into wedges. With your fingers, carefully loosen skin from both sides of chicken breast. Place orange slices under the skin. Place orange wedges inside cavity and sprinkle the chicken with ¼ tsp. pepper.

2. Tuck wings under chicken. Place breast side up on a rack in a shallow roasting pan. Combine the butter, garlic, basil, salt, onion powder, marjoram and remaining pepper; rub over chicken.

3. Bake chicken, uncovered, at 350° for 30 minutes. Meanwhile, in a large bowl, combine champagne, onions, broth and orange juice; pour into pan. Bake until a thermometer reads 175°, 1½-2 hours longer, basting occasionally with pan juices. Cover loosely with foil if chicken browns too quickly. Cover and let stand for 15 minutes before slicing.

4. To make gravy, pour drippings and loosened browned bits into a measuring cup. Skim fat, reserving 1 Tbsp. Add enough broth to drippings to measure 1 cup. In a small saucepan, melt butter and reserved fat. Stir in the flour until smooth; gradually add broth mixture. Bring to a boil; cook and stir gravy until thickened, about 2 minutes. Serve with the chicken.

6 oz. cooked chicken with 2 Tbsp. gravy: 731 cal., 41g fat (15g sat. fat), 204mg chol., 798mg sod., 17g carb. (9g sugars, 2g fiber), 58g pro.

REAL SOUTHERN FRIED CHICKEN

A Yankee originally from Vermont, I didn't know one fried chicken from another. They all seemed pretty much the same to me. Tasting the southern version opened my eyes! A side of hot biscuits served with butter and honey is practically mandatory.
—*Lily Julow, Lawrenceville, GA*

PREP: 20 min. + marinating • **COOK:** 30 min.
MAKES: 6 servings

- 3 cups buttermilk, divided
- 3 tsp. kosher salt, divided
- 1 tsp. coarsely ground pepper, divided
- 1 broiler/fryer chicken (3 to 4 lbs.), cut up
  Oil for deep-fat frying
- 2 cups all-purpose flour
- 1 tsp. onion powder
- 1 tsp. garlic powder
- 1 tsp. paprika

1. In a shallow bowl, whisk together 2 cups buttermilk, 1 tsp. salt and ⅛ tsp. pepper. Add the chicken; turn to coat. Refrigerate, covered, overnight.

2. In an electric skillet or deep fryer, heat oil to 375°. Meanwhile, place remaining buttermilk in a shallow bowl. In another shallow bowl, whisk flour, onion powder, garlic powder, paprika and remaining salt and pepper. Place half of the flour mixture in another shallow bowl (for a second coat of breading). Drain chicken, discarding marinade; pat chicken dry. Dip in flour mixture to coat both sides; shake off excess. Dip in buttermilk, allowing excess to drain off. For the second coat of breading, dip chicken in remaining flour mixture, patting to help coating adhere.

3. Fry chicken, a few pieces at a time, 4-5 minutes on each side or until browned and juices run clear. Drain on paper towels.

1 serving: 580 cal., 39g fat (7g sat. fat), 106mg chol., 628mg sod., 19g carb. (3g sugars, 1g fiber), 37g pro.

GARLIC-ROASTED CHICKEN & VEGETABLES

GARLIC-ROASTED CHICKEN & VEGETABLES

The first time my Greek father-in-law made this chicken, he proudly shared the recipe with me. It's become my favorite way to roast chicken.
—*Jessica Pardalos, Shelton, WA*

PREP: 20 min. • **BAKE:** 2 hours + standing
MAKES: 10 servings

- 1 roasting chicken (5 to 6 lbs.)
- 4 Tbsp. butter, softened, divided
- 15 garlic cloves, halved
- 1 can (14½ oz.) chicken broth, divided
- ¼ cup olive oil
- ¼ cup lemon juice
- 1 to 2 Tbsp. dried oregano
- 1 tsp. salt
- ½ tsp. pepper
- ¼ tsp. garlic powder
- 10 red potatoes (about 1½ lbs.), cut into large chunks
- 2 cups baby carrots
- 1 medium red onion, thinly sliced

1. Rub the inside of the chicken with 2 Tbsp. butter. With a sharp knife, cut 16 small slits in the chicken breast, drumsticks and thighs. Place a halved garlic clove in each slit. Place chicken on a rack in a shallow roasting pan; tie the drumsticks together.

2. Place remaining garlic in pan. Pour half of the broth over chicken. Combine oil and lemon juice; pour half over the chicken. Rub remaining butter over chicken. Combine the oregano, salt, pepper and garlic powder; sprinkle half over chicken. Cover and bake at 350° for 45 minutes.

3. Place the potatoes, carrots and onion in pan. Drizzle remaining oil mixture and broth over chicken and vegetables. Sprinkle remaining oregano mixture over chicken. Cover and bake chicken 30 minutes longer; baste. Bake chicken, uncovered, for 45-50 minutes or until a thermometer reads 170°-175°, basting several times. Thicken pan juices if desired. Cover and let stand for 10 minutes before serving.

1 serving: 460 cal., 26g fat (8g sat. fat), 103mg chol., 567mg sod., 24g carb. (3g sugars, 3g fiber), 31g pro.

ROASTED CHICKEN & RED POTATOES

ROASTED CHICKEN & RED POTATOES

Pop this homey dinner in the oven for about an hour, then enjoy! It has so much flavor—the meat juices help cook the veggies just perfectly.

—*Sherri Melotik, Oak Creek, WI*

PREP: 15 min. • **BAKE:** 55 min.
MAKES: 6 servings

- 2   lbs. red potatoes, cut into 1-in. pieces
- 1   pkg. (9 oz.) fresh spinach
- 1   large onion, cut into 1-in. pieces
- 2   Tbsp. olive oil
- 4   garlic cloves, minced
- 1   tsp. salt, divided
- 1   tsp. dried thyme
- ¾   tsp. pepper, divided
- 6   chicken leg quarters
- ¾   tsp. paprika

1. Preheat oven to 375°. Place potatoes, spinach and onion in a greased shallow roasting pan. Add the oil, garlic, ¾ tsp. salt, thyme and ½ tsp. pepper; toss to combine.

2. Arrange chicken over vegetables; sprinkle with paprika and remaining salt and pepper. Roast on an upper oven rack 55-60 minutes or until a thermometer inserted in chicken reads 170°-175° and potatoes are tender.

1 chicken leg quarter with 1 cup vegetable mixture: 449 cal., 21g fat (5g sat. fat), 105mg chol., 529mg sod., 29g carb. (3g sugars, 4g fiber), 35g pro.

TEST KITCHEN TIP

Common olive oil works better for cooking at high heat than virgin or extra-virgin oil. The higher grades have ideal flavor for cold foods, but they smoke at lower temperatures than the less-expensive oils.

🍎 BAKED BUFFALO CHICKEN

When I make this tangy chicken, I have to double the recipe because it disappears so fast. Better to have leftovers, especially since they make delicious sandwiches and salads.

—Beth Zimmerman, Willingboro, NJ

PREP: 20 min. + marinating • **BAKE:** 25 min.
MAKES: 4 servings

¾ cup Buffalo wing sauce, divided
4   boneless skinless chicken breast halves (6 oz. each)
¾ cup all-purpose flour
¾ tsp. dried tarragon
½ tsp. pepper
1¼ cups panko bread crumbs

1. Pour ⅓ cup wing sauce into a shallow dish. Add chicken breasts and turn to coat. Let chicken stand 15 minutes or refrigerate, covered, up to 24 hours.

2. Preheat oven to 400°. Drain chicken, discarding marinade. In a shallow bowl, mix flour, tarragon and pepper. Place bread crumbs and remaining wing sauce in separate shallow bowls. Dip chicken in flour mixture to coat all sides; shake off excess. Dip in wing sauce, then in bread crumbs, patting to help the coating adhere.

3. Place chicken pieces on a rack in a 15x10x1-in. baking pan. Bake for 25-30 minutes or until a thermometer reads 165°.

1 chicken breast half : 277 cal., 5g fat (1g sat. fat), 94mg chol., 811mg sod., 18g carb. (1g sugars, 1g fiber), 37g pro.
Diabetic exchanges: 5 lean meat, 1 starch.

ROAST CHICKEN WITH CREOLE STUFFING

ROAST CHICKEN WITH CREOLE STUFFING

I've used this recipe ever since I roasted my first chicken. Our whole family looks forward to it. The combination of shrimp, sausage, ham, vegetables and seasonings makes the stuffing unique and delicious.
—*Ruth Bates, Temecula, CA*

- -

PREP: 50 min. • **BAKE:** 3 hours
MAKES: 8 servings (8 cups stuffing)

1½ cups uncooked brown rice
2 Italian sausage links
2 Tbsp. vegetable oil
1 cup chopped onion
5 garlic cloves, minced
½ cup diced green pepper
½ cup diced sweet red pepper
1 can (14½ oz.) diced tomatoes, undrained
1 Tbsp. lemon juice
1 tsp. dried basil
½ tsp. sugar
½ tsp. hot pepper sauce
½ tsp. chicken bouillon granules
¼ tsp. chili powder
¼ tsp. pepper
⅛ tsp. dried thyme
1¼ tsp. salt, divided
1 cup diced fully cooked ham
1 cup cooked small shrimp, peeled and deveined, optional
3 Tbsp. minced fresh parsley
1 roasting chicken (5 to 6 lbs.)
½ tsp. paprika
   Dash pepper

1. In a large saucepan, cook the rice according to the package directions. Meanwhile, in a skillet, cook sausages in oil until a thermometer reads 160°. Remove sausages, reserving drippings. When cool enough to handle, cut the sausages in half lengthwise, then into ¼-in. pieces; set aside.

2. Saute onion, garlic and peppers in drippings until tender, about 4 minutes. Add the tomatoes, lemon juice, basil, sugar, hot pepper sauce, bouillon, chili powder, pepper, thyme and 1 tsp. salt; cook and stir for 5 minutes. Add to the cooked rice. Stir in the ham, shrimp, if desired, parsley and sausage; mix lightly.

3. Just before baking, stuff the chicken with about 3½ cups stuffing. Place the remaining stuffing in a greased 1½-qt. baking dish; cover and refrigerate. Place chicken on a rack in a roasting pan; tie drumsticks together. Combine paprika, pepper and remaining salt; rub over chicken.

4. Bake chicken, uncovered, at 350° for 1½ hours, basting every 30 minutes. Cover and bake 1½ hours longer or until juices run clear. Bake additional stuffing for the last 40 minutes of baking time, uncovering during the last 10 minutes.

1 serving: 472 cal., 24g fat (6g sat. fat), 106mg chol., 766mg sod., 27g carb. (3g sugars, 2g fiber), 36g pro.

⏱ CRISPY GARLIC-BROILED CHICKEN THIGHS

These garlicky chicken thighs are also great on the grill.

—*Kelley French, Colchester, VT*

TAKES: 25 min. • **MAKES:** 4 servings

- ⅓ cup butter, melted
- ¼ cup reduced-sodium soy sauce
- 7 garlic cloves, minced
- ½ tsp. pepper
- 8 bone-in chicken thighs (about 3 lbs.)

1. In a large bowl, mix the butter, soy sauce, garlic and pepper. Reserve ¼ cup soy mixture for basting. Add chicken to remaining soy mixture; turn to coat.

2. Place chicken on a broiler pan, skin side down. Broil 4-6 in. from the heat for 10-15 minutes on each side or until a thermometer reads 170°-175°. Brush occasionally with reserved soy mixture during the last 10 minutes of cooking.

2 chicken thighs: 598 cal., 44g fat (18g sat. fat), 201mg chol., 833mg sod., 3g carb. (0 sugars, 0 fiber), 46g pro.

GLAZED ROAST CHICKEN

GLAZED ROAST CHICKEN

A few pantry items inspired this recipe, which I've since made for small weeknight meals or for big parties. The quince jelly comes from my boss, who grows the fruit in his own backyard.

—*Victoria Miller, San Ramon, CA*

PREP: 15 min. • **BAKE:** 1½ hours + standing
MAKES: 6 servings

- 1 cup white wine or chicken broth
- 1 cup apricot preserves or quince jelly
- 1 Tbsp. stone-ground mustard
- 1 broiler/fryer chicken (3 to 4 lbs.)
- ¾ tsp. salt
- ½ tsp. pepper

1. Preheat oven to 375°. In a small saucepan, bring wine to a boil; cook until the wine is reduced by half, 3-4 minutes. Stir in preserves and mustard. Reserve half of the glaze for serving.

2. Place chicken on a rack in a shallow roasting pan, breast side up. Sprinkle with salt and pepper. Tuck wings under chicken; tie drumsticks together.

3. Roast 45 minutes; baste with glaze. Continue roasting chicken until a thermometer inserted in thigh reads 170°-175°, basting occasionally with glaze. Cover loosely with foil if chicken browns too quickly. Remove chicken from the oven; tent with foil. Let stand 15 minutes before carving. Serve with remaining reserved glaze.

1 serving: 437 cal., 17g fat (5g sat. fat), 104mg chol., 458mg sod., 35g carb. (23g sugars, 0 fiber), 34g pro.

BALSAMIC ROASTED CHICKEN THIGHS WITH ROOT VEGETABLES

I will always remember the way my grandmother's house smelled when she made this chicken every Sunday. Ever since she gave me the recipe, the heartwarming flavors always take me back to my childhood.
—Erin Chilcoat, Central Islip, NY

- -

PREP: 15 min. + marinating • **BAKE:** 35 min.
MAKES: 6 servings

- 4 Tbsp. olive oil, divided
- 3 Tbsp. stone-ground mustard
- 2 Tbsp. balsamic vinaigrette
- ¾ tsp. kosher salt, divided
- ¾ tsp. freshly ground pepper, divided
- 6 bone-in chicken thighs (about 2¼ lbs.)
- 4 medium parsnips, peeled and cut into ½-in. pieces
- 1 medium sweet potato, peeled and cut into ½-in. pieces
- 4 shallots, chopped
- ¼ tsp. caraway seeds
- 4 Tbsp. minced fresh parsley, divided
- 3 bacon strips, cooked and crumbled, divided

1. In a bowl, whisk 3 Tbsp. oil, mustard, vinaigrette and ½ tsp. each salt and pepper until blended. Add chicken, turning to coat. Refrigerate, covered, 6 hours or overnight.

2. Preheat oven to 425°. Place the chicken, skin side up, on half of a greased 15x10x1-in. baking pan. Place parsnips and sweet potato in a large bowl; add shallots, caraway seeds and the remaining oil, salt and pepper and toss to combine. Arrange in a single layer on remaining half of pan.

3. Roast chicken and vegetables 20 minutes. Stir vegetables; roast chicken and vegetables until a thermometer inserted in chicken reads 170°-175° and vegetables are tender, 15-20 minutes longer.

4. Transfer vegetables to a bowl; toss with 2 Tbsp. parsley and half of the bacon. Serve chicken with vegetables; sprinkle chicken with the remaining parsley and bacon.

1 serving: 480 cal., 27g fat (6g sat. fat), 85mg chol., 604mg sod., 33g carb. (10g sugars, 5g fiber), 27g pro.

WHY YOU'LL LOVE IT...

"I used parchment for easy cleanup. I did not have parsnips and shallots. I used yellow potatoes, sweet potatoes, carrots, and onions. The chicken skin came out nice and crispy. The vegetables were extra flavorful. I am sure the bacon would be a great addition, but I did not take the time to add it. It was a winner even without it."
—SUSANFOOTE, TASTEOFHOME.COM

BALSAMIC ROASTED CHICKEN THIGHS WITH ROOT VEGETABLES

CHICKEN CLUB PIZZA

🍎 SPICY OVEN-FRIED CHICKEN

My family adores this chicken recipe. The coating keeps the chicken nice and moist, and with the taste enhanced by marinating, the result is delicious.
—*Stephanie Otten, Byron Center, MI*

PREP: 25 min. + marinating • **BAKE:** 35 min.
MAKES: 8 servings

- 2 cups buttermilk
- 2 Tbsp. Dijon mustard
- 2 tsp. salt
- 2 tsp. hot pepper sauce
- 1½ tsp. garlic powder
- 8 bone-in chicken breast halves, skin removed (8 oz. each)
- 2 cups soft bread crumbs
- 1 cup cornmeal
- 2 Tbsp. canola oil
- ½ tsp. poultry seasoning
- ½ tsp. ground mustard
- ½ tsp. paprika
- ½ tsp. cayenne pepper
- ¼ tsp. dried oregano
- ¼ tsp. dried parsley flakes

1. Preheat oven to 400°. In a large bowl or dish, combine the first 5 ingredients. Add the chicken pieces and turn to coat. Refrigerate 1 hour or overnight.
2. Drain chicken, discarding marinade. In a large bowl, combine remaining ingredients. Add chicken, 1 piece at a time, and coat with crumb mixture. Place on a parchment-lined baking sheet. Bake 35-40 minutes or until a thermometer reads 170°.
Note: To make soft bread crumbs, tear bread into pieces and place in a food processor or blender. Cover and pulse until crumbs form. One slice of bread yields ½-¾ cup crumbs.
1 chicken breast half: 296 cal., 7g fat (2g sat. fat), 103mg chol., 523mg sod., 15g carb. (2g sugars, 1g fiber), 40g pro.
Diabetic exchanges: 6 lean meat, 1 starch, ½ fat.

🕐 CHICKEN CLUB PIZZA

A co-worker shared how to replace pizza crust with crescent rolls. I used that idea to turn an awesome sandwich recipe into an even more fabulous pizza. After baking, top it with shredded lettuce.
—*Sherri Cox, Lucasville, OH*

TAKES: 30 min. • **MAKES:** 6 pieces

- 1 tube (8 oz.) refrigerated crescent rolls
- 2 tsp. sesame seeds
- ¼ cup mayonnaise
- 1 tsp. dried basil
- ¼ tsp. grated lemon zest
- 1 cup shredded Monterey Jack cheese
- 4 oz. roasted deli chicken, cut into 1-in. strips
- 6 bacon strips, cooked and crumbled
- 2 plum tomatoes, thinly sliced
- ½ cup shredded Swiss cheese

1. Preheat oven to 375°. Unroll crescent dough and separate into 8 triangles; arrange in a single layer on a greased 12-in. pizza pan. Press onto pan to form a crust and seal seams; sprinkle with sesame seeds. Bake 8-10 minutes or until edge is lightly browned.
2. In a small bowl, mix the mayonnaise, basil and lemon zest. Spread over the crust; top with Monterey Jack cheese, chicken, bacon, tomatoes and Swiss cheese. Bake 8-12 minutes or until crust is golden and cheese is melted.
1 piece: 387 cal., 28g fat (10g sat. fat), 47mg chol., 782mg sod., 17g carb. (3g sugars, 0 fiber), 16g pro.

SPICY
OVEN-FRIED
CHICKEN

BAKE JUICY
—NOT DRY—
CHICKEN
BREASTS
Just hover your
camera here.

SHEET-PAN
TANDOORI CHICKEN,
PAGE 189

FROM AROUND THE GLOBE

🍲 ZA'ATAR CHICKEN

It's hard to find a dinner that both my husband and kids will enjoy—and even harder to find one that's fast and easy. This is it! No matter how much I make of this dish, every last morsel is eaten.
—*Esther Erani, Brooklyn, NY*

- -

PREP: 20 min. • **COOK:** 5 hours
MAKES: 6 servings

- ¼ cup za'atar seasoning
- ¼ cup olive oil
- 3 tsp. dried oregano
- 1 tsp. salt
- ½ tsp. ground cumin
- ½ tsp. ground turmeric
- 3 lbs. bone-in chicken thighs
- 1 cup pimiento-stuffed olives
- ½ cup dried apricots
- ½ cup pitted dried plums
- ¼ cup water
  Hot cooked basmati rice, optional

1. In a large bowl, combine the first 6 ingredients. Add chicken; toss to coat.
2. Arrange olives, apricots and plums on the bottom of a 4- or 5-qt. slow cooker. Add ¼ cup water; top with chicken. Cook, covered, on low until chicken is tender, 5-6 hours. If desired, serve with rice.
1 serving: 484 cal., 32g fat (7g sat. fat), 107mg chol., 1367mg sod., 18g carb. (10g sugars, 2g fiber), 30g pro.

TEST KITCHEN TIPS
- If you have a few minutes to spare, try browning the chicken in a little oil before placing it in the slow cooker.
- Make your own za'atar spice by mixing 1 Tbsp. each fresh chopped oregano, ground sumac, ground cumin and sesame seeds; and 1 tsp. each kosher salt and fresh ground pepper.

ZA'ATAR CHICKEN

🕐 🍎 MARRAKESH CHICKEN & COUSCOUS

I love to make fast dinners with boxed grains. They already have a flavor packet, and the sky's the limit on their possibilities. Here, I transformed the couscous into a one-pot delight that transports you to a faraway land of exotic flavor! My family loves this recipe.
—*Devon Delaney, Westport, CT*

TAKES: 30 min. • **MAKES:** 6 servings

- 1 Tbsp. olive oil
- 1 lb. boneless skinless chicken thighs, cut into 1¼-in. pieces
- 1 can (14½ oz.) diced tomatoes, undrained
- 1 jar (7½ oz.) marinated quartered artichoke hearts, drained
- ¼ cup lemon juice
- 2 Tbsp. apricot preserves
- ½ tsp. salt
- ½ tsp. ground cumin
- ¼ tsp. crushed red pepper flakes
- ⅛ tsp. ground cinnamon
- 1 pkg. (5.8 oz.) roasted garlic and olive oil couscous
  Chopped smoked almonds, optional

1. In a 6-qt. stockpot, heat the oil over medium-high heat. Brown chicken on both sides. Stir in tomatoes, artichoke hearts, lemon juice, preserves, salt, spices and seasoning packet from couscous; bring to a boil. Reduce heat; simmer, covered, 10 minutes to allow flavors to develop and for chicken to cook through.
2. Stir in couscous; remove from heat. Let stand, covered, 5 minutes. If desired, sprinkle with almonds.
1⅓ cups: 326 cal., 14g fat (3g sat. fat), 50mg chol., 751mg sod., 30g carb. (8g sugars, 2g fiber), 19g pro. **Diabetic exchanges:** 3 lean meat, 2 starch, ½ fat.

THAI PEANUT CHICKEN & NOODLES

🕐 THAI PEANUT CHICKEN & NOODLES

This versatile chicken recipe is very similar to chicken pad thai but is easier to make and tastes just as good. Rice noodles can be replaced with mung bean noodles or any type of egg noodles.
—*Kristina Segarra, Yonkers, NY*

TAKES: 30 min. • **MAKES:** 4 servings

- ½ cup water
- ¼ cup soy sauce
- 2 Tbsp. rice vinegar
- 2 Tbsp. creamy peanut butter
- 3 garlic cloves, minced
- 1 to 2 tsp. Sriracha chili sauce
- 1 tsp. sesame oil
- 1 tsp. molasses
- 1 pkg. (6.75 oz.) thin rice noodles
- 2 Tbsp. peanut oil, divided
- 1 lb. chicken tenderloins, cut into ¾-in. pieces
- 1 medium onion, chopped
  Optional: Halved cucumber slices and chopped peanuts

1. For sauce, whisk together the first 8 ingredients. Bring a large saucepan of water to a boil; remove from heat. Add noodles; let stand until noodles are tender but firm, 3-4 minutes. Drain; rinse with cold water and drain well.
2. In a large skillet, heat 1 Tbsp. peanut oil over medium-high heat; saute the chicken until no longer pink, 5-7 minutes. Remove from pan.
3. In same pan, saute onion in remaining oil over medium-high heat until tender, 2-3 minutes. Stir in sauce; cook and stir over medium heat until slightly thickened. Add noodles and chicken; heat through, tossing to combine. If desired, top with cucumber slices and chopped peanuts. Serve immediately.
2 cups: 444 cal., 13g fat (2g sat. fat), 56mg chol., 1270mg sod., 48g carb. (6g sugars, 2g fiber), 34g pro.

🕐 🍎 WHOLE GRAIN CHOW MEIN

My kids are picky eaters, but a little sweet hoisin sauce works wonders—and I love the healthy goodness of whole grain pasta.
—*Kelly Shippey, Orange, CA*

TAKES: 30 min. • **MAKES:** 6 servings

- 6 oz. uncooked whole wheat spaghetti
- 2 Tbsp. canola oil
- 2 cups small fresh broccoli florets
- 2 bunches baby bok choy, trimmed and cut into 1-in. pieces (about 2 cups)
- ¾ cup fresh baby carrots, halved diagonally
- ½ cup reduced-sodium chicken broth, divided
- 3 Tbsp. reduced-sodium soy sauce, divided
- ¼ tsp. pepper
- 4 green onions, diagonally sliced
- 2 Tbsp. hoisin sauce
- 12 oz. refrigerated fully cooked teriyaki and pineapple chicken meatballs or frozen fully cooked turkey meatballs, thawed
- 1 cup bean sprouts
   Additional sliced green onions

1. Cook spaghetti according to package directions; drain.

2. In a large nonstick skillet, heat oil over medium-high heat. Add the broccoli, bok choy and carrots; stir-fry 4 minutes. Stir in ¼ cup broth, 1 Tbsp. soy sauce and pepper; reduce heat to medium. Cook, covered, 3-5 minutes or until vegetables are crisp-tender. Stir in green onions; remove from pan.

3. In same skillet, mix hoisin sauce and the remaining broth and soy sauce; add meatballs. Cook, covered, over medium-low heat 4-5 minutes or until heated through, stirring occasionally.

4. Add bean sprouts, spaghetti and broccoli mixture; heat through, tossing to combine. Top with additional sliced green onions.

1⅓ cups: 305 cal., 15g fat (3g sat. fat), 54mg chol., 758mg sod., 30g carb. (5g sugars, 4g fiber), 18g pro. **Diabetic exchanges:** 3 lean meat, 2 starch, 1 fat.

WHOLE GRAIN CHOW MEIN

FILIPINO CHICKEN ADOBO

FILIPINO CHICKEN ADOBO

My mom always makes her saucy chicken adobo recipe when I come home to visit. I think it's even better the next day as leftovers —she says it's because of the vinegar.

—*Michael Moya, New York, NY*

PREP: 10 min. + marinating • **COOK:** 30 min.
MAKES: 6 servings

- 1 cup white vinegar
- ¼ cup soy sauce
- 1 whole garlic bulb, smashed and peeled
- 2 tsp. kosher salt
- 1 tsp. coarsely ground pepper
- 1 bay leaf
- 2 lbs. bone-in chicken thighs or drumsticks
- 1 Tbsp. canola oil
- 1 cup water

1. In a shallow dish, combine the first 6 ingredients. Add chicken; refrigerate, covered, 20-30 minutes. Drain chicken, reserving marinade. Pat chicken dry.
2. In a large skillet, heat oil over medium-high heat; brown chicken. Stir in water and reserved marinade. Bring to a boil. Reduce heat; simmer, uncovered, until chicken is no longer pink and sauce is slightly reduced, 20-25 minutes. Discard bay leaf. If desired, serve chicken with the cooking sauce.

1 serving: 234 cal., 15g fat (4g sat. fat), 71mg chol., 1315mg sod., 2g carb. (0 sugars, 0 fiber), 22g pro.

⏱ 🍎 MEDITERRANEAN CHICKEN

As special as it is simple to prepare, this moist, flavorful chicken is dressed in tomatoes, olives and capers. It's a knockout main dish for guests.
—*Mary Relyea, Canastota, NY*

TAKES: 25 min. • **MAKES:** 4 servings

- 4 boneless skinless chicken breast halves (6 oz. each)
- ¼ tsp. salt
- ¼ tsp. pepper
- 3 Tbsp. olive oil
- 1 pint grape tomatoes
- 16 pitted Greek or ripe olives, sliced
- 3 Tbsp. capers, drained

1. Sprinkle chicken with salt and pepper. In a large ovenproof skillet, cook chicken in the oil over medium heat until golden brown, 2-3 minutes on each side. Add the tomatoes, olives and capers.
2. Bake the chicken, uncovered, at 475° until a thermometer reads 165°, 10-14 minutes.
1 serving: 336 cal., 18g fat (3g sat. fat), 94mg chol., 631mg sod., 6g carb. (3g sugars, 2g fiber), 36g pro. **Diabetic exchanges:** 5 lean meat, 3 fat, 1 vegetable.

NEW ENGLAND BEAN & BOG CASSOULET

NEW ENGLAND BEAN & BOG CASSOULET

When I moved to New England, I embraced the local cuisine. My cassoulet with baked beans pays tribute to a French classic, too.
—*Devon Delaney, Westport, CT*

PREP: 20 min. • **BAKE:** 35 min.
MAKES: 8 servings (3½ qt.)

- 5 Tbsp. olive oil, divided
- 8 boneless skinless chicken thighs (about 2 lbs.)
- 1 pkg. (12 oz.) fully cooked Italian chicken sausage links, cut into ½-in. slices
- 4 shallots, finely chopped
- 2 tsp. minced fresh rosemary or ½ tsp. dried rosemary, crushed
- 2 tsp. minced fresh thyme or ½ tsp. dried thyme
- 1 can (28 oz.) fire-roasted diced tomatoes, undrained
- 1 can (16 oz.) baked beans
- 1 cup chicken broth
- ½ cup fresh or frozen cranberries
- 3 day-old croissants, cubed (about 6 cups)
- ½ tsp. lemon-pepper seasoning
- 2 Tbsp. minced fresh parsley

1. Preheat oven to 400°. In a Dutch oven, heat 2 Tbsp. oil over medium heat. In batches, brown the chicken thighs on both sides; remove from pan, reserving drippings. Add sausage; cook and stir until lightly browned. Remove from pan.
2. In same pan, heat 1 Tbsp. oil over medium heat. Add shallots, rosemary and thyme; cook and stir until shallots are tender, 1-2 minutes. Stir in the tomatoes, beans, broth and cranberries. Return chicken and sausage to pan; bring to a boil. Bake, covered, until chicken is tender, 20-25 minutes.
3. Toss croissant pieces with remaining 2 Tbsp. oil; sprinkle with lemon pepper. Arrange over chicken mixture. Bake, uncovered, until croissants are golden brown, 12-15 minutes. Sprinkle with fresh parsley.
1¾ cups: 500 cal., 26g fat (7g sat. fat), 127mg chol., 1050mg sod., 32g carb. (6g sugars, 5g fiber), 35g pro.

THAI CHICKEN
LINGUINE

🕐 🍎 THAI CHICKEN LINGUINE

When I'm feeding a crowd, I multiply this recipe for Thai-inspired chicken with pasta and snow peas. The merrymaking begins when everybody digs in, even the kids.
—*Teri Rumble, Jensen Beach, FL*

- -

TAKES: 30 min. • **MAKES:** 6 servings

- 8   oz. uncooked whole wheat linguine
- ⅓   cup reduced-sodium soy sauce
- ¼   cup lime juice
- 3   Tbsp. brown sugar
- 2   Tbsp. rice vinegar
- 1   Tbsp. Thai chili sauce
- 2   Tbsp. peanut oil, divided
- 1   lb. boneless skinless chicken breasts, cubed
- 1   cup fresh snow peas
- 1   medium sweet red pepper, julienned
- 4   garlic cloves, minced
- 2   large eggs, beaten
- ⅓   cup chopped unsalted peanuts

1. Cook linguine according to package directions. Meanwhile, in a small bowl, mix soy sauce, lime juice, brown sugar, vinegar and chili sauce until blended.
2. In a large nonstick skillet, heat 1 Tbsp. oil over medium-high heat. Add chicken; stir-fry 5-7 minutes or until no longer pink. Remove from pan. Stir-fry snow peas and pepper in remaining oil until vegetables are crisp-tender. Add garlic; cook 1 minute longer. Add eggs; cook and stir until set.
3. Drain linguine; add to the vegetable mixture. Stir soy sauce mixture and add to pan. Bring to a boil. Add chicken; heat through. Sprinkle with peanuts.
1⅓ cups: 377 cal., 13g fat (2g sat. fat), 104mg chol., 697mg sod., 44g carb. (12g sugars, 5g fiber), 25g pro. **Diabetic exchanges:** 3 starch, 3 lean meat, 2 fat.

⏱ FAMILY-FAVORITE ITALIAN CHICKEN

Crispy chicken is treated to a jazzed-up sauce in this simple main dish that's so comforting and tasty.
—*Carol Heeren, Parker, SD*

TAKES: 30 min. • **MAKES:** 4 servings

- 2   cans (8 oz. each) tomato sauce
- 2   tsp. dried basil
- ½   tsp. garlic powder
- 4   boneless skinless chicken breast halves (4 oz. each)
- ¾   cup dry bread crumbs
- 2   tsp. dried oregano
- ¼   tsp. salt
- 2   large eggs
- 2   Tbsp. water
- ½   cup all-purpose flour
- ¼   cup olive oil
- 1   cup shredded part-skim mozzarella cheese
- ¼   cup shredded Parmesan cheese
      Hot cooked angel hair pasta

1. In a small saucepan, combine the tomato sauce, basil and garlic powder; heat through.
2. Meanwhile, flatten chicken breasts to ¼-in. thickness. In a shallow bowl, combine the bread crumbs, oregano and salt. In a separate shallow bowl, whisk eggs and water. Place flour in another shallow bowl. Coat chicken with flour, then dip in egg mixture and coat with bread crumb mixture.
3. In a large skillet, cook chicken in oil in batches for 4-6 minutes on each side or until juices run clear. Spoon sauce over chicken; sprinkle with cheeses. Serve with pasta.
1 serving: 483 cal., 25g fat (7g sat. fat), 188mg chol., 1050mg sod., 23g carb. (4g sugars, 2g fiber), 39g pro.

⏱ SMOKY SPANISH CHICKEN

After enjoying a similar dish at a Spanish tapas restaurant, my husband and I were eager to make our own version of this saucy chicken at home. If I want to make it extra healthy, I remove the skin from the chicken after browning.
—*Ryan Haley, San Diego, CA*

TAKES: 30 min. • **MAKES:** 4 servings

- 3   tsp. smoked paprika
- ½   tsp. salt
- ¼   tsp. pepper
- 1   Tbsp. water
- 4   bone-in chicken thighs
- 1½   cups baby portobello mushrooms, quartered
- 1   cup chopped green onions, divided
- 1   can (14½ oz.) fire-roasted diced tomatoes, undrained

1. Mix seasonings; rub over chicken.
2. Place a large skillet over medium heat. Add the chicken, skin side down. Cook until browned, 4-5 minutes per side; remove from the pan. Remove all but 1 Tbsp. drippings from pan.
3. In drippings, saute mushrooms and ½ cup green onions over medium heat until tender, 1-2 minutes. Stir in the tomatoes. Add chicken; bring to a boil. Reduce heat; simmer, covered, until a thermometer inserted in chicken reads 170°, 10-12 minutes. Top with the remaining green onions.
1 serving: 272 cal., 15g fat (4g sat. fat), 81mg chol., 646mg sod., 10g carb. (4g sugars, 2g fiber), 25g pro.

TEST KITCHEN TIPS

- Baby portobello mushrooms, also known as cremini mushrooms, have a firmer texture and deeper, earthier flavor than regular white mushrooms.
- Smoked paprika is made from peppers that are dried over wood fires, giving it a rich, smoky flavor.
- Make the most of the flavorful sauce and serve this with a starchy side like couscous or rice.

SMOKY SPANISH CHICKEN

CASSOULET
FOR TODAY

EASY SLOW-COOKER CHICKEN ROPA VIEJA

When discussing the various methods of cooking ropas, a friend of mine told me her sister adds apple juice. I thought a Granny Smith apple might give the dish an extra kick—and it does. The ropas may also be served with hominy or tortillas, but I think the plantains add a special touch.
—*Arlene Erlbach, Morton Grove, IL*

PREP: 20 min. • **COOK:** 5 hours
MAKES: 6 Servings

- 2 medium sweet red peppers, sliced
- 1 medium Granny Smith apple, peeled and chopped
- 1 cup fresh cilantro leaves
- 1 cup chunky salsa
- 2 Tbsp. tomato paste
- 1 garlic clove, minced
- 1 tsp. ground cumin
- 5 tsp. adobo seasoning, divided
- 1½ lbs. boneless skinless chicken thighs
- 3 to 6 tsp. lime juice
- ¼ cup butter
- 3 ripe plantains, peeled and sliced into thin rounds
  Optional: Hot cooked rice, lime wedges and additional fresh cilantro leaves

1. Place the first 7 ingredients and 1 tsp. adobo in a 5- or 6-qt. slow cooker. Rub the remaining adobo seasoning over the chicken; add to slow cooker. Cook, covered, on low until chicken is tender, 5-6 hours. Using 2 forks, shred chicken. Stir in lime juice to taste; heat through.
2. Meanwhile, heat butter in a large skillet over medium heat. Cook the plantains in batches until tender and golden brown, about 3 minutes per side. Drain on paper towels.
3. Serve chicken with plantains using a slotted spoon. If desired, serve with rice, lime wedges and cilantro.
1 serving: 387 cal., 16g fat (7g sat. fat), 96mg chol., 1428mg sod., 39g carb. (20g sugars, 4g fiber), 23g pro.

CASSOULET FOR TODAY

Traditionally cooked for hours, this version of the rustic French cassoulet offers the same homey taste in less time. It's easy on the wallet, too.
—*Virginia C. Anthony, Jacksonville, FL*

PREP: 45 min. • **BAKE:** 50 min.
MAKES: 6 servings

- 6 boneless skinless chicken thighs (about 1½ lbs.)
- ¼ tsp. salt
- ¼ tsp. coarsely ground pepper
- 3 tsp. olive oil, divided
- 1 large onion, chopped
- 1 garlic clove, minced
- ½ cup white wine or chicken broth
- 1 can (14½ oz.) diced tomatoes, drained
- 1 bay leaf
- 1 tsp. minced fresh rosemary or ¼ tsp. dried rosemary, crushed
- 1 tsp. minced fresh thyme or ¼ tsp. dried thyme
- 2 cans (15 oz. each) cannellini beans, rinsed and drained
- ¼ lb. smoked turkey kielbasa, chopped
- 3 bacon strips, cooked and crumbled

TOPPING
- ½ cup soft whole wheat bread crumbs
- ¼ cup minced fresh parsley
- 1 garlic clove, minced

1. Preheat oven to 325°. Sprinkle the chicken with salt and pepper. In a broiler-safe Dutch oven, heat 2 tsp. oil over medium heat; brown chicken on both sides. Remove from pan.
2. In same pan, saute onion in remaining oil over medium heat until crisp-tender. Add garlic; cook 1 minute. Add wine; bring to a boil, stirring to the loosen browned bits from pan. Add tomatoes, herbs and chicken; return to a boil.
3. Transfer to the oven; bake, covered, 30 minutes. Stir in beans and kielbasa; bake, covered, until chicken is tender, 20-25 minutes longer.
4. Remove from oven; preheat broiler. Discard bay leaf; stir in bacon. Toss bread crumbs with parsley and garlic; sprinkle over top. Place in oven so surface of cassoulet is 4-5 in. from the heat; broil until crumbs are golden brown, 2-3 minutes.
1 serving: 394 cal., 14g fat (4g sat. fat), 91mg chol., 736mg sod., 29g carb. (4g sugars, 8g fiber), 33g pro. **Diabetic exchanges:** 4 lean meat, 2 starch, ½ fat.

⏱ 🍎 CARIBBEAN JERK CHICKEN BOWLS

Fruit cocktail in stir-fry? You might be surprised by how good this dish is. It's a promising go-to option when time's tight.
—*Jeanne Holt, St. Paul, MN*

TAKES: 25 min. • **MAKES:** 4 servings

- 2 tsp. cornstarch
- ¼ cup water
- 1 lb. boneless skinless chicken breasts, cut into ½-in. strips
- 2 tsp. Caribbean jerk seasoning
- 1 can (15 oz.) mixed tropical fruit, drained and coarsely chopped
- 2 pkg. (8.8 oz. each) ready-to-serve brown rice

1. In a small bowl, mix cornstarch and water until smooth.
2. Coat a large skillet with cooking spray; heat over medium-high heat. Add the chicken; sprinkle with jerk seasoning. Stir-fry 3-5 minutes or until no longer pink. Stir cornstarch mixture and add to the pan. Add the fruit. Bring to a boil; cook and stir 1-2 minutes or until sauce is thickened.
3. Meanwhile, heat rice according to package directions. Serve with chicken.

½ cup stir-fry with ½ cup rice: 432 cal., 5g fat (1g sat. fat), 63mg chol., 210mg sod., 60g carb. (0 sugars, 3g fiber), 28g pro.

CHICKEN TAMALES

I love to make tamales. They take a little time but are so worth the effort. I usually make them for Christmas, but my family wants them more often, so I freeze a big batch.
—*Cindy Pruitt, Grove, OK*

PREP: 2½ hours + soaking • **COOK:** 50 min.
MAKES: 20 tamales

- 24 dried corn husks
- 1 broiler/fryer chicken (3 to 4 lbs.), cut up
- 1 medium onion, quartered
- 2 tsp. salt
- 1 garlic clove, crushed
- 3 qt. water

DOUGH
- 1 cup shortening
- 3 cups masa harina

FILLING
- 6 Tbsp. canola oil
- 6 Tbsp. all-purpose flour
- ¾ cup chili powder
- ½ tsp. salt
- ¼ tsp. garlic powder
- ¼ tsp. pepper
- 2 cans (2¼ oz. each) sliced ripe olives, drained
  Hot water

1. Cover corn husks with cold water; soak until softened, at least 2 hours.
2. Place chicken, onion, salt and garlic in a 6-qt. stockpot. Pour in 3 qt. water; bring to a boil. Reduce heat; simmer, covered, until the chicken is tender, 45-60 minutes. Remove chicken from broth. When cool enough to handle, remove bones and skin; discard. Shred chicken. Strain cooking juices; skim fat. Reserve 6 cups stock.
3. For dough, beat shortening until light and fluffy, about 1 minute. Beat in small amounts of masa harina alternately with small amounts of reserved stock, using no more than 2 cups stock. Drop a small amount of dough into a cup of cold water; dough should float. If not, continue beating, rechecking every 1 2 minutes.
4. For filling, heat oil in a Dutch oven; stir in flour until blended. Cook and stir over medium heat until lightly browned, 7-9 minutes. Stir in seasonings, chicken and the remaining stock; bring to a boil. Reduce the heat; simmer, uncovered, stirring occasionally, until thickened, about 45 minutes.
5. Drain the corn husks and pat dry; tear 4 husks to make 20 strips for tying tamales. (To prevent husks from drying out, cover with a damp towel until ready to use.) On wide end of each remaining husk, spread 3 Tbsp. dough to within ½ in. of side edges; top each with 2 Tbsp. chicken filling and 2 tsp. olives. Fold long sides of husk over filling, overlapping slightly. Fold over narrow end of husk; tie with a strip of husk to secure.
6. Place a large steamer basket in the stockpot over water; place tamales upright in the steamer. Bring to a boil; steam, covered, adding hot water as needed, until dough peels away from husk, about 45 minutes.

2 tamales: 564 cal., 35g fat (7g sat. fat), 44mg chol., 835mg sod., 43g carb. (2g sugars, 7g fiber), 20g pro.

TEST KITCHEN TIP

Fresh masa (dough made from stone-ground corn flour, called masa harina) is the foundation of a perfect tamale. You can find masa harina and corn husks in the international foods aisle or online.

Make Tamales

1. Soak the corn husks.
2. Prepare masa dough.
3. Fill husks with dough and filling.
4. Wrap each tamale to enclose the filling.
5. Tie to secure if desired.
6. Steam according to recipe directions.

CHICKEN TAMALES

EASY CARIBBEAN CHICKEN

⏱ 🍎 EASY CARIBBEAN CHICKEN

This is a very simple recipe that uses easy-to-find ingredients. Serve with steamed vegetables for a complete meal. You can also use cubes of pork or even shrimp instead of the chicken.
—*Courtney Stultz, Weir, KS*

- -

TAKES: 20 min. • **MAKES:** 4 servings

- 1 Tbsp. olive oil
- 1 lb. boneless skinless chicken breasts, cut into 1-in. pieces
- 2 tsp. garlic-herb seasoning blend
- 1 can (14½ oz.) fire-roasted diced tomatoes
- 1 can (8 oz.) unsweetened pineapple chunks
- ¼ cup barbecue sauce
  Hot cooked rice
  Fresh cilantro leaves, optional

In a large nonstick skillet, heat oil over medium-high heat. Add chicken and seasoning; saute until chicken is lightly browned and no longer pink, about 5 minutes. Add tomatoes, pineapple and barbecue sauce. Bring to a boil; cook and stir until flavors blend and chicken is cooked through, 5-7 minutes. Serve with rice and, if desired, cilantro.
1 cup chicken mixture: 242 cal., 6g fat (1g sat. fat), 63mg chol., 605mg sod., 20g carb. (15g sugars, 1g fiber), 24g pro. **Diabetic exchanges:** 3 lean meat, 1 starch, ½ fat.

TEST KITCHEN TIPS

- Fresh pineapple can be used instead of canned. Use about 1 cup.
- The flavors of this dish will remind you of a pineapple barbecue chicken pizza.

FILIPINO ADOBO AROMATIC CHICKEN

🍲 FILIPINO ADOBO AROMATIC CHICKEN

This saucy chicken packs a wallop of flavor—salty, sweet, sour, slightly spicy and even a little umami. It can be made on the stove, too. Any way I make it, I think it tastes even better the next day served over warm rice.
—*Loanne Chiu, Fort Worth, TX*

- -

PREP: 30 min. • **COOK:** 3 hours 20 min.
MAKES: 6 servings

- 8 bacon strips, chopped
- 3 lbs. boneless skinless chicken thighs
- 1 large onion, chopped
- 4 garlic cloves, minced
- 2 medium limes
- ¼ cup dry sherry
- 3 Tbsp. soy sauce
- 3 Tbsp. molasses
- 2 Tbsp. minced fresh gingerroot
- 3 bay leaves
- 1 tsp. pepper
- ½ tsp. chili garlic sauce
  Minced fresh cilantro and toasted sesame seeds
  Hot cooked rice
  Lime wedges, optional

1. In a large skillet, cook bacon over medium heat until crisp, stirring occasionally. Remove with a slotted spoon; drain on paper towels. Discard drippings, reserving 1 Tbsp. in pan. Brown the chicken in bacon drippings in batches. Transfer the chicken to a 4- or 5-qt. slow cooker.
2. Add onion to the same pan; cook and stir until tender, 3-5 minutes. Add garlic; cook and stir 1 minute longer. Finely grate enough zest from the limes to measure 2 tsp. Cut limes crosswise in half; squeeze juice from limes.
3. Add the lime juice and zest, sherry, soy sauce, molasses, ginger, bay leaves, pepper and chili sauce to pan; cook and stir to loosen browned bits. Pour over chicken. Cook, covered, on high until a thermometer reads 165°, 3-4 hours.
4. Remove chicken; shred meat with 2 forks, keep warm. If desired, slightly thicken juices by cooking over medium-high heat in a saucepan. Remove bay leaves. Stir in bacon. Pour over chicken; sprinkle with the cilantro and sesame seeds. Serve with rice and, if desired, lime wedges.
6 oz. cooked chicken with ¼ cup sauce: 474 cal., 23g fat (7g sat. fat), 164mg chol., 865mg sod., 15g carb. (9g sugars, 1g fiber), 47g pro.

🕐 TUSCAN CHICKEN FOR TWO

Have dinner on the table in no time flat! This chicken dish comes together in 15 minutes and is sized perfectly for two.
—*Debra Legrand, Port Orchard, WA*

TAKES: 15 min. • **MAKES:** 2 servings

- 2 boneless skinless chicken breast halves (5 oz. each)
- ¼ tsp. salt
- ¼ tsp. pepper
- 1 garlic clove, sliced
- 1 tsp. dried rosemary, crushed
- ¼ tsp. rubbed sage
- ¼ tsp. dried thyme
- 1 Tbsp. olive oil

1. Flatten chicken to ½-in. thickness; sprinkle with salt and pepper.
2. In a large skillet over medium heat, cook and stir the garlic, rosemary, sage and thyme in oil for 1 minute. Add the chicken; cook for 5-7 minutes on each side or until the chicken juices run clear.
1 chicken breast half : 217 cal., 10g fat (2g sat. fat), 78mg chol., 364mg sod., 1g carb. (0 sugars, 1g fiber), 29g pro.
Diabetic exchanges: 4 lean meat, 1 fat.

VIETNAMESE CHICKEN BANH MI SANDWICHES

🕐 VIETNAMESE CHICKEN BANH MI SANDWICHES

My version of the classic Vietnamese sandwich combines the satisfying flavor of chicken sausage with tangy vegetables pickled in rice vinegar. Stuff the ingredients in a hoagie bun and lunch is ready to go!
—*Angela Spengler, Niceville, FL*

TAKES: 25 min. • **MAKES:** 4 servings

- 1 pkg. (12 oz.) fully cooked spicy chicken sausage links
- 2 tsp. olive oil, divided
- ⅓ cup hoisin sauce
- 1 Tbsp. honey
- 2 tsp. reduced-sodium soy sauce
- 1 garlic clove, minced
- ¼ tsp. Chinese five-spice powder
- 1 medium onion, thinly sliced
- ½ cup shredded cabbage
- ½ cup shredded carrots
- 2 tsp. rice vinegar
- 4 hoagie buns, split
- 4 lettuce leaves

1. Cut each sausage in half lengthwise. In a large skillet, brown the sausage in 1 tsp. oil. Remove and keep warm.
2. Add the hoisin, honey, soy sauce, garlic and five-spice powder to skillet. Bring to a boil. Cook and stir until garlic is tender and sauce is thickened. Return sausages to pan; toss to coat.
3. In a small skillet, saute the onion, cabbage and carrots in remaining oil until crisp-tender. Stir in vinegar. Serve the sausage in buns with lettuce and onion mixture.
1 sandwich: 452 cal., 15g fat (3g sat. fat), 66mg chol., 1,331mg sod., 57g carb., 3g fiber, 25g pro.

DID YOU KNOW?

Hoisin sauce is a thick, sweet and somewhat spicy condiment popular in Chinese cooking. It's often made with fermented soybeans (miso), garlic, spices and sweet ingredients such as plums or sweet potatoes.

CHICKEN
CHIMICHANGAS

🍎 CHICKEN CHIMICHANGAS

I developed this quick and easy recipe through trial and error. I used to garnish with sour cream, but eliminated it in order to lighten the recipe. My friends all love it when I cook these, and they're much healthier than deep-fried chimichangas.
—*Rickey Madden, Clinton, SC*

PREP: 20 min. • **BAKE:** 20 min.
MAKES: 6 servings

1½ cups cubed cooked chicken breast
1½ cups picante sauce, divided
½ cup shredded reduced-fat cheddar cheese
⅔ cup chopped green onions, divided
1 tsp. ground cumin
1 tsp. dried oregano
6 flour tortillas (8 in.), warmed
1 Tbsp. butter, melted
Sour cream, optional

1. Preheat oven to 375°. In small bowl, combine the chicken, ¾ cup picante sauce, cheese, ¼ cup onions, cumin and oregano. Spoon ½ cup mixture down the center of each tortilla. Fold sides and ends over filling and roll up. Place seam side down in a 15x10x1-in. baking pan coated with cooking spray. Brush with melted butter.
2. Bake, uncovered, until heated through, 20-25 minutes. If desired, broil until browned, about 1 minute. Top with remaining picante sauce and onions. If desired, serve with sour cream.
Freeze option: Cool the baked chimichangas; wrap and freeze for up to 3 months. Place chimichangas on a baking sheet coated with cooking spray. Preheat oven to 400°. Bake until heated through, 10-15 minutes.
1 chimichanga: 269 cal., 8g fat (3g sat. fat), 39mg chol., 613mg sod., 31g carb. (3g sugars, 1g fiber), 17g pro. **Diabetic exchanges:** 2 lean meat, 1½ starch, 1 vegetable, ½ fat.

THAI PEANUT CHICKEN CASSEROLE

I used traditional pizza sauce and toppings in this recipe for years. After becoming a fan of Thai peanut chicken pizza, I decided to use those flavors instead. Serve the casserole with stir-fried vegetables or a salad with sesame dressing for an easy, delicious meal.
—*Katherine Wollgast, Troy, MO*

PREP: 30 min. • **BAKE:** 40 min.
MAKES: 10 servings

- 2 tubes (12 oz. each) refrigerated buttermilk biscuits
- 3 cups shredded cooked chicken
- 1 cup sliced fresh mushrooms
- 1 bottle (11½ oz.) Thai peanut sauce, divided
- 2 cups shredded mozzarella cheese, divided
- ½ cup chopped sweet red pepper
- ½ cup shredded carrot
- 4 green onions, sliced
- ¼ cup honey-roasted peanuts, coarsely chopped

1. Preheat oven to 350°. Cut each biscuit into 4 pieces. Place in a greased 13x9-in. baking pan.
2. In a large bowl, combine chicken, mushrooms and 1 cup peanut sauce; spread over biscuits. Top with 1 cup cheese, red pepper, carrot and green onions. Sprinkle with remaining cheese.
3. Bake until topping is set, cheese is melted and biscuits have cooked all the way through, about 40 minutes. Sprinkle with peanuts and serve with remaining peanut sauce.
1 serving: 490 cal., 25g fat (8g sat. fat), 55mg chol., 1013mg sod., 43g carb. (13g sugars, 1g fiber), 26g pro.

TEST KITCHEN TIP

This dish needs to bake until the centers of the biscuits aren't doughy. The only reliable way to make sure they're cooked through is to cut into a biscuit near the center of the dish.

🕐 🍎 APPLE CHICKEN CURRY

When she was in college, my daughter introduced me to curry dishes. Now we love the aroma of apples simmering with chicken, curry and coconut milk.
—*Dawn Elliott, Greenville, MI*

TAKES: 30 min. • **MAKES:** 4 servings

- 4 boneless skinless chicken thighs (about 1 lb.)
- ¾ tsp. salt, divided
- ¼ tsp. pepper
- 1 Tbsp. olive oil
- 1 medium sweet red pepper, julienned
- 1 small onion, halved and thinly sliced
- 3 tsp. curry powder
- 2 garlic cloves, minced
- 2 medium Granny Smith apples, cut into ¾-in. pieces
- 1 cup frozen peas
- 1 cup light coconut milk
- 2 cups hot cooked brown rice

1. Sprinkle chicken with ½ tsp. salt and pepper. In a large skillet, heat oil over medium-high heat. Brown chicken on both sides; remove from pan.
2. Add red pepper and onion to skillet; cook and stir 5 minutes. Stir in curry powder and garlic; cook 1 minute longer. Stir in apples, peas, coconut milk and remaining salt.
3. Return chicken to the pan; bring to a boil. Reduce heat; simmer, covered, for 8-10 minutes or until a thermometer inserted in chicken reads 170°. Serve with rice.
1 serving: 435 cal., 17g fat (6g sat. fat), 76mg chol., 550mg sod., 43g carb. (13g sugars, 7g fiber), 26g pro. **Diabetic exchanges:** 3 lean meat, 2½ starch, 2 fat, ½ fruit.

THAI PEANUT CHICKEN CASSEROLE

VIETNAMESE
CRUNCHY
CHICKEN SALAD

VIETNAMESE CRUNCHY CHICKEN SALAD

When I lived in Cleveland, I dined at a great Vietnamese restaurant. There was a dish that I couldn't get enough of. Because I had it so often, I figured out the components and created my own easy version.
—Erin Schillo, Northfield, OH

PREP: 30 min. + marinating • COOK: 10 min.
MAKES: 4 servings

- 3 Tbsp. olive oil
- 2 Tbsp. lime juice
- 1 Tbsp. minced fresh cilantro
- 1½ tsp. grated lime zest
- ½ tsp. salt
- ½ tsp. pepper
- ¼ tsp. cayenne pepper
- 1 lb. boneless skinless chicken breasts, cut into thin strips

DRESSING
- ½ cup olive oil
- ¼ cup lime juice
- 2 Tbsp. rice vinegar
- 2 Tbsp. sugar
- 1 Tbsp. grated lime zest
- ¾ tsp. salt
- ½ tsp. crushed red pepper flakes
- ¼ tsp. pepper

SALAD
- 5 cups thinly sliced cabbage (about 1 lb.)
- 1 cup minced fresh cilantro
- 1 cup julienned carrots
- 1 cup salted peanuts, coarsely chopped

1. In a large bowl, mix the first 7 ingredients; add chicken and toss to coat. Refrigerate, covered, 30 minutes. In a small bowl, whisk dressing ingredients.
2. In a large skillet over medium-high heat, stir-fry half the chicken mixture for 4-5 minutes or until no longer pink. Remove from pan; repeat with the remaining chicken. Cool slightly.
3. In a large bowl, combine cabbage, cilantro, carrots and chicken; toss to combine. Add peanuts and dressing; toss to coat. Serve immediately.
2 cups: 743 cal., 59g fat (9g sat. fat), 63mg chol., 1068mg sod., 25g carb. (12g sugars, 7g fiber), 35g pro.

🕐 SIZZLING CHICKEN LO MEIN

All the high school students at the school where I work love this scrumptious chicken dish. It is the most-requested recipe in my cooking classes.
—Kris Campion, Marshall, MN

TAKES: 30 min. • MAKES: 4 servings

- 8 oz. uncooked linguine
- ¾ lb. boneless skinless chicken breasts, cubed
- 2 Tbsp. olive oil
- 5 Tbsp. stir-fry sauce, divided
- 4 Tbsp. teriyaki sauce, divided
- 1 pkg. (12 oz.) frozen stir-fry vegetable blend

1. Cook linguine according to package directions. Meanwhile, in a large skillet or wok, stir-fry chicken in oil until no longer pink. Add 2 Tbsp. each stir fry sauce and teriyaki sauce. Remove the chicken from pan.
2. Stir-fry vegetables and 1 Tbsp. each stir-fry sauce and teriyaki sauce in the same pan for 4-6 minutes or until vegetables are crisp-tender. Drain the linguine. Add the linguine, chicken and remaining sauces to the pan; stir-fry for 2-3 minutes or until heated through.
2 cups: 445 cal., 10g fat (2g sat. fat), 47mg chol., 1324mg sod., 59g carb. (11g sugars, 4g fiber), 29g pro.

🍎🍲 CHICKEN MOLE

Even if you're not familiar with mole, don't be shy to try this versatile Mexican sauce. I love sharing this recipe, which is a tasty introduction to a classic dish.
—*Darlene Morris, Franklinton, LA*

PREP: 25 min. • **COOK:** 6 hours
MAKES: 12 servings

- 12 bone-in chicken thighs (about 4½ lbs.), skin removed
- 1   tsp. salt

MOLE SAUCE
- 1   can (28 oz.) whole tomatoes, drained
- 1   medium onion, chopped
- 2   dried ancho chiles, stems and seeds removed
- ½   cup sliced almonds, toasted
- ¼   cup raisins
- 3   oz. bittersweet chocolate, chopped
- 3   Tbsp. olive oil
- 1   chipotle pepper in adobo sauce
- 3   garlic cloves, peeled and halved
- ¾   tsp. ground cumin
- ½   tsp. ground cinnamon
      Fresh cilantro leaves, optional

1. Sprinkle chicken with salt; place in a 5- or 6-qt. slow cooker. Place the tomatoes, onion, chiles, almonds, raisins, chocolate, oil, chipotle pepper, garlic, cumin and cinnamon in a food processor; cover and process until blended. Pour over chicken.
2. Cover and cook on low until chicken is tender, 6-8 hours; skim fat. Sprinkle servings with cilantro if desired.
Freeze option: Cool chicken in mole sauce. Freeze in freezer containers. To use, partially thaw in refrigerator overnight. Heat through slowly in a covered skillet or Dutch oven until a thermometer inserted in chicken reads 170°-175°, stirring occasionally; add broth or water if necessary.
1 chicken thigh with ⅓ cup sauce: 311 cal., 18g fat (5g sat. fat), 86mg chol., 378mg sod., 12g carb. (7g sugars, 3g fiber), 26g pro.

CHICKEN MOLE

ASIAN GLAZED CHICKEN THIGHS

Everyone goes for this super moist, garlicky chicken, including my fussy kids. For your holiday buffet or family gathering, serve it with rice or noodles.
—*Carole Lotito, Hillsdale, NJ*

TAKES: 25 min. • **MAKES:** 4 servings

- ¼ cup rice vinegar
- 3 Tbsp. reduced-sodium soy sauce
- 2 Tbsp. honey
- 2 tsp. canola oil
- 4 boneless skinless chicken thighs (about 1 lb.)
- 3 garlic cloves, minced
- 1 tsp. minced fresh gingerroot or ½ tsp. ground ginger
  Toasted sesame seeds, optional

1. In a small bowl, whisk vinegar, soy sauce and honey until blended. In a large nonstick skillet, heat oil over medium-high heat. Brown chicken on both sides.

2. Add garlic and ginger to skillet; cook and stir 1 minute (do not allow garlic to brown). Stir in vinegar mixture; bring to a boil. Reduce heat; simmer, covered, 8-10 minutes or until a thermometer inserted in chicken reads 170°.

3. Uncover; simmer 1-2 minutes longer or until sauce is slightly thickened. If desired, sprinkle with sesame seeds before serving.

1 serving: 247 cal., 11g fat (2g sat. fat), 76mg chol., 735mg sod., 15g carb. (14g sugars, 0 fiber), 22g pro. **Diabetic exchanges:** 3 lean meat, 1 starch, ½ fat.

WHY YOU'LL LOVE IT...

"Delicious. The sauce did not thicken very much but was tasty over brown rice. Definitely a 5-star recipe."
—MARINEMOM_TEXAS, TASTEOFHOME.COM

SO-EASY
COQ AU VIN

SO-EASY COQ AU VIN

Here's my adaptation of the beloved French dish. I substituted boneless skinless chicken breasts for a lighter version that still showcases traditional and memorable flavors.
—*Sonya Labbe, West Hollywood, CA*

PREP: 20 min. • **COOK:** 5 hours
MAKES: 4 servings

- 3 bacon strips, chopped
- 4 boneless skinless chicken breast halves (4 oz. each)
- ½ lb. sliced fresh mushrooms
- 1 medium onion, chopped
- 4 garlic cloves, minced
- 1 bay leaf
- ⅓ cup all-purpose flour
- ½ cup red wine
- ½ cup chicken broth
- ½ tsp. dried thyme
- ¼ tsp. pepper
  Hot cooked noodles, optional

1. In large skillet, cook bacon over medium heat until crisp, stirring occasionally. Remove with a slotted spoon; drain on paper towels. Brown chicken on both sides in drippings over medium heat. Transfer chicken to a 3-qt. slow cooker.

2. Add the mushrooms, onion and garlic to skillet; cook and stir just until tender, 1-2 minutes. Spoon over chicken; add bay leaf.

3. In a small bowl, whisk the flour, wine, broth, thyme and pepper until smooth; pour over chicken.

4. Cover; cook on low until chicken is tender, 5-6 hours. Discard bay leaf. If desired, serve with noodles. Sprinkle with bacon.

1 chicken breast half with ½ cup mushroom sauce: 299 cal., 11g fat (3g sat. fat), 75mg chol., 324mg sod., 16g carb. (4g sugars, 2g fiber), 28g pro. **Diabetic exchanges:** 3 lean meat, 1½ fat, 1 vegetable, ½ starch.

Build a Better Sheet-Pan Dinner

Sheet-pan dinners are a quick and easy way to put a one-dish meal on the table. Follow these tips to whip up supper in a flash.

- Invest in a sturdy sheet pan with a rim that will stop juices and sauces from spilling over.
- Line the pan for easy cleanup, or at least coat it with oil or nonstick cooking spray.
- Don't forget to toss the ingredients with a little oil first.
- Season generously.
- Don't overcrowd the pan.
- Elevate the ingredients on an ovenproof wire cooling rack to crisp things up.
- Give hearty vegetables (such as potatoes or winter squash) a head start before adding other ingredients.
- Rotate the pan halfway through cooking for best results.

SHEET-PAN TANDOORI CHICKEN

SHEET-PAN TANDOORI CHICKEN

This tandoori chicken recipe is easy for weeknights since it uses just one pan, but it's also special enough for company. The best part is there isn't much to cleanup when dinner is over!
—*Anwar Khan, Iriving, TX*

- -

PREP: 20 min. + marinating • **BAKE:** 25 min.
MAKES: 4 servings

- 1 cup plain Greek yogurt
- 3 Tbsp. tandoori masala seasoning
- ⅛ to ¼ tsp. crushed red pepper flakes, optional
- 8 bone-in chicken thighs (about 3 lbs.), skin removed
- 2 medium sweet potatoes, peeled and cut into ½-in. wedges
- 1 Tbsp. olive oil
- 16 cherry tomatoes
  Lemon slices
  Optional: Minced fresh cilantro and naan flatbreads

1. In a large bowl, whisk yogurt, tandoori seasoning and, if desired, pepper flakes until blended. Add chicken and turn to coat. Cover and refrigerate 6-8 hours, turning occasionally.
2. Preheat oven to 450°. Drain chicken, discarding marinade. Place chicken in a greased 15x10x1-in. baking pan. Add the sweet potatoes; drizzle with the oil. Bake 15 minutes. Add the tomatoes and lemon slices. Bake until a thermometer inserted into chicken reads 170°-175°, 10-15 minutes longer. Broil 4-5 in. from the heat until browned, 4-5 minutes. If desired, serve with cilantro and naan.
2 chicken thighs with 1 cup sweet potatoes and 4 tomatoes: 589 cal., 27g fat (9g sat. fat), 186mg chol., 187mg sod., 29g carb. (13g sugars, 6g fiber), 52g pro.

🍲 SLOW-COOKER MALAYSIAN CHICKEN

Malaysian food has influences from the Malays, Chinese, Indians, Thai, British and Portuguese. In this dish, Asian ingredients combine for maximum flavor and sweet potatoes thicken the sauce as the meal slowly cooks.
—*Suzanne Banfield, Basking Ridge, NJ*

- -

PREP: 20 min. • **COOK:** 5 hours
MAKES: 6 servings

- 1 cup coconut milk
- 2 Tbsp. brown sugar
- 2 Tbsp. soy sauce
- 2 Tbsp. creamy peanut butter
- 1 Tbsp. fish sauce
- 2 tsp. curry powder
- 2 garlic cloves, minced
- ½ tsp. salt
- ½ tsp. pepper
- 1 can (14½ oz.) diced tomatoes, undrained
- 2 medium sweet potatoes, peeled and cut into ½-in. thick slices
- 2 lbs. boneless skinless chicken thighs
- 2 Tbsp. cornstarch
- 2 Tbsp. water

1. In a bowl, whisk together the first 9 ingredients; stir in tomatoes. Place sweet potatoes in a 5- or 6-qt. slow cooker; top with chicken. Pour tomato mixture over top. Cook, covered, on low until the chicken is tender and a thermometer reads 170°, 5-6 hours.
2. Remove chicken and sweet potatoes; keep warm. Transfer the cooking juices to a saucepan. In a small bowl, mix the cornstarch and water until smooth; stir into cooking juices. Bring to a boil; cook and stir 1-2 minutes or until thickened. Serve sauce with chicken and potatoes.
1 serving: 425 cal., 20g fat (10g sat. fat), 101mg chol., 964mg sod., 28g carb. (14g sugars, 4g fiber), 33g pro.

TZATZIKI CHICKEN

I like to make classic chicken recipes for my family but the real fun is trying a fresh new twist.

—Kristen Heigl, Staten Island, NY

TAKES: 30 min. • **MAKES:** 4 servings

- 1½ cups finely chopped peeled English cucumber
- 1 cup plain Greek yogurt
- 2 garlic cloves, minced
- 1½ tsp. chopped fresh dill
- 1½ tsp. olive oil
- ⅛ tsp. salt

CHICKEN

- ⅔ cup all-purpose flour
- 1 tsp. salt
- 1 tsp. pepper
- ¼ tsp. baking powder
- 1 large egg
- ⅓ cup 2% milk
- 4 boneless skinless chicken breast halves (6 oz. each)
- ¼ cup canola oil
- ¼ cup crumbled feta cheese
  Lemon wedges, optional

1. For sauce, mix the first 6 ingredients; refrigerate until serving.

2. In a shallow bowl, whisk together flour, salt, pepper and baking powder. In another bowl, whisk together egg and milk. Pound chicken breasts with a meat mallet to ½-in. thickness. Dip in flour mixture to coat both sides; shake off excess. Dip in egg mixture, then again in flour mixture.

3. In a large skillet, heat oil over medium heat. Cook chicken until golden brown and the juices run clear, 5-7 minutes per side. Top with cheese. Serve with sauce and, if desired, lemon wedges.

1 chicken breast half with ⅓ cup sauce: 482 cal., 27g fat (7g sat. fat), 133mg chol., 737mg sod., 17g carb. (4g sugars, 1g fiber), 41g pro.

TEST KITCHEN TIP

An English cucumber works well in this recipe because it's seedless and won't thin out the sauce. But regular cucumber can be used, too—just seed before chopping. Make the sauce before preparing the rest of the recipe so the garlic mellows and flavors meld.

CHINESE TAKEOUT-ON-A-STICK

I like to serve chicken and broccoli with rice, and a side of pineapple or other fresh fruit. Leftovers (if there are any) are great the next day when used in a salad or wrapped in a flour tortilla with a little mayonnaise.

—Bethany Seeley, Warwick, RI

TAKES: 30 min. • **MAKES:** 4 servings

- 3 Tbsp. reduced-sodium soy sauce
- 3 Tbsp. sesame oil
- 4 tsp. brown sugar
- 4 tsp. minced fresh gingerroot
- 2 garlic cloves, minced
- ½ tsp. crushed red pepper flakes
- 1 lb. boneless skinless chicken breasts, cut into 1-in. cubes
- 3 cups fresh broccoli florets

1. In a large bowl, combine the first 6 ingredients; remove 3 Tbsp. for basting. Add chicken to remaining soy sauce mixture; toss to coat. On 4 metal or soaked wooden skewers, alternately thread chicken and broccoli.

2. Place skewers on greased grill rack. Cook, covered, over medium heat or broil 4 in. from the heat until chicken is no longer pink, 10-15 minutes, turning occasionally. Baste with reserved soy mixture during the last 4 minutes of cooking.

1 skewer: 261 cal., 13g fat (2g sat. fat), 63mg chol., 534mg sod., 10g carb. (5g sugars, 2g fiber), 25g pro. **Diabetic exchanges:** 3 lean meat, 2 fat, ½ starch.

TZATZIKI CHICKEN

STICKY ASIAN CHICKEN

As a working mom with three children, I need dishes that hit the spot and come together fast. I double this Asian-style chicken because leftovers are awesome.
—*Jennifer Carnegie, Lake Oswego, OR*

TAKES: 25 min. • **MAKES:** 6 servings

- 1 Tbsp. canola oil
- 6 boneless skinless chicken thighs (about 1½ lbs.)
- ⅓ cup soy sauce
- ⅓ cup white wine or reduced-sodium chicken broth
- 3 Tbsp. sugar
- 3 garlic cloves, minced
- 1 Tbsp. cornstarch
- 3 Tbsp. water

1. In a large skillet, heat the oil over medium-high heat. Brown chicken on both sides.
2. In a small bowl, mix soy sauce, wine, sugar and garlic; pour over chicken. Bring to a boil. Reduce the heat and simmer, covered, 5-7 minutes or until a thermometer inserted in chicken reads 170°. Remove chicken; keep warm.
3. Remove cooking juices from pan; skim fat and return juices to pan. In a small bowl, mix cornstarch and water until smooth; stir into juices. Bring to a boil, stirring constantly; cook and stir 1-2 minutes or until thickened. Serve with chicken.
1 chicken thigh with 1 Tbsp. sauce: 229 cal., 11g fat (2g sat. fat), 76mg chol., 881mg sod., 8g carb. (6g sugars, 0 fiber), 23g pro.

SLOW-COOKER CHICKEN TIKKA MASALA

SLOW-COOKER CHICKEN TIKKA MASALA

Just a small dash of garam marsala adds lots of flavor. The bright red sauce coats the caramelized chicken beautifully.
—*Anwar Khan, Iriving, TX*

PREP: 25 min. • **COOK:** 3 hours 10 min.
MAKES: 4 Servings

- 1 can (15 oz.) tomato puree
- 1 small onion, grated
- 3 garlic cloves, minced
- 2 Tbsp. tomato paste
- 1 tsp. grated lemon zest
- 1 Tbsp. lemon juice
- 1 tsp. hot pepper sauce
- 1 Tbsp. canola oil
- 1 tsp. curry powder
- 1 tsp. salt
- ¼ tsp. pepper
- ¼ tsp. garam masala
- 4 bone-in chicken thighs
- 3 Tbsp. plain Greek yogurt, plus more for topping
- 1 Tbsp. unsalted butter, melted
  Optional: Chopped cilantro and grated lemon zest
  Hot cooked rice

1. Combine the first 12 ingredients in a 3- or 4-qt. slow cooker. Add the chicken and stir gently to coat. Cook, covered, on low 3-4 hours or until chicken is tender.
2. Preheat broiler. Using a slotted spoon, transfer chicken to a broiler-safe baking pan lined with foil. Broil 4-6 in. from heat for 3-4 minutes on each side or until lightly charred.
3. Meanwhile, transfer cooking juices from the slow cooker to saucepan. Cook, uncovered, over medium-high heat until slightly thickened, 6-8 minutes. Remove from heat and gently stir in yogurt and butter. Serve the chicken with sauce. If desired, garnish with chopped cilantro, lemon zest and additional yogurt. Serve with hot cooked rice.
1 chicken thigh: 364 cal., 22g fat (7g sat. fat), 91mg chol., 705mg sod., 12g carb. (4g sugars, 3g fiber), 25g pro.

SPANISH-STYLE
PAELLA

SPANISH-STYLE PAELLA

If you enjoy serving ethnic foods, this hearty rice dish is a great one. It's brimming with generous chunks of chicken, sausage, shrimp and veggies.
—Taste of Home *Test Kitchen*

PREP: 10 min. • **COOK:** 35 min.
MAKES: 8 servings

- ½ lb. Spanish chorizo links, sliced
- ½ lb. boneless skinless chicken breasts, cubed
- 1 Tbsp. olive oil
- 1 garlic clove, minced
- 1 cup uncooked short grain rice
- 1 cup chopped onion
- 1½ cups chicken broth
- 1 can (14½ oz.) stewed tomatoes, undrained
- ½ tsp. paprika
- ¼ tsp. ground cayenne pepper
- ¼ tsp. salt
- 10 strands saffron, crushed or ⅛ tsp. ground saffron
- ½ lb. uncooked medium shrimp, peeled and deveined
- ½ cup sweet red pepper strips
- ½ cup green pepper strips
- ½ cup frozen peas
  Optional: Minced fresh parsley and lemon wedges

1. In a large saucepan or skillet over medium-high heat, cook the sausage and chicken in oil for 5 minutes or until sausage is lightly browned and chicken is no longer pink, stirring frequently. Add garlic; cook 1 minute longer. Drain if necessary.
2. Stir in rice and onion. Cook until onion is tender and the rice is lightly browned, stirring frequently. Add broth, tomatoes, paprika, cayenne, salt and saffron. Bring to a boil. Reduce the heat to low; cover and cook for 10 minutes.
3. Stir in the shrimp, peppers and peas. Cover and cook 10 minutes longer or until rice is tender, shrimp turn pink and liquid is absorbed. Top with minced parsley and lemon wedges, if desired.

1 cup: 237 cal., 7g fat (2g sat. fat), 62mg chol., 543mg sod., 27g carb. (5g sugars, 2g fiber), 16g pro.

JAMAICAN CHICKEN WITH COUSCOUS

⏱ 🍎 JAMAICAN CHICKEN WITH COUSCOUS

Fantabulous is a word I use for fantastic dishes such as this jerk-seasoned chicken. It's a mouth full of yum.
—*Joni Hilton, Rocklin, CA*

TAKES: 30 min. • **MAKES:** 6 servings

- 1 can (20 oz.) unsweetened pineapple tidbits, undrained
- 1 tsp. salt, divided
- 1 cup uncooked whole wheat couscous
- ⅓ cup all-purpose flour
- 2 Tbsp. minced fresh cilantro
- 1½ lbs. boneless skinless chicken breasts, cut into ½-in.-thick strips
- 2 tsp. Caribbean jerk seasoning
- 3 Tbsp. olive oil, divided
  Additional minced fresh cilantro, optional

1. In a large saucepan, combine the pineapple and ½ tsp. salt; bring to a boil. Stir in couscous. Remove from heat; let stand, covered, 5 minutes or until liquid is absorbed. Fluff with a fork.
2. Meanwhile, in a shallow bowl, mix flour and 2 Tbsp. cilantro. Toss chicken with jerk seasoning and remaining salt. Add to flour mixture, a few pieces at a time, and toss to coat lightly; shake off any excess.
3. In a large skillet, heat 1 Tbsp. oil. Add a third of the chicken; cook 1-2 minutes on each side or until strips are no longer pink. Repeat twice with the remaining oil and chicken. Serve with couscous. If desired, sprinkle with cilantro.

3 oz. cooked chicken with ⅔ cup couscous mixture: 374 cal., 10g fat (2g sat. fat), 63mg chol., 542mg sod., 42g carb. (12g sugars, 5g fiber), 29g pro.
Diabetic exchanges: 3 starch, 3 lean meat, 1 fat.

ON THE
GRILL

APPLE-MARINATED
CHICKEN & VEGETABLES,
PAGE 201

GRILLED CHICKEN RANCH BURGERS

This is one of the most fantastic, flavorful burgers I've ever made. Ranch is a favorite in dips and dressings, and believe me, it doesn't disappoint in these burgers, either!
—*Kari Shifflett, Lake Mills, IA*

PREP: 15 min. + chilling • **GRILL:** 10 min.
MAKES: 16 servings

- ¾ cup ranch salad dressing
- ¾ cup panko bread crumbs
- ¾ cup grated Parmesan cheese
- 3 Tbsp. Worcestershire sauce
- 3 garlic cloves, minced
- 3 tsp. pepper
- 4 lbs. ground chicken
- 3 Tbsp. olive oil
- 16 hamburger buns, split
  Optional toppings: Tomato slices, lettuce leaves, sliced red onion, sliced cucumber, sliced avocado and ranch dip

1. In a large bowl, mix first 6 ingredients. Add chicken; mix lightly but thoroughly. Shape mixture into sixteen ½-in.-thick patties. Brush both sides with oil; refrigerate, covered, 15 minutes to allow patties to firm up.
2. Grill the burgers, covered, over medium heat or broil 3-4 in. from heat 5-6 minutes on each side or until a thermometer reads 165°. Serve on buns with toppings as desired.

1 burger: 371 cal., 19g fat (5g sat. fat), 79mg chol., 498mg sod., 26g carb. (4g sugars, 1g fiber), 24g pro.

GRILLED CHICKEN RANCH BURGERS

WHISKEY PINEAPPLE CHICKEN

WHISKEY PINEAPPLE CHICKEN

Everyone in my family loves this recipe and its sweet marinade with ginger, pineapple and a splash of whiskey. Want even more intense flavor? Let the chicken marinate for two full days. Wow!
—*Jodi Taffel, Altadena, CA*

- -

PREP: 20 min. + marinating • **GRILL:** 15 min.
MAKES: 10 servings

- 2 cups bourbon
- 2 cups unsweetened pineapple juice
- 1 cup hoisin sauce
- 2 Tbsp. minced fresh gingerroot
- 2 Tbsp. coarsely ground pepper, divided
- 4 tsp. Worcestershire sauce
- 8 garlic cloves, minced
- 1 Tbsp. kosher salt, divided
- 5 lbs. boneless skinless chicken thighs
- 1 cup sliced sweet red pepper
- 1 cup sliced yellow onions
- 2 Tbsp. olive oil

1. Whisk together bourbon, pineapple juice, hoisin sauce, ginger, 1 Tbsp. pepper, Worcestershire sauce, garlic and 1 tsp. salt until blended. Place chicken in a shallow dish. Add half the marinade; turn to coat. Cover and refrigerate overnight, turning occasionally. Cover and refrigerate remaining marinade.
2. Drain chicken, discarding marinade. Grill chicken, covered, on a greased grill rack over medium-high direct heat until a thermometer reads 170°, 5-6 minutes on each side.
3. Meanwhile, toss pepper and onion slices in oil and remaining salt and pepper. Grill, turning frequently, until soft, 5-7 minutes. In a small saucepan on grill, cook reserved marinade over medium heat, stirring occasionally, until slightly thickened, about 10 minutes. Chop pepper and onion. Sprinkle over chicken; serve with sauce.
1 serving: 439 cal., 20g fat (5g sat. fat), 152mg chol., 735mg sod., 13g carb. (8g sugars, 1g fiber), 43g pro.

TEST KITCHEN TIP

It's important to use coarsely crushed pepper. Anything finer and the pepper flavor will be overpowering. If finely ground is all you have, reduce the amount of pepper by about a third.

⏱ CHICKEN WITH BLACK BEAN SALSA

There's nothing timid about the flavors in this southwestern-style entree. Prepared on the grill or broiled, it's a fast, fun meal for a busy weeknight or a weekend get-together with friends.
—*Trisha Kruse, Eagle, ID*

- -

TAKES: 25 min. • **MAKES:** 4 servings

- 1 can (15 oz.) black beans, rinsed and drained
- 1 can (8 oz.) unsweetened crushed pineapple, drained
- 1 small red onion, chopped
- 1 plum tomato, chopped
- 1 garlic clove, minced
- 2 Tbsp. lime juice
- ¼ tsp. salt
- ¼ tsp. coarsely ground pepper

RUB
- 1 Tbsp. brown sugar
- 1 tsp. hot pepper sauce
- ½ tsp. garlic powder
- ½ tsp. salt
- ½ tsp. coarsely ground pepper
- 4 boneless skinless chicken breast halves (4 oz. each)

1. For salsa, in a large bowl, combine the first 8 ingredients; refrigerate until serving. Combine the brown sugar, pepper sauce, garlic powder, salt and pepper; rub over both sides of chicken.
2. Grill chicken on an oiled rack, covered, over medium heat or broil 4 in. from heat for 4-7 minutes on each side or until a thermometer reads 170°. Serve with salsa.
1 serving: 269 cal., 3g fat (1g sat. fat), 63mg chol., 710mg sod., 31g carb. (13g sugars, 5g fiber), 29g pro.
Diabetic exchanges: 3 lean meat, 1½ starch, ½ fruit.

GLAZED SPATCHCOCKED CHICKEN

LEARN HOW TO GRILL SPATCHCOCKED CHICKEN

Just hover your camera here.

GLAZED SPATCHCOCKED CHICKEN

A few pantry items inspired this recipe, which I've since made for small weeknight meals or for big parties.

—*James Schend, Pleasant Prairie, WI*

- -

PREP: 15 min.
GRILL: 40 min. + standing
MAKES: 6 servings

- 1 cup white wine or chicken broth
- 1 cup apricot preserves or quince jelly
- 1 Tbsp. stone-ground mustard
- 1 broiler/fryer chicken (3 to 4 lbs.)
- ¾ tsp. salt
- ½ tsp. pepper

1. In a small saucepan, bring wine to a boil; cook 3-4 minutes or until wine is reduced by half. Stir in preserves and mustard. Reserve half the glaze for basting.

2. Cut the chicken along each side of the backbone with shears. Remove the backbone. Turn the chicken breast side up, and press to flatten. Sprinkle with salt and pepper.

3. Prepare grill for indirect medium heat. Place chicken on greased grill grate, skin side down, covered, over direct heat 10-15 minutes or until nicely browned. Turn chicken and place over indirect heat until a thermometer reads 170°-175° in the thickest part of the thigh, brushing chicken occasionally with reserved sauce mixture, about 30 minutes.

4. Remove chicken from grill. Let stand 15 minutes before carving; serve with remaining glaze.

5 oz. cooked chicken: 437 cal., 17g fat (5g sat. fat), 104mg chol., 458mg sod., 35g carb. (23g sugars, 0 fiber), 34g pro.

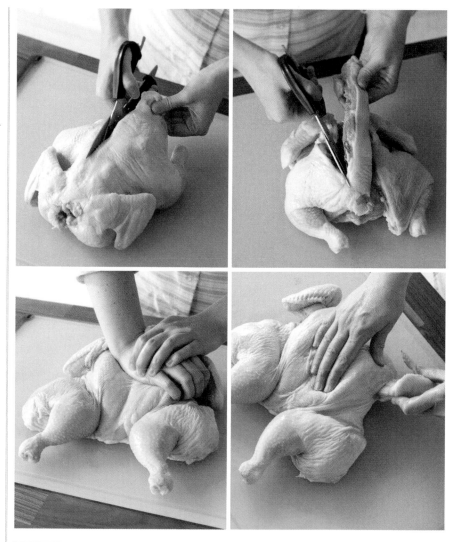

HOW-TO

Spatchcock a Chicken

- **Cut along backbone.** Use kitchen shears to cut as close along the spine as possible. If you feel any resistance cutting through rib bones, press down on the shears with both hands.
- **Remove the backbone.** Rotate the chicken 180° so the uncut side is closer to your dominant hand. Cut along the bone again and remove the backbone.
- **Flatten the bird.** Flip the chicken over so the breast side is facing upward. With two hands, press down firmly on the center of the bird until you hear the wishbone crack.
- **Tuck the wings under.** Give the wings a quick twist and tuck them underneath the body of the bird so the chicken lies flat.

SPICED GRILLED CHICKEN WITH CILANTRO LIME BUTTER

This grilled chicken gets a lovely pop of color and flavor from the lime butter—don't skip it!
—*Diane Halferty, Corpus Christi, TX*

- -

PREP: 20 min. • **GRILL:** 35 min.
MAKES: 6 servings

1 Tbsp. chili powder
1 Tbsp. brown sugar
2 tsp. ground cinnamon
1 tsp. baking cocoa
½ tsp. salt
½ tsp. pepper
3 Tbsp. olive oil
1 Tbsp. balsamic vinegar
6 bone-in chicken breast halves (8 oz. each)

CILANTRO LIME BUTTER

⅓ cup butter, melted
¼ cup minced fresh cilantro
2 Tbsp. finely chopped red onion
1 Tbsp. lime juice
1 serrano pepper, finely chopped
⅛ tsp. pepper

1. In a small bowl, combine the first 8 ingredients. Brush over chicken.
2. Place chicken skin side down on grill rack. Grill, covered, over indirect medium heat for 15 minutes. Turn; grill 20-25 minutes longer or until a thermometer reads 165°.
3. Meanwhile, in a small bowl, combine the butter ingredients. Drizzle over chicken before serving.
Note: Wear disposable gloves when cutting hot peppers; the oils can burn skin. Avoid touching your face.

1 chicken breast half with 1 Tbsp. lime butter: 430 cal., 27g fat (10g sat. fat), 138mg chol., 411mg sod., 5g carb. (3g sugars, 1g fiber), 40g pro.

TEST KITCHEN TIPS

- This recipe gives you a hint of classic mole flavor. Mole is a Mexican sauce that can be made in many ways but includes the standout flavors of cumin, cinnamon and cocoa.
- Bone-in chicken means juicier, more flavorful meat than using boneless chicken breasts.
- Shred leftover chicken and make chicken tacos for a quick follow-up meal later in the week.

SPICED GRILLED CHICKEN WITH CILANTRO LIME BUTTER

⏱ 🍎 MAPLE-THYME CHICKEN THIGHS

We eat a lot of chicken at our house, and figuring out different ways to serve it gets challenging. My family went nuts for the cozy maple flavors in this recipe, so now I share it at potlucks, too.
—Lorraine Caland, Shuniah, ON

TAKES: 15 min. • **MAKES:** 6 servings

- 2 Tbsp. stone-ground mustard
- 2 Tbsp. maple syrup
- 1 tsp. minced fresh thyme or ½ tsp. dried thyme
- ½ tsp. salt
- ½ tsp. pepper
- 6 boneless skinless chicken thighs (about 1½ lbs.)

1. In a small bowl, mix the first 5 ingredients.
2. Grill the chicken on an oiled rack, covered, over medium heat 4-5 minutes on each side or until a thermometer reads 170°. Brush frequently with the mustard mixture during the last 4 minutes of cooking.
1 chicken thigh: 188 cal., 9g fat (2g sat. fat), 76mg chol., 363mg sod., 5g carb. (5g sugars, 0 fiber), 21g pro. **Diabetic exchanges:** 3 lean meat.
Brown Sugar-Mustard Chicken: Mix ⅓ cup yellow or Dijon mustard, ¼ cup brown sugar, and ¼ tsp. each ground allspice and crushed red pepper flakes. Set aside 3 Tbsp. for serving. Toss the chicken with remaining mixture; grill as directed. Serve with reserved mixture.
Orange Chicken: Simmer ⅓ cup brown sugar, ⅓ cup sugar, ¼ tsp. salt and 1 cup orange juice until mixture reaches a glaze consistency. Stir in 1 Tbsp. Dijon and 2 tsp. grated orange peel. Season chicken with ½ tsp. lemon-pepper seasoning; grill as directed. Serve with sauce.

APPLE-MARINATED CHICKEN & VEGETABLES

🍎 APPLE-MARINATED CHICKEN & VEGETABLES

I actually created this at a campground, so you know it's easy. Using the same marinade for the chicken and veggies keeps it simple so we can spend more time outside and less time making dinner.
—Jayme Schertz, Clintonville, WI

PREP: 20 min. + marinating
GRILL: 25 min. • **MAKES:** 6 servings

- 1 cup apple juice
- ½ cup canola oil
- ¼ cup packed brown sugar
- ¼ cup reduced-sodium soy sauce
- 3 Tbsp. lemon juice
- 2 Tbsp. minced fresh parsley
- 3 garlic cloves, minced
- 6 boneless skinless chicken breast halves (6 oz. each)
- 4 large carrots
- 2 medium zucchini
- 2 medium yellow summer squash

1. In a small bowl, whisk the first 7 ingredients until blended. In a bowl, place 1 cup marinade and chicken; turn to coat. Cover and refrigerate 6 hours or overnight. Cover and refrigerate remaining marinade.
2. Cut the carrots, zucchini and squash lengthwise into quarters; cut crosswise into 2-in. pieces. Toss with ½ cup reserved marinade.
3. Drain chicken, discarding marinade in bowl. Grill chicken, covered, over medium heat or broil 4 in. from heat 6-8 minutes on each side or until a thermometer reads 165°, basting frequently with remaining reserved marinade during the last 5 minutes. Keep warm.
4. Transfer vegetables to a grill wok or basket; place on grill rack. Grill, covered, over medium heat 10-12 minutes or until crisp-tender, stirring frequently. Serve with chicken.
1 chicken breast half with 1 cup vegetables: 367 cal., 16g fat (2g sat. fat), 94mg chol., 378mg sod., 19g carb. (13g sugars, 3g fiber), 37g pro.

GRILLED PINEAPPLE CHIMICHURRI CHICKEN

Classic chimichurri gets a Hawaiian twist thanks to pineapple and macadamia nuts. For a spicier version, substitute red serrano pepper for the bell pepper.
—*Naylet LaRochelle, Miami, FL*

TAKES: 30 min. • **MAKES:** 4 servings

- ½ small sweet red pepper, stemmed and seeded
- 2 slices fresh pineapple (½ in.)
- ⅔ cup fresh cilantro leaves
- ⅔ cup parsley sprigs (stems removed)
- 4 tsp. lime juice
- ¼ cup canola oil
- ¼ cup island teriyaki sauce
- 1 Tbsp. minced fresh gingerroot
- 4 boneless skinless chicken breast halves (6 oz. each)
  Hot cooked couscous, optional
- 2 green onions, sliced
- ¼ cup chopped macadamia nuts, toasted

1. Place pepper and pineapple on an oiled grill rack over medium heat; grill, covered, until lightly browned, 3-4 minutes per side.

2. For chimichurri, place cilantro, parsley and lime juice in a food processor; pulse until herbs are finely chopped. Continue processing while slowly adding oil. Chop grilled pepper and pineapple; stir into herb mixture.

3. Mix teriyaki sauce and ginger. Place chicken on an oiled grill rack over medium heat; grill, covered, until a thermometer reads 165°, 5-7 minutes per side. Brush with some teriyaki mixture during the last 4 minutes.

4. Brush chicken with remaining teriyaki mixture before serving. If desired, serve with couscous. Top with chimichurri, green onions and macadamia nuts.

Note: To toast nuts, cook in a skillet over low heat until lightly browned, stirring occasionally.

1 chicken breast half with about ¼ cup sauce : 428 cal., 24g fat (3g sat. fat), 94mg chol., 686mg sod., 19g carb. (13g sugars, 2g fiber), 37g pro.

FAVORITE BARBECUED CHICKEN

GRILLED PINEAPPLE CHIMICHURRI CHICKEN

FAVORITE BARBECUED CHICKEN

Is there a place better than Texas to find a terrific barbecue sauce? That's where this one is from—it's my father-in-law's own recipe. We have served it at many family reunions and think it's the best!
—*Bobbie Morgan, Woodstock, GA*

- -

PREP: 15 min. • **GRILL:** 35 min.
MAKES: 12 servings

  2 **broiler/fryer chickens
     (3 to 4 lbs. each),
     cut into 8 pieces each
     Salt and pepper**
BARBECUE SAUCE
  2 **Tbsp. canola oil**
  2 **small onions, finely chopped**
  2 **cups ketchup**
  ¼ **cup lemon juice**
  2 **Tbsp. brown sugar**
  2 **Tbsp. water**
  1 **tsp. ground mustard**
  ½ **tsp. garlic powder**
  ¼ **tsp. pepper**
  ⅛ **tsp. salt**
  ⅛ **tsp. hot pepper sauce**

1. Sprinkle chicken pieces with salt and pepper. Grill skin side down, uncovered, on a greased grill rack over medium heat for 20 minutes.
2. Meanwhile, in a small saucepan, make barbecue sauce by heating oil over medium heat. Add onion; saute until tender. Stir in remaining sauce ingredients and bring to a boil. Reduce the heat; simmer, uncovered, for 10 minutes.
3. Turn chicken; brush with barbecue sauce. Grill 15-25 minutes longer, brushing frequently with sauce, until a thermometer reads 165° when inserted in the breast and 170°-175° in the thigh.
1 serving: 370 cal., 19g fat (5g sat. fat), 104mg chol., 622mg sod., 15g carb. (14g sugars, 0 fiber), 33g pro.

🕐 JALAPENO-LIME CHICKEN DRUMSTICKS

Bottled hot sauce isn't my thing, so I developed a fresh pepper glaze for grilled chicken. These drumsticks practically fly off the plate.
—*Kristeen DeVorss, Farmington, NM*

- -

TAKES: 25 min. • **MAKES:** 6 servings

- 1 jar (10 oz.) red jalapeno pepper jelly
- ¼ cup lime juice
- 12 chicken drumsticks (about 3 lbs.)
- 1 tsp. salt
- ½ tsp. pepper

1. In a small saucepan, heat jelly and lime juice over medium heat until melted. Set aside ½ cup for serving.
2. Sprinkle chicken with salt and pepper. On a greased grill rack, grill chicken, covered, over medium heat 15-20 minutes or until a thermometer reads 170°-175°, turning occasionally and basting with remaining jelly mixture during the last 5 minutes of cooking. Serve with reserved jelly mixture.
2 chicken drumsticks: 361 cal., 12g fat (3g sat. fat), 95mg chol., 494mg sod., 34g carb. (24g sugars, 1g fiber), 29g pro.

GRILLED CHICKEN, MANGO & BLUE CHEESE TORTILLAS

🕐 🍎 GRILLED CHICKEN, MANGO & BLUE CHEESE TORTILLAS

Tortillas packed with chicken, mango and blue cheese make a fabulous appetizer to welcome summer. We double or triple the ingredients when we host parties.
—*Josee Lanzi, New Port Richey, FL*

- -

TAKES: 30 min. • **MAKES:** 16 appetizers

- 1 boneless skinless chicken breast (8 oz.)
- 1 tsp. blackened seasoning
- ¾ cup plain yogurt
- 1½ tsp. grated lime zest
- 2 Tbsp. lime juice
- ¼ tsp. salt
- ⅛ tsp. pepper
- 1 cup finely chopped peeled mango
- ⅓ cup finely chopped red onion
- 4 flour tortillas (8 in.)
- ½ cup crumbled blue cheese
- 2 Tbsp. minced fresh cilantro

1. Sprinkle chicken with blackened seasoning. On a lightly oiled rack, grill chicken, covered, over medium heat 6-8 minutes on each side or until a thermometer reads 165°.
2. Meanwhile, in a small bowl, mix yogurt, lime zest, lime juice, salt and pepper. Cool chicken slightly; finely chop and transfer to a small bowl. Stir in mango and onion.
3. Grill tortillas, uncovered, over medium heat 2-3 minutes or until puffed. Turn; top with the chicken mixture and blue cheese. Grill, covered, 2-3 minutes longer or until bottoms of tortillas are lightly browned. Drizzle with yogurt mixture; sprinkle with cilantro. Cut each tortilla into 4 wedges.
1 wedge: 85 cal., 3g fat (1g sat. fat), 12mg chol., 165mg sod., 10g carb. (2g sugars, 1g fiber), 5g pro. **Diabetic exchanges:** 1 lean meat, ½ starch.

SESAME CHICKEN
WITH CREAMY
SATAY SAUCE

SESAME CHICKEN WITH CREAMY SATAY SAUCE

These skewers taste as if they came from your favorite takeout place, but they are surprisingly simple to make at home. The sesame dressing keeps the chicken juicy.
—*Kathi Jones-DelMonte, Rochester, NY*

PREP: 20 min. + marinating • **GRILL:** 10 min.
MAKES: 4 servings

- ¾ cup Asian toasted sesame salad dressing
- 1 lb. boneless skinless chicken breast halves, cut into 1-in. strips
- ½ cup reduced-fat cream cheese
- ¼ cup coconut milk
- 3 Tbsp. creamy peanut butter
- 2 Tbsp. lime juice
- 1 Tbsp. reduced-sodium soy sauce
- ½ tsp. crushed red pepper flakes
- 1 Tbsp. minced fresh cilantro

1. In a bowl or shallow dish, add salad dressing and chicken; turn chicken to coat. Cover and refrigerate for 4 hours or overnight.
2. Drain and discard marinade. Thread the chicken onto metal or soaked wooden skewers.
3. Grill the skewers on an oiled rack, covered, over medium heat or broil 4 in. from the heat for 10-15 minutes or until no longer pink, turning once.
4. Meanwhile, in a small bowl, combine the cream cheese, coconut milk, peanut butter, lime juice, soy sauce and pepper flakes; sprinkle with cilantro. Serve chicken with sauce.
1 serving: 356 cal., 22g fat (9g sat. fat), 83mg chol., 692mg sod., 10g carb. (7g sugars, 1g fiber), 30g pro.

LOADED GRILLED CHICKEN SANDWICH

I threw these ingredients together on a whim and the sandwich turned out so well, I surprised myself! If you're in a rush, microwave the bacon—just cover it with a paper towel to keep it from spattering too much.
—Dana York, Kennewick, WA

TAKES: 30 min. • **MAKES:** 4 servings

- 4 boneless skinless chicken breast halves (4 oz. each)
- 2 tsp. Italian salad dressing mix
- 4 slices pepper jack cheese
- 4 ciabatta or kaiser rolls, split
- 2 Tbsp. mayonnaise
- ¾ tsp. Dijon mustard
- 4 cooked bacon strips, halved
- 4 slices tomato
- ½ medium ripe avocado, peeled and thinly sliced
- ½ lb. deli coleslaw (about 1 cup)

1. Pound chicken with a meat mallet to flatten slightly; sprinkle both sides with dressing mix.

2. On a greased grill, cook the chicken, covered, over medium heat or broil 4 in. from heat 4-6 minutes on each side or until a thermometer reads 165°. Place cheese on the chicken; grill, covered, 1-2 minutes longer or until cheese is melted. Meanwhile, grill rolls, cut side down, 1-2 minutes or until toasted.

3. Mix mayonnaise and mustard; spread on roll tops. Layer roll bottoms with chicken, bacon, tomato, avocado and coleslaw. Replace tops.

1 sandwich: 764 cal., 32g fat (9g sat. fat), 108mg chol., 1260mg sod., 82g carb. (12g sugars, 6g fiber), 43g pro.

LOADED GRILLED CHICKEN SANDWICH

KEEP GRILLED CHICKEN JUICY
Just hover your camera here.

SWEET TEA BARBECUED CHICKEN

Marinades sometimes use coffee or espresso, and that inspired me to try tea and apple juice to perk up this sauce.
—Kelly Williams, Forked River, NJ

PREP: 15 min. • **COOK:** 1 hour
MAKES: 8 servings

- 1 cup unsweetened apple juice
- 1 cup water
- 2 tsp. seafood seasoning
- 1 tsp. paprika
- 1 tsp. garlic powder
- 1 tsp. coarsely ground pepper
- 1 chicken (4 to 5 lbs.), cut up
- 1 cup barbecue sauce
- ½ cup sweet tea

1. Preheat oven to 350°. Pour apple juice and water into a large shallow roasting pan. Mix seafood seasoning, paprika, garlic powder and pepper; rub over chicken. Place in roasting pan.

2. Bake, covered, until juices run clear and a thermometer reads 170°-175°, 50-60 minutes. Transfer chicken to a foil-lined 15x10x1-in. baking pan. Whisk barbecue sauce and sweet tea; brush some mixture over chicken.

3. Place chicken on greased grill rack; grill over medium heat 3-4 minutes per side, brushing occasionally with remaining sauce.

1 piece: 374 cal., 17g fat (5g sat. fat), 104mg chol., 608mg sod., 19g carb. (16g sugars, 1g fiber), 33g pro.

CHIPOTLE-LIME
CHICKEN THIGHS

● CHIPOTLE-LIME CHICKEN THIGHS

You can put leftovers from this recipe to good use—use the chicken bones to make your own stock, or freeze remaining chipotle peppers and sauce for a smoky Sunday chili.
—Nancy Brown, Dahinda, IL

- -

PREP: 15 min. + chilling • **GRILL:** 20 min.
MAKES: 4 servings

  2 garlic cloves, peeled
  ¾ tsp. salt
  1 Tbsp. lime juice
  1 Tbsp. minced chipotle pepper
     in adobo sauce
  2 tsp. adobo sauce
  1 tsp. chili powder
  4 bone-in chicken thighs
     (about 1½ lbs.)

1. Place garlic on a cutting board; sprinkle with salt. Using flat side of a knife, mash garlic. Continue to mash until it reaches a paste consistency; transfer to a small bowl.
2. Stir in the lime juice, pepper, adobo sauce and chili powder. Gently loosen skin from chicken thighs; rub the garlic mixture under skin. Cover and refrigerate overnight.
3. On a lightly oiled grill rack, grill the chicken, covered, over medium-low heat for 20-25 minutes or until a thermometer reads 170°-175°, turning once. Remove and discard the skin before serving.
1 chicken thigh: 209 cal., 11g fat (3g sat. fat), 87mg chol., 596mg sod., 2g carb. (1g sugars, 0 fiber), 25g pro.
Diabetic exchanges: 3 lean meat.

● BLACKENED CHICKEN

This spicy standout packs a one-two punch of flavor. The grilled chicken is basted with a peppery white sauce, and there's always plenty of extra sauce left over for dipping.
—Stephanie Kenney, Falkville, AL

- -

TAKES: 25 min. • **MAKES:** 4 servings

  1   Tbsp. paprika
  4   tsp. sugar, divided
  1½ tsp. salt, divided
  1   tsp. garlic powder
  1   tsp. dried thyme
  1   tsp. lemon-pepper seasoning
  1   tsp. cayenne pepper
  1½ to 2 tsp. pepper, divided
  4   boneless skinless chicken breast
      halves (4 oz. each)
  1⅓ cups mayonnaise
  2   Tbsp. water
  2   Tbsp. cider vinegar

1. In a small bowl, combine the paprika, 1 tsp. sugar, 1 tsp. salt, garlic powder, thyme, lemon pepper, cayenne and ½-1 tsp. pepper; sprinkle over both sides of chicken. Set aside.
2. In another bowl, combine the mayonnaise, water, vinegar, and the remaining sugar, salt and pepper; cover and refrigerate 1 cup for serving. Save remaining sauce for basting.
3. Grill chicken, covered, over indirect medium heat for 4-6 minutes on each side or until a thermometer reads 170°, basting frequently with the remaining sauce. Serve with reserved sauce.
1 serving: 704 cal., 62g fat (9g sat. fat), 100mg chol., 1465mg sod., 7g carb. (5g sugars, 1g fiber), 27g pro.

WHY YOU'LL LOVE IT...

"Whoa—this recipe has a ton of flavor! It does have a little kick, but we served it over creamy pasta and it was perfect!"
—LPHJKITCHEN, TASTEOFHOME.COM

HERBED BEER CAN CHICKEN

SPICY BARBECUED CHICKEN

This zesty chicken is great served with basil-buttered grilled corn on the cob and fresh coleslaw.
—*Rita Wintrode, Corryton, TN*

TAKES: 30 min. • **MAKES:** 8 servings

- 1 Tbsp. canola oil
- 2 garlic cloves, minced
- ½ cup chili sauce
- 3 Tbsp. brown sugar
- 2 tsp. salt-free seasoning blend, divided
- ¾ tsp. cayenne pepper, divided
- 2 tsp. ground mustard
- 2 tsp. chili powder
- 8 boneless skinless chicken breast halves (4 oz. each)

1. In a small saucepan, heat oil over medium heat. Add garlic; cook and stir 1 minute. Add chili sauce, brown sugar, 1 tsp. seasoning blend and ¼ tsp. cayenne. Bring to a boil; cook and stir for 1 minute. Remove from heat.
2. In a small bowl, mix mustard, chili powder and remaining seasoning blend and cayenne; rub over chicken.
3. Lightly coat grill rack with cooking oil. Grill chicken, covered, over medium heat for 4 minutes. Turn chicken; grill 4-6 minutes longer or until a thermometer reads 165°, brushing the tops occasionally with chili sauce mixture.

1 chicken breast half : 179 cal., 5g fat (1g sat. fat), 63mg chol., 293mg sod., 10g carb. (8g sugars, 0 fiber), 23g pro.
Diabetic exchanges: 3 lean meat, ½ starch, ½ fat.

HERBED BEER CAN CHICKEN

Our Fourth of July tradition is to grill a chicken standing up on a can of beer. It might look slightly silly when you're making it, but it's such a fun conversation piece—and you can't beat the tender taste.
—*Karen Barros, Bristol, RI*

PREP: 15 min. • **GRILL:** 1¼ hours + standing
MAKES: 4 servings

- 2 Tbsp. canola oil
- 1 Tbsp. minced fresh tarragon or 1 tsp. dried tarragon
- 1 Tbsp. minced fresh basil or 1 tsp. dried basil
- 2 tsp. minced fresh parsley
- 1 tsp. garlic powder
- ½ tsp. salt
- ¼ tsp. pepper
- 3 garlic cloves, minced, divided
- 1 broiler/fryer chicken (3 to 4 lbs.)
- 1 can (12 oz.) beer
- 1 fresh rosemary sprig

1. In a small bowl, combine the first 7 ingredients; stir in half the minced garlic. Rub mixture over outside and inside of chicken. Tuck wings under the chicken.
2. Prepare the grill for indirect heat. Completely cover all sides of an 8- or 9-in. round baking pan with foil. Place a beer-can chicken rack in pan. Remove ⅓ cup beer from can; save for another use. Using a can opener, make additional large holes in top of can. Insert rosemary and remaining garlic into can. Add beer can to rack.
3. Place chicken vertically onto rack. Place pan on grill rack. Grill, covered, over indirect medium heat 1¼-1½ hours or until a thermometer inserted in thigh reads 180°.
4. Remove pan from grill; tent chicken with foil. Let stand 15 minutes. Carefully remove chicken from rack.

6 oz. cooked chicken: 474 cal., 28g fat (6g sat. fat), 131mg chol., 412mg sod., 4g carb. (3g sugars, 0 fiber), 42g pro.

SPICY BARBECUED CHICKEN

Grill Boneless Skinless Chicken Breasts

- Place marinade in a bowl or shallow dish, then add the chicken. Turn to coat. Cover and refrigerate for 30 minutes. Drain and discard the marinade.
- Clean grill grates. Moisten a paper towel with cooking oil. Holding it with long-handled tongs, use it to lightly coat the grill rack. Get the heat up to medium and use tongs to place the chicken breasts on the grill. Cover the grill, let the chicken cook for 5-7 minutes, then use tongs to flip the chicken breasts. Grill for 5-7 minutes longer or until a thermometer reads 165°.

CHICKEN ALFREDO WITH GRILLED APPLES

🕐 CHICKEN ALFREDO WITH GRILLED APPLES

If you've never grilled apples before, here's your excuse to start. I created this Alfredo-style chicken for a party. By the number of recipe requests, I knew it was a hit.
—*Richard Robinson, Park Forest, IL*

TAKES: 25 min. • **MAKES:** 4 servings

4	boneless skinless chicken breast halves (6 oz. each)
4	tsp. chicken seasoning
1	large Braeburn or Gala apple, cut into ½-in. wedges
1	Tbsp. lemon juice
4	slices provolone cheese
½	cup Alfredo sauce, warmed
¼	cup crumbled blue cheese

1. Sprinkle both sides of chicken with chicken seasoning. In a small bowl, toss apple wedges with lemon juice.
2. Place chicken on an oiled grill rack. Grill chicken, covered, over medium heat 5-8 minutes on each side or until a thermometer reads 165°. Grill apple, covered, over medium heat 2-3 minutes on each side or until lightly browned. Top chicken with provolone cheese; cook, covered, 1-2 minutes longer or until cheese is melted.
3. Serve chicken with Alfredo sauce and apple. Sprinkle with blue cheese.
Note: This recipe was tested with McCormick's Montreal Chicken Seasoning. Look for it in the spice aisle.
1 serving: 352 cal., 16g fat (8g sat. fat), 124mg chol., 684mg sod., 9g carb. (5g sugars, 1g fiber), 43g pro.

KENTUCKY GRILLED CHICKEN

This chicken is perfect for an outdoor summer meal, and my family thinks it's marvelous. It takes about an hour on the grill but is worth the wait. I use a new paintbrush to mop on the basting sauce.
—*Jill Evely, Wilmore, KY*

PREP: 5 min. + marinating • **GRILL:** 40 min.
MAKES: 10 servings

- 1 cup cider vinegar
- ½ cup canola oil
- 5 tsp. Worcestershire sauce
- 4 tsp. hot pepper sauce
- 2 tsp. salt
- 10 bone-in chicken breast halves (10 oz. each)

1. In a bowl or shallow dish, combine the first 5 ingredients. Pour 1 cup marinade into a separate bowl; add the chicken. Turn to coat; cover and refrigerate for at least 4 hours. Cover and refrigerate the remaining marinade for basting.

2. Drain and discard marinade from chicken. Prepare grill for indirect heat, using a drip pan.

3. Place the chicken, breast bone side down, on an oiled rack. Grill, covered, over indirect medium heat until a thermometer reads 170°, basting occasionally with reserved marinade, 20 minutes on each side.

1 chicken breast half: 284 cal., 11g fat (2g sat. fat), 113mg chol., 406mg sod., 0 carb. (0 sugars, 0 fiber), 41g pro. **Diabetic exchanges:** 6 lean meat, 2 fat.

CHICKEN & VEGETABLE KABOBS

In the summer, my husband and I love to cook out, especially vegetables. These kabobs not only taste delicious but look amazing, too!
—*Tina Oles, Nashwauk, MN*

TAKES: 30 min. • **MAKES:** 4 servings

- 1 lb. boneless skinless chicken breasts, cut into 1½-in. cubes
- 1 medium sweet red pepper, cut into 1½-in. pieces
- 1 medium zucchini, cut into 1½-in. pieces
- 1 medium red onion, cut into thick wedges
- ⅔ cup sun-dried tomato salad dressing, divided

1. In a large bowl, combine chicken and vegetables. Drizzle with ⅓ cup dressing and toss to coat. Alternately thread chicken and vegetables onto 4 metal or soaked wooden skewers.

2. Grill kabobs, covered, over medium heat or broil 4 in. from heat until chicken is no longer pink, 8-10 minutes, turning occasionally and basting with remaining dressing during the last 3 minutes.

1 kabob: 228 cal., 10g fat (1g sat. fat), 63mg chol., 515mg sod., 11g carb. (7g sugars, 2g fiber), 24g pro. **Diabetic exchanges:** 3 lean meat, 1 vegetable, 1 fat.

LEARN TO CLEAN YOUR GRILL
Just hover your camera here.

KENTUCKY GRILLED CHICKEN

SWEET SRIRACHA WINGS

Serve these fiery hot wings on game day or any time friends and family gather. If you don't like a ton of sweetness, add the honey slowly and taste as you go.
—*Logan Holser, Clarkston, MI*

PREP: 20 min. + marinating • **GRILL:** 15 min.
MAKES: 1 dozen

12 chicken wings (about 3 lbs.)
1 Tbsp. canola oil
2 tsp. ground coriander
½ tsp. garlic salt
¼ tsp. pepper

SAUCE

¼ cup butter, cubed
½ cup orange juice
⅓ cup Sriracha chili sauce
3 Tbsp. honey
2 Tbsp. lime juice
¼ cup chopped fresh cilantro

1. Place chicken wings in a large bowl. Mix oil, coriander, garlic salt and pepper; add to wings and toss to coat. Refrigerate, covered, 2 hours or overnight.

2. For sauce, in a small saucepan, melt butter. Stir in orange juice, chili sauce, honey and lime juice until blended.

3. Grill wings, covered, over medium heat 15-18 minutes or until juices run clear, turning occasionally; brush with some of the sauce during the last 5 minutes of grilling.

4. Transfer chicken to a large bowl; add remaining sauce and toss to coat. Sprinkle with cilantro.

1 chicken wing: 201 cal., 13g fat (5g sat. fat), 46mg chol., 321mg sod., 8g carb. (7g sugars, 0 fiber), 12g pro.

TEST KITCHEN TIP

Scrub grill grates clean with wadded aluminum foil. Keep a spray bottle on hand for flare-ups.

SWEET SRIRACHA WINGS

*GRILLED CHICKEN &
MANGO SKEWERS*

HERBED BARBECUED CHICKEN

Garlic, rosemary, sage and thyme help season the marinade for this moist, tender chicken. A friend gave me the recipe years ago and my family never tires of it.
—*Dawn Sowders, Harrison, OH*

- -

PREP: 10 min. + marinating • **GRILL:** 10 min.
MAKES: 4 servings

  2   Tbsp. olive oil
  2   Tbsp. reduced-sodium soy sauce
  2   Tbsp. Worcestershire sauce
  1   garlic clove, minced
  1   Tbsp. dried parsley flakes
  ½   tsp. dried rosemary, crushed
  ½   tsp. rubbed sage
  ¼   tsp. dried oregano
  ¼   tsp. dried thyme
  ¼   tsp. pepper
  4   boneless skinless chicken breast
      halves (4 oz. each)

1. In a bowl or shallow dish, combine the first 10 ingredients; add chicken. Turn to coat; cover and refrigerate for 8 hours or overnight.
2. Drain and discard marinade. Grill chicken on an oiled rack, covered, over medium heat or broil 4 in. from the heat for 5-8 minutes on each side or until a thermometer reads 170°.
1 serving: 159 cal., 6g fat (1g sat. fat), 63mg chol., 248mg sod., 1g carb. (0 sugars, 0 fiber), 23g pro. **Diabetic exchanges:** 3 lean meat, ½ fat.

🕐 🍎 GRILLED CHICKEN & MANGO SKEWERS

The inspiration for this recipe came from the charbroiled chicken skewers I used to enjoy while strolling along Calle Ocho in Miami on Sunday afternoons. Feel free to garnish them with sesame seeds or spritz them with fresh lime juice.
—*Wolfgang Hanau, West Palm Beach, FL*

- -

TAKES: 30 min. • **MAKES:** 4 servings

  3   medium ears sweet corn
  1   Tbsp. butter
  ⅓   cup plus 3 Tbsp. sliced
      green onions, divided
  1   lb. boneless skinless
      chicken breasts, cut into 1-in. cubes
  ½   tsp. salt
  ¼   tsp. pepper
  1   medium mango, peeled and
      cut into 1-in. cubes
  1   Tbsp. extra virgin olive oil
      Lime wedges, optional

1. Cut corn from cobs. In a large skillet, heat butter over medium-high heat; saute cut corn until crisp-tender, about 5 minutes. Stir in ⅓ cup green onions. Keep warm.
2. Toss chicken with salt and pepper. Alternately thread the chicken and mango onto 4 metal or soaked wooden skewers. Brush with oil.
3. Grill, covered, over medium heat or broil 4 in. from heat until chicken is no longer pink, 10-12 minutes, turning occasionally. Serve with corn mixture; sprinkle with remaining green onions. If desired, serve with lime wedges.
1 skewer with ½ cup corn mixture: 297 cal., 10g fat (3g sat. fat), 70mg chol., 387mg sod., 28g carb. (16g sugars, 3g fiber), 26g pro. **Diabetic exchanges:** 3 lean meat, 2 starch, 1½ fat.

GRILLED CHICKEN WITH HERBED STUFFING

Plain grilled chicken breasts can get boring after a while, so I like to stuff them with a bunch of herbs, bread crumbs and garlic. I think they taste infinitely better this way, and the stuffing and lemon butter help keep the chicken moist. Any leftover chicken goes well in a salad or tossed with some pasta the following day.
—*Joy McMillan, The Woodlands, TX*

TAKES: 30 min. • **MAKES:** 4 servings

- 5 tsp. butter, divided
- ½ cup finely chopped onion
- 1 garlic clove, minced
- ½ cup soft bread crumbs
- 1 Tbsp. minced fresh parsley
- ¼ tsp. salt, divided
- ⅛ tsp. dried marjoram
- ⅛ tsp. dried thyme
- 4 boneless skinless chicken breast halves (6 oz. each)
- 1 tsp. grated lemon zest

1. In a small nonstick skillet, heat 2 tsp. butter. Add onion and garlic; cook and stir until tender. Stir in the bread crumbs, parsley, ⅛ tsp. salt, marjoram and thyme.

2. Cut a pocket in the thickest part of each chicken breast. Fill with bread crumb mixture; secure with toothpicks. Sprinkle chicken with remaining salt. In a microwave, melt remaining butter; stir in lemon zest.

3. Place chicken on greased grill rack. Grill over medium heat 6-9 minutes on each side or until chicken is no longer pink, brushing occasionally with butter mixture during the last 5 minutes of cooking. Discard toothpicks.

1 stuffed chicken breast half: 250 cal., 9g fat (4g sat. fat), 107mg chol., 296mg sod., 5g carb. (1g sugars, 1g fiber), 35g pro. **Diabetic exchanges:** 5 lean meat, 1 fat.

MATT'S JERK CHICKEN

MATT'S JERK CHICKEN

Get ready for a trip to the Islands. You may think jerk chicken is complicated but, really, all it takes is time. Throw on some tunes, grab an icy drink and prepare to be transported. Have a smoker? You can smoke the chicken first and finish it on the grill.

—Jenn Hall, Collingswood, NJ

- -

PREP: 25 min. + marinating
GRILL: 50 min.
MAKES: 16 servings

- 1 large onion, chopped
- 3 green onions, chopped
- ¾ cup white vinegar
- ½ cup orange juice
- ¼ cup dark rum
- ¼ cup olive oil
- ¼ cup soy sauce
- 2 Tbsp. lime juice
- 1 habanero or Scotch bonnet pepper, seeded and minced
- 2 Tbsp. garlic powder
- 1 Tbsp. sugar
- 1 Tbsp. ground allspice
- 1 Tbsp. dried thyme
- 1½ tsp. cayenne pepper
- 1½ tsp. rubbed sage
- 1½ tsp. pepper
- ¾ tsp. ground nutmeg
- ¾ tsp. ground cinnamon
- 8 lbs. bone-in chicken breast halves and thighs
- ½ cup whole allspice berries
- 1 cup applewood chips
- ½ cup ketchup

1. Process first 18 ingredients, covered, in a blender until smooth. Divide chicken into 2 large bowls; pour half the onion mixture in each. Turn chicken to coat. Cover and refrigerate overnight.
2. Soak allspice berries in water for 30 minutes. Drain chicken, reserving 1½ cups marinade. Preheat grill and prepare for indirect heat. On a piece of heavy-duty foil (12 in. square), place soaked allspice berries; fold foil around berries to form a packet, crimping edges to seal. Using a small skewer, poke holes in packet. Repeat process for the applewood chips. Place packets over heat on grate of gas grill or in coals of charcoal grill.
3. Place the chicken on greased grill rack, skin side down. Grill, covered, over indirect medium heat until a thermometer reads 165° when inserted into the breasts and 170°-175° when inserted into thighs, 50-60 minutes.
4. Meanwhile, in a small saucepan over high heat, bring reserved marinade to a full rolling boil for at least 1 minute. Add ketchup; cook and stir until heated through. Remove from heat.
5. To serve Jamaican-style, remove meat from bones and chop with a cleaver. Toss chicken with sauce.

Freeze option: Arrange grilled chicken pieces in a greased 13x9-in. baking dish; add sauce. Cool; cover and freeze. To use, partially thaw in refrigerator overnight. Remove from refrigerator 30 minutes before baking. Preheat oven to 350°. Reheat chicken, covered, until a thermometer reads 165°, 40-50 minutes.
Note: Wear disposable gloves when cutting hot peppers; the oils can burn skin. Avoid touching your face.
1 serving: 346 cal., 18g fat (5g sat. fat), 109mg chol., 419mg sod., 7g carb. (4g sugars, 1g fiber), 36g pro.

WHY YOU'LL LOVE IT...

"This is so flavorful and tasty! It takes a little effort to make, as there are a lot of ingredients, but they all blend together very well! I broiled the chicken as opposed to grilling it. I also omitted the habanero pepper, but the recipe still had plenty of zip to it!"

—REMENEC, TASTEOFHOME.COM

TURN YOUR GRILL INTO A SMOKER
Just hover your camera here.

RHUBARB-APRICOT BARBECUED CHICKEN

Springtime brings back memories of the rhubarb that grew beside my childhood home. When I found ruby red stalks in the store, I created this recipe for them. My family gives this a big thumbs up.
—*Laurie Hudson, Westville, FL*

- -

PREP: 30 min. • **GRILL:** 30 min.
MAKES: 6 servings

- 1   Tbsp. olive oil
- 1   cup finely chopped sweet onion
- 1   garlic clove, minced
- 2   cups chopped fresh or frozen rhubarb
- ¾   cup ketchup
- ⅔   cup water
- ⅓   cup apricot preserves
- ¼   cup cider vinegar
- ¼   cup molasses
- 1   Tbsp. honey Dijon mustard
- 2   tsp. finely chopped chipotle pepper in adobo sauce
- 5   tsp. barbecue seasoning, divided
- 1¼ tsp. salt, divided
- ¾   tsp. pepper, divided
- 12 chicken drumsticks (about 4 lbs.)

1. In a large saucepan, heat oil over medium heat. Add onion; cook and stir until tender, 4-6 minutes. Add garlic; cook 1 minute longer. Stir in rhubarb, ketchup, water, preserves, vinegar, molasses, mustard, chipotle pepper, 1 tsp. barbecue seasoning, ¼ tsp. salt and ¼ tsp. pepper. Bring to a boil. Reduce heat; simmer, uncovered, until rhubarb is tender, 8-10 minutes. Puree rhubarb mixture using an immersion blender, or cool slightly and puree in a blender. Reserve 2 cups sauce for serving.

2. Meanwhile, in a small bowl, mix the remaining 4 tsp. barbecue seasoning, 1 tsp. salt and ½ tsp. pepper; sprinkle over chicken. On a lightly oiled grill rack, grill chicken, covered, over indirect medium heat 15 minutes. Turn; grill until a thermometer reads 170°-175°, 15-20 minutes longer, brushing occasionally with remaining sauce. Serve with reserved sauce.

Note: If using frozen rhubarb, measure rhubarb while still frozen, then thaw completely. Drain in a colander, but do not press liquid out.

2 chicken drumsticks with ⅓ cup sauce: 469 cal., 19g fat (5g sat. fat), 126mg chol., 1801mg sod., 35g carb. (28g sugars, 1g fiber), 39g pro.

RHUBARB-APRICOT BARBECUED CHICKEN

CHICKEN YAKITORI

⏱ CHICKEN YAKITORI

I grew up in Tokyo, and some of my favorite memories include eating street food like this dish with my friends. Although we now live thousands of miles apart, my friends and I still reminisce about our nights sharing secrets and bonding over delicious meals. This one is easy to re-create at home, which makes it perfect for when I'm feeling homesick. I like to serve it with rice.
—*Lindsay Howerton-Hastings, Greenville, SC*

TAKES: 30 min. • **MAKES:** 6 servings

- ½ cup mirin (sweet rice wine)
- ½ cup sake
- ½ cup soy sauce
- 1 Tbsp. sugar
- 2 large sweet red peppers, cut into 2-in. pieces
- 2 lbs. boneless skinless chicken thighs, cut into 1½-in. pieces
- 1 bunch green onions

1. In a small saucepan, combine first 4 ingredients. Bring to a boil over medium-high heat. Remove from heat; set aside half the mixture for serving.

2. Thread peppers onto 2 metal or soaked wooden skewers. Thread chicken onto 6 metal or soaked wooden skewers.
3. Grill chicken, covered, over medium heat until no longer pink, 10-12 minutes, turning occasionally and basting frequently with soy sauce mixture during last 3 minutes. Grill peppers, covered, until tender, 4-5 minutes, turning occasionally. Grill onions, covered, until lightly charred, 1-2 minutes, turning occasionally. Serve chicken and vegetables with reserved sauce for dipping.
1 serving: 332 cal., 11g fat (3g sat. fat), 101mg chol., 1316mg sod., 14g carb. (11g sugars, 1g fiber), 32g pro.

TEST KITCHEN TIP

When stored in a shallow, airtight container or tightly wrapped in foil, the cooked chicken skewers will keep in the refrigerator for 3-4 days. The sauce, on its own, can be kept in an airtight container for 2-3 months.

GRILLED CAESAR CHICKEN BREASTS

Marinated overnight in creamy Caesar dressing, this chicken grills up juicy and tender. It's a real hit with foodie friends, and it couldn't be easier.
—*Marcia Wallenfeldt, Kent, OH*

PREP: 10 min. + marinating • **GRILL:** 15 min.
MAKES: 4 servings

- ½ cup creamy Caesar salad dressing
- 3 Tbsp. olive oil
- 3 Tbsp. Dijon mustard
- 6 garlic cloves, minced
- 4 boneless skinless chicken breast halves (6 oz. each)

1. In a shallow dish, combine dressing, oil, mustard and garlic. Add chicken; turn to coat. Cover and refrigerate for 8 hours or overnight.
2. Drain and discard marinade. Grill chicken, covered, over medium heat or broil 4 in. from the heat until a thermometer reads 165°, 7-8 minutes on each side.

1 chicken breast half: 318 cal., 18g fat (3g sat. fat), 100mg chol., 395mg sod., 2g carb. (0 sugars, 0 fiber), 35g pro.

INSTANT POT, AIR FRYER & SLOW COOKER

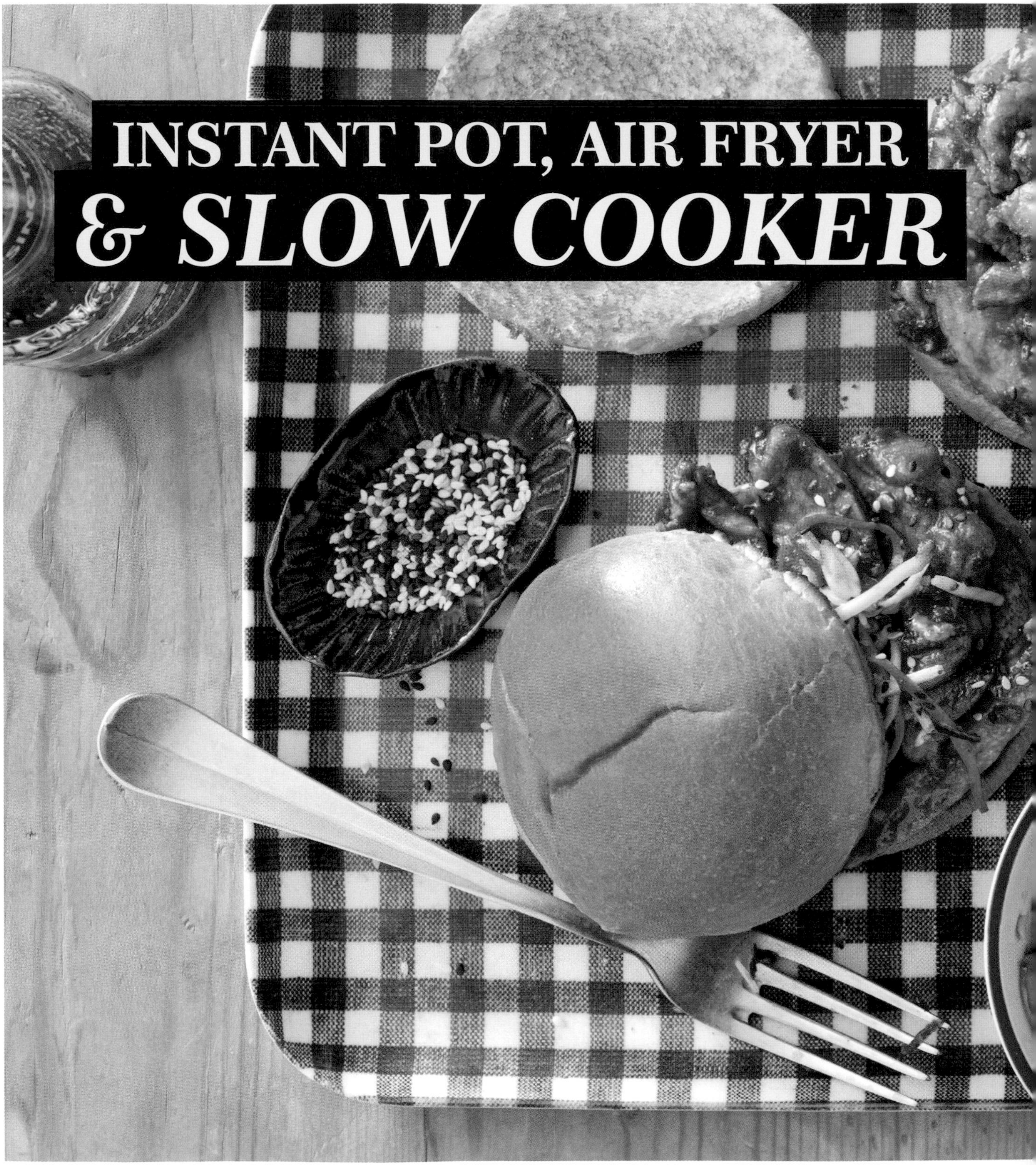

GENERAL TSO'S
CHICKEN SANDWICH WITH
BROCCOLI SLAW, PAGE 232

PRESSURE-COOKER ORANGE CHIPOTLE CHICKEN

PRESSURE-COOKER ORANGE CHIPOTLE CHICKEN

The citrus in this delicious chicken dish keeps things fresh and lively. We're big on spice in our house, so sometimes I use two chipotle peppers.
—*Deborah Biggs, Omaha, NE*

TAKES: 25 min. • **MAKES:** 6 servings

- ½ cup plus 2 Tbsp. cold water, divided
- ½ cup thawed orange juice concentrate
- ¼ cup barbecue sauce
- 1 chipotle pepper in adobo sauce
- ¼ tsp. salt
- ¼ tsp. garlic powder
- 6 boneless skinless chicken breast halves (6 oz. each)
- ¼ cup chopped red onion
- 4 tsp. cornstarch
  Grated orange zest

1. Place ½ cup water, juice concentrate, barbecue sauce, chipotle pepper, salt and garlic powder in a blender; cover and process until blended.

2. Place the chicken and onion in a 6-qt. electric pressure cooker; top with juice mixture. Lock the lid; close pressure-release valve. Adjust to pressure-cook on high for 6 minutes.

3. Quick-release pressure. When a thermometer is inserted in chicken, it should read at least 165°. Remove chicken from the pressure cooker; keep warm.

4. In a small bowl, mix cornstarch and remaining 2 Tbsp. water until smooth; gradually stir into pressure cooker. Select saute setting and adjust for low heat. Simmer, stirring constantly, until thickened, 1-2 minutes. Spoon over chicken; top with orange zest.

1 chicken breast with ¼ cup sauce: 246 cal., 4g fat (1g sat. fat), 94mg chol., 315mg sod., 15g carb. (11g sugars, 1g fiber), 35g pro. **Diabetic exchanges:** 5 lean meat, 1 starch.

YES, YOU CAN COOK FROZEN CHICKEN IN THE INSTANT POT
Just hover your camera here.

🍎 🍲 GENERAL TSO'S STEW

I love Asian food and wanted a chili-like soup with the distinctive flavors of General Tso's chicken. The slow cooker makes this super easy, and you can use any meat you like. It's wonderful with turkey, ground meats or leftover pork.
—*Lori McLain, Denton, TX*

- -

PREP: 10 min. • **COOK:** 2 hours
MAKES: 6 servings

- 1 cup tomato juice
- ½ cup pickled cherry peppers, chopped
- 2 Tbsp. soy sauce
- 2 Tbsp. hoisin sauce
- 1 Tbsp. peanut oil
- 1 to 2 tsp. crushed red pepper flakes
- 1 lb. shredded cooked chicken
- 1½ cups chopped onion
- 1 cup chopped fresh broccoli
- ¼ cup chopped green onions
- 1 tsp. sesame seeds, toasted

In a 4- or 5-qt. slow cooker, combine the first 6 ingredients. Stir in chicken, onion and broccoli. Cook, covered, on low about 2 hours, until vegetables are tender. Top with green onions and sesame seeds to serve.
1 cup: 222 cal., 9g fat (2g sat. fat), 67mg chol., 791mg sod., 10g carb. (5g sugars, 2g fiber), 25g pro. **Diabetic exchanges:** 3 lean meat, 2 vegetable, ½ fat.

SLOW-COOKER CHICKEN TINGA

🍲 SLOW-COOKER CHICKEN TINGA

I first fell in love with this traditional Mexican dish at a taco stand inside a gas station. This is how I now make it at home. My version has a nice zing without being overly spicy.
—*Ramona Parris, Canton, GA*

- -

PREP: 25 min. • **COOK:** 4 hours
MAKES: 8 servings

- 8 oz. fresh chorizo
- 1½ lbs. boneless, skinless chicken thighs
- 1 large onion, cut into wedges
- 1 can (14½ oz.) fire-roasted diced tomatoes
- ½ cup chicken broth
- 3 Tbsp. minced chipotle peppers in adobo sauce
- 3 garlic cloves, minced
- 2 tsp. ground cumin
- 1 tsp. dried oregano
- ½ tsp. salt
- 16 corn tortillas (6 in.)
  Optional: Shredded lettuce and pico de gallo

1. In a small skillet, fully cook chorizo over medium heat, breaking meat into crumbles, 6-8 minutes; drain. Transfer to a 3- or 4-qt. slow cooker. Add next 9 ingredients; stir to combine. Cook, covered, on low 4-5 hours or until chicken is tender.
2. Remove chicken; cool slightly. Shred with 2 forks. Remove and discard the onions; strain cooking juices and skim fat. Return cooking juices and chicken to slow cooker; heat through. Serve the chicken in corn tortillas. If desired, top with shredded lettuce and pico de gallo.
Freeze option: Freeze cooled chicken mixture in freezer containers. To use, partially thaw in refrigerator overnight. Heat through in a saucepan, stirring occasionally; add broth if necessary.
2 tacos: 363 cal., 16g fat (5g sat. fat), 82mg chol., 800mg sod., 27g carb. (3g sugars, 4g fiber), 25g pro.

*AIR-FRYER
CHICKEN PICCATA
POCKETS*

🔲 AIR-FRYER CHICKEN PICCATA POCKETS

My husband loves chicken piccata. This puff pastry version tastes sensational. When he took leftovers to work, everyone asked what smelled so amazing.
—*Arlene Erlbach, Morton Grove, IL*

- -

PREP: 15 min. • **COOK:** 20 min.
MAKES: 4 servings

1	pkg. (8 oz.) cream cheese, softened
2	Tbsp. lemon juice
¼	tsp. salt
¼	tsp. pepper
2	Tbsp. capers, drained
1	large shallot, finely chopped
1	sheet frozen puff pastry, thawed
4	chicken tenderloins, cubed
1	large egg, well beaten
1	Tbsp. water
4	thin lemon slices
2	Tbsp. chopped fresh parsley

1. Preheat air fryer to 425°. Beat cream cheese, lemon juice, salt and pepper on medium speed until well combined. Fold in capers and shallot.

2. Unfold the puff pastry; roll dough into a 12-in. square. Cut pastry into 4 smaller squares. Spread cream cheese mixture over squares to within ¼ in. of edges; top with chicken.

3. Fold a corner of each pastry square over chicken, forming a triangle. Pinch triangle edges to seal and flatten with fork for tighter seal. Whisk the egg and water; brush over the pastry pocket, including edges. Discard leftover egg mixture. Pierce each pocket twice with a fork to vent.

4. Place in a single layer on greased tray in air-fryer basket. Cook until golden brown, 18-25 minutes. Remove from air fryer; cool 5 minutes. Serve pockets with lemon slices and parsley.

Freeze option: Cover and freeze the unbaked pockets on a waxed paper-lined baking sheet until firm. Transfer to an airtight container; return to freezer. To use, cook as directed, increasing time about 5 minutes.

1 chicken pocket: 564 cal., 38g fat (16g sat. fat), 120mg chol., 669mg sod., 41g carb. (3g sugars, 5g fiber), 18g pro.

🍲 EASY LEMON-ROSEMARY CHICKEN

This slow-cooker chicken is perfect for spring gatherings with its light and fresh lemon and rosemary flavor. It pairs well with a variety of sides. Plus, the slow cooker does most of the work!
—*Courtney Stultz, Weir, KS*

- -

PREP: 10 min. • **COOK:** 4 hours + standing
MAKES: 6 servings

1	broiler/fryer chicken (3 to 4 lbs.)
2	celery ribs, cut into 1-in. pieces
1	medium onion, chopped
1	medium apple, sliced
1	Tbsp. olive oil
1	Tbsp. minced fresh rosemary or 1 tsp. dried rosemary, crushed
2	tsp. sea salt
1½	tsp. minced fresh thyme or ½ tsp. dried thyme
1½	tsp. paprika
1	garlic clove, minced
1	tsp. pepper
1	medium lemon, sliced

1. Fill chicken cavity with celery, onion and apple. Tuck wings under chicken; tie drumsticks together. Place chicken in a 6-qt. slow cooker, breast side up. Rub chicken with oil; rub with rosemary, salt, thyme, paprika, garlic and pepper. Top with lemon.

2. Cook chicken, covered, on low until a thermometer inserted in thickest part of thigh reads at least 170°-175°, 4-5 hours. Remove chicken from slow cooker; tent with foil. Discard vegetables and apple. Let chicken stand 15 minutes before carving.

5 oz. cooked chicken: 318 cal., 19g fat (5g sat. fat), 104mg chol., 730mg sod., 1g carb. (0 sugars, 0 fiber), 33g pro.

EASY
LEMON-ROSEMARY
CHICKEN

Truss a Chicken

- Place aromatics in bird, if using. Place kitchen twine under the tail and loop around the ankles, pulling up tightly.
- After making an "X" with the string, reverse your grip on the twine and cross the ends down and around the ankles in a figure-eight pattern. Pull tightly so the legs move together: The goal is to create a tight, compact shape.
- Pull twine up around the thighs and hook it under the wing joints.
- Flip the chicken and tie the twine in a firm knot. Tuck wings under bird and trim any excess twine.

🦉 AIR-FRYER FAJITA-STUFFED CHICKEN

I had all the ingredients for this fajita-inspired dish , but instead of heating up my big oven I decided to try out the air fryer. Since mine is a small one, I wanted to get as much filling as possible in each stuffed chicken breast. Cutting slits in the breasts and then filling them did the trick.
—*Joan Hallford, North Richland Hills, TX*

PREP: 20 min. • **COOK:** 15 min./batch • **MAKES:** 4 servings

- 4 boneless skinless chicken breast halves (6 oz. each)
- 1 small onion, halved and thinly sliced
- ½ medium green pepper, thinly sliced
- 1 Tbsp. olive oil
- 1 Tbsp. chili powder
- 1 tsp. ground cumin
- ½ tsp. salt
- ¼ tsp. garlic powder
- 4 oz. cheddar cheese, cut into 4 slices
  Optional: Salsa, sour cream, minced fresh cilantro, jalapeno slices and guacamole

1. Preheat air fryer to 375°. Cut a pocket horizontally in the thickest part of each chicken breast. Fill with onion and green pepper. In a small bowl, combine olive oil and seasonings; rub over chicken.
2. In batches, place chicken on greased tray in air-fryer basket. Cook 6 minutes. Top chicken with cheese slices; secure with toothpicks. Cook stuffed breasts until a thermometer inserted in chicken reads at least 165°, 6-8 minutes longer. Discard toothpicks. If desired, serve chicken with toppings of your choice.
1 chicken breast half: 347 cal., 17g fat (7g sat. fat), 126mg chol., 628mg sod., 5g carb. (1g sugars, 1g fiber), 42g pro.

SLOW-COOKER PUMPKIN CHICKEN TAGINE

🍎🍲 SLOW-COOKER PUMPKIN CHICKEN TAGINE

I first discovered tagines—Moroccan stews—when my oldest son was a baby, and I've loved them ever since. I used a slow cooker for my first version and that has stayed my preferred method. The pumpkin mixture is supposed to be thick, but stir in chicken broth if you like a thinner consistency.
—*Necia Blundy, Bothell, WA*

PREP: 35 min. • **COOK:** 5 hours
MAKES: 4 servings

- 1 lb. boneless skinless chicken thighs, cut into ½-in. pieces
- 1 can (15 oz.) garbanzo beans or chickpeas, rinsed and drained
- 1 can (14½ oz.) diced tomatoes, undrained
- 1 medium green pepper, chopped
- 1 cup canned pumpkin
- ¼ cup golden raisins
- 1 Tbsp. maple syrup
- 2 tsp. ground cumin
- 1 tsp. ground cinnamon
- ½ tsp. salt
- ½ tsp. ground coriander
- ¼ tsp. cayenne pepper
- ¼ tsp. ground cloves
- ¼ tsp. ground allspice
- 1 Tbsp. olive oil
- 1 medium onion, chopped
- 2 garlic cloves, minced
- 1 tsp. minced fresh gingerroot
  Hot cooked couscous and chopped fresh cilantro

1. In a 3- or 4-qt. slow cooker, combine the first 14 ingredients. In a small skillet, heat oil over medium heat. Add onion; cook and stir until tender, 5-7 minutes. Add garlic and ginger; cook 1 minute longer. Stir into slow cooker.
2. Cook, covered, on low until chicken is cooked through and vegetables are tender, 5-6 hours. Serve with couscous; sprinkle with cilantro.

GET OUR MEAL PLAN USING SLOW-COOKED CHICKEN
Just hover your camera here.

1 serving: 400 cal., 14g fat (3g sat. fat), 76mg chol., 668mg sod., 42g carb. (18g sugars, 10g fiber), 28g pro.

🍲 SPICED LIME & CILANTRO CHICKEN

As a working mom and home cook, I strive to have fabulous flavor-packed dinners that will make my family smile. Nothing is more awesome than a slow-cooker recipe that makes it seem as though you've been cooking in the kitchen all day!
—*Mari Smith, Ashburn, VA*

PREP: 15 min. • **COOK:** 3 hours
MAKES: 6 servings

- 2 tsp. chili powder
- 1 tsp. sea salt
- 1 tsp. ground cumin
- 1 tsp. pepper
- ¼ tsp. cayenne pepper
- 6 bone-in chicken thighs (about 2¼ lbs.)
- ⅓ cup lime juice (about 3 limes)
- 1 Tbsp. olive oil
- ½ cup fresh cilantro leaves
- 5 garlic cloves, halved

1. Combine the first 5 ingredients; rub over chicken thighs . Place in a 4- or 5-qt. slow cooker. Combine remaining ingredients in a blender; cover and process until pureed. Pour over chicken.
2. Cook, covered, on low until a thermometer inserted in chicken reads 170°-175°, 3-4 hours.
1 chicken thigh: 253 cal., 17g fat (4g sat. fat), 81mg chol., 390mg sod., 2g carb. (0 sugars, 0 fiber), 23g pro.

PRESSURE-COOKER GARDEN CHICKEN CACCIATORE

Treat company to this perfect Italian meal. You'll have time to visit with your guests while it simmers, and it has won rave reviews. I like to serve it with pasta or couscous, green beans and dry red wine.
—*Martha Schirmacher, Sterling Heights, MI*

TAKES: 25 min. • **MAKES:** 12 servings

- 12 boneless skinless chicken thighs (about 3 lbs.)
- 2 medium green peppers, chopped
- 1 can (14½ oz.) diced tomatoes with basil, oregano and garlic, undrained
- 1 can (6 oz.) tomato paste
- 1 medium onion, chopped
- ½ cup reduced-sodium chicken broth
- ¼ cup dry red wine or additional reduced-sodium chicken broth
- 3 garlic cloves, minced
- ¾ tsp. salt
- ⅛ tsp. pepper
- 2 Tbsp. cornstarch
- 2 Tbsp. cold water
  Minced fresh parsley, optional

1. Place chicken in an 6- or 8-qt. electric pressure cooker. Combine the green peppers, tomatoes, tomato paste, onion, broth, wine, garlic, salt and pepper; pour over chicken. Lock lid; close pressure-release valve. Adjust to pressure-cook on high for 10 minutes. Quick-release pressure. A thermometer inserted in chicken should read at least 170°.

2. Remove chicken to a platter; keep warm. In a small bowl, mix cornstarch and water until smooth; stir into broth mixture. Select saute setting and adjust for low heat. Simmer, stirring constantly, until thickened, 1-2 minutes.

3 oz. cooked chicken with about ½ cup sauce: 206 cal., 8g fat (2g sat. fat), 76mg chol., 353mg sod., 8g carb. (3g sugars, 2g fiber), 23g pro. **Diabetic exchanges:** 3 lean meat, 1 vegetable.

PRESSURE-COOKER GARDEN CHICKEN CACCIATORE

SLOW-COOKER CARIBBEAN MOO SHU CHICKEN

A tropical twist on a takeout favorite, this slow-cooker creation is simple, satisfying and destined to become a new favorite of your family!
—Shannon Kohn, Simpsonville, SC

PREP: 10 min. • **COOK:** 3 hours
MAKES: 8 servings

- 6 boneless skinless chicken breast halves (about 6 oz. each)
- 1½ cups chopped onions (about 2 medium)
- 1 cup chopped sweet red pepper
- ⅔ cup chopped dried pineapple
- ½ cup chopped dried mango
- 1 can (14½ oz.) fire-roasted diced tomatoes, drained
- ⅔ cup hoisin sauce
- 3 Tbsp. hot pepper sauce
- 16 flour tortillas (6 in.), warmed
- 4 cups coleslaw mix
- ½ cup chopped dry roasted peanuts

1. In a 4- or 5-qt. slow cooker, combine first 5 ingredients. In a small bowl, stir together tomatoes, hoisin sauce and hot pepper sauce. Pour tomato mixture over chicken mixture. Cook, covered, on low until the chicken is tender, 3-4 hours. Remove the meat. When cool enough to handle, shred with 2 forks; return meat to slow cooker. Heat through.
2. To serve, divide mixture evenly among tortillas. Top with coleslaw and peanuts.
1 serving: 552 cal., 15g fat (4g sat. fat), 71mg chol., 1122mg sod., 66g carb. (24g sugars, 7g fiber), 35g pro.

TEST KITCHEN TIP
Try serving the chicken over steamed jasmine or basmati rice.

MOROCCAN APRICOT CHICKEN

MOROCCAN APRICOT CHICKEN

Chili sauce, apricots and Moroccan seasoning create an incredible sauce for slow-cooked chicken thighs. Traditional Moroccan apricot chicken typically includes chili pepper paste, but I use chili sauce in my version. Serve alone or with couscous for a heartier meal.
—Arlene Erlbach, Morton Grove, IL

PREP: 25 min. • **COOK:** 4¼ hours
MAKES: 6 servings

- 1 tsp. olive oil
- ½ cup slivered almonds
- 6 bone-in chicken thighs (about 2¼ lbs.)
- ¾ cup chili sauce
- ½ cup apricot preserves
- ½ cup dried apricots, quartered
- 4 tsp. Moroccan seasoning (ras el hanout)
- 1 Tbsp. vanilla extract
- 1½ tsp. garlic powder
- 1 can (15 oz.) garbanzo beans or chickpeas, rinsed and drained
- ¼ cup orange juice
  Chopped fresh parsley, optional

1. In a large skillet, heat oil over medium heat. Add almonds; cook and stir until lightly browned, 2-3 minutes. Remove with a slotted spoon; drain on paper towels. In the same skillet, brown the chicken on both sides. Remove from heat. Transfer chicken to a 4- or 5-qt. slow cooker. Stir chili sauce, preserves, apricots, Moroccan seasoning, vanilla and garlic powder into drippings. Pour over chicken.
2. Cook mixture, covered, on low until a thermometer inserted in chicken reads 170°-175°, 4-4½ hours. Stir in garbanzo beans and orange juice. Cook, covered, on low until heated through, 15-30 minutes longer. Serve with almonds. If desired, sprinkle with parsley.
1 chicken thigh with ¾ cup chickpea mixture: 482 cal., 21g fat (4g sat. fat), 81mg chol., 633mg sod., 47g carb. (27g sugars, 5g fiber), 28g pro.

SWEET & SPICY PINEAPPLE CHICKEN SANDWICHES

My kids often ask for chicken sloppy joes, and this version has a bonus of sweet pineapple. It is a perfect recipe to double for a potluck. Try topping the sandwiches with smoked Gouda cheese.
—*Nancy Heishman, Las Vegas, NV*

PREP: 15 min. • **COOK:** 2¾ hours
MAKES: 8 servings

- 2½ lbs. boneless skinless chicken breasts
- 1 bottle (18 oz.) sweet and spicy barbecue sauce, divided
- 2 Tbsp. honey mustard
- 1 can (8 oz.) unsweetened crushed pineapple, undrained
- 8 hamburger buns, split and toasted Optional: Bibb lettuce leaves and thinly sliced red onion

1. Place chicken breasts in a 4-qt. slow cooker. Combine ¼ cup barbecue sauce and mustard; pour over chicken. Cover and cook on low 2½-3 hours or until chicken is tender.
2. Remove chicken; discard liquid. Shred chicken with 2 forks; return to slow cooker. Add crushed pineapple and remaining barbecue sauce; cover and cook on high for 15 minutes.
3. Serve on toasted buns, with lettuce and onion if desired.
Freeze option: Place shredded chicken in freezer containers. Cool and freeze. To use, partially thaw in refrigerator overnight. Heat through in a covered saucepan, stirring gently; add broth if necessary.
1 sandwich: 415 cal., 6g fat (1g sat. fat), 78mg chol., 973mg sod., 56g carb. (30g sugars, 2g fiber), 34g pro.

SLOW & EASY BARBECUED CHICKEN

I rely on this yummy recipe often during the summer and fall when I know I'm going to be out working in the yard all day. I just pair it with a side vegetable and salad, and supper is served!
—*Dreama Hughes, London, KY*

PREP: 20 min. • **COOK:** 3 hours
MAKES: 4 servings

- ¼ cup water
- 3 Tbsp. brown sugar
- 3 Tbsp. white vinegar
- 3 Tbsp. ketchup
- 2 Tbsp. butter
- 2 Tbsp. Worcestershire sauce
- 1 Tbsp. lemon juice
- 1 tsp. salt
- 1 tsp. paprika
- 1 tsp. ground mustard
- ½ tsp. cayenne pepper
- 1 broiler/fryer chicken (3 lbs.), cut up and skin removed
- 4 tsp. cornstarch
- 1 Tbsp. cold water

1. In a small saucepan, combine the first 11 ingredients. Bring to a boil. Reduce heat; simmer, uncovered, for 5 minutes. Remove from the heat.
2. Place the chicken in a 3-qt. slow cooker. Top with sauce. Cover and cook on low for 3-4 hours or until chicken juices run clear.
3. Remove chicken to a serving platter; keep warm. Skim the fat from cooking juices; transfer to a small saucepan. Bring the liquid to a boil. Combine cornstarch and water until smooth. Gradually stir into the pan. Bring to a boil; cook and stir for 2 minutes or until thickened. Spoon some of the sauce over chicken and serve the remaining sauce on the side.
1 serving: 319 cal., 13g fat (6g sat. fat), 107mg chol., 947mg sod., 18g carb. (11g sugars, 0 fiber), 31g pro.

SWEET & SPICY PINEAPPLE CHICKEN SANDWICHES

AIR-FRYER CRISPY CHICKEN WINGS

You can't go wrong with air-fryer chicken
wings. Our spice rub has a nice kick from
the cayenne seasoning.
—Taste of Home *Test Kitchen*

- -

PREP: 15 min. • **COOK:** 20 min. /batch
MAKES: 2 dozen

- 2 tsp. garlic powder
- 1 tsp. garlic salt
- 1 tsp. each ground mustard,
  ginger and nutmeg
- ½ tsp. pepper
- ½ tsp. ground allspice
- ½ tsp. baking soda
- ½ tsp. cayenne pepper
- 12 whole chicken wings (2½ lbs.)
  Optional: Ranch salad dressing,
  Buffalo sauce or barbecue sauce

1. Preheat air fryer to 300°. In a large
bowl, combine the garlic powder, garlic
salt, mustard, ginger, nutmeg, pepper,
allspice, baking soda and cayenne.
2. Cut chicken wings into 3 sections;
discard wing tip sections. Add to bowl
with spices and stir to coat. In batches,
arrange wings in a single layer on tray
in a greased air-fryer basket. Cook
15 minutes. Increase temperature
to 400°; cook until chicken juices run
clear and wings are golden brown,
20-25 minutes. Repeat with remaining
wings. Serve hot with sauce if desired.
1 piece: 54 cal., 4g fat (1g sat. fat), 15mg
chol., 102mg sod., 0 carb. (0 sugars,
0 fiber), 5g pro.

TEST KITCHEN TIP

Garam masala is a good substitute
for allspice in savory recipes.
Or use a dash of nutmeg (and
cinnamon, if you like it).

**AIR-FRYER
CRISPY
CHICKEN WINGS**

PRESSURE-COOKER SHREDDED CHICKEN GYROS

Our family has no links of any kind to Greece, but we always have such a marvelous time at the annual Salt Lake City Greek Festival. One of my favorite parts is all the awesome food. This meal is a good way to mix up our menu, and my kids are big fans.
—*Camille Beckstrand, Layton, UT*

TAKES: 30 min • **MAKES:** 8 servings

- 2 medium onions, chopped
- 6 garlic cloves, minced
- 1 tsp. lemon-pepper seasoning
- 1 tsp. dried oregano
- ½ tsp. ground allspice
- ½ cup lemon juice
- ¼ cup red wine vinegar
- 2 Tbsp. olive oil
- 2 lbs. boneless skinless chicken breasts
- 8 whole pita breads

Toppings: Tzatziki sauce, torn romaine and sliced tomato, cucumber and onion

1. In a 6-qt. electric pressure cooker, combine the first 8 ingredients; add chicken. Lock lid; close pressure-release valve. Adjust to pressure-cook on high for 6 minutes. Quick-release pressure. A thermometer inserted in chicken should read at least 165°.

2. Remove chicken; shred with 2 forks. Return to pressure cooker. Using tongs, place chicken mixture on pita breads. Serve with toppings.

Freeze option: Freeze cooled meat mixture and juices in freezer containers. To use, partially thaw in refrigerator overnight. Heat through in a saucepan, stirring occasionally; add water if necessary.

1 gyro: 335 cal., 7g fat (1g sat. fat), 63mg chol., 418mg sod., 38g carb. (2g sugars, 2g fiber), 29g pro. **Diabetic exchanges:** 3 lean meat, 2½ starch, ½ fat.

PRESSURE-COOKER ROAST CHICKEN

PRESSURE-COOKER SHREDDED CHICKEN GYROS

PRESSURE-COOKER ROAST CHICKEN

We love rotisserie chicken and now with an Instant Pot I can have it ready to eat in an hour or so. I combined several recipes to come up with this one— it's our favorite. If you are new to the Instant Pot this is a great recipe to begin with as it is so easy.
—*Joan Hallford, North Richland Hills, TX*

PREP: 10 min. • **COOK:** 30 min. + releasing
MAKES: 6 servings

- 2 Tbsp. dried thyme
- 2 Tbsp. dried rosemary, crushed
- 2 Tbsp. rubbed sage
- 1 Tbsp. kosher salt
- 1 Tbsp. pepper
- 1 small lemon, quartered, optional
- 1 small onion, quartered, optional
- 3 garlic cloves, smashed, optional
- 1 broiler/fryer chicken (3 to 4 lbs.)
- 2 Tbsp. olive oil, divided
- 1 cup chicken broth or water

1. In a small bowl, combine the first 5 ingredients. If desired, insert lemon, onion and garlic into the cavity of the chicken. Brush with 1 Tbsp. oil and sprinkle with herb mixture.
2. Select the saute setting on a 6-qt. electric pressure cooker. Adjust for medium heat; add the remaining 1 Tbsp. oil. When oil is hot, sear chicken, breast side down, until browned, 4-5 minutes. Press cancel; remove chicken. Place trivet insert and broth in pressure cooker. Place chicken on top of trivet. Lock lid; close pressure-release valve. Adjust to pressure-cook on high for 25 minutes. Let pressure release naturally.
5 oz. cooked chicken: 345 cal., 22g fat (5g sat. fat), 104mg chol., 1051mg sod., 3g carb. (0 sugars, 1g fiber), 33g pro.

🪷 GENERAL TSO'S CHICKEN SANDWICH WITH BROCCOLI SLAW

I turned a classic takeout dinner into a sandwich that's easy to make at home. The air fryer keeps it lighter but still crunchy, and the recipe can be prepped in 30 minutes, which is a must for our active family. We like spicy foods, so this sauce has a good amount of heat.
—*Julie Peterson, Crofton, MD*

PREP: 30 min. • **COOK:** 10 min./batch
MAKES: 4 servings

- ½ cup reduced-fat mayonnaise
- 2 Tbsp. honey
- 1 Tbsp. rice vinegar
- 2 tsp. hoisin sauce
- 3 cups broccoli coleslaw mix
- ½ cup sliced almonds
- 1 lb. boneless skinless chicken thighs, cut into ½-in. strips
- 4 Tbsp. cornstarch
- ½ tsp. salt
- ¼ tsp. pepper

SAUCE
- ¼ cup hoisin sauce
- 3 Tbsp. reduced-sodium soy sauce
- 3 Tbsp. honey
- 1 Tbsp. minced fresh gingerroot
- 2 garlic cloves, minced
- ½ to 1 tsp. crushed red pepper flakes
  Sesame seeds
- 4 brioche hamburger buns, split

1. In a large bowl, combine mayonnaise, honey, vinegar and hoisin sauce. Stir in coleslaw mix and almonds; refrigerate until serving.
2. Preheat air fryer to 400°. Toss the chicken with cornstarch, salt and pepper. In batches, arrange chicken in a single layer on greased tray in air-fryer basket. Cook until lightly browned and chicken is no longer pink, 4-5 minutes on each side.
3. Meanwhile, in a small saucepan, combine hoisin sauce, soy sauce, honey, ginger, garlic and pepper flakes; bring to a boil. Reduce heat; simmer, uncovered, until sauce thickens, about 5 minutes. Add cooked chicken; toss to coat.
4. Spoon chicken on bun bottoms; top with coleslaw mix and sprinkle with sesame seeds. Replace tops.

1 sandwich: 678 cal., 29g fat (5g sat. fat), 117mg chol., 1587mg sod., 75g carb. (37g sugars, 6g fiber), 32g pro.

GENERAL TSO'S CHICKEN SANDWICH WITH BROCCOLI SLAW

WHY YOU'LL LOVE IT...

"I love the use of the air fryer for this recipe. Made for an easy and fun weeknight meal. It was a hit with the family. If you can't find broccoli coleslaw mix, the cabbage coleslaw mix tastes great with these flavors as well."
—ANGEL182009, TASTEOFHOME.COM

🍎 🗑 PRESSURE-COOKER ASIAN WRAPS

This recipe is similar to other Asian wraps but it's packed with even more deliciously healthy flavor. Instead of ordering Chinese, why not try making these yourself?
—*Melissa Hansen, Ellison Bay, WI*

- -

PREP: 30 min. • **COOK:** 10 min.
MAKES: 1 dozen

- 2 lbs. boneless skinless chicken breast halves
- ¼ cup reduced-sodium soy sauce
- 6 Tbsp. water, divided
- ¼ cup ketchup
- ¼ cup honey
- 2 Tbsp. minced fresh gingerroot
- 2 Tbsp. sesame oil
- 1 small onion, finely chopped
- 2 Tbsp. cornstarch
- 12 spring roll wrappers or rice papers (8 in.)
- 3 cups broccoli coleslaw mix
- ¾ cup crispy chow mein noodles

1. Place the chicken in a 6-qt. electric pressure cooker. In a small bowl, whisk soy sauce, ¼ cup water, ketchup, honey, ginger and oil; stir in onion. Pour over the chicken. Lock lid; close pressure-release valve. Adjust to pressure-cook on high for 7 minutes. Quick-release pressure. A thermometer inserted in chicken should read at least 165°. Remove the chicken; shred with 2 forks. Set aside.

2. Mix the cornstarch and remaining 2 Tbsp. water until smooth; gradually stir into pressure cooker. Select saute setting and adjust for low heat. Simmer, stirring constantly 1-2 minutes, or until thickened. Remove sauce from pressure cooker. Toss chicken with ¾ cup sauce; reserve remaining sauce for serving.

3. Fill a large shallow dish partway with water. Dip a spring roll wrapper into the water just until pliable, about 45 seconds (do not soften completely); allow excess water to drip off.

4. Place wrapper on a flat surface. Layer ¼ cup coleslaw, ⅓ cup chicken mixture and 1 Tbsp. noodles across the bottom third of wrapper. Fold in both sides of wrapper; fold bottom over filling, then roll up tightly. Place on a serving plate, seam side down. Repeat with remaining ingredients. Serve with reserved sauce.

1 wrap: 195 cal., 5g fat (1g sat. fat), 42mg chol., 337mg sod., 21g carb. (8g sugars, 1g fiber), 17g pro. **Diabetic exchanges:** 2 lean meat, 1½ starch, ½ fat.

PRESSURE-COOKER
ASIAN WRAPS

INGREDIENT CLOSE-UP

Spring Roll Wrappers

Thin and delicate spring roll wrappers are like super thin crepes made from rice flour and tapioca flour. To soften wrappers, dip them briefly in water and work with one at a time. The spring rolls may be made in advance: just cover with damp paper towels to keep them moist and refrigerate in a covered container. Spring rolls (made with the season's first spring vegetables) are a classic dish for Chinese New Year.

🌷 SOUTHERN-STYLE CHICKEN

I call this America's best-loved air-fryer chicken. The secret is in the breading, which makes the chicken super moist, flavorful, herby and golden brown.
—*Elaina Morgan, Rickman, TN*

- -

PREP: 15 min. • **COOK:** 20 min./batch
MAKES: 6 servings

- 2   cups crushed Ritz crackers (about 50)
- 1   Tbsp. minced fresh parsley
- 1   tsp. garlic salt
- 1   tsp. paprika
- ½   tsp. pepper
- ¼   tsp. ground cumin
- ¼   tsp. rubbed sage
- 1   large egg, beaten
- 1   broiler/fryer chicken (3 to 4 lbs.), cut up
     Cooking spray

1. Preheat air fryer to 375°. In a shallow bowl, mix the first 7 ingredients. Place egg in a separate shallow bowl. Dip the chicken in egg, then in cracker mixture, patting to help the coating adhere. In batches, place chicken in a single layer on greased tray in air-fryer basket; spritz with cooking spray.
2. Cook 10 minutes. Turn chicken and spritz with cooking spray. Cook until chicken is golden brown and juices run clear, 10-20 minutes longer.
5 oz. cooked chicken: 410 cal., 23g fat (6g sat. fat), 135mg chol., 460mg sod., 13g carb. (2g sugars, 1g fiber), 36g pro.

TEST KITCHEN TIP

In our testing, we have found cook times vary dramatically among brands of air fryers. So, we provide a wider than normal range of suggested cook times.

🍅🍲 SLOW-COOKER BUFFALO CHICKEN LASAGNA

When I make this tasty chicken lasagna at home, I use a whole bottle of Buffalo wing sauce because my family likes it nice and spicy. Increase the pasta sauce and use less wing sauce if you prefer.
—*Heidi Pepin, Sykesville, MD*

- -

PREP: 25 min. • **COOK:** 4 hours + standing
MAKES: 8 servings

- 1½ lbs. ground chicken
- 1   Tbsp. olive oil
- 1   bottle (12 oz.) Buffalo wing sauce
- 1½ cups meatless spaghetti sauce
- 1   carton (15 oz.) ricotta cheese
- 2   cups shredded part-skim mozzarella cheese
- 9   no-cook lasagna noodles
- 2   medium sweet red peppers, chopped
- ½   cup crumbled blue cheese or feta cheese
     Optional: Chopped celery and additional crumbled blue cheese

1. In a Dutch oven, cook chicken in oil over medium heat until no longer pink; drain. Stir in wing sauce and spaghetti sauce. In a small bowl, mix ricotta and mozzarella cheeses.
2. Spread 1 cup sauce onto the bottom of an oval 6-qt. slow cooker. Layer with 3 noodles (breaking the noodles to fit), 1 cup sauce, a third of the peppers and a third of the cheese mixture. Repeat layers twice. Top with remaining sauce; sprinkle with blue cheese.
3. Cover and cook on low for 4-5 hours or until noodles are tender. Let stand for 15 minutes before serving. Top the lasagna with celery and additional blue cheese if desired.
1 piece: 445 cal., 23g fat (11g sat. fat), 104mg chol., 1996mg sod., 28g carb. (9g sugars, 3g fiber), 33g pro.

SOUTHERN-STYLE CHICKEN

⏱ 🍎 🍲 PRESSURE-COOKER MUSHROOM CHICKEN & PEAS

Some amazingly fresh mushrooms I found at our local farmers market inspired this recipe. When you start with the best ingredients, you can't go wrong.
—*Jenn Tidwell, Fair Oaks, CA*

TAKES: 20 min. • **MAKES:** 4 servings

- 4 boneless skinless chicken breast halves (6 oz. each)
- 1 envelope onion mushroom soup mix
- ½ lb. baby portobello mushrooms, sliced
- 1 medium onion, chopped
- ¾ cup water
- 4 garlic cloves, minced
- 2 cups frozen peas, thawed

1. Place chicken in a 6-qt. electric pressure cooker. Sprinkle with soup mix, pressing to help the seasonings adhere. Add mushrooms, onion, water and garlic. Lock lid; close pressure-release valve. Adjust to pressure-cook on high for 6 minutes.
2. Quick-release the pressure. A thermometer inserted in chicken should read at least 165°. Select the saute setting and adjust for low heat. Add the peas; simmer, uncovered, until tender, 3-5 minutes, stirring the mixture occasionally.

1 chicken breast half with ¾ cup vegetable mixture: 282 cal., 5g fat (1g sat. fat), 94mg chol., 558mg sod., 18g carb. (6g sugars, 4g fiber), 41g pro. **Diabetic exchanges:** 5 lean meat, 1 starch, 1 vegetable.

PRESSURE-COOKER CREAMY PESTO CHICKEN STEW

⏱ 🍲 PRESSURE-COOKER CREAMY PESTO CHICKEN STEW

I am a fan of thick stews and soups, and this dish is perfect! It's similar to a creamy broccoli soup. I replaced the rice with riced cauliflower for my low-carb-loving family.
—*Kim Banick, Turner, OR*

TAKES: 20 min. **MAKES:** 6 servings

- 1 jar (15 oz.) Alfredo sauce with mushrooms
- ½ cup prepared pesto
- 1 Tbsp. canola oil
- 1½ lbs. boneless skinless chicken breasts, cubed
- ½ tsp. salt
- ½ tsp. pepper
- ½ cup chopped onion
- 8 oz. whole cremini mushrooms, quartered
- 1 pkg. (10 oz.) frozen broccoli spears
- 1 pkg. (10 oz.) frozen riced cauliflower
  Optional: Shredded Parmesan and fresh basil leaves

1. Combine Alfredo sauce and pesto in a medium-sized bowl. Set aside.
2. Select saute setting on a 6-qt. electric pressure cooker and adjust for medium heat; add the oil. When oil is hot, add chicken; season with salt and pepper. Cook and stir until lightly browned, 3-4 minutes. Add onion; cook and stir until tender, 2-3 minutes. Press cancel.
3. Layer the mushrooms, broccoli, cauliflower and reserved sauce in pressure cooker. Lock lid; close the pressure-release valve. Adjust to pressure-cook on high for 10 minutes. Let pressure release naturally for 3 minutes, then quick-release any remaining pressure.
4. Stir mixture to combine. If desired, top with Parmesan and basil leaves.

1 cup: 530 cal., 31g fat (9g sat. fat), 138mg chol., 1527mg sod., 19g carb. (8g sugars, 5g fiber), 44g pro.

🍎🍲 SLOW-COOKER BUTTER CHICKEN

I spent several years in Malaysia eating a variety of Middle Eastern and Southeast Asian food—and this was one of my favorites! There are many versions of butter chicken, but this is similar to the Middle Eastern version I had.
—*Shannon Copley, Upper Arlington, OH*

PREP: 10 min. • **COOK:** 3 hours
MAKES: 8 servings

- 2 Tbsp. butter
- 1 medium onion, chopped
- 4 garlic cloves, peeled, thinly sliced
- 2 tsp. garam masala
- 2 tsp. red curry powder
- ½ tsp. chili powder
- 1 tsp. ground ginger
- 2 Tbsp. whole wheat flour
- 1 Tbsp. olive oil
- 1 can (14 oz.) coconut milk
- ¼ cup tomato paste
- 1 tsp. salt
- ¼ tsp. pepper
- 3 lbs. boneless skinless chicken breasts, cut into 1-in. pieces
   Hot cooked rice
   Optional: Fresh cilantro leaves and naan bread

1. Heat large saucepan over medium-high heat; add the butter and onion. Cook and stir until onions are tender, 2-3 minutes. Add garlic, cook until fragrant, about 1 minute. Add garam marsala, curry powder, chili powder and ginger; cook and stir 1 minute longer. Add the flour. Drizzle in olive oil until a paste
is formed. Whisk in coconut milk and tomato paste; cook until combined and slightly thickened, 1-2 minutes. Season with salt and pepper.
2. Using an immersion blender, carefully puree spice mixture. Transfer mixture into a 5-qt. slow cooker. Add chicken; gently stir to combine.
3. Cover and cook on low until chicken is no longer pink, 3-4 hours. Serve with rice. If desired, sprinkle with cilantro and serve with naan bread.
1 cup: 242 cal., 9g fat (3g sat. fat), 102mg chol., 407mg sod., 4g carb. (1g sugars, 1g fiber), 35g pro. **Diabetic exchanges:** 5 lean meat, 1 fat.

🍲 CHICKEN & ARTICHOKE LASAGNA

My family loves lasagna and I love the slow cooker. I wanted to try something a little different from the classic lasagna we usually make. This recipe not only tastes incredible, it's hearty and convenient, too.
—*Kelly Silvers, Edmond, OK*

PREP: 30 min. • **COOK:** 3 hours + standing
MAKES: 8 servings

- 2 cans (14 oz. each) water-packed artichoke hearts, drained and finely chopped
- 1 cup shredded Parmesan cheese, divided
- ¼ cup loosely packed basil leaves, finely chopped
- 3 garlic cloves, minced, divided
- 1 lb. ground chicken
- 1 Tbsp. canola oil
- 1 cup finely chopped onion
- ¾ tsp. salt
- ½ tsp. pepper
- ½ cup white wine
- 1 cup half-and-half cream
- 1 pkg. (8 oz.) cream cheese, softened
- 1 cup shredded Monterey Jack cheese
- 1 large egg
- 1½ cups 2% cottage cheese
- 9 no-cook lasagna noodles
- 2 cups shredded part-skim mozzarella cheese
   Optional: Prepared pesto and additional basil

1. Fold two 18-in. square pieces of foil into thirds. Crisscross strips and place strips on bottom and up the sides of a 6-qt. slow cooker. Coat the strips with cooking spray. Combine artichoke hearts, ½ cup Parmesan cheese, basil and 2 garlic cloves.
2. In a large skillet, crumble chicken over medium heat 6-8 minutes or until no longer pink; drain. Set chicken aside. Add oil and onion; cook and stir just until tender, 6-8 minutes. Add salt, pepper and the remaining garlic; cook 1 minute longer. Stir in the wine. Bring to a boil; cook until the liquid is reduced by half, 4-5 minutes. Stir in the cream, cream cheese and Monterey Jack cheese. Return chicken to the pan. In a bowl, combine the egg, cottage cheese and the remaining Parmesan.
3. Spread ¾ cup meat mixture into slow cooker. Layer with 3 noodles (breaking noodles as necessary to fit), ¾ cup meat mixture, ½ cup cottage cheese mixture, 1 cup artichoke mixture and ½ cup mozzarella cheese. Repeat layers twice; top with remaining mozzarella cheese. Cook, covered, on low until noodles are tender, 3-4 hours. Remove slow cooker insert and let stand 30 minutes. If desired, serve with pesto and sprinkle with additional basil.
1 piece: 588 cal., 34g fat (18g sat. fat), 144mg chol., 1187mg sod., 31g carb. (6g sugars, 1g fiber), 36g pro.

CHICKEN &
ARTICHOKE
LASAGNA

PRESSURE-COOKER BLACK BEAN CHICKEN NACHOS

One of my favorite local restaurants, Zeppelins, has the best chicken nachos. Their famous dish inspired me to create my own but with the added convenience of using the pressure cooker. I recommend fresh cilantro because it's economical and makes the dish pop with flavor.
—*Natalie Hess, Pennsville, NJ*

TAKES: 18 min. • **MAKES:** 8 servings

- 1½ lbs. boneless skinless chicken breasts
- 2 jars (16 oz. each) black bean and corn salsa
- 1 medium green pepper, chopped
- 1 medium sweet red pepper, chopped
- 1 pkg. (12 oz.) tortilla chips
- 2 cups shredded Mexican cheese blend
  Optional toppings: Minced fresh cilantro, pickled jalapeno slices and sour cream

1. Place chicken, salsa and peppers in a 6-qt. electric pressure cooker. Lock lid; close pressure-release valve. Adjust to pressure-cook on high for 7 minutes. Quick-release pressure. A thermometer inserted in the chicken should read at least 165°.
2. Remove chicken; shred with 2 forks. Return to the pressure cooker. Using a slotted spoon, serve chicken over chips; sprinkle with cheese and, if desired, cilantro. Add toppings if desired.
1 serving: 280 cal., 11g fat (5g sat. fat), 72mg chol., 708mg sod., 20g carb. (5g sugars, 8g fiber), 27g pro.

PRESSURE-COOKER
BLACK BEAN
CHICKEN NACHOS

PRESSURE-COOKER LEMON CHICKEN WITH BASIL

No matter when I eat it, this tangy chicken dish reminds me of summer meals with friends and family. The recipe produces a lot of lovely sauce; serve it as is or spoon it over some lightly herbed couscous.
—*Deborah Posey, Virginia Beach, VA*

TAKES: 20 min. • **MAKES:** 4 servings

- 4 boneless skinless chicken breast halves (6 oz. each)
- 2 medium lemons
- 1 bunch fresh basil leaves (¾ oz.)
- 2 cups chicken stock

1. Place chicken in a 6-qt. electric pressure cooker. Finely grate enough zest from lemons to measure 4 tsp. Cut lemons in half; squeeze juice. Add zest and juice to pressure cooker.
2. Tear basil leaves directly into pressure cooker; add chicken stock. Lock lid; close pressure-release valve. Adjust to pressure-cook on high for 6 minutes. Quick-release pressure. A thermometer inserted in chicken should read at least 165°. When cool enough to handle, shred meat with 2 forks; return to pressure cooker. If desired, stir in additional lemon zest and chopped basil. Serve with a slotted spoon.
Freeze option: Place chicken and cooking liquid in freezer containers. Cool and freeze. To use, partially thaw in refrigerator overnight. Microwave, covered, on high in a microwave-safe dish until heated through, stirring gently.
5 oz. cooked chicken: 200 cal., 4g fat (1g sat. fat), 94mg chol., 337mg sod., 3g carb. (1g sugars, 0 fiber), 37g pro.
Diabetic exchanges: 5 lean meat.

🍎 🍲 SLOW-COOKED CHICKEN A LA KING

When I know I'll be having a busy day with little time to prepare a meal, I use my slow cooker to make chicken a la king. It smells so good while it's cooking.
—Eleanor Mielke, Snohomish, WA

PREP: 10 min. • **COOK:** 7½ hours
MAKES: 6 servings

- 1 can (10¾ oz.) reduced-fat reduced-sodium condensed cream of chicken soup, undiluted
- 3 Tbsp. all-purpose flour
- ¼ tsp. pepper
  Dash cayenne pepper
- 1 lb. boneless skinless chicken breasts, cubed
- 1 celery rib, chopped
- ½ cup chopped green pepper
- ¼ cup chopped onion
- 1 pkg. (10 oz.) frozen peas, thawed
- 2 Tbsp. diced pimientos, drained
  Hot cooked rice

1. In a 3-qt. slow cooker, combine soup, flour, pepper and cayenne until smooth. Stir in the chicken, celery, green pepper and onion.

2. Cover and cook on low for 7-8 hours or until meat is no longer pink. Stir in peas and pimientos. Cook 30 minutes longer or until heated through. Serve with rice.

1 cup chicken mixture: 174 cal., 3g fat (1g sat. fat), 44mg chol., 268mg sod., 16g carb. (6g sugars, 3g fiber), 19g pro. **Diabetic exchanges:** 2 lean meat, 1 starch.

WHY YOU'LL LOVE IT...

"Just like Mom's, only easier because of the slow cooker."
BJSILVO, TASTEOFHOME.COM

PRESSURE-COOKER
SPRING-THYME
CHICKEN STEW

🍎 🍲 PRESSURE-COOKER SPRING-THYME CHICKEN STEW

During a long winter (and spring), we were in need of something warm, comforting and bright. This stew always reminds me of the days Mom would make her chicken soup for me.
—Amy Chase, Vanderhoof, BC

PREP: 25 min. • **COOK:** 10 min.
MAKES: 4 servings

- 1 lb. small red potatoes, halved
- 1 large onion, finely chopped
- ¾ cup shredded carrots
- 6 garlic cloves, minced
- 2 tsp. grated lemon zest
- 2 tsp. dried thyme
- ½ tsp. salt
- ¼ tsp. pepper
- 1½ lbs. boneless skinless chicken thighs, cut into 1-in. pieces
- 2 cups reduced-sodium chicken broth, divided
- 2 bay leaves
- 3 Tbsp. all-purpose flour
- 2 Tbsp. minced fresh parsley

1. Place potatoes, onion and carrots in a 6-qt. electric pressure cooker. Top with garlic, lemon zest, thyme, salt and pepper. Place chicken over top. Add 1¾ cups broth and bay leaves.

2. Lock lid; close pressure-release valve. Adjust to pressure-cook on high for 5 minutes. Quick-release pressure. A thermometer inserted in chicken should read at least 170°.

3. Remove chicken; keep warm. Discard bay leaves. In a small bowl, mix the flour and remaining ¼ cup broth until smooth; stir into pressure cooker. Select saute setting and adjust for low heat. Simmer, stirring constantly, until slightly thickened, 1-2 minutes. Return chicken to pressure cooker; heat through. Sprinkle servings with parsley.

1 serving: 389 cal., 13g fat (3g sat. fat), 113mg chol., 699mg sod., 31g carb. (4g sugars, 4g fiber), 37g pro. **Diabetic exchanges:** 5 lean meat, 2 vegetable, 1½ starch.

🍲 SLOW-COOKER CHICKEN PARMESAN

I love to make this satisfying dish—it's easy and elegant, and the slow cooker minimizes my time in the kitchen. I often make it during football season. For game days, I skip the pasta and serve the chicken on submarine rolls with a bit of the sauce and some chopped lettuce. You could also cut the chicken breasts in half and make sliders.
—Bonnie Hawkins, Elkhorn, WI

- -

PREP: 25 min. • **COOK:** 4 hours 10 min.
MAKES: 4 servings

- ½ cup seasoned bread crumbs
- ½ cup grated Parmesan cheese
- ½ tsp. Italian seasoning
- ½ tsp. pepper
- ¼ tsp. salt
- 1 large egg, lightly beaten
- 1 Tbsp. water
- 4 (6 oz. each) boneless skinless chicken breast halves
- 1 jar (24 oz.) marinara sauce
- 4 slices part-skim mozzarella cheese
  Hot cooked pasta, optional

1. In a shallow bowl, combine bread crumbs, Parmesan cheese, Italian seasoning, pepper and salt. In another bowl, combine egg and water. Dip the chicken in egg mixture, then in crumb mixture to coat both sides, patting to help coating adhere.

2. Transfer chicken to a 4- or 5-qt. slow cooker. Pour sauce over chicken. Cook, covered, on low for 4-6 hours or until a thermometer inserted in chicken reads 165°. Top with cheese, recover, and cook for 10-15 minutes, until cheese is melted. If desired, serve with pasta.

1 serving: 475 cal., 17g fat (7g sat. fat), 171mg chol., 1689mg sod., 27g carb. (11g sugars, 4g fiber), 50g pro.

SLOW-COOKER CHICKEN PARMESAN

WATCH US MAKE IT
Just hover your camera here.

PRESSURE-COOKER
CURRIED CHICKEN
MEATBALL WRAPS

🍎 🥘 PRESSURE-COOKER CURRIED CHICKEN MEATBALL WRAPS

My strategy to get picky kids to eat healthy: Let everyone make their dinner at the table. We love these easy meatball wraps topped with crunchy veggies and peanuts, sweet raisins and a creamy dollop of yogurt.
—*Jennifer Beckman, Falls Church, VA*

PREP: 35 min. • **COOK:** 10 min.
MAKES: 2 dozen

- 1 large egg, lightly beaten
- 1 small onion, finely chopped
- ½ cup Rice Krispies
- ¼ cup golden raisins
- ¼ cup minced fresh cilantro
- 2 tsp. curry powder
- ½ tsp. salt
- 1 lb. lean ground chicken
- 2 Tbsp. olive oil

SAUCE
- 1 cup plain yogurt
- ¼ cup minced fresh cilantro

WRAPS
- 24 small Bibb or Boston lettuce leaves
- 1 medium carrot, shredded
- ½ cup golden raisins
- ½ cup chopped salted peanuts

1. In a large bowl, combine the first 7 ingredients. Add chicken; mix lightly but thoroughly (mixture will be soft). With wet hands, shape mixture into 24 balls (about 1¼-in.). Select saute or browning setting on a 6-qt. electric pressure cooker. Adjust for medium heat; add oil. When oil is hot, brown meatballs in batches; remove and keep warm. Add 1 cup water to the pressure cooker. Cook 1 minute, stirring to loosen browned bits from pan. Press cancel.

2. Place trivet insert in pressure cooker. Place meatballs on trivet, overlapping if needed. Lock lid; close pressure-release valve. Adjust to pressure-cook on high for 7 minutes. Quick-release pressure.

3. In a small bowl, mix sauce ingredients. To serve, place 2 tsp. sauce and 1 meatball in each lettuce leaf; top with remaining ingredients. If desired, serve with additional minced cilantro.

1 wrap: 82 cal., 4g fat (1g sat. fat), 22mg chol., 88mg sod., 6g carb. (4g sugars, 1g fiber), 6g pro. **Diabetic exchanges:** 1 lean meat, ½ starch.

**BUFFALO CHICKEN
LASAGNA, PAGE 262**

CASSEROLES, POTPIES & OTHER OVEN GREATS

EASY CHICKEN
ENCHILADAS

EASY CHICKEN ENCHILADAS

This recipe is so quick and easy, and I always receive compliments. It quickly becomes a favorite of friends whenever I share a batch. Modify the spiciness with the intensity of the salsa and chiles to suit your taste.

—*Kristi Black, Harrison Township, MI*

PREP: 20 min. • **BAKE:** 25 min.
MAKES: 5 servings

- 1 can (10 oz.) enchilada sauce, divided
- 4 oz. cream cheese, cubed
- 1½ cups salsa
- 2 cups cubed cooked chicken
- 1 can (15 oz.) pinto beans, rinsed and drained
- 1 can (4 oz.) chopped green chiles
- 10 flour tortillas (6 in.)
- 1 cup shredded Mexican cheese blend
  Optional: Shredded lettuce, chopped tomato, sour cream and sliced ripe olives

1. Spoon ½ cup enchilada sauce into a greased 13x9-in. baking dish. In a large saucepan, cook and stir the cream cheese and salsa over medium heat until blended, 2-3 minutes. Stir in the chicken, beans and chiles.
2. Place about ⅓ cup chicken mixture down the center of each tortilla. Roll up and place seam side down over sauce. Top with remaining enchilada sauce; sprinkle with cheese.
3. Cover and bake at 350° until heated through, 25-30 minutes. If desired, serve with the lettuce, tomato, sour cream and sliced olives.
2 enchiladas: 468 cal., 13g fat (6g sat. fat), 75mg chol., 1394mg sod., 51g carb. (6g sugars, 8g fiber), 34g pro.

SEE HOW SIMPLE THESE ARE
Just hover your camera here.

HOT CHICKEN SALAD PIES

These tasty pies come together in a snap! They're perfect for when you have leftover chicken on hand and need to use it up.
—*Shirley Gudenschwager, Orchard, NE*

PREP: 20 min. • **BAKE:** 30 min.
MAKES: 2 pies (6 servings each)

  2 sheets refrigerated pie crust
  3 cups diced cooked chicken
  2 cups cooked long grain rice
  4 hard-boiled large eggs, chopped
  1 can (10¾ oz.) condensed cream of mushroom soup, undiluted
  1 cup mayonnaise
  1 medium onion, chopped
  ½ cup chopped celery
  ¼ cup lemon juice
  1 tsp. salt
  1½ cups crushed cornflakes
  ¼ cup butter, melted

1. Unroll crusts into 9-in. pie plates; flute edges. Refrigerate 30 minutes. Preheat oven to 400°. Line unpricked crust with a double thickness of foil. Fill with pie weights, dried beans or uncooked rice. Bake on a lower oven rack until edges are light golden brown, 10-15 minutes. Remove foil and weights; bake until bottom is golden brown, 3-6 minutes longer. Cool on a wire rack; reduce the heat to 350°.
2. In a large bowl, combine chicken, rice, eggs, soup, mayonnaise, onion, celery, lemon juice and salt. Spoon chicken mixture into crusts. Combine cornflakes and butter; sprinkle over tops. Bake on lowest oven rack until lightly browned, 20-25 minutes.
1 piece: 505 cal., 32g fat (10g sat. fat), 112mg chol., 771mg sod., 38g carb. (3g sugars, 1g fiber), 15g pro.

LEEK & HERB STUFFED CHICKEN

LEEK & HERB STUFFED CHICKEN

You're likely to find a lot of herb-stuffed chicken breast recipes out there, but this chicken leek recipe is unique. It makes great use of leeks, an aromatic that's uncommon on the dinner table, but easy to find.
—*Shirley Glaab, Hattiesburg, MS*

PREP: 30 min. • **BAKE:** 35 min.
MAKES: 4 servings

  3 medium leeks (white and light green portions only), cleaned and chopped
  1 Tbsp. olive oil
  ½ tsp. dried rosemary, crushed
  ½ tsp. dried thyme
  ¼ tsp. salt
  ¼ tsp. pepper
  4 boneless skinless chicken breast halves (6 oz. each)
PECAN CRUST
  ¼ cup finely chopped pecans
  ¼ cup dry bread crumbs
  ¼ tsp. dried rosemary, crushed
  ¼ tsp. dried thyme
  ½ tsp. salt
  ¼ tsp. pepper
  ¼ cup Dijon mustard
  1 Tbsp. olive oil

1. In a small skillet, saute leeks in oil until almost tender. Add the rosemary, thyme, salt and pepper; saute 1 minute longer. Remove from the heat; cool.
2. Flatten each chicken breast half to ¼-in. thickness; top with leek mixture. Roll up and secure with toothpicks.
3. In a small shallow bowl, combine the pecans, bread crumbs, rosemary, thyme, salt and pepper. Brush mustard over chicken, then coat with pecan mixture. Place seam side down in a greased 11x7-in. baking dish. Drizzle with oil.
4. Bake chicken, uncovered, at 375° for 35-40 minutes or until the chicken is no longer pink. Discard toothpicks.
1 chicken breast half: 333 cal., 15g fat (2g sat. fat), 73mg chol., 929mg sod., 16g carb. (3g sugars, 2g fiber), 29g pro.

ROAST CHICKEN BREASTS WITH PEPPERS

Garden-fresh peppers and onions smother seasoned chicken breasts in a dish that's a real winner with my family.
—*Melissa Galinat, Lakeland, FL*

TAKES: 30 min. • **MAKES:** 4 servings

- ¾ tsp. fennel seed, crushed
- ¾ tsp. salt, divided
- ½ tsp. pepper, divided
- ¼ tsp. garlic powder
- ¼ tsp. dried oregano
- 4 boneless skinless chicken breast halves (5 oz. each)
- 2 tsp. plus 1 Tbsp. olive oil, divided
- 1 large sweet red pepper, thinly sliced
- 1 medium sweet yellow pepper, thinly sliced
- 4 shallots, thinly sliced
- 1 cup chicken broth
- 1½ tsp. minced fresh rosemary
- 1 Tbsp. balsamic vinegar

1. In a large dry skillet, toast the fennel, ½ tsp. salt, ¼ tsp. pepper, garlic powder and oregano over medium heat for 1-2 minutes or until aromatic, stirring frequently. Cool slightly. Sprinkle over the chicken.

2. In the same skillet, heat 2 tsp. oil over medium-high heat. Brown the chicken, about 2 minutes on each side. Transfer to an ungreased 15x10x1-in. baking pan. Bake at 450° for 10-15 minutes or until a thermometer reads 170°.

3. Meanwhile, heat remaining oil in the same skillet. Add peppers and shallots; cook and stir over medium heat until crisp-tender.

4. Add the broth and rosemary, stirring to loosen browned bits from pan. Bring to a boil; cook for 4-6 minutes or until broth is almost evaporated. Stir in the vinegar and remaining salt and pepper. Serve with chicken.

1 chicken breast with ⅔ cup peppers: 267 cal., 9g fat (2g sat. fat), 80mg chol., 765mg sod., 14g carb. (6g sugars, 2g fiber), 31g pro. **Diabetic exchanges:** 4 lean meat, 1 vegetable, 1 fat.

EASY CHEDDAR CHICKEN POTPIE

My kids love chicken potpie, and I really like that this is so quick and easy to put together with frozen veggies and store-bought gravy. To make it even simpler, my friend and I decided to top it with a biscuit crust instead of homemade pastry. It's delicious!
—*Linda Drees, Palestine, TX*

PREP: 20 min. • **BAKE:** 25 min.
MAKES: 6 servings

- 1 pkg. (16 oz.) frozen vegetables for stew, thawed and coarsely chopped
- 1 jar (12 oz.) chicken gravy
- 2 cups shredded cheddar cheese
- 2 cups cubed cooked chicken
- 2 cups biscuit/baking mix
- 1 tsp. minced fresh or ¼ tsp. dried thyme
- 2 large eggs, room temperature
- ¼ cup 2% milk

1. Combine vegetables and gravy in a large saucepan. Bring to a boil. Reduce heat; stir in cheese and chicken. Cook and stir until cheese is melted. Pour mixture into a greased 2-qt. round or 11x7-in. baking dish.

2. Combine biscuit mix and thyme in a small bowl. In another bowl, whisk eggs and milk; stir into dry ingredients just until moistened. Drop by tablespoonfuls over chicken mixture; spread gently.

3. Bake, uncovered, at 375° until golden brown, 23-27 minutes. Let stand for 5 minutes before serving.

1 serving: 481 cal., 22g fat (10g sat. fat), 146mg chol., 977mg sod., 41g carb. (3g sugars, 2g fiber), 29g pro.

SALSA VERDE CHICKEN CASSEROLE

This is a rich and tasty combination of a number of Tex-Mex dishes blended into one packed, beautiful casserole. Best of all, it's ready in hardly any time!
—*Janet McCormick, Proctorville, OH*

TAKES: 30 min. • **MAKES:** 6 servings

- 2 cups shredded rotisserie chicken
- 1 cup sour cream
- 1½ cups salsa verde, divided
- 8 corn tortillas (6 in.)
- 2 cups chopped tomatoes
- ¼ cup minced fresh cilantro
- 2 cups shredded Monterey Jack cheese
  Optional toppings: Avocado slices, thinly sliced green onions or fresh cilantro leaves

1. In a small bowl, combine the chicken, sour cream and ¾ cup salsa. Spread ¼ cup salsa on the bottom of a greased 8-in. square baking dish.

2. Layer with half of the tortillas and chicken mixture; sprinkle with half the tomatoes, minced cilantro and half of the cheese. Repeat the layers with remaining tortillas, chicken mixture, tomatoes and cheese.

3. Bake, uncovered, at 400° until bubbly, 20-25 minutes. Serve with remaining salsa and, if desired, optional toppings.

1 serving: 400 cal., 23g fat (13g sat. fat), 102mg chol., 637mg sod., 22g carb. (5g sugars, 3g fiber), 26g pro.

TEST KITCHEN TIPS

- If substituting canned tomatoes for fresh, drain them well.
- Flour tortillas also work well.
- Leftovers make a hearty breakfast. Serve with a fried or poached egg.

GOLDEN CHICKEN POTPIE

GOLDEN CHICKEN POTPIE

The golden crust and creamy sauce make this veggie-packed pie a surefire hit. Mild and comforting, the family favorite has convenient freezer instructions for a night when there's no time for prep.
—Taste of Home *Test Kitchen*

- -

PREP: 20 min. • **BAKE:** 35 min.
MAKES: 2 potpies (6 servings each)

- 4 cups cubed cooked chicken
- 4 cups frozen cubed hash brown potatoes, thawed
- 1 pkg. (16 oz.) frozen mixed vegetables, thawed and drained
- 1 can (10½ oz.) condensed cream of chicken soup, undiluted
- 1 can (10½ oz.) condensed cream of onion soup, undiluted
- 1 cup whole milk
- 1 cup sour cream
- 2 Tbsp. all-purpose flour
- ½ tsp. salt
- ½ tsp. pepper
- ¼ tsp. garlic powder
- 2 sheets refrigerated pie crust

1. Preheat oven to 400°. Combine the first 11 ingredients. Divide between two 9-in. deep-dish pie plates.
2. Roll out crusts to fit top of each pie. Place over filling; trim, seal and flute edges. Cut slits in top. Bake until golden brown, 35-40 minutes.
Freeze option: Cover and freeze unbaked pies up to 3 months. To use, remove from freezer 30 minutes before baking (do not thaw). Preheat oven to 425°. Place pie on a baking sheet; cover edges loosely with foil. Bake 30 minutes. Reduce heat to 350°. Remove foil and bake until golden brown or until heated through and a thermometer inserted in center reads 165°, 50-55 minutes longer.
1 serving: 415 cal., 19g fat (8g sat. fat), 69mg chol., 706mg sod., 39g carb. (5g sugars, 3g fiber), 20g pro.

CHICKEN TAMALE BAKE

When I serve this Mexican-style casserole, everyone ends up with clean plate awards. Offer fresh toppings like green onions, tomatoes and avocado.
—*Jennifer Stowell, Deep River, IA*

PREP: 10 min. • **BAKE:** 25 min. + standing
MAKES: 8 servings

- 1 large egg, lightly beaten
- 1 can (14¾ oz.) cream-style corn
- 1 pkg. (8½ oz.) cornbread/muffin mix
- 1 can (4 oz.) chopped green chiles
- ⅓ cup 2% milk
- ¼ cup shredded Mexican cheese blend

TOPPING
- 2 cups coarsely shredded cooked chicken
- 1 can (10 oz.) enchilada sauce
- 1 tsp. ground cumin
- ½ tsp. onion powder
- 1¾ cups shredded Mexican cheese blend
  Optional: Chopped green onions, tomatoes and avocado

1. Preheat oven to 400°. In a large bowl, combine the first 6 ingredients; stir just until the dry ingredients are moistened. Transfer to a greased 13x9-in. baking dish. Bake until light golden brown and a toothpick inserted in center comes out clean, 15-18 minutes.
2. In a large skillet, combine chicken, enchilada sauce, cumin and onion powder; bring to a boil, stirring occasionally. Reduce heat; simmer, uncovered, 5 minutes. Spread over cornbread layer; sprinkle with cheese.
3. Bake until the cheese is melted, 10-12 minutes longer. Let stand 10 minutes before serving. If desired, top with green onions, tomatoes and avocado.
1 piece: 364 cal., 17g fat (7g sat. fat), 81mg chol., 851mg sod., 35g carb. (9g sugars, 4g fiber), 21g pro.

CHICKEN & SWISS CASSEROLE

It's nice to have an alternative to the traditional baked ham on Easter. This comforting casserole is always a crowd-pleaser. Using rotisserie chicken from the deli makes prep simple.
—*Christina Petri, Alexandria, MN*

PREP: 30 min. • **BAKE:** 10 min.
MAKES: 8 servings

- 5½ cups uncooked egg noodles (about ½ lb.)
- 3 Tbsp. olive oil
- 3 shallots, chopped
- 3 small garlic cloves, minced
- ⅓ cup all-purpose flour
- 2 cups chicken broth
- ¾ cup 2% milk
- 1½ tsp. dried thyme
- ¾ tsp. grated lemon zest
- ½ tsp. salt
- ¼ tsp. ground nutmeg
- ¼ tsp. pepper
- 5 cups cubed rotisserie chicken
- 1½ cups frozen peas
- 2 cups shredded Swiss cheese
- ¾ cup dry bread crumbs
- 2 Tbsp. butter, melted

1. Preheat oven to 350°. Cook noodles according to package directions; drain. In a large skillet, heat oil over medium heat. Add shallots and garlic; cook and stir 45 seconds. Stir in flour; cook and stir 1 minute. Add broth, milk, thyme, lemon zest, salt, nutmeg and pepper. Stir in chicken and peas; heat through. Stir in noodles and cheese.
2. Transfer to a greased 13x9-in. baking dish. In a small bowl, mix bread crumbs and butter; sprinkle over the top. Bake 8-10 minutes or until top is browned.
1¼ cups: 551 cal., 25g fat (10g sat. fat), 136mg chol., 661mg sod., 38g carb. (4g sugars, 3g fiber), 41g pro.

CHICKEN &
SWISS CASSEROLE

HOW-TO

Make Homemade Bread Crumbs

- Pulse three to four bread slices in a food processor until coarse crumbs form. If desired, you can sprinkle in some dried herbs for flavor.
- Spread crumbs on an ungreased baking sheet and bake at 350° for 8-10 minutes or until dried and just starting to brown, stirring after 5 minutes.

CASHEW CHICKEN CASSEROLE

I especially like this dish because I can get it ready the day before I need it. It's easy to whip up with common pantry items that I seem to always have on hand, including macaroni, canned soup and saltine crackers.
—Julie Ridlon, Solway, MN

PREP: 15 min. + chilling • **BAKE:** 35 min.
MAKES: 8 servings

- 2 cups uncooked elbow macaroni
- 3 cups cubed cooked chicken
- ½ cup Velveeta
- 1 small onion, chopped
- ½ cup chopped celery
- ½ cup chopped green pepper
- 1 can (8 oz.) sliced water chestnuts, drained
- 1 can (10¾ oz.) condensed cream of mushroom soup, undiluted
- 1 can (10¾ oz.) condensed cream of chicken soup, undiluted
- 1⅓ cups whole milk
- 1 can (14½ oz.) chicken broth
- ¼ cup butter, melted
- ⅔ cup crushed saltines (about 20 crackers)
- ¾ cup cashew halves

1. In a greased 13x9-in. baking dish, layer the first 7 ingredients in the order listed. In a large bowl, combine soups, milk and broth. Pour mixture over the water chestnuts. Cover the bowl and refrigerate overnight.
2. Toss butter and cracker crumbs; sprinkle over casserole. Top with the cashews. Bake, uncovered, at 350° for 35-40 minutes or until the macaroni is tender.
1¼ cups: 464 cal., 25g fat (9g sat. fat), 79mg chol., 1095mg sod., 36g carb. (6g sugars, 4g fiber), 24g pro.

CHICKEN MANICOTTI

When a girlfriend came home from the hospital with her newborn, I sent over this freezer casserole. She and her family raved over how good it was.
—Jamie Valocchi, Mesa, AZ

PREP: 25 min. • **BAKE:** 45 min.
MAKES: 2 casseroles (4 servings each)

- 1 Tbsp. garlic powder
- 1½ lbs. boneless skinless chicken breasts
- 16 uncooked manicotti shells
- 2 jars (26 oz. each) spaghetti sauce, divided
- 1 lb. bulk Italian sausage, cooked and drained
- ½ lb. fresh mushrooms, sliced
- 4 cups shredded part-skim mozzarella cheese
- ⅔ cup water

1. Preheat oven to 375°. Rub the garlic powder over chicken; cut into 1-in. strips. Stuff the chicken into the manicotti shells. Spread 1 cup sauce on the bottom of each of 2 greased 13x9-in. baking dishes.
2. Place 8 stuffed manicotti shells in each dish. Sprinkle with sausage and mushrooms. Pour the remaining spaghetti sauce over the top. Sprinkle with cheese.
3. Drizzle water around the edge of each dish. Cover and bake 45-55 minutes or until chicken is no longer pink and pasta is tender.
Freeze option: Cover and freeze unbaked casseroles for up to 1 month. To use, partially thaw in refrigerator overnight. Remove from refrigerator 30 minutes before baking. Preheat oven to 375°. Bake casseroles as directed, increasing time as necessary to heat through and for a thermometer inserted in center to read 165°.
2 stuffed shells: 546 cal., 26g fat (11g sat. fat), 115mg chol., 980mg sod., 37g carb. (8g sugars, 3g fiber), 41g pro.

CASHEW CHICKEN CASSEROLE

CHICKEN ALFREDO LASAGNA

My family was growing tired of traditional red sauce lasagna, so I created this fun twist using a creamy homemade Alfredo sauce. Store-bought rotisserie chicken keeps prep simple and fast.
—*Caitlin MacNeilly, Uncasville, CT*

PREP: 35 min. • **BAKE:** 45 min. + standing
MAKES: 12 servings

- 4 oz. thinly sliced pancetta, cut into strips
- 3 oz. thinly sliced prosciutto or deli ham, cut into strips
- 3 cups shredded rotisserie chicken
- 5 Tbsp. unsalted butter, cubed
- ¼ cup all-purpose flour
- 4 cups whole milk
- 2 cups shredded Asiago cheese, divided
- 2 Tbsp. minced fresh parsley, divided
- ¼ tsp. coarsely ground pepper
    Pinch ground nutmeg
- 9 no-cook lasagna noodles
- 1½ cups shredded part-skim mozzarella cheese
- 1½ cups shredded Parmesan cheese

1. In a large skillet, cook pancetta and prosciutto over medium heat until browned. Drain on paper towels. Transfer to a large bowl; add chicken and toss to combine.
2. For sauce, in a large saucepan, melt butter over medium heat. Stir in flour until smooth; gradually whisk in milk. Bring to a boil, stirring constantly; cook and stir 1-2 minutes or until thickened. Remove from heat; stir in ½ cup Asiago cheese, 1 Tbsp. parsley and seasonings.
3. Preheat oven to 375°. Spread ½ cup sauce into a greased 13x9-in. baking dish. Layer with a third of each of the following: noodles, sauce, meat mixture, Asiago, mozzarella and Parmesan cheeses. Repeat layers twice.
4. Bake, covered, 30 minutes. Uncover; bake 15 minutes longer or until bubbly. Sprinkle with remaining parsley. Let stand 10 minutes before serving.

1 piece: 421 cal., 25g fat (13g sat. fat), 99mg chol., 688mg sod., 18g carb. (5g sugars, 1g fiber), 31g pro.

TEST KITCHEN TIPS

- Swap bacon for the pancetta if you want a little smoky action in your lasagna. *Mmm.*
- Rotisserie chicken keeps this dish ultra simple, but any leftover pulled or cubed chicken will do.

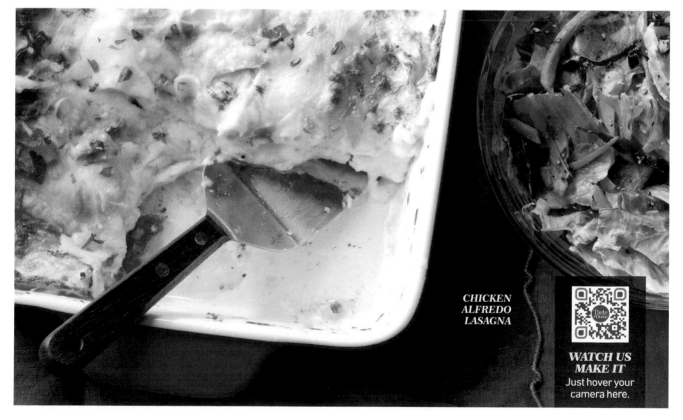

CHICKEN ALFREDO LASAGNA

WATCH US MAKE IT
Just hover your camera here.

GREEK SPAGHETTI WITH CHICKEN

When this flavorful spaghetti emerges from the oven, it's time for true comfort food. Serve up a dinner rich with chicken, spinach and two types of cheese.
—*Melanie Dalbec, Inver Grove, MN*

PREP: 25 min. • **BAKE:** 25 min.
MAKES: 10 servings

- 1 pkg. (16 oz.) spaghetti, broken into 2-in. pieces
- 4 cups cubed cooked chicken breast
- 2 pkg. (10 oz. each) frozen chopped spinach, thawed and squeezed dry
- 2 cans (10¾ oz. each) condensed cream of chicken soup, undiluted
- 1 cup mayonnaise
- 1 cup sour cream
- 3 celery ribs, chopped
- 1 small onion, chopped
- ½ cup chopped green pepper
- 1 jar (2 oz.) diced pimientos, drained
- ½ tsp. lemon-pepper seasoning
- 1 cup shredded Monterey Jack cheese
- ½ cup soft bread crumbs
- ½ cup shredded Parmesan cheese

1. Cook spaghetti according to package directions; drain. Return spaghetti to saucepan. Stir in the chicken, spinach, soup, mayonnaise, sour cream, celery, onion, green pepper, pimientos and lemon pepper.

2. Transfer to a greased 13x9-in. baking dish (dish will be full). Top mixture with Monterey Jack cheese, bread crumbs and Parmesan cheese. Bake, uncovered, at 350° for 25-30 minutes or until dish is heated through.

Note: To make soft bread crumbs, tear bread into pieces and place in a food processor or blender. Cover and pulse until crumbs form. One slice of bread yields ½-¾ cup crumbs.

1⅓ cups: 594 cal., 32g fat (10g sat. fat), 68mg chol., 815mg sod., 45g carb. (4g sugars, 5g fiber), 31g pro.

GREEK SPAGHETTI WITH CHICKEN

CREAMY CHICKEN ENCHILADAS

My daughter, Lisa Sand, brought 10 pans of these yummy chicken enchiladas to my wedding reception and they were the biggest hit of all the food. So many guests wanted the recipe, we sent it out with our Christmas cards.
—*Pat Coffee, Kingston, WA*

- -

PREP: 30 min. • **BAKE:** 35 min.
MAKES: 10 servings

- 1 pkg. (8 oz.) cream cheese, softened
- 2 Tbsp. water
- 2 tsp. onion powder
- 2 tsp. ground cumin
- ½ tsp. salt
- ¼ tsp. pepper
- 5 cups diced cooked chicken
- 20 flour tortillas (6 in.), room temperature
- 2 cans (10½ oz. each) condensed cream of chicken soup, undiluted
- 2 cups sour cream
- 1 cup 2% milk
- 2 cans (4 oz. each) chopped green chiles
- 2 cups shredded cheddar cheese

1. Preheat oven to 350°. In a large bowl, beat the cream cheese, water, onion powder, cumin, salt and pepper until smooth. Stir in chicken.
2. Place ¼ cup chicken mixture down the center of each tortilla. Roll up and place seam side down in 2 greased 13x9-in. baking dishes. In a large bowl, combine soup, sour cream, milk and chiles; pour over enchiladas.
3. Bake, uncovered, 30-40 minutes or until heated through. Sprinkle with cheese; bake 5 minutes longer or until cheese is melted.
2 enchiladas: 651 cal., 38g fat (18g sat. fat), 151mg chol., 1392mg sod., 37g carb. (3g sugars, 1g fiber), 37g pro.

MILE-HIGH CHICKEN POTPIE

MILE-HIGH CHICKEN POTPIE

Classic chicken potpie gets extra homey when it's loaded with a creamy filling and baked tall in a springform pan. This deep-dish marvel is perfect for Sunday dinners.
—*Shannon Norris, Cudahy, WI*

- -

PREP: 40 min. + chilling
BAKE: 50 min. + standing
MAKES: 6 servings

- 1 large egg, separated
- 4 to 6 Tbsp. cold water, divided
- 2 cups all-purpose flour
- ¼ tsp. salt
- ⅔ cup cold butter, cubed
- **FILLING**
- 3 Tbsp. butter
- 2 medium potatoes, peeled and cut into ½-in. cubes
- 4 medium carrots, thinly sliced
- 2 celery ribs, finely chopped
- ¼ cup finely chopped onion
- 3 Tbsp. all-purpose flour
- 2 Tbsp. chicken bouillon granules
- 1½ tsp. dried tarragon
- ½ tsp. coarsely ground pepper
- 1½ cups half-and-half cream
- 2½ cups cubed cooked chicken
- 1½ cups fresh peas or frozen peas
- ½ to 1 tsp. celery seed

1. In a small bowl, beat egg yolk with 2 Tbsp. water. In a large bowl, combine flour and salt; cut in butter until crumbly. Gradually add yolk mixture, tossing with a fork; add additional water 1 Tbsp. at a time, as needed, until dough forms a ball. Divide dough into 2 portions, 1 with three-quarters of the dough and 1 with the remainder. Shape each portion into a disk; cover and refrigerate 1 hour or overnight.
2. For filling, in a Dutch oven, melt butter. Saute potatoes, carrots, celery and onion until crisp-tender, 5-7 minutes. Stir in flour, bouillon, tarragon and pepper. Gradually stir in cream. Bring to a boil; cook and stir until thickened, about 2 minutes. Stir in chicken and peas; set aside to cool completely.
3. On a lightly floured surface, roll out larger portion of dough to fit bottom and up the sides of an 8-in. springform pan. Place dough in pan; add cooled filling. Roll remaining dough to fit over the top. Place over filling. Trim, seal and flute edge. Cut slits in top. Chill pie for at least 1 hour.
4. Lightly the beat egg white with 1 tsp. water. Brush over the top crust; sprinkle with celery seed. Place pie on a rimmed baking tray.
5. Bake at 400° until the crust is golden brown and the filling is bubbly, 50-55 minutes. Cool on a wire rack for at least 30 minutes before serving.
1 piece: 700 cal., 38g fat (22g sat. fat), 183mg chol., 1282mg sod., 58g carb. (8g sugars, 6g fiber), 29g pro.

NACHO CHICKEN

I have been serving this rich and zippy chicken casserole for several years, and it's a favorite of my family and friends. It's sure to disappear quickly at potluck suppers.
—*Thom Britton, Three Rivers, MI*

PREP: 15 min. • **BAKE:** 30 min.
MAKES: 10 servings

- 4 cups cubed cooked chicken
- 1 lb. Velveeta, cubed
- 2 cans (10¾ oz. each) condensed cream of chicken soup, undiluted
- 1 can (10 oz.) diced tomatoes and green chiles, undrained
- 1 cup chopped onion
- ½ tsp. garlic salt
- ¼ tsp. pepper
- 1 pkg. (14½ oz.) nacho cheese tortilla chips
  Optional: Sliced jalapeno pepper and diced tomato

In a large bowl, combine the first 7 ingredients; mix well. Crush chips; set aside 1 cup for topping. Add remaining chips to chicken mixture. Spoon into a greased 13x9-in. baking dish; sprinkle with reserved chips. Bake, uncovered, at 350° until cheese is melted and edges are bubbly, 30 minutes. Serve with sliced jalapenos and diced tomatoes if desired.

1 cup: 496 cal., 27g fat (11g sat. fat), 81mg chol., 1299mg sod., 32g carb. (8g sugars, 2g fiber), 29g pro.

CHICKEN POTPIE GALETTE WITH CHEDDAR-THYME CRUST

CHICKEN POTPIE GALETTE WITH CHEDDAR-THYME CRUST

This gorgeous galette takes traditional chicken potpie and gives it a fun open-faced spin. The rich filling and flaky cheddar-flecked crust make it taste so homey.

—Elisabeth Larsen, Pleasant Grove, UT

PREP: 45 min. + chilling
BAKE: 30 min. + cooling
MAKES: 8 servings

1¼ cups all-purpose flour
½ cup shredded sharp cheddar cheese
2 Tbsp. minced fresh thyme
¼ tsp. salt
½ cup cold butter, cubed
¼ cup ice water

FILLING
3 Tbsp. butter
2 large carrots, sliced
1 celery rib, diced
1 small onion, diced
8 oz. sliced fresh mushrooms
3 cups julienned Swiss chard
3 garlic cloves, minced
1 cup chicken broth
3 Tbsp. all-purpose flour
½ tsp. salt
¼ tsp. pepper
2 cups shredded cooked chicken
½ tsp. minced fresh oregano
2 Tbsp. minced fresh parsley

1. Combine flour, cheese, thyme and salt; cut in the butter until crumbly. Gradually add ice water, tossing with a fork until dough holds together when pressed. Shape into a disk; refrigerate 1 hour.

2. For filling, melt butter in a large saucepan over medium-high heat. Add carrots, celery and onion; cook and stir until slightly softened, 5-7 minutes. Add mushrooms; cook 3 minutes longer. Add Swiss chard and garlic; cook until chard is wilted, 2-3 minutes.

3. Whisk together the broth, flour, salt and pepper; slowly pour liquid over vegetables, stirring constantly. Cook until thickened, 2-3 minutes. Stir in chicken and oregano.

4. Preheat oven to 400°. On a floured sheet of parchment, roll dough into a 12-in. circle. Transfer to a baking sheet. Spoon filling over crust to within 2 in. of the edge. Fold the crust edge over filling, pleating as you go, leaving the center uncovered. Bake on a lower oven rack until crust is golden brown and filling is bubbly, 30-35 minutes. Cool 15 minutes before slicing. Sprinkle with parsley.

1 piece: 342 cal., 21g fat (12g sat. fat), 81mg chol., 594mg sod., 22g carb. (2g sugars, 2g fiber), 16g pro.

TEST KITCHEN TIP

Fill the potpie with any meat/cheese/veggie combo you like. It would be just as amazing, for example, with sausage, golden beets and kale. The filling may start to bubble up a bit near the end of baking, so be sure to use parchment paper or a silicone mat to catch drips.

LEARN HOW WE MADE IT
Just hover your camera here.

🕐 🍎 CHICKEN VEGGIE PACKETS

People think I went to a lot of trouble when I serve these packets. Individual aluminum foil pouches hold juices in during baking to keep the herbed chicken moist and tender. It saves time and makes cleanup a breeze.
—Edna Shaffer, Beulah, MI

TAKES: 30 min. • **MAKES:** 4 servings

  4 boneless skinless chicken breast
     halves (4 oz. each)
  ½ lb. sliced fresh mushrooms
  1½ cups fresh baby carrots
  1 cup pearl onions
  ½ cup julienned sweet red pepper
  ¼ tsp. pepper
  3 tsp. minced fresh thyme
  ½ tsp. salt, optional
     Lemon wedges, optional

1. Preheat oven to 375°. Flatten chicken breasts to ½-in. thickness; place each on a piece of heavy-duty foil (about 12 in. square). Layer with mushrooms, carrots, onions and red pepper; sprinkle with pepper, thyme and, if desired, salt.
2. Fold foil around the chicken and vegetables and seal tightly. Place on a baking sheet. Bake until chicken juices run clear, about 20 minutes. If desired, serve with lemon wedges.

1 serving: 175 cal., 3g fat (1g sat. fat), 63mg chol., 100mg sod., 11g carb. (6g sugars, 2g fiber), 25g pro. **Diabetic exchanges:** 3 lean meat, 2 vegetable.

WHY YOU'LL LOVE IT...

"My whole family loves this recipe! If I don't have pearl onions on hand, I substitute chopped sweet onion. My 8-year-old daughter likes to help me fix the packets as well."
—LKDUNCAN1, TASTEOFHOME.COM

CHICKEN VEGGIE PACKETS

🍎 SPICY ROASTED SAUSAGE, POTATOES & PEPPERS

I love to share my cooking, and this hearty sheet-pan dinner has built a reputation for being tasty. People have actually approached me in public to ask for the recipe.
—Laurie Sledge, Brandon, MS

PREP: 20 min. • **BAKE:** 30 min.
MAKES: 4 servings

  1 lb. potatoes (about 2 medium), peeled
     and cut into ½-in. cubes
  1 pkg. (12 oz.) fully cooked andouille
     chicken sausage links or flavor of
     your choice, cut into 1-in. pieces
  1 medium red onion, cut into wedges
  1 medium sweet red pepper, cut into
     1-in. pieces
  1 medium green pepper, cut into
     1-in. pieces
  ½ cup pickled pepper rings
  1 Tbsp. olive oil
  ½ to 1 tsp. Creole seasoning
  ¼ tsp. pepper

1. Preheat oven to 400°. In a large bowl, combine potatoes, sausage, onion, red pepper, green pepper and pepper rings. Mix oil, Creole seasoning and pepper; drizzle over potato mixture and toss to coat.
2. Transfer to a 15x10x1-in. baking pan coated with cooking spray. Roast until vegetables are tender, stirring occasionally, 30-35 minutes.

1½ cups: 257 cal., 11g fat (3g sat. fat), 65mg chol., 759mg sod., 24g carb. (5g sugars, 3g fiber), 17g pro. **Diabetic exchanges:** 3 lean meat, 1 starch, 1 vegetable, 1 fat.

CHICKEN LOAF WITH MUSHROOM GRAVY

CHICKEN LOAF WITH MUSHROOM GRAVY

Try a twist on traditional meat loaf with this delightful chicken version. Mushroom gravy creates an upscale topping.
—*Keri Schofield Lawson, Brea, CA*

PREP: 25 min. • **BAKE:** 55 min. + standing
MAKES: 10 servings

- 1¼ lbs. boneless skinless chicken breast halves
- 1¼ lbs. boneless skinless chicken thighs
- 2 large eggs, lightly beaten
- ½ cup panko bread crumbs
- ½ cup mayonnaise
- 1 envelope onion soup mix
- 2 Tbsp. minced fresh parsley
- 1 Tbsp. prepared horseradish
- ½ tsp. salt
- ½ tsp. garlic powder
- ½ tsp. dried sage leaves
- ½ tsp. dried thyme
- ½ tsp. pepper

GRAVY

- 2 cups sliced fresh mushrooms
- 1 Tbsp. butter
- 3 cups reduced-sodium chicken broth
- 1 tsp. dried rosemary, crushed
- ½ tsp. salt
- ¼ tsp. white pepper
- 3 Tbsp. cornstarch
- ¼ cup white wine or additional reduced-sodium chicken broth

1. Place chicken in the freezer for 15-20 minutes or until it begins to freeze. Cut into 1-in. pieces. In a food processor, cover and process chicken in batches until ground.
2. Preheat oven to 350°. In a large bowl, combine eggs, bread crumbs, mayonnaise, soup mix, parsley, horseradish, salt, garlic powder, sage, thyme and pepper. Crumble the chicken over mixture and mix lightly but thoroughly.
3. Shape mixture into a loaf; place in a greased 13x9-in. baking dish. Bake, uncovered, until no pink remains and a thermometer reads 165°, 55-60 minutes. Let stand for 10 minutes before slicing.
4. Meanwhile, in a large saucepan, saute mushrooms in butter until tender. Add the broth, rosemary, salt and white pepper. Bring to a boil. Combine the cornstarch and wine until smooth; gradually stir into mushroom mixture. Bring to a boil; cook and stir for 2 minutes or until thickened. Serve with meat loaf.
Note: You may substitute 2½ pounds ground chicken for the chicken breast halves and thighs.
1 piece with ⅓ cup gravy: 290 cal., 17g fat (4g sat. fat), 118mg chol., 807mg sod., 8g carb. (1g sugars, 1g fiber), 25g pro.

ENCHILADA CASSEROLE WITH CHICKEN

My brother brought this recipe home from Scout camp when he was young, and it quickly became a family favorite. Now that my five siblings and I live away from home, we often make this dish for ourselves.
—*Kristi Larson, Milwaukee, WI*

PREP: 15 min. • **COOK:** 30 min.
MAKES: 10 servings

- 1 can cream of chicken soup
- 1 can cream of mushroom soup
- 16 oz. sour cream
- 1 bunch green onions, chopped
- 1 can (4 oz.) chopped green chiles
- 8 flour tortillas (8 in.)
- 3 cups shredded cooked chicken breast
- 1 cup shredded cheddar cheese
- 1 cup shredded pepper jack cheese
  Optional: Chopped tomatoes, sliced black olives, green onions and sour cream

1. Preheat oven to 350°.
2. Combine soups, sour cream, green onions and green chiles in a bowl. Spray a 13x9-in. pan with cooking spray, then spread ¼ of the soup mixture in the pan.
3. Place 4 tortillas on top, tearing to overlap. Spread with half the chicken, half the remaining soup mixture, and ½ cup each of shredded cheddar and pepper jack cheese. Repeat layers.
4. Bake, uncovered for 30 minutes or until casserole is bubbly and cheese is melted. Add toppings if desired.
1 piece: 391 cal., 21g fat (10g sat. fat), 82mg chol., 777mg sod., 30g carb. (2g sugars, 3g fiber), 21g pro.

CHICKEN BURRITOS

This mouthwatering southwestern recipe makes enough for two casseroles, so you can enjoy one today and freeze the other for a busy weeknight. These burritos are super to have on hand for quick meals or to take to potlucks.

—Sonya Nightingale, Burley, ID

- -

PREP: 20 min. • **BAKE:** 35 min.
MAKES: 2 casseroles (6 servings each)

- 6 Tbsp. butter
- 1 large onion, chopped
- ¼ cup chopped green pepper
- ½ cup all-purpose flour
- 3 cups chicken broth
- 1 can (10 oz.) diced tomatoes and green chiles, undrained
- 1 tsp. ground cumin
- 1 tsp. chili powder
- ½ tsp. garlic powder
- ½ tsp. salt
- 2 Tbsp. chopped jalapeno pepper, optional
- 1 can (15 oz.) chili with beans
- 1 pkg. (8 oz.) cream cheese, cubed
- 8 cups cubed cooked chicken
- 24 flour tortillas (6 in.), warmed
- 6 cups shredded Colby-Monterey Jack cheese
   Salsa, optional

1. Preheat oven to 350°. In a Dutch oven, heat butter over medium-high heat. Add the onion and pepper; cook and stir until tender. Stir in the flour until blended; gradually stir in the broth. Bring to a boil; cook and stir 2 minutes. Reduce heat; stir in tomatoes, seasonings and, if desired, jalapeno. Cook 5 minutes. Add chili and cream cheese; stir until cream cheese is melted. Stir in chicken.

2. Spoon about ½ cup filling across center of each tortilla; sprinkle each with ¼ cup Colby-Monterey Jack cheese. Fold bottom and sides over filling and roll up. Place in 2 greased 13x9-in. baking dishes.

3. Bake, covered, 35-40 minutes or until heated through. If desired, serve with salsa.

Freeze option: Cool unbaked burritos; cover and freeze. To use, partially thaw in refrigerator overnight. Remove from refrigerator 30 minutes before baking. Preheat oven to 350°. Cover burritos with foil; bake as directed, increasing baking time to 50-55 minutes or until heated through and a thermometer inserted in center reads 160°.

Note: Wear disposable gloves when cutting hot peppers; the oils can burn skin. Avoid touching your face.

2 burritos: 760 cal., 44g fat (23g sat. fat), 177mg chol., 1608mg sod., 40g carb. (2g sugars, 2g fiber), 51g pro.

WHY YOU'LL LOVE IT...

"Huge hit. I left out the jalapeno pepper for the kids. I used an Anaheim instead. I loved the creamy texture the cream cheese gave the burritos. I froze the leftover for lunches. The burritos reheat in the microwave well. This recipe made it into my permanent cookbook and will be used many times!"

—JENANDBRY, TASTEOFHOME.COM

CHICKEN BURRITOS

CREAMY CHICKEN TETRAZZINI CASSEROLE

This creamy tetrazzini has been one of my favorite recipes for over 20 years. I always hear, Yum! Is there any more? Even overnight guests ask for leftovers the next day.
—*Amanda Hertz-Crisel, Eagle Point, OR*

- -

PREP: 30 min. • **BAKE:** 30 min.
MAKES: 6 servings

12 oz. uncooked spaghetti
1 small onion, chopped
1 celery rib, chopped
¼ cup butter, cubed
1 can (14 oz.) chicken broth
1½ cups half-and-half cream
1 pkg. (8 oz.) cream cheese, cubed
2 cups cubed cooked chicken
1 can (4 oz.) mushroom stems and pieces, drained
2 to 4 Tbsp. sliced pimientos
½ tsp. salt
¼ tsp. pepper
½ cup sliced almonds, toasted
¼ cup grated Parmesan cheese
¼ cup crushed potato chips

1. Cook spaghetti according to package directions. Meanwhile, in a large skillet, saute onion and celery in butter until tender. Stir in the broth, cream and cream cheese. Cook and stir just until cheese is melted. Remove from the heat.
2. Stir in the chicken, mushrooms, pimientos, salt and pepper. Drain spaghetti; add to chicken mixture and toss to coat. Transfer to a greased 13x9-in. baking dish.
3. Bake, uncovered, at 350° for 20 minutes. Sprinkle with almonds, Parmesan cheese and chips. Bake 10-15 minutes longer or until heated through and topping is golden brown.
1½ cups: 665 cal., 37g fat (19g sat. fat), 134mg chol., 871mg sod., 52g carb. (6g sugars, 3g fiber), 29g pro.

Seed a Tomato

Seeding a tomato eliminates some of the juice that can make a dish too watery. To seed a tomato, cut the fruit in half and remove the stem. Holding one half over a bowl, scrape out the seeds with a small spoon or with your fingertip. Then cut as the recipe directs.

CHICKEN CLUB CASSEROLES

Here's a warm and welcoming casserole that tastes as fresh and delicious after it's frozen as it does right out of the oven!
—*Janine Smith, Columbia, SC*

- -

PREP: 20 min. • **BAKE:** 35 min.
MAKES: 2 casseroles (5 servings each)

- 4 **cups uncooked spiral pasta**
- 4 **cups cubed cooked chicken**
- 2 **cans (10¾ oz. each) condensed cheddar cheese soup, undiluted**
- 1 **cup crumbled cooked bacon**
- 1 **cup 2% milk**
- 1 **cup mayonnaise**
- 4 **medium tomatoes, seeded and chopped**
- 3 **cups fresh baby spinach, chopped**
- 2 **cups shredded Colby-Monterey Jack cheese**

1. Preheat oven to 375°. Cook pasta according to package directions.
2. Meanwhile, in a large bowl, combine the chicken, soup, bacon, milk and mayonnaise. Stir in the tomatoes and spinach.
3. Drain pasta; stir into chicken mixture. Transfer to 2 greased 8-in. square baking dishes. Sprinkle with cheese.
4. Cover and bake 35-40 minutes or until bubbly and cheese is melted, .
Freeze option: Cover and freeze the unbaked casseroles for up to 3 months. To use, thaw in the refrigerator overnight. Remove from refrigerator 30 minutes before baking. Preheat oven to 375°. Cover and bake until bubbly, 60-70 minutes.
1⅓ cups: 584 cal., 34g fat (10g sat. fat), 93mg chol., 1161mg sod., 36g carb. (5g sugars, 2g fiber), 33g pro.

CHICKEN CLUB CASSEROLES

CHICKEN PENNE CASSEROLE

CHICKEN CORDON BLEU BAKE

A friend shared this awesome hot dish recipe with me. I freeze several pans to share with neighbors or for days when I'm scrambling at mealtime.
—*Rea Newell, Decatur, IL*

- -

PREP: 20 min. • **BAKE:** 40 min.
MAKES: 2 casseroles (6 servings each)

> 2 pkg. (6 oz. each) reduced-sodium stuffing mix
> 1 can (10¾ oz.) condensed cream of chicken soup, undiluted
> 1 cup 2% milk
> 8 cups cubed cooked chicken
> ½ tsp. pepper
> ¾ lb. sliced deli ham, cut into 1-in. strips
> 1 cup shredded Swiss cheese
> 3 cups shredded cheddar cheese

1. Preheat oven to 350°. Prepare stuffing mixes according to package directions. Meanwhile, whisk together the soup and milk.
2. Toss chicken with pepper; divide between 2 greased 13x9-in. baking dishes. Layer with ham, Swiss cheese, 1 cup cheddar cheese, soup mixture and stuffing. Sprinkle with remaining cheddar cheese.
3. Bake casserole, covered, 30 minutes. Uncover; bake until cheese is melted, 10-15 minutes.
Freeze option: Cover and freeze unbaked casseroles. To use, partially thaw in refrigerator overnight. Remove from refrigerator 30 minutes before baking. Preheat oven to 350°. Bake, covered, until heated through and a thermometer inserted in center reads 165°, about 45 minutes. Uncover; bake until cheese is melted, 10-15 minutes.
1 cup: 555 cal., 29g fat (15g sat. fat), 158mg chol., 1055mg sod., 26g carb. (5g sugars, 1g fiber), 46g pro.

CHICKEN PENNE CASSEROLE

I make this family favorite casserole every week or two and we never tire of it. I like that I can put it together and then relax while it bakes.
—*Carmen Vanosch, Vernon, BC*

- -

PREP: 35 min. • **BAKE:** 45 min.
MAKES: 4 servings

> 1½ cups uncooked penne pasta
> 1 Tbsp. canola oil
> 1 lb. boneless skinless chicken thighs, cut into 1-in. pieces
> ½ cup chopped onion
> ½ cup chopped green pepper
> ½ cup chopped sweet red pepper
> 1 tsp. dried basil
> 1 tsp. dried oregano
> 1 tsp. dried parsley flakes
> ½ tsp. salt
> ½ tsp. crushed red pepper flakes
> 3 garlic cloves, minced
> 1 can (14½ oz.) diced tomatoes, undrained
> 3 Tbsp. tomato paste
> ¾ cup chicken broth
> 2 cups shredded part-skim mozzarella cheese
> ½ cup grated Romano cheese

1. Preheat oven to 350°. Cook pasta according to the package directions. Meanwhile, in a large saucepan, heat oil over medium heat. Add chicken, onion, peppers and seasonings; saute until chicken is no longer pink. Add garlic; cook 1 minute longer.
2. In a blender, pulse tomatoes and tomato paste, covered, until blended. Add to chicken mixture. Stir in broth; bring to a boil over medium-high heat. Reduce heat; cover and simmer until slightly thickened, 10-15 minutes.
3. Drain pasta; toss with the chicken mixture. Spoon half of the mixture into a greased 2-qt. baking dish. Sprinkle with half of the cheeses. Repeat layers.
4. Cover casserole and bake 30 minutes. Uncover; bake until heated through, 15-20 minutes longer.
1½ cups: 579 cal., 28g fat (12g sat. fat), 128mg chol., 1357mg sod., 36g carb. (9g sugars, 4g fiber), 47g pro.
Chicken Pasta Casserole: Substitute chicken breast for the chicken thighs, spiral pasta for the penne and shredded provolone for the mozzarella. Proceed as directed.

BUFFALO CHICKEN LASAGNA

BUFFALO CHICKEN LASAGNA

This recipe was inspired by my daughter's favorite food—Buffalo wings! It tastes just like it came from a restaurant.
—*Melissa Millwood, Lyman, SC*

PREP: 1½ hours • **BAKE:** 40 min. + standing
MAKES: 12 servings

 1 Tbsp. canola oil
1½ lbs. ground chicken
 1 small onion, chopped
 1 celery rib, finely chopped
 1 large carrot, grated
 2 garlic cloves, minced
 1 can (14½ oz.) diced tomatoes, drained
 1 bottle (12 oz.) Buffalo wing sauce
 ½ cup water
1½ tsp. Italian seasoning
 ½ tsp. salt
 ¼ tsp. pepper
 9 lasagna noodles
 1 carton (15 oz.) ricotta cheese
1¾ cups crumbled blue cheese, divided
 ½ cup minced Italian flat-leaf parsley
 1 large egg, lightly beaten
 3 cups shredded part-skim mozzarella cheese
 2 cups shredded white cheddar cheese

1. In a Dutch oven, heat oil over medium heat. Add chicken, onion, celery and carrot; cook and stir until meat is no longer pink and vegetables are tender. Add garlic; cook 2 minutes longer. Stir in tomatoes, wing sauce, water and seasonings; bring to a boil. Reduce heat; cover and simmer 1 hour.
2. Meanwhile, cook noodles according to package directions; drain. In a small bowl, mix the ricotta cheese, ¾ cup blue cheese, parsley and egg. Preheat oven to 350°.
3. Spread 1½ cups wing sauce into a greased 13x9-in. baking dish. Layer with 3 noodles, 1½ cups sauce, ⅔ cup ricotta mixture, 1 cup mozzarella cheese, ⅔ cup cheddar cheese and ⅓ cup blue cheese. Repeat layers twice.
4. Bake, covered, 20 minutes. Uncover; bake until bubbly and cheese is melted, 20-25 minutes. Let stand 10 minutes before serving.
1 piece: 466 cal., 28g fat (15g sat. fat), 124mg chol., 1680mg sod., 22g carb. (6g sugars, 2g fiber), 33g pro.

CHICKEN AMANDINE

CHICKEN AMANDINE

With colorful green beans and pimientos, this attractive casserole is terrific for the holidays or family dinners. This is true comfort food at its finest.

—Kat Woolbright, Wichita Falls, TX

PREP: 35 min. • **BAKE:** 30 min.
MAKES: 8 servings

- ¼ cup chopped onion
- 1 Tbsp. butter
- 1 pkg. (6 oz.) long grain and wild rice
- 2¼ cups chicken broth
- 3 cups cubed cooked chicken
- 2 cups frozen french-style green beans, thawed
- 1 can (10¾ oz.) condensed cream of chicken soup, undiluted
- ¾ cup sliced almonds, divided
- 1 jar (4 oz.) diced pimientos, drained
- 1 tsp. pepper
- ½ tsp. garlic powder
- 1 bacon strip, cooked and crumbled

1. In a large saucepan, saute onion in butter until tender. Add rice with contents of seasoning packet and broth. Bring to a boil. Reduce heat; cover and simmer until liquid is absorbed, about 25 minutes. Uncover; set aside to cool.
2. In a large bowl, combine chicken, green beans, soup, ½ cup almonds, pimientos, pepper and garlic powder. Stir in rice.
3. Transfer to a greased 2½-qt. baking dish. Sprinkle with bacon and remaining ¼ cup almonds. Cover and bake at 350° until heated through, 30-35 minutes.
1 cup: 297 cal., 13g fat (3g sat. fat), 54mg chol., 912mg sod., 24g carb. (3g sugars, 3g fiber), 22g pro.

BBQ CHICKEN &
APPLE BREAD
PUDDING

BBQ CHICKEN & APPLE BREAD PUDDING

To me, bread pudding is the epitome of comfort food and it's simply too good to reserve only for dessert. This sweet-and-savory twist on the classic is a delicious new way to enjoy an old favorite.
—*Shauna Havey, Roy, UT*

PREP: 45 min. + cooling • **BAKE:** 35 min.
MAKES: 8 servings

- 1 pkg. (8½ oz.) cornbread/muffin mix
- 6 Tbsp. butter, divided
- 1 large sweet onion, thinly sliced
- ⅔ cup barbecue sauce, divided
- 2 cups diced cooked chicken
- 2 large eggs, beaten
- 1 cup half-and-half cream
- 1 tsp. salt
- ½ tsp. pepper
- 1¼ cups shredded Monterey Jack cheese
- 1 small green apple, peeled and diced
  Minced chives

1. Prepare cornbread according to package directions and bake using a greased and floured 8-in. square baking pan. Cool. Reduce oven setting to 375°. Meanwhile, in a small skillet, heat 2 Tbsp. butter over medium heat. Add the onion; cook and stir until softened. Reduce heat to medium-low; cook until deep golden brown and caramelized, 30-40 minutes. Remove from heat and set aside.
2. Pour ¼ cup barbecue sauce over chicken; toss to coat.
3. Cube cornbread. Microwave remaining butter, covered, on high until melted, about 30 seconds. Whisk in eggs, cream, salt and pepper. Add caramelized onions. Pour egg mixture over cornbread cubes. Add chicken, cheese and apple. Toss gently to combine.
4. Pour the mixture into a greased 8-in. square or 1½-qt. baking dish; bake until bubbly and top is golden brown,

about 35 minutes. Drizzle remaining barbecue sauce over bread pudding. Sprinkle with chives.
1 serving: 465 cal., 25g fat (13g sat. fat), 156mg chol., 1028mg sod., 37g carb. (19g sugars, 3g fiber), 21g pro.

BAKED NECTARINE CHICKEN SALAD

Folks love the crunchy chow mein noodles on top of my nectarine chicken casserole. I love that I can make it a day in advance and refrigerate until it's time to serve. Serve with hot bread or rolls.
—*Faye Robinson, Pensacola, FL*

PREP: 15 min. • **BAKE:** 20 min.
MAKES: 8 servings

- 1⅓ cups mayonnaise
- ½ cup shredded Parmesan cheese
- 2 Tbsp. lemon juice
- 1 tsp. salt
- 1 tsp. onion powder
- 4 cups cubed cooked chicken
- 8 celery ribs, thinly sliced
- 4 medium nectarines, coarsely chopped
- 8 green onions, sliced
- 2 cans (3 oz. each) crispy chow mein noodles

1. Preheat oven to 375°. In a small bowl, mix the first 5 ingredients. In a large bowl, combine the chicken, celery, nectarines and onions. Add mayonnaise mixture; toss gently to coat.
2. Transfer to greased 13x9-in. baking dish. Sprinkle with noodles. Bake the dish, uncovered, until heated through, 20-25 minutes.
Note: This can be made a day in advance. Before adding noodles, cover and refrigerate. Remove the dish from the refrigerator 30 minutes before baking. Sprinkle with noodles. Bake as directed.
1¼ cups: 539 cal., 37g fat (7g sat. fat), 69mg chol., 911mg sod., 26g carb. (8g sugars, 3g fiber), 25g pro.

🍎 CHICKEN TOSTADA CUPS

I tried a version of these cups at a restaurant in Santa Fe, and I wanted to create my own spin .
—*Marla Clark, Moriarty, NM*

PREP: 25 min. • **BAKE:** 15 min.
MAKES: 6 servings

- 12 corn tortillas (6 in.), warmed
  Cooking spray
- 2 cups shredded rotisserie chicken
- 1 cup salsa
- 1 can (16 oz.) refried beans
- 1 cup shredded reduced-fat Mexican cheese blend
  Optional toppings: Shredded lettuce, reduced-fat sour cream, sliced ripe olives, sliced green onions, chopped cilantro, sliced radishes, diced avocado and additional salsa

1. Preheat oven to 425°. Press warm tortillas into 12 muffin cups coated with cooking spray, pleating sides as needed. Spritz with additional cooking spray.
2. Bake cups until lightly browned, 5-7 minutes. Toss chicken with salsa. Layer each cup with beans, chicken mixture and cheese.
3. Bake until cups are heated through, 9-11 minutes. Serve with toppings as desired.
2 tostada cups: 338 cal., 11g fat (4g sat. fat), 52mg chol., 629mg sod., 35g carb. (2g sugars, 6g fiber), 25g pro. **Diabetic exchanges:** 3 lean meat, 2 starch, 1 fat.

TORTELLINI CHICKEN AU GRATIN

I have a number of easy planned-leftover meals in my recipe arsenal, having them is especially useful during the holiday season, when people are coming and going (and staying!). This is a favorite: Pasta from Monday plus roasted chicken from Tuesday equals this delicious dish on Wednesday.
—Brenda Cole, Reisterstown, MD

- -

PREP: 15 min. • **BAKE:** 30 min.
MAKES: 6 servings

- 2 cans (14 oz. each) water-packed artichoke hearts
- 3 cups shredded cooked chicken
- 3 cups refrigerated spinach tortellini, cooked
- 1½ cups mayonnaise
- 1½ cups grated Asiago cheese, divided
  Fresh basil, optional

Preheat oven to 350°. Drain artichoke hearts, reserving ¼ cup of juices. Coarsely chop; combine with chicken, tortellini, mayonnaise, 1 cup cheese and reserved artichoke liquid. Place the artichoke mixture in a greased 13x9-in. baking dish; sprinkle with remaining cheese. Bake until dish is bubbly and starting to brown, about 30 minutes. If desired, garnish with basil leaves.

1⅓ cups: 709 cal., 54g fat (13g sat. fat), 101mg chol., 859mg sod., 19g carb. (1g sugars, 2 fiber), 34g pro.

TEST KITCHEN TIP
For a delightful crunch, stir in a little finely chopped celery or red bell pepper.

TORTELLINI CHICKEN AU GRATIN

*CHICKEN PARMESAN
STUFFED SHELLS*

CHICKEN PARMESAN STUFFED SHELLS

When chicken Parmesan meets stuffed shells, it's love at first bite.
—*Cyndy Gerken, Naples, FL*

PREP: 45 min. • **BAKE:** 40 min.
MAKES: 12 servings

- 1   pkg. (12 oz.) uncooked jumbo pasta shells
- 2   Tbsp. olive oil

FILLING
- 1   lb. boneless skinless chicken breasts, cut into ½-in. cubes
- 1½ tsp. Italian seasoning
- 1   tsp. salt, divided
- ½   tsp. pepper, divided
- 1   Tbsp. olive oil
- 2   Tbsp. butter
- ⅓   cup seasoned bread crumbs
- 3   cups part-skim ricotta cheese
- 1   cup shredded part-skim mozzarella cheese
- ½   cup grated Parmesan cheese
- ½   cup 2% milk
- ¼   cup chopped fresh Italian parsley

ASSEMBLY
- 4   cups meatless pasta sauce
- ¼   cup grated Parmesan cheese
- 8   oz. fresh mozzarella cheese, thinly sliced and halved

1. Preheat oven to 375°. Cook shells according to package directions for al dente; drain. Toss with oil; spread in an even layer on a baking sheet.
2. For filling, toss chicken with Italian seasoning, ½ tsp. salt and ¼ tsp. pepper. In a large skillet, heat oil over medium-high heat; saute chicken just until lightly browned, about 2 minutes. Reduce heat to medium; stir in butter until melted. Stir in bread crumbs; cook until crumbs are slightly toasted, 2-3 minutes, stirring occasionally. Cool slightly.
3. In a large bowl, mix cheeses, milk, parsley and the remaining salt and pepper. Fold in chicken.
4. Spread 2 cups pasta sauce into a greased 13x9-in. baking dish. Fill each shell with 2½ Tbsp. cheese mixture; place over sauce. Top with remaining sauce and cheeses (dish will be full).
5. Cover with greased foil; bake 30 minutes. Uncover; bake until heated through, 10-15 minutes.
1 serving: 431 cal., 19g fat (10g sat. fat), 71mg chol., 752mg sod., 36g carb. (8g sugars, 2g fiber), 28g pro.

GLAZED CORNISH HENS
WITH PECAN-RICE
STUFFING, PAGE 285

EXTRA POULTRY FAVORITES

LIGHT CHICKEN & BROCCOLI BAKE

🕐🍎 LIGHT CHICKEN & BROCCOLI BAKE

Cheesy chicken and broccoli bakes are the ultimate comfort food, but I wanted to give the classic casserole a healthier spin. Mine cuts down on fat and calories, but keeps the same cozy flavor.
—*Jenny Dubinsky, Inwood, WV*

- -

TAKES: 30 min. • **MAKES:** 4 servings

- 2   large eggs
- 1   cup fat-free milk
- ½   cup reduced-fat biscuit/baking mix
- ½   tsp. salt
- ¼   tsp. pepper
- 4   cups frozen broccoli florets (about 9 oz.), thawed and drained
- 1   cup shredded rotisserie chicken
- 1   small onion, chopped
- ½   cup shredded cheddar cheese, divided

1. Preheat oven to 400°. In a large bowl, whisk together first 5 ingredients. Stir in broccoli, chicken, onion and ¼ cup cheese. Transfer to a greased 9-in. pie plate. Sprinkle with remaining cheese.
2. Bake until golden brown and a knife inserted near the center comes out clean, 15-20 minutes. Let stand for 10 minutes before serving.
1 serving: 274 cal., 11g fat (4g sat. fat), 139mg chol., 667mg sod., 20g carb. (7g sugars, 3g fiber), 22g pro. **Diabetic exchanges:** 3 lean meat, 1½ fat, 1 starch, 1 vegetable.

TEST KITCHEN TIP

Allowing the egg bake to stand before cutting will help you cut clean slices. If you can't wait, use a serving spoon to dish this up to hungry family members.

HOMEMADE CHICKEN STOCK

Rich in chicken flavor, this traditional broth is lightly seasoned with herbs. In addition to making wonderful chicken soups, it can be used in casseroles, rice dishes and any other recipes that call for chicken broth.
—Taste of Home *Test Kitchen*

- -

PREP: 10 min. • **COOK:** 3¼ hours + chilling
MAKES: about 6 cups

- 2½   lbs. bone-in chicken pieces (legs, wings, necks or back bones)
- 2   celery ribs with leaves, cut into chunks
- 2   medium carrots, cut into chunks
- 2   medium onions, quartered
- 2   bay leaves
- ½   tsp. dried rosemary, crushed
- ½   tsp. dried thyme
- 8   to 10 whole peppercorns
- 2   qt. cold water

1. Place all ingredients in a soup kettle or Dutch oven. Slowly bring to a boil; reduce heat until the mixture is just at a simmer. Simmer, uncovered, for 3-4 hours, skimming foam as needed.
2. Set chicken aside until cool enough to handle. Remove meat from bones. Discard bones; save meat for another use. Strain broth, discarding vegetables and seasonings. Refrigerate for 8 hours or overnight. Skim fat from surface.
1 cup: 25 cal., 0 fat (0 sat. fat), 0 chol., 130mg sod., 2g carb. (0 sugars, 0 fiber), 4g pro.

HOMEMADE CHICKEN STOCK

LEARN HOW TO MAKE YOUR OWN CHICKEN STOCK
Just hover your camera here.

*TROPICAL CHICKEN
CAULIFLOWER RICE
BOWLS*

🍎 TROPICAL CHICKEN CAULIFLOWER RICE BOWLS

This tropical favorite is a tasty and healthy dinner and is bursting with flavor! You can use regular rice instead of cauliflower rice.
—*Bethany DiCarlo, Harleysville, PA*

PREP: 40 min. + marinating
GRILL: 10 min. • **MAKES:** 4 servings

- 1   fresh pineapple, peeled, cored and cubed (about 3 cups), divided
- ½   cup plain or coconut Greek yogurt
- 2   Tbsp. plus ½ cup chopped fresh cilantro, divided
- 3   Tbsp. lime juice, divided
- ¾   tsp. salt, divided
- ¼   tsp. crushed red pepper flakes
- ⅛   tsp. chili powder
- 4   boneless skinless chicken breast halves (6 oz. each)
- 3   cups fresh cauliflower florets (about ½ small cauliflower)
- 1   Tbsp. canola oil
- 1   small red onion, finely chopped
      Optional: Toasted sweetened shredded coconut or lime wedges

1. For marinade, place 1 cup pineapple, yogurt, 2 Tbsp. each cilantro and lime juice, ¼ tsp. salt, pepper flakes and chili powder in a food processor; process until blended. In a large bowl, toss the chicken with the marinade; refrigerate, covered, 1-3 hours.

2. In a clean food processor, pulse cauliflower until it resembles rice (do not overprocess). In a large skillet, heat oil over medium-high heat; saute onion until lightly browned, 3-5 minutes. Add cauliflower; cook and stir until lightly browned, 5-7 minutes. Stir in 1 cup pineapple and the remaining lime juice and salt; cook, covered, over medium until cauliflower is tender, 3-5 minutes. Stir in remaining cilantro. Keep warm.

3. Preheat grill or broiler. Drain chicken, discarding marinade. Place chicken on an oiled grill rack over medium heat or in a greased foil-lined 15x10x1-in. pan. Grill, covered, or broil 4 in. from the heat until a thermometer reads at least 165°, 4-6 minutes per side. Let chicken stand 5 minutes before slicing.

4. To serve, divide cauliflower mixture among 4 bowls. Top with the chicken, remaining pineapple and, if desired, shredded coconut and lime wedges.

Note: To toast coconut, bake in a shallow pan in a 350° oven for 5-10 minutes or cook in a skillet over low heat until golden brown, stirring occasionally.

1 serving: 325 cal., 10g fat (3g sat. fat), 100mg chol., 529mg sod., 22g carb. (15g sugars, 4g fiber), 38g pro. **Diabetic exchanges:** 5 lean meat, 1 fruit, 1 vegetable, 1 fat.

TEST KITCHEN TIP

To save time, buy cauliflower that's already been processed. Look for "riced" cauliflower in the refrigerated section of the produce department. You'll need 3 cups.

ALABAMA WHITE BBQ SAUCE

ALABAMA WHITE BBQ SAUCE

When my boys spent their summers with their grandmother in Alabama, she would bring them to a local restaurant that served chicken with white barbecue sauce. Making this reminds me of those times. Brush on the sauce only at the very end of the grilling.
—*Sabrina Everett, Thomasville, GA*

PREP: 5 min. + chilling • **MAKES:** 3 cups

- 2   cups mayonnaise
- 1   cup cider vinegar
- 2   Tbsp. pepper
- 2   Tbsp. lemon juice
- 1   tsp. salt
- ½   tsp. cayenne pepper

In a small bowl, whisk all ingredients. Refrigerate for at least 8 hours. Brush sauce over meats during the last few minutes of grilling. Serve remaining sauce on the side for dipping.

2 Tbsp.: 124 cal., 13g fat (2g sat. fat), 1mg chol., 192mg sod., 1g carb. (0 sugars, 0 fiber), 0 pro.

FALAFEL CHICKEN BURGERS WITH LEMON SAUCE

This recipe for falafel burgers with a lemon yogurt sauce was the first one I created myself. Use leftover falafel mix to bread fish, chicken and vegetables, or use it in meatballs.

—*Nicole Mederos, Hoboken, NJ*

- -

PREP: 35 min. • **COOK:** 10 min.
MAKES: 4 servings

4 frozen onion rings, optional
SAUCE
1 carton (5.3 oz.) fat-free lemon Greek yogurt
¼ tsp. ground cumin
¼ tsp. dill weed
⅛ tsp. salt
⅛ tsp. paprika
BURGERS
¼ cup minced fresh parsley
3 Tbsp. crumbled cooked bacon
3 garlic cloves, minced
¾ tsp. salt
¾ tsp. curry powder
½ tsp. pepper
¼ tsp. ground cumin

1 lb. ground chicken
1 pkg. (6 oz.) falafel mix
4 tsp. canola oil
4 sesame seed hamburger buns, split
1 cup fresh arugula or baby spinach
   Optional: Sliced tomato and cucumber

1. If desired, prepare onion rings according to package directions.
2. Meanwhile, in a small bowl, mix sauce ingredients. In a large bowl, mix the first 7 burger ingredients. Add chicken; mix lightly but thoroughly. Shape into four ½-in.-thick patties. Place ½ cup falafel mix in a shallow bowl (save remaining mix for another use). Press the patties into the falafel mix, patting to help the coating adhere.
3. In a large nonstick skillet, heat the oil over medium-high heat. Add burgers; cook 4-5 minutes on each side or until a thermometer reads 165°. Serve burgers on the buns with sauce and arugula. If desired, add an onion ring and sliced tomato and cucumber to each.
1 burger: 435 cal., 22g fat (5g sat. fat), 86mg chol., 1036mg sod., 33g carb. (9g sugars, 3g fiber), 32g pro.

HOW-TO
Keep Parsley Fresh
To keep parsley fresh for up to a month, trim the stems and place the bunch in a tumbler with an inch of water. Be sure no leaves are in the water. Tie a produce bag around the tumbler to trap humidity; store in the refrigerator. Each time you use the parsley, change the water and turn the produce bag inside out so any moisture that has built up inside the bag can escape.

*FALAFEL CHICKEN
BURGERS WITH
LEMON SAUCE*

HERB-STUFFED ROASTED CORNISH HENS

If you're looking for an elegant dinner for two, we suggest these delightful Cornish game hens. As a bonus, the crisp, tasty potatoes cook right alongside the birds.
—Taste of Home *Test Kitchen*

- -

PREP: 20 min. • **BAKE:** 70 min.
MAKES: 2 servings

2	Cornish game hens (20 to 24 oz. each)
12	fresh sage leaves
4	lemon wedges
6	green onions, cut into 2-in. lengths, divided
2	Tbsp. butter, melted
1	Tbsp. olive oil
1	Tbsp. lemon juice
2	garlic cloves, minced
1	tsp. kosher salt or sea salt
¼	tsp. coarsely ground pepper
6	small red potatoes, halved

1. Preheat oven to 375°. Gently lift skin from hen breasts and place sage leaves under skin. Place lemon wedges and a third of the onions in the cavities. Tuck wings under hens; tie legs together. Place in a small greased roasting pan.
2. Combine butter, oil, lemon juice and garlic; spoon half of mixture over hens. Sprinkle with salt and pepper.
3. Bake 30 minutes. Add potatoes and remaining onions to pan. Brush the hens with remaining butter mixture. Bake until a thermometer inserted in the thickest part of the thigh reads 170°-175° and the potatoes are tender, 40-45 minutes longer.
4. Remove hens to a serving platter. Stir potatoes and onions to coat with pan drippings. Serve with hens.
1 hen: 980 cal., 67g fat (22g sat. fat), 379mg chol., 1,398mg sod., 29g carb., 4g fiber, 63g pro.

🕐 SUPER QUICK CHICKEN FRIED RICE

After my first child was born, I needed meals that were satisfying and fast. This fried rice is now part of our dinner routine.
—*Alicia Gower, Auburn, NY*

TAKES: 30 min. • **MAKES:** 6 servings

- 1 pkg. (12 oz.) frozen mixed vegetables
- 2 Tbsp. olive oil, divided
- 2 large eggs, lightly beaten
- 4 Tbsp. sesame oil, divided
- 3 pkg. (8.8 oz. each) ready-to-serve garden vegetable rice
- 1 rotisserie chicken, skin removed, shredded
- ¼ tsp. salt
- ¼ tsp. pepper

1. Prepare frozen vegetables according to package directions. Meanwhile, in a large skillet, heat 1 Tbsp. olive oil over medium-high heat. Pour in eggs; cook and stir until eggs are thickened and no liquid egg remains. Remove from pan.
2. In same skillet, heat 2 Tbsp. sesame oil and remaining olive oil over medium-high heat. Add rice; cook and stir until rice begins to brown, 10-12 minutes.
3. Stir in chicken, salt and pepper. Add eggs and vegetables; heat through, breaking eggs into small pieces and stirring to combine. Drizzle with the remaining sesame oil.
1½ cups: 548 cal., 25g fat (5g sat. fat), 163mg chol., 934mg sod., 43g carb. (3g sugars, 3g fiber), 38g pro.

SUPER QUICK
CHICKEN FRIED RICE

SEE HOW QUICK IT TRULY IS
Just hover your camera here.

SIMPLE MARINATED CHICKEN

This is the best fooler recipe I've ever used. It takes just a few minutes but looks like you worked all day. You can even place frozen chicken breasts in the marinade and allow them to defrost and marinate in the refrigerator overnight.
—Nan Haring, Portage, MI

- -

PREP: 5 min. + marinating • **GRILL:** 10 min.
MAKES: 8 servings

- 1 envelope Italian salad dressing mix
- ¼ cup red wine vinegar
- ¼ cup soy sauce
- 2 lbs boneless skinless chicken breasts

1. In a large container, combine the dressing mix, red wine vinegar and soy sauce. Add chicken breasts. Cover and refrigerate for several hours.

2. Remove chicken from the marinade and grill over medium-hot heat for 5-6 minutes on each side or until the chicken juices run clear.

3 oz. cooked chicken: 130 cal., 3g fat (1g sat. fat), 63mg chol., 724mg sod., 1g carb. (1g sugars, 0g fiber), 24g pro. **Diabetic exchanges:** 3 lean meat.

WHY YOU'LL LOVE IT...

"Just used this for the second time last night—took the marinated and grilled chicken to a potluck, and it received rave reviews. It smelled wonderful as it was grilling, and it tasted great. This one is definitely going in my recipe box."
—TAXMASTER, TASTEOFHOME.COM

CREAMY CHICKEN VOL-AU-VENT

CREAMY CHICKEN VOL-AU-VENT

I have been getting together with friends for special ladies lunches for years. These pastry cups are the perfect no-fuss fancy food; they look complicated, but are simple and fun to make. Whenever I think of good friends and good company, I think of these savory pastries.
—Shauna Havey, Roy, UT

- -

PREP: 20 min. + chilling • **BAKE:** 20 min.
MAKES: 6 servings

- 1 pkg. (17.30 oz.) frozen puff pastry, thawed
- 1 large egg
- 1 Tbsp. water
- 6 bacon strips
- 2 medium leeks (white parts only), sliced
- 1 medium sweet yellow pepper, diced
- 1 cup shredded rotisserie chicken
- 8 oz. cream cheese, softened
- ¼ tsp. salt
- ¼ tsp. pepper
  Minced fresh parsley plus additional ground pepper

1. Preheat oven to 400°. On a lightly floured surface, unfold 1 puff pastry sheet. Using a 3¼-in. round cutter, cut out 6 circles. Place on a parchment-lined baking sheet.

2. Unfold remaining pastry sheet. Cut 6 more circles out with the 3¼-in. cutter. With a 2½-in. round cutter, cut centers out of the circles. Place the rings on top of the circles on the baking sheet. Place the cut-out circles on the baking sheet. In a small bowl, whisk egg and water; brush over pastries. Chill 15 minutes. Bake until the pastries are dark golden brown, 20-25 minutes. Remove to a wire rack to cool.

3. Meanwhile, in a large skillet, cook the bacon over medium heat until crisp. Remove to paper towels to drain. Discard all but 1 Tbsp. drippings. Add leeks and pepper to drippings; cook and stir over medium-high heat until tender, 5-7 minutes. Reduce heat to low; stir in bacon, chicken, cream cheese, salt and pepper. Cook and stir until blended; remove from heat.

4. When cool enough to handle, hollow out pastries with a small knife. Fill with chicken mixture. Sprinkle with parsley and pepper. Serve with small center pastries on the side.

1 filled pastry: 669 cal., 45g fat (16g sat. fat), 108mg chol., 670mg sod., 47g carb. (4g sugars, 6g fiber), 19g pro.

*SLOW-SIMMERED
CHICKEN RAGU*

🍲 SLOW-SIMMERED CHICKEN RAGU

After a day of simmering in the slow cooker, this ragu is not your typical spaghetti sauce. It's so hearty, it's almost like a stew.
—*Laurie LaClair, North Richland Hills, TX*

PREP: 30 min. • **COOK:** 6 hours
MAKES: 10 servings

- 1 jar (24 oz.) tomato basil pasta sauce
- 1 can (14½ oz.) Italian diced tomatoes, undrained
- 2 jars (6 oz. each) sliced mushrooms, drained
- 1 can (8 oz.) tomato sauce
- 1 jar (3½ oz.) prepared pesto
- 1½ lbs. chicken tenderloins
- 1 medium sweet red pepper, chopped
- ½ cup chopped pepperoni
- ½ cup pitted ripe olives, halved
- 1 tsp. dried oregano
- ½ tsp. hot pepper sauce
- 1 lb. Italian sausage links, cut into 1-in. pieces
- 1 medium onion, chopped
  Hot cooked angel hair pasta

1. In a 5- or 6-qt. slow cooker, combine the first 11 ingredients. Heat a large skillet over medium heat. Add sausage and onion; cook and stir until sausage is no longer pink and onion is tender. Drain. Add to slow cooker.
2. Cook, covered, on low 6-8 hours or until chicken is tender. Serve with pasta.
Freeze option: Do not cook or add the pasta. Freeze cooled sauce in freezer containers. To use, partially thaw in the refrigerator overnight. Cook the pasta according to package directions. Place meat mixture in a large saucepan; heat through, stirring occasionally; add water if necessary. Proceed as directed.
1 cup: 341 cal., 20g fat (5g sat. fat), 64mg chol., 1294mg sod., 18g carb. (10g sugars, 4g fiber), 26g pro.

CHICKEN PARMESAN BURGERS

⏱ CHICKEN PARMESAN BURGERS

A restaurant-quality burger that's topped with marinara and loaded with cheese—what's not to love? Add fresh basil for even more flavor if you'd like.
—*Brooke Petras, Alpine, CA*

TAKES: 30 min. • **MAKES:** 4 servings

- 3 Tbsp. olive oil, divided
- 1 small onion, finely chopped
- 2 garlic cloves, minced
- ¾ cup marinara sauce, divided
- ½ cup finely chopped or shredded part-skim mozzarella cheese
- ½ cup dry bread crumbs
- 1 tsp. Italian seasoning
- 1 tsp. dried oregano
- ½ tsp. salt
- ½ tsp. pepper
- 1 lb. ground chicken
- 4 slices part-skim mozzarella cheese
- 4 hamburger buns, split and toasted
- ¼ cup shredded Parmesan cheese
  Fresh basil leaves, optional

1. In a large skillet, heat 1 Tbsp. oil over medium-high heat. Add onion; cook and stir until tender, about 3 minutes. Add garlic; cook 1 minute longer. Remove from heat; cool slightly.
2. In a large bowl, combine ¼ cup marinara sauce, chopped mozzarella cheese, bread crumbs, seasonings and onion mixture. Add chicken; mix lightly but thoroughly. With wet hands, shape into four ½-in.-thick patties.
3. In the same skillet, heat remaining 2 Tbsp. oil over medium heat. Cook burgers until a thermometer reads 165°, 4-5 minutes on each side. Top with sliced mozzarella cheese; cook, covered, until cheese is melted, 1-2 minutes.
4. Serve in buns; top with remaining ½ cup marinara sauce, Parmesan cheese and, if desired, basil leaves.
1 burger: 603 cal., 33g fat (10g sat. fat), 108mg chol., 1275mg sod., 41g carb. (8g sugars, 3g fiber), 38g pro.

BUFFALO CHICKEN MEAT LOAF

Here's a great way to spice up a plain chicken meat loaf. It combines two of my favorite Sunday afternoon foods into one easy-to-make meal that's a huge hit with my family.
—*Holly Jones, Kennesaw, GA*

PREP: 25 min. • **BAKE:** 45 min. + standing
MAKES: 6 servings

- 1   cup dry whole wheat bread crumbs
- 2   celery ribs, chopped
- 1   small onion, chopped
- 2   large eggs, lightly beaten
- ½   cup Buffalo wing sauce
- 3   garlic cloves, minced
- 1   tsp. pepper
- 1   cup crumbled blue cheese, divided
- 1   lb. ground chicken
- 6   bacon strips

GLAZE
- ¼   cup Buffalo wing sauce
- 4   tsp. prepared mustard
- 4   tsp. honey
    Additional chopped celery, optional

1. Preheat oven to 350°. In a large bowl, combine the first 7 ingredients; stir in ¾ cup cheese. Add chicken; mix lightly but thoroughly. Shape chicken mixture into an 8x4-in. loaf placed on a greased 15x10x1-in. baking pan. Arrange bacon over top.
2. For glaze, in a small bowl, mix wing sauce, mustard and honey; spoon over meat loaf. Bake until a thermometer reads 165°, 45-50 minutes. Sprinkle with remaining blue cheese and, if desired, additional celery. Let stand 10 minutes before slicing.
2 pieces: 427 cal., 26g fat (10g sat. fat), 147mg chol., 1570mg sod., 25g carb. (6g sugars, 3g fiber),25g pro.

BUFFALO
CHICKEN
MEAT LOAF

BARBECUED
CHICKEN
MARINADE

🕐 BARBECUED CHICKEN MARINADE

When the family comes together, I pull out the chili powder, Worcestershire and garlic for a marinade that makes my chicken a home run.
—*Barbara Blickens Derfer, Edgewater, FL*

TAKES: 10 min. • **MAKES:** 1½ cups

- 1 large onion, chopped
- ⅔ cup butter, melted
- ⅓ cup cider vinegar
- 4 tsp. sugar
- 1 Tbsp. chili powder
- 2 tsp. salt
- 2 tsp. Worcestershire sauce
- 1½ tsp. pepper
- 1½ tsp. ground mustard
- 2 garlic cloves, minced
- ½ tsp. hot pepper sauce

In a small bowl, mix all ingredients. Use to marinate chicken.
¼ cup: 218 cal., 21g fat (13g sat. fat), 55mg chol., 1012mg sod., 7g carb. (4g sugars, 1g fiber), 1g pro.

🕐 ST. LOUIS BBQ SAUCE

This barbecue sauce is versatile and can be used on chicken, beef or pork.
—*David Boehm, Glendale, AZ*

PREP/COOK TIME: 20 min.
MAKES: 1½ cups

- 1 cup ketchup
- 3 Tbsp. packed brown sugar
- 1 Tbsp. cider vinegar
- 1 Tbsp. yellow mustard
- 2 tsp. Worcestershire sauce
- ½ tsp. salt
- ½ tsp. hot pepper sauce
- 1 to 2 Tbsp. water, optional

In a small saucepan, combine all ingredients; bring to a boil. Reduce heat; simmer, uncovered until slightly thickened, 5-10 minutes, stirring occasionally. Refrigerate leftovers.
2 Tbsp.: 17 cal., 0 fat (0 sat. fat), 0 chol., 188mg sod., 4g carb. (4g sugars, 0 fiber), 0 pro.

KALE & FENNEL SKILLET

🍎 KALE & FENNEL SKILLET

I love to combine vegetables and use different herbs and spices to change things up. If you can't find apple sausage for this skillet, a good mild Italian sausage would work just fine.
—*Patricia Levenson, Santa Ana, CA*

PREP: 10 min. • **COOK:** 25 min.
MAKES: 6 servings

- 2 Tbsp. extra virgin olive oil
- 1 small onion, thinly sliced
- 1 small fennel bulb, thinly sliced
- ½ lb. fully cooked apple chicken sausage links or cooked Italian sausage links, halved lengthwise and sliced into half-moons
- 2 garlic cloves, minced
- 3 Tbsp. dry sherry or dry white wine
- 1 Tbsp. herbes de Provence
- ⅛ tsp. salt
- ⅛ tsp. pepper
- 1 bunch kale, trimmed and torn into bite-sized pieces

1. In a large cast-iron or other heavy skillet, heat olive oil over medium-high heat. Add onion and fennel; cook and stir until the onion begins to brown, 6-8 minutes. Add the sausage, garlic, sherry and seasonings; cook until the sausage starts to caramelize, 4-6 minutes.
2. Add the kale; cook, covered, stirring occasionally, until leaves are tender, 15-17 minutes.
Note: Look for herbes de Provence in the spice aisle.
¾ cup: 167 cal., 8g fat (2g sat. fat), 27mg chol., 398mg sod., 16g carb. (6g sugars, 3g fiber), 9g pro. **Diabetic exchanges:** 2 vegetable, 1 lean meat, 1 fat.

TEST KITCHEN TIP

If you've never been a fan of kale because the mature leaves seem too tough, try the baby variety. Available at most supermarkets, the leaves are more tender, mild and palatable.

🕐 BLUE CHEESE CHICKEN SALAD SANDWICHES

I'm a big fan of blue cheese dressing, so I tried it in chicken salad instead of mayonnaise. It's so tangy! Serve the chicken mixture on a bed of lettuce if you're in the mood for salad instead.
—*Giovanna Kranenberg, Cambridge, MN*

TAKES: 15 min. • **MAKES:** 6 servings

- ⅔ cup chunky blue cheese salad dressing
- 1 celery rib, diced
- ½ cup seeded and diced cucumber
- ⅓ cup diced carrot
- 2 Tbsp. finely chopped onion
- 1 garlic clove, minced
- ¼ tsp. salt
- ¼ tsp. pepper
- 2 cups shredded rotisserie chicken, chilled
- 12 slices sourdough bread
  Crumbled blue cheese, optional

Mix first 8 ingredients; stir in chicken. Spread over half of the bread slices. If desired, sprinkle with blue cheese. Top with remaining bread.
1 sandwich: 418 cal., 19g fat (4g sat. fat), 50mg chol., 747mg sod., 40g carb. (5g sugars, 2g fiber), 22g pro.

BLUE CHEESE CHICKEN SALAD SANDWICHES

⏱ 🍎 EAST CAROLINA BARBECUE SAUCE

On a recent trip to the East Coast, I came across this bold, spicy barbecue sauce in the Carolinas. I'm not a fan of the thick and sugary sauces you typically see, so this really intrigued me. It was served with pulled pork, but I've tried it on chicken and it works beautifully.
—*Susan Hein, Burlington, WI*

TAKES: 5 min. • **MAKES:** 1 cup

- 1 cup cider vinegar
- 1 Tbsp. brown sugar
- 2 tsp. coarsely ground pepper
- 2 to 3 tsp. hot pepper sauce
- 1 tsp. salt
- ½ to 1 tsp. crushed red pepper flakes

Combine all ingredients in a jar or shaker. Seal and shake until sugar has completely dissolved. Use or store at room temperature for up to 2 weeks.
2 Tbsp.: 15 cal., 0 fat (0 sat. fat), 0 chol., 305mg sod., 2g carb. (2g sugars, 0 fiber), 0 pro.

GLAZED CORNISH HENS WITH PECAN-RICE STUFFING

Cornish hens bake up with a lovely golden brown shine when they are basted with my sweet and tangy glaze. The traditional rice stuffing gets some added interest with the crunchy pecans and sweet golden raisins.
—*Agnes Ward, Stratford, ON*

PREP: 1 hour
BAKE: 1 hour 25 min. + standing
MAKES: 8 servings

- 8 Cornish game hens (20 to 24 oz. each)
- ¼ cup butter, softened
- ½ tsp. salt
- ½ tsp. pepper
- 2 cups unsweetened apple juice
- 1 Tbsp. honey
- 1 Tbsp. Dijon mustard

PECAN RICE

- 2 Tbsp. butter
- 1½ cups uncooked long grain rice
- 2 tsp. ground cumin
- 1 tsp. curry powder
- 4 cups reduced-sodium chicken broth
- 1 cup chopped pecans, toasted
- 3 green onions, thinly sliced
- ½ cup golden raisins

1. Tuck wings under the hens; tie drumsticks together. Rub skin with butter; sprinkle with salt and pepper. Place hens breast side up in a shallow roasting pan.

2. Bake, uncovered, at 350° for 1 hour. Meanwhile, place apple juice in a small saucepan. Bring to a boil; cook juice until reduced by half. Remove from heat. Stir in honey and mustard. Set aside ½ cup for serving.

3. Brush hens with apple juice mixture. Bake, basting occasionally with the pan drippings, until a thermometer reads 180°, 25-35 minutes longer. Cover the hens loosely with foil if they brown too quickly.

4. For pecan rice, heat butter in a large saucepan over medium heat. Add rice, cumin and curry; cook and stir until rice is lightly browned, 2-3 minutes. Stir in broth. Bring to a boil. Reduce the heat; simmer, covered, until rice is tender, 15-20 minutes. Stir in pecans, onions and raisins.

5. Cover hens; let stand 10 minutes before serving. Serve with rice and reserved sauce.

1 hen with 1 Tbsp. sauce: 1075 cal., 68g fat (20g sat. fat), 371mg chol., 905mg sod., 48g carb. (16g sugars, 3g fiber), 65g pro.

GLAZED CORNISH HENS WITH PECAN-RICE STUFFING

DR PEPPER BBQ SAUCE

My family is stationed in Italy with my husband, Lt. William Robert Blackman. William grew up in Memphis, Tennessee, and I'm from Texas, so the dish that spells home for us is a good ol' barbecue. I have my own recipe for sauce that we like to pour all over sliced brisket. Eating it reminds us of family barbecues.
—*Tina Blackman, Naples, Italy*

PREP: 5 min. • **COOK:** 35 min.
MAKES: 1 cup

- 1 can (12 oz.) Dr Pepper
- 1 cup crushed tomatoes
- ¼ cup packed brown sugar
- 2 Tbsp. spicy brown mustard
- 1 Tbsp. orange juice
- 1 Tbsp. Worcestershire sauce
- 1 garlic clove, minced
- ¼ tsp. salt
- ⅛ tsp. pepper

In a small saucepan, combine all the ingredients; bring to a boil. Reduce the heat; simmer, uncovered, 30-35 minutes or until the sauce is slightly thickened, stirring occasionally. Refrigerate the leftover sauce.

2 Tbsp.: 60 cal., 0 fat (0 sat. fat), 0 chol., 193mg sod., 15g carb. (12g sugars, 1g fiber), 1g pro.

WHY YOU'LL LOVE IT...

"This is a great BBQ sauce. Made the recipe as is and also made it using Diet Dr Pepper— both are excellent! Family enjoyed it on pulled pork and on ribs. I will definitely make it often."
—AMEHART, TASTEOFHOME.COM

DR PEPPER
BBQ SAUCE

Dr Pepper
BBQ
Sauce

BUFFALO CHICKEN-TOPPED POTATOES

Cheesy potatoes meet spicy Buffalo chicken wings in this irresistible recipe! Loaded with cheese, sour cream and onions, these hearty stuffed potatoes get a sassy bite from mild wing sauce.
—*Michelle Gauer, Spicer, MN*

PREP: 70 min. • **BAKE:** 10 min.
MAKES: 8 servings

- 4 medium potatoes (about 1½ lbs.)
- ¾ cup shredded cheddar cheese, divided
- ½ cup sour cream
- 2 Tbsp. Buffalo wing sauce, divided
- 1 lb. boneless skinless chicken breasts, cubed
- ¼ tsp. salt
- ¼ tsp. chili powder
- 1 Tbsp. canola oil
- 2 Tbsp. white vinegar
- 2 Tbsp. butter
  Additional sour cream and chopped green onions

1. Scrub and pierce potatoes. Bake at 375° for 1 hour or until tender. When cool enough to handle, cut each potato in half lengthwise. Scoop out the pulp, leaving thin shells.
2. In a large bowl, mash the pulp with ½ cup cheese, sour cream and 1 Tbsp. wing sauce. Spoon into potato shells; top with remaining cheese.
3. Place on baking sheet. Bake potatoes 8-12 minutes or until heated through.
4. Meanwhile, sprinkle chicken with salt and chili powder. In a large skillet, cook the chicken in oil over medium heat for 6-8 minutes or until no longer pink. Add the vinegar, butter and remaining wing sauce; cook and stir 2-3 minutes longer.
5. Spoon chicken mixture over potatoes. Serve with the additional sour cream and onions.
1 potato: 254 cal., 12g fat (6g sat. fat), 60mg chol., 198mg sod., 20g carb. (2g sugars, 2g fiber), 16g pro.

HASH BROWN & CHICKEN BRUNCH CASSEROLE

HASH BROWN & CHICKEN BRUNCH CASSEROLE

My husband and I love a hot breakfast, but find it difficult with two kids. This dish is excellent to prepare the night before and bake the next day for your family or to take in to work to share with co-workers—there are never any leftovers.
—*Jennifer Berry, Lexington, OH*

PREP: 20 min. + chilling • **BAKE:** 1¼ hours
MAKES: 12 servings

- 15 large eggs, beaten
- 1 pkg. (28 oz.) frozen potatoes O'Brien
- 1 rotisserie chicken, skin removed, shredded
- 1½ cups 2% milk
- 1 can (10 oz.) diced tomatoes and green chiles, undrained
- 2 cups shredded cheddar cheese, divided
- 5 green onions, chopped
- 3 Tbsp. minced fresh cilantro
- 1 tsp. ground cumin
- 1½ tsp. salt
- ½ tsp. pepper

1. In a very large bowl, combine the eggs, potatoes, chicken, milk, tomatoes, 1 cup cheese, green onions, cilantro and seasonings until blended. Transfer to a greased 13x9-in. baking dish; sprinkle with remaining cheese. Refrigerate, covered, several hours or overnight.
2. Preheat oven to 350°. Remove the casserole from refrigerator while oven heats. Bake, uncovered, until golden brown and a knife inserted in the center comes out clean, 1¼-1½ hours. Let stand 5-10 minutes before serving.
1 piece: 432 cal., 20g fat (8g sat. fat), 348mg chol., 705mg sod., 14g carb. (3g sugars, 2g fiber), 45g pro.

BUFFALO CHICKEN EMPANADAS WITH BLUE CHEESE SAUCE

BUFFALO CHICKEN EMPANADAS WITH BLUE CHEESE SAUCE

These little golden brown pockets are fun to eat and feature the popular taste of Buffalo wings. Rotisserie chicken and refrigerated pie crusts make them easy.
—*Melissa Millwood, Lyman, SC*

- -

PREP: 35 min. • **BAKE:** 10 min./batch
MAKES: 6¼ dozen (1 cup sauce)

- 1   small onion, chopped
- 1   small green pepper, chopped
- 4½ tsp. canola oil
- 2   garlic cloves, minced
- 3   cups finely chopped rotisserie chicken
- 1½ cups shredded part-skim mozzarella cheese
- ½   cup Buffalo wing sauce
- ¼   tsp. salt
- ¼   tsp. pepper
- 5   sheets refrigerated pie crust
- 2   large eggs
- 2   Tbsp. water
- 1   cup heavy whipping cream
- 1   cup crumbled blue cheese

1. In a small skillet, saute onion and green pepper in oil until crisp-tender. Add garlic; cook 1 minute longer.

2. In a large bowl, combine the chicken, mozzarella cheese, wing sauce, salt and pepper. Stir in the onion mixture.

3. On a lightly floured surface, unroll 1 pie crust. Roll out into a 12-in. circle. Cut circles with a floured 3-in. biscuit cutter. Remove excess and reroll scraps. Repeat with remaining pie crusts.

4. Beat eggs and water; brush over edges of 3-in. pie crust circles. Place heaping teaspoons of filling in the centers. Fold crust in half over filling. Press edges with a fork to seal.

5. Place 2 in. apart on greased baking sheets. Brush with the remaining egg mixture. Bake at 400° until golden brown, 9-12 minutes.

6. Meanwhile, in a small saucepan, bring cream to a boil. Reduce heat; simmer, uncovered, until cream thickens slightly, 5-7 minutes, stirring occasionally. Add blue cheese; cook and stir until cheese is melted and sauce thickens, about 2 minutes longer. Serve with the empanadas.

1 empanada with ½ tsp. sauce: 104 cal., 7g fat (2g sat. fat), 19mg chol., 153mg sod., 7g carb. (1g sugars, 0 fiber), 3g pro.

Make Ahead: Unbaked empanadas may be frozen for up to 2 months. Bake as directed for 12-16 minutes.

CHICKEN-PROSCIUTTO PINWHEELS IN WINE SAUCE

We host a large group for holiday meals, and these pinwheels always go over well alongside the other dishes. I often double this recipe and use two 13x9-in. pans.
—*Johnna Johnson, Scottsdale, AZ*

- -

PREP: 30 min. + chilling • **BAKE:** 30 min.
MAKES: 6 servings

- 6   boneless skinless chicken breast halves (6 oz. each)
- 6   thin slices prosciutto or deli ham
- 6   slices part-skim mozzarella cheese
- 2   large eggs, lightly beaten
- ½   cup Italian-style panko bread crumbs
- ½   cup butter, cubed
- 1   shallot, finely chopped
- 2   garlic cloves, minced
- 3   cups Madeira wine

1. Pound chicken breasts with a meat mallet to ¼-in. thickness; layer with prosciutto and mozzarella. Roll up chicken from a short side; secure with toothpicks.

2. Place eggs and bread crumbs in separate shallow bowls. Dip chicken in eggs, then roll in crumbs to coat. Cut each chicken breast crosswise into 3 slices; place in a greased 13x9-in. baking dish, cut side down. Refrigerate, covered, overnight.

3. Preheat oven to 350°. Remove the chicken from refrigerator; uncover and let stand while oven heats. In a small saucepan, heat butter over medium-high heat. Add shallot and garlic; cook and stir until tender, 1-2 minutes. Add wine. Bring to a boil; cook until liquid is reduced to 1½ cups. Pour over chicken.

4. Bake, uncovered, until a thermometer reads 165°, 30-35 minutes. Discard toothpicks before serving.

3 pinwheels: 581 cal., 30g fat (15g sat. fat), 227mg chol., 827mg sod., 15g carb. (5g sugars, 0 fiber), 48g pro.

**CHICKEN-PROSCIUTTO
PINWHEELS
IN WINE SAUCE**

CHICKEN CORNBREAD DRESSING

Even though Mom passed away years ago, her wonderful cornbread dressing lives on each year at our Christmas dinner. It just wouldn't be the same holiday without it!
—*Fay Miller, Denham Springs, LA*

PREP: 1 hour 40 min. • **BAKE:** 1 hour
MAKES: 12 servings

- 1 broiler/fryer chicken (3 to 3½ lbs.)
- 2½ qt. water
- 2 to 3 celery ribs with leaves
- 1 large onion, cut into chunks

DRESSING
- 4 celery ribs, chopped
- 2 small onions, chopped
- ½ cup butter
- 1 tsp. salt
- ¼ tsp. rubbed sage
- ¼ tsp. pepper
- ⅛ tsp. cayenne pepper
- 6 cups crumbled cornbread
- 1 cup chopped green onions
- ¾ cup chopped pecans, toasted
- ½ cup minced fresh parsley
- 2 large eggs, lightly beaten

1. Place chicken in a soup kettle. Add the water, celery and onion; bring to a boil. Reduce heat; cover and simmer for 1-1½ hours or until the chicken is tender. Remove chicken from broth. Strain broth, discarding vegetables; set broth aside. When cool enough to handle, remove chicken from bones; dice and place in a large bowl.
2. In a large skillet, saute celery and onions in butter until tender; stir in the salt, sage, pepper and cayenne. Add to chicken. Stir in the cornbread, green onions, pecans, parsley and eggs. Add 1¼-1½ cups of reserved broth, stirring gently to mix. (Refrigerate remaining broth for another use.)
3. Transfer chicken cornbread dressing to greased 13x9-in. baking dish. Cover dish and bake at 325° for 45 minutes. Uncover; bake 15-20 minutes or until a thermometer reads 160°.
½ cup: 383 cal., 22g fat (7g sat. fat), 100mg chol., 663mg sod., 27g carb. (4g sugars, 3g fiber), 19g pro.

CRUSTLESS CHICKEN QUICHE

This is a very easy brunch dish that also keeps well if there are leftovers. Thick and cheesy, it's nearly impossible not to enjoy this savory recipe!
—*Susie Baumberger, Lancaster, CA*

PREP: 15 min. • **BAKE:** 35 min. + standing
MAKES: 6 servings

- 1 large sweet onion, chopped
- 2 Tbsp. olive oil
- 2 tsp. minced garlic
- 6 large eggs, lightly beaten
- ¾ cup heavy whipping cream
- 2 cups cubed cooked rotisserie chicken
- 2 cups shredded cheddar cheese
- 5 bacon strips, cooked and crumbled

1. In a small skillet, saute onion in oil until tender. Add garlic; cook 1 minute longer. In a large bowl, combine eggs and cream. Stir in the chicken, cheese, bacon and onion mixture. Pour into a greased 9-in. deep-dish pie plate.
2. Bake at 375° for 35-45 minutes or until a knife inserted in the center comes out clean. Let quiche stand for 10 minutes before cutting.
Freeze option: Cover and freeze for up to 2 months. To use the frozen quiche, thaw in the refrigerator. Remove from refrigerator 30 minutes before baking. Bake according to directions.
1 piece: 498 cal., 39g fat (19g sat. fat), 337mg chol., 696mg sod., 5g carb. (1g sugars, 0 fiber), 31g pro.

ROASTED CORNISH HENS WITH VEGETABLES

Roasting simply seasoned Cornish game hens and vegetables in one pan results in a full-flavored meal in one.
—*Lily Julow, Lawrenceville, GA*

PREP: 20 min. • **BAKE:** 1¼ hours
MAKES: 6 servings

- 6 medium potatoes, quartered
- 6 medium carrots, cut in half lengthwise and cut into chunks
- 1 large sweet onion, cut into wedges
- ½ cup butter, melted
- 2 tsp. dried oregano
- 2 tsp. dried rosemary, crushed
- 1½ tsp. garlic salt
- 6 Cornish game hens (20 to 24 oz. each)
- 1 Tbsp. olive oil
- ¼ tsp. salt
- ¼ tsp. pepper
- 6 bacon strips

1. Preheat oven to 350°. In a large bowl, combine first 7 ingredients. Transfer to a large shallow roasting pan.
2. Brush hens with oil; sprinkle with salt and pepper. Wrap a bacon strip around each hen; secure bacon with a wooden toothpick. Tie legs together. Place hen, breast side up, over vegetables.
3. Bake, uncovered, 1¼-1¾ hours or until a thermometer inserted in thigh reads 170-175° and vegetables are tender. Remove hens to a serving platter; serve with vegetables.
1 hen: 1164 cal., 77g fat (27g sat. fat), 404mg chol., 1268mg sod., 49g carb. (9g sugars, 6g fiber), 68g pro.

**BBQ CHICKEN
GRITS BITES**

BBQ CHICKEN GRITS BITES

I love grits and barbecued chicken, so
I decided to combine them into a fun and
tasty appetizer. You can also use shredded
pork instead of chicken.
—*Jamie Jones, Madison, GA*

PREP: 30 min. • **BAKE:** 15 min.
MAKES: 2½ dozen

2 cups 2% milk
¾ cup quick-cooking grits
¼ tsp. salt
⅛ tsp. pepper
4 oz. crumbled goat cheese, divided
¼ cup apricot preserves
¼ cup barbecue sauce
1½ cups chopped rotisserie chicken
3 green onions, thinly sliced

1. Preheat oven to 350°. Grease
30 mini-muffin cups.
2. In a large saucepan, bring milk to a
boil. Slowly stir in grits, salt and pepper.
Reduce the heat to medium-low; cook,
covered, until grit mixture is thickened,
about 5 minutes, stirring occasionally.
Stir in half of the cheese. Spoon 1 Tbsp.
mixture into each prepared muffin cup.
3. In a bowl, mix preserves and
barbecue sauce; toss with chicken.
Spoon about 1 tsp. chicken mixture
into each cup; press lightly into grits.
4. Bake appetizers until heated through,
15-20 minutes. Top with the remaining
cheese; sprinkle with green onions. Cool
5 minutes before removing from pans.
Serve warm.
1 appetizer: 56 cal., 2g fat (1g sat. fat),
12mg chol., 76mg sod., 7g carb. (3g
sugars, 0 fiber), 4g pro.

BONUS: TURKEY SPECIALTIES

TURKEY LATTICE PIE,
PAGE 300

FAMILY-FAVORITE TURKEY EGG ROLLS

Finger foods give mealtime extra flair! This recipe is so easy, kids can help prepare it. Serve with sweet-and-sour or hot mustard dipping sauce.
—Virginia Rehm, Waynesville, MO

PREP: 25 min. • **COOK:** 5 min./batch
MAKES: 1 dozen

½ lb. ground turkey
4½ cups coleslaw mix
3 Tbsp. sesame seeds
1 Tbsp. reduced-sodium soy sauce
2 tsp. Worcestershire sauce
¾ tsp. ground ginger
½ tsp. seasoned salt
12 egg roll wrappers
Oil for deep-fat frying
Sweet-and-sour sauce

1. In a large skillet, cook turkey over medium heat until no longer pink; drain. Stir in the coleslaw mix, sesame seeds, soy sauce, Worcestershire sauce, ginger and seasoned salt. Cook for 3-4 minutes or until cabbage is crisp-tender.
2. Place ¼ cup of turkey mixture in the center of 1 egg roll wrapper. (Keep remaining wrappers covered with a damp paper towel until ready to use.) Fold bottom corner over filling. Fold sides toward center over filling. Moisten remaining corner with water; roll up tightly to seal. Repeat.
3. In an electric skillet or deep-fat fryer, heat oil to 375°. Fry egg rolls, a few at a time, for 3-4 minutes or until golden brown, turning often. Drain on paper towels. Serve with sweet-and-sour sauce.
1 egg roll: 199 cal., 10g fat (1g sat. fat), 16mg chol., 332mg sod., 21g carb. (1g sugars, 1g fiber), 7g pro.

MOM'S TURKEY TETRAZZINI

If you're looking for stick-to-your-ribs comfort food, this hearty dish will meet your needs.
—Judy Batson, Tampa, FL

PREP: 25 min. • **BAKE:** 25 min. + standing
MAKES: 6 servings

1 pkg. (12 oz.) fettuccine
½ lb. sliced fresh mushrooms
1 medium onion, chopped
¼ cup butter, cubed
3 Tbsp. all-purpose flour
1 cup white wine or chicken broth
3 cups 2% milk
3 cups cubed cooked turkey
¾ tsp. salt
½ tsp. pepper
½ tsp. hot pepper sauce
½ cup shredded Parmesan cheese
Paprika, optional

1. Preheat oven to 375°. Cook fettuccine according to the package directions.
2. Meanwhile, in a large skillet, saute mushrooms and onion in butter until tender. Stir in flour until blended; whisk in wine until smooth, about 2 minutes. Slowly whisk in milk. Bring to a boil; cook and stir until thickened. Stir in turkey, salt, pepper and pepper sauce.
3. Drain the fettuccine. Layer half of the fettuccine, turkey mixture and cheese in a greased 13x9-in. baking dish. Repeat layers. Sprinkle with paprika if desired.
4. Cover and bake 25-30 minutes or until heated through. Let stand for 10 minutes before serving.
1 cup: 516 cal., 17g fat (9g sat. fat), 87mg chol., 596mg sod., 53g carb. (10g sugars, 4g fiber), 37g pro.

*BUFFALO
TURKEY BURGERS*

BUFFALO TURKEY BURGERS

Celery and blue cheese dressing help tame the hot sauce on these juicy burgers. For an even lighter version, pass on the buns and serve with lettuce leaves, sliced onion and chopped tomato.

—Mary Pax-Shipley, Bend, OR

TAKES: 25 min. • **MAKES:** 4 servings

2	Tbsp. Louisiana-style hot sauce, divided
2	tsp. ground cumin
2	tsp. chili powder
2	garlic cloves, minced
½	tsp. salt
⅛	tsp. pepper
1	lb. lean ground turkey
4	whole wheat hamburger buns, split
1	cup shredded lettuce
2	celery ribs, chopped
2	Tbsp. fat-free blue cheese salad dressing

1. In a large bowl, combine 1 Tbsp. hot sauce, cumin, chili powder, garlic, salt and pepper. Add the turkey; mix lightly but thoroughly. Shape into four ½-in.-thick patties.

2. In a large nonstick skillet, cook the burgers over medium heat 4-6 minutes on each side or until a thermometer reads 165°.

3. Serve burgers on buns with lettuce, celery, salad dressing and remaining hot sauce.

Freeze option: Place patties on a waxed paper-lined baking sheet; cover and freeze until firm. Remove from pan and transfer to an airtight container; return to freezer. To use, cook frozen patties as directed, increasing time as necessary for a thermometer to read 165°.

1 burger: 312 cal., 12g fat (3g sat. fat), 90mg chol., 734mg sod., 28g carb. (5g sugars, 5g fiber), 24g pro. **Diabetic exchanges:** 3 lean meat, 2 starch, ½ fat.

AIR-FRYER
TURKEY
CROQUETTES

🍎 🍽 AIR-FRYER TURKEY CROQUETTES

I grew up in a family that looked forward to leftovers, especially on the day after Thanksgiving. But we didn't just reheat turkey and spuds in the microwave—we took our culinary creativity to a new level with recipes likes these croquettes.
—*Meredith Coe, Charlottesville, VA*

PREP: 20 min. • **COOK:** 10 min./batch
MAKES: 6 servings

- 2 cups mashed potatoes (with added milk and butter)
- ½ cup grated Parmesan cheese
- ½ cup shredded Swiss cheese
- 1 shallot, finely chopped
- 2 tsp. minced fresh rosemary or ½ tsp. dried rosemary, crushed
- 1 tsp. minced fresh sage or ¼ tsp. dried sage leaves
- ½ tsp. salt
- ¼ tsp. pepper
- 3 cups finely chopped cooked turkey
- 1 large egg
- 2 Tbsp. water
- 1¼ cups panko bread crumbs
  Butter-flavored cooking spray
  Sour cream, optional

1. Preheat air fryer to 350°. In a large bowl, combine the mashed potatoes, cheeses, shallot, rosemary, sage, salt and pepper; stir in turkey. Mix lightly but thoroughly. Shape mixture into twelve 1-in.-thick patties.
2. In a shallow bowl, whisk egg and water. Place bread crumbs in another shallow bowl. Dip croquettes in egg mixture, then in bread crumbs, patting to help coating adhere.
3. In batches, place croquettes in a single layer on greased tray in air-fryer basket; spritz with cooking spray. Cook until golden brown, 4-5 minutes. Turn; spritz with cooking spray. Cook until golden brown; 4-5 minutes. If desired, serve with sour cream.

2 croquettes: 322 cal., 12g fat (6g sat. fat), 124mg chol., 673mg sod., 22g carb. (2g sugars, 2g fiber), 29g pro. **Diabetic exchanges:** 4 lean meat, 1½ starch, 1 fat.

🕐 🍎 CURRY TURKEY STIR-FRY

Just open the fridge and go to town making this throw-together curry. We prefer turkey, but if you like chicken, shrimp, or even bean sprouts and carrots, feel free to use them.
—*Lauren Rush, Clark, NJ*

TAKES: 20 min. • **MAKES:** 4 servings

- ½ tsp. cornstarch
- 2 Tbsp. reduced-sodium soy sauce
- 1 Tbsp. minced fresh cilantro
- 1 Tbsp. honey
- 1 tsp. curry powder
- 1 tsp. sesame or canola oil
- 1 garlic clove, minced
- ⅛ tsp. crushed red pepper flakes, optional
- 1 Tbsp. canola oil
- 1 large sweet red pepper, julienned
- 3 green onions, cut into 2-in. pieces
- 2 cups cubed cooked turkey breast
- 2 cups hot cooked brown rice

1. Mix first 7 ingredients and, if desired, pepper flakes. In a large skillet, heat 1 Tbsp. canola oil over medium-high heat; stir-fry red pepper until crisp-tender, about 2 minutes. Add the green onions; stir-fry until tender, 1-2 minutes.
2. Stir cornstarch mixture and add to pan. Bring to a boil; cook and stir until thickened, 1-2 minutes. Stir in turkey; heat through. Serve with rice.

¾ cup turkey mixture with ½ cup rice: 287 cal., 7g fat (1g sat. fat), 60mg chol., 351mg sod., 31g carb. (7g sugars, 3g fiber), 25g pro. **Diabetic exchanges:** 3 lean meat, 2 starch, 1 fat.

STUFFING & TURKEY CASSEROLE

This makes a plate full of love, comfort and goodness.
—*Debbie Fabre, Fort Myers, FL*

PREP: 15 min. • **BAKE:** 45 min. + standing
MAKES: 12 servings

- 4 cups leftover stuffing
- 1 cup dried cranberries
- 1 cup chopped pecans
- ¾ cup chicken broth
- 1 large egg, lightly beaten
- 2 cups shredded part-skim mozzarella cheese
- 1 cup whole-milk ricotta cheese
- 4 cups cubed cooked turkey, divided
- 1 cup shredded cheddar cheese

1. Preheat oven to 350°. Place stuffing, cranberries and pecans in a large bowl; stir in broth. In a small bowl, mix egg and the mozzarella and ricotta cheeses.
2. In a greased 13x9-in. baking dish, layer 2 cups turkey, 3 cups stuffing mixture, and the cheese mixture. Top with remaining turkey and stuffing mixture. Sprinkle with cheddar cheese.
3. Bake, covered, 40-45 minutes or until heated through. Bake, uncovered, 5 minutes longer. Let stand 10 minutes before serving.

1 piece: 418 cal., 24g fat (8g sat. fat), 91mg chol., 640mg sod., 26g carb. (10g sugars, 3g fiber), 27g pro.

CLASSIC
STUFFED
TURKEY

HOW-TO

Stuff, Roast and Carve a Whole Turkey

STEP 1. Tuck wing tips under body to aid in even cooking.

STEP 2. Combine stuffing as the recipe directs, but do not stuff the turkey until you're ready to place it in the oven. Once you're ready to cook the bird, spoon the stuffing loosely into cavity.

STEP 3. Tie drumsticks together with kitchen string.

STEP 4. Place turkey, breast side up, on a rack in a shallow roasting pan. Brush with oil or melted butter if desired. Insert an oven-safe thermometer into thick area of inner thigh, not touching bone. Or use an instant-read thermometer to check the temperature near the end of the roasting time.

STEP 5. Roast turkey as the recipe directs, basting with the pan juices if desired.

STEP 6. Once turkey breast has browned, cover it loosely with foil to prevent overbrowning. Continue roasting until a thermometer reads 165° in the center of the stuffing and at least 170° in thigh. Let turkey stand, covered, at least 20 minutes.

STEP 7. Place bird on a carving board and remove any stuffing. Holding the drumstick, pull leg away from the body and cut through the hip joint. Remove leg. Repeat on other side.

STEP 8. Cut through joint to separate drumstick and thigh.

STEP 9. Cut meat into ¼-in. slices while holding drumstick by the end. Cut thigh meat into ¼-in. slices.

STEP 10. Hold the bird with a meat fork and make a deep horizontal cut into the breast meat just above the wing area.

STEP 11. Slice down from the top of the breast into the cut made in the previous step. Slice the meat ¼ in. thick. Repeat these steps on the other side of bird.

STEP 12. Cut through joints to separate the wings.

CLASSIC STUFFED TURKEY

For years, my mother has made this moist stuffed turkey recipe. Now, I do the same thing. The turkey stuffing compliments the tender, juicy slices of oven-roasted turkey.
—*Kathi Graham, Naperville, IL*

- -

PREP: 20 min. • **BAKE:** 3¾ hours + standing
MAKES: 12 servings (10 cups stuffing)

- 2 large onions, chopped
- 2 celery ribs, chopped
- ½ lb. fresh mushrooms, sliced
- ½ cup butter
- 1 can (14½ oz.) chicken broth
- ⅓ cup minced fresh parsley
- 2 tsp. rubbed sage
- 1 tsp. salt
- 1 tsp. poultry seasoning
- ½ tsp. pepper
- 12 cups unseasoned stuffing cubes
  Warm water
- 1 turkey (14 to 16 lbs.)
  Melted butter

1. In a large skillet, saute the onions, celery and mushrooms in butter until tender. Add broth and seasonings; mix well. Place bread cubes in a large bowl; add mushroom mixture and toss to coat. Stir in enough warm water to reach desired moistness.

2. Just before baking, loosely stuff turkey. Place any remaining stuffing in a greased baking dish; cover and refrigerate until ready to bake. Skewer the turkey openings; tie drumsticks together with kitchen string. Place breast side up on a rack in a roasting pan. Brush with melted butter.

3. Bake turkey, uncovered, at 325° for 3¾-4½ hours or until a thermometer reads 165° when inserted in center of stuffing and the thigh reaches at least 170°, basting occasionally with pan drippings. (Cover loosely with foil if turkey browns too quickly.)

4. Bake additional stuffing, covered, for 30-40 minutes. Uncover; bake 10 minutes longer or until lightly browned. Cover turkey with foil and let stand for 20 minutes before removing the stuffing and carving. If desired, thicken pan drippings for gravy.

1 serving: 571 cal., 26g fat (11g sat. fat), 153mg chol., 961mg sod., 42g carb. (5g sugars, 4g fiber), 44g pro.

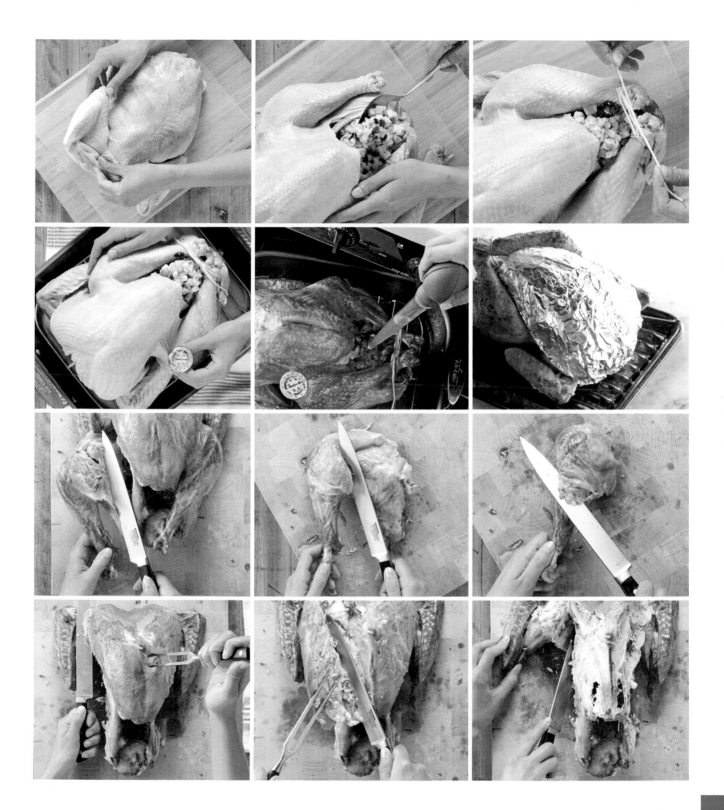

TURKEY LATTICE PIE

With its pretty lattice crust, this cheesy baked dish is as appealing as it is tasty. It's easy to make, too, since it uses ready-to-go crescent roll dough.
—*Lorraine Naig, Emmetsburg, IA*

PREP: 20 min. • **BAKE:** 20 min.
MAKES: 12 servings

- 3 tubes (8 oz. each) refrigerated crescent rolls
- 4 cups cubed cooked turkey
- 1½ cups shredded cheddar or Swiss cheese
- 3 cups frozen chopped broccoli, thawed and drained
- 1 can (10¾ oz.) condensed cream of chicken soup, undiluted
- 1⅓ cups 2% milk
- 2 Tbsp. Dijon mustard
- 1 Tbsp. dried minced onion
- ½ tsp. salt
  Dash pepper
- 1 large egg, lightly beaten

1. Preheat oven to 375°. Unroll 2 tubes of crescent roll dough; separate into rectangles. Place rectangles in an ungreased 15x10x1-in. baking pan. Press onto the bottom and ¼ in. up the sides of pan to form a crust; seal seams and perforations. Bake for 5-7 minutes or until light golden brown.
2. Meanwhile, in a large bowl, combine the turkey, cheese, broccoli, soup, milk, mustard, onion, salt and pepper. Spoon over crust.
3. Unroll remaining dough; divide into 2 rectangles. Seal perforations. Cut each rectangle lengthwise into 1-in. strips. Using strips, make a lattice design on top of turkey mixture. Brush with egg. Bake 17-22 minutes longer or until top crust is golden brown and filling is bubbly.
1 serving: 396 cal., 20g fat (4g sat. fat), 81mg chol., 934mg sod., 30g carb. (8g sugars, 2g fiber), 24g pro.

CURRY-ROASTED TURKEY & POTATOES

Honey mustard is the condiment of choice around here, so I wanted a healthy recipe to serve it with. Roasted turkey with a dash of curry is perfect.
—*Carol Witczak, Tinley Park, IL*

TAKES: 30 min. • **MAKES:** 4 servings

- 1 lb. Yukon Gold potatoes (about 3 medium), cut into ½-in. cubes
- 2 medium leeks (white portion only), thinly sliced
- 2 Tbsp. canola oil, divided
- ½ tsp. pepper, divided
- ¼ tsp. salt, divided
- 3 Tbsp. Dijon mustard
- 3 Tbsp. honey
- ¾ tsp. curry powder
- 1 pkg. (17.6 oz.) turkey breast cutlets
  Optional: Minced fresh cilantro or thinly sliced green onions

1. Preheat oven to 450°. Place potatoes and leeks in a 15x10x1-in. baking pan coated with cooking spray. Drizzle with 1 Tbsp. oil; sprinkle with ¼ tsp. pepper and ⅛ tsp. salt. Stir to coat. Roast for 15 minutes, stirring once.
2. Meanwhile, in a small bowl, combine the mustard, honey, curry powder and remaining oil. Sprinkle the turkey with remaining salt and pepper.
3. Drizzle 2 Tbsp. mustard mixture over potatoes; stir to coat. Place turkey over potato mixture; drizzle with remaining mustard mixture. Roast 6-8 minutes longer or until turkey is no longer pink and potatoes are tender. If desired, sprinkle with cilantro.
3 oz. cooked turkey with ¾ cup potato mixture: 393 cal., 9g fat (1g sat. fat), 71mg chol., 582mg sod., 44g carb. (16g sugars, 3g fiber), 33g pro. **Diabetic exchanges:** 4 lean meat, 3 starch, 1½ fat.

TURKEY LATTICE PIE

🕐 🍎 GRILLED GROUND TURKEY BURGERS

We especially like to grill these burgers, but you could also pan-fry them.
—*Sherry Hulsman, Louisville, KY*

TAKES: 30 min. • **MAKES:** 6 servings

- 1 large egg, lightly beaten
- ⅔ cup soft whole wheat bread crumbs
- ½ cup finely chopped celery
- ¼ cup finely chopped onion
- 1 Tbsp. minced fresh parsley
- 1 tsp. Worcestershire sauce
- 1 tsp. dried oregano
- ½ tsp. salt
- ¼ tsp. pepper
- 1¼ lbs. lean ground turkey
- 6 whole wheat hamburger buns, split

1. In a small bowl, combine the egg, bread crumbs, celery, onion, parsley, Worcestershire sauce and seasonings. Crumble turkey into bowl and mix lightly but thoroughly. Shape into 6 patties.
2. On a greased grill, cook, covered, over medium heat or broil 4 in. from the heat for 5-6 minutes on each side or until a thermometer reads 165° and juices run clear. Serve on buns.
1 burger: 293 cal., 11g fat (3g sat. fat), 110mg chol., 561mg sod., 27g carb. (3g sugars, 4g fiber), 22g pro. **Diabetic exchanges:** 3 lean meat, 2 starch.

SLOW-COOKER
TURKEY PESTO
LASAGNA

🍲 SLOW-COOKER TURKEY PESTO LASAGNA

My cheesy lasagna makes any slow-cooker skeptic a believer. It's easy to prep while my kids nap, and dinner's ready when their dad walks in the door at night. We bring more pesto and marinara to the table for our resident sauce lovers.
—*Blair Lonergan, Rochelle, VA*

PREP: 25 min. • **COOK:** 3 hours + standing
MAKES: 8 servings

- 1 lb. ground turkey
- 1 small onion, chopped
- 2 tsp. Italian seasoning
- ½ tsp. salt
- 2 cups shredded part-skim mozzarella cheese, divided
- 1 container (15 oz.) whole-milk ricotta cheese
- ¼ cup prepared pesto
- 1 jar (24 oz.) marinara sauce
- 9 no-cook lasagna noodles
  Grated Parmesan cheese

1. Cut three 25x3-in. strips of heavy-duty foil; crisscross so they resemble spokes of a wheel. Place strips on bottom and up sides of a greased 5-qt. slow cooker. Coat strips with cooking spray.
2. In a large skillet, cook the turkey and onion over medium heat 6-8 minutes or until turkey is no longer pink, breaking up turkey into crumbles; drain. Stir in Italian seasoning and salt.
3. In a small bowl, mix 1 cup mozzarella cheese, ricotta cheese and pesto. In a prepared slow cooker, layer a third of each of the following: marinara sauce, noodles (breaking noodles if necessary to fit), turkey mixture and cheese mixture. Repeat layers twice. Sprinkle with remaining mozzarella cheese.
4. Cook, covered, on low until noodles are tender, 3-4 hours. Turn off slow cooker; remove insert. Let stand, uncovered, 30 minutes before serving. Using foil strips, remove lasagna to a platter. Serve with Parmesan cheese.
1 piece: 397 cal., 19g fat (8g sat. fat), 79mg chol., 883mg sod., 28g carb. (9g sugars, 3g fiber), 28g pro.

RASPBERRY TURKEY TENDERLOINS

Fast to prep and even quicker to grill, this dish is always a winner at my house. We love the raspberry-Dijon sauce.
—*JoAnn Handley, Mount Dora, FL*

PREP: 20 min. • **GRILL:** 15 min.
MAKES: 6 servings

- ½ cup seedless raspberry jam
- ⅓ cup cider vinegar
- ¼ cup Dijon mustard
- 1 tsp. grated orange zest
- ½ tsp. minced fresh thyme or ⅛ tsp. dried thyme
- 4 turkey breast tenderloins (6 oz. each)
- ⅛ tsp. salt

1. In a small saucepan, combine first 5 ingredients. Cook and stir until heated through. Set aside ¼ cup for serving.
2. Sprinkle turkey with salt. On a lightly oiled rack, grill turkey, covered, over medium heat or broil 4 in. from the heat for 13-18 minutes or until a thermometer reads 170°, turning occasionally. Baste with reserved sauce in last 5 minutes of cooking. Let stand for 5 minutes before slicing. Serve with reserved sauce.
1 serving: 199 cal., 2g fat (0 sat. fat), 56mg chol., 351mg sod., 20g carb. (16g sugars, 0 fiber), 26g pro. **Diabetic exchanges:** 3 lean meat, 1 starch.

DID YOU KNOW?

Dijon, a town in eastern France's Burgundy wine-growing region, is home to Dijon mustard. Mustard is a popular cover crop, grown among the vines. The plants attract beneficial insects and give nutrients to the soil. The scores of tiny mustard seeds mean the crop replants itself each year. Dijon is made with wine instead of vinegar.

ROASTED SAGE TURKEY WITH VEGETABLE GRAVY

ROASTED SAGE TURKEY WITH VEGETABLE GRAVY

There's no prep like home-style when roasting the big bird. Instead of sage stuffing with turkey, fill this bird with fresh sage and thyme sprigs for the same delicious flavors.

—*Beth Jacobson, Milwaukee, WI*

PREP: 30 min. + chilling
BAKE: 2 hours 10 min. + standing
MAKES: 16 servings (3½ cups gravy)

- 1 turkey (14 to 16 lbs.)
- 1 Tbsp. kosher salt
- 1 tsp. ground sage
- ½ tsp. garlic powder
- 1 large onion, chopped
- 3 celery ribs, chopped
- 3 medium carrots, chopped
- 1¼ cups water, divided
- 3 Tbsp. canola oil
- ½ tsp. freshly ground pepper
- ¾ cup white wine
- 3 fresh sage sprigs
- 4 fresh thyme sprigs

GRAVY
- 1 to 1½ cups reduced-sodium chicken broth or homemade chicken stock
- ¼ cup all-purpose flour
- ¼ tsp. minced fresh sage
- ¼ tsp. freshly ground pepper

1. Remove giblets and neck from turkey. Reserve turkey neck; refrigerate, covered, overnight. Place turkey in a 15x10x1-in. baking pan, breast side up. Secure skin to underside of neck cavity with toothpicks. Mix salt, sage and garlic powder. Tuck wings under turkey; tie drumsticks together. Pat turkey dry. Rub outside of turkey with salt mixture. Refrigerate turkey, loosely covered, overnight.
2. Preheat oven to 475°. Place onion, celery, carrots and reserved neck in bottom of a broiler pan; add ½ cup water. Place broiler pan rack over top;

transfer turkey to rack. Rub outside of the turkey with oil; sprinkle with pepper. Pour wine and remaining water into turkey cavity; add sage and thyme sprigs.
3. Place turkey in oven, legs facing toward back of oven. Roast, uncovered, 40 minutes.
4. Reduce oven setting to 350°. Cover breast tightly with a double thickness of foil. Roast until a thermometer inserted in thickest part of thigh reads 170°-175° (thermometer should not touch bone or fat), 1½-2 hours longer.
5. Remove turkey from oven. Let stand, uncovered, 20 minutes before carving. Using a turkey baster, remove the liquid from turkey cavity to a large measuring cup. Line a strainer or colander with cheesecloth; place over measuring cup. With a slotted spoon, remove vegetables from bottom of broiler pan, reserving 1¼ cups. Discard turkey neck. Strain the cooking liquid into measuring cup. Skim the fat, reserving ¼ cup fat. Add enough broth to the cooking liquid to measure 2 cups.
6. In a large saucepan, mix flour and reserved fat until smooth; gradually whisk in broth mixture. Bring to a boil over medium-high heat, stirring constantly; cook and stir until thickened, 1-2 minutes. Add half of the reserved vegetables. Puree the gravy using an immersion blender; or cool the gravy slightly and puree in a blender. Stir in sage, pepper and remaining vegetables; heat through. Serve with turkey.

9 oz. cooked turkey with about ¼ cup gravy: 514 cal., 24g fat (6g sat. fat), 215mg chol., 562mg sod., 4g carb. (1g sugars, 1g fiber), 64g pro.

HOW-TO

Troubleshoot Holiday Turkey Problems

- **Pale appearance**
  If your turkey is cooked but not browned, stop basting and increase the heat to 450°. It should get golden in a few minutes.
- **Thighs are underdone**
  Remove legs and thighs from the turkey and place them back in the roasting pan. Continue cooking until thickest part of the thigh reaches 170°-175°.
- **Dry meat**
  Slice the meat and place in a single layer in a baking dish. Add enough warm turkey or chicken stock to cover slices; cover and bake at 350° for 10-15 minutes.
- **Gravy is wrong consistency**
  To thicken a gravy, stir cold turkey or chicken stock (or water) into a bit of cornstarch. Gradually whisk into simmering gravy. Alternatively, thin a too-thick gravy with whatever stock or broth you have on hand.
- **Lumpy gravy**
  Give it a whir in the blender to work things out.
- **Soggy stuffing**
  Spread on a cookie sheet and bake at 350° for 10 minutes. Still mushy? Stir and repeat.

🍲 FAMILY-PLEASING TURKEY CHILI

My children really love this recipe—it's one of their favorite comfort foods. I like that it's relatively inexpensive, and the leftovers are wonderful!
—*Sheila Christensen, San Marcos, CA*

- -

PREP: 25 min. • **COOK:** 4 hours
MAKES: 6 servings (2¼ qt.)

- 1   lb. lean ground turkey
- 1   medium green pepper, finely chopped
- 1   small red onion, finely chopped
- 2   garlic cloves, minced
- 1   can (28 oz.) diced tomatoes, undrained
- 1   can (16 oz.) kidney beans, rinsed and drained
- 1   can (15 oz.) black beans, rinsed and drained
- 1   can (14½ oz.) reduced-sodium chicken broth
- 1¾ cups frozen corn, thawed
- 1   can (6 oz.) tomato paste
- 1   Tbsp. chili powder
- ½   tsp. pepper
- ¼   tsp. ground cumin
- ¼   tsp. garlic powder
    Optional toppings: Reduced-fat sour cream and minced fresh cilantro

1. In a large nonstick skillet, cook the turkey, green pepper and onion over medium heat until meat is no longer pink, breaking it into crumbles. Add garlic; cook 1 minute longer. Drain.
2. Transfer to a 4-qt. slow cooker. Stir in tomatoes, kidney beans, black beans, broth, corn, tomato paste, chili powder, pepper, cumin and garlic powder.
3. Cover and cook on low until heated through, 4-5 hours. If desired, serve with sour cream and cilantro.
1½ cups: 349 cal., 7g fat (2g sat. fat), 60mg chol., 725mg sod., 47g carb. (11g sugars, 12g fiber), 27g pro.
Diabetic exchanges: 3 lean meat, 2 starch, 2 vegetable.

FAMILY-PLEASING
TURKEY CHILI

CRANBERRY, BRIE & TURKEY PIZZA

🕐 CRANBERRY, BRIE & TURKEY PIZZA

While traveling in New Zealand, my husband and I discovered turkey pizza. We came up with our own version for a creative way to use leftovers.
—*Kristin Stone, Little Elm, TX*

TAKES: 25 min. • **MAKES:** 6 servings

1 prebaked 12-in. pizza crust
1 cup whole-berry cranberry sauce
1 tsp. grated orange zest
2 cups shredded part-skim mozzarella cheese
1 cup coarsely shredded cooked turkey
½ small red onion, thinly sliced
4 oz. Brie cheese, cubed
1 Tbsp. minced fresh rosemary

1. Preheat oven to 450°. Place crust on an ungreased baking sheet.
2. In a small bowl, mix cranberry sauce and orange zest; spread over crust. Top with mozzarella, turkey, onion and Brie cheese; sprinkle with rosemary. Bake 10-12 minutes or until cheese is melted.
1 piece: 456 cal., 17g fat (9g sat. fat), 67mg chol., 768mg sod., 49g carb. (14g sugars, 2g fiber), 27g pro.

INGREDIENT CLOSE-UP
Brie Cheese
With a buttery texture and an edible, slightly salty rind, Brie cheese goes great with fruit, nuts and slightly sweet foods such as cranberry sauce or berry preserves. Experiment with this pizza by adding caramelized onions, golden raisins, pecan halves, or sliced almonds and apples. Substitute Camembert for Brie if you prefer a more earthy, intense flavor.

🍲 STUFFED TURKEY WITH MOJO SAUCE

I love Latin food so I created a recipe that combines wonderful spices and fresh ingredients. This is a traditional turkey recipe with a healthier twist because it uses chicken sausage instead of chorizo.
—*Melissa Lauer, San Antonio, TX*

PREP: 45 min. • **COOK:** 5 hours + standing
MAKES: 8 servings (about 1 cup sauce)

- 1 medium green pepper, finely chopped
- 1 medium onion, finely chopped
- 2 garlic cloves, minced
- 2 tsp. ground coriander
- 1 tsp. ground cumin
- ⅛ tsp. cayenne pepper
- 1 lb. uncooked chicken sausage links, casings removed
- 1 fresh boneless turkey breast (4 lbs.)
- ¼ tsp. salt
- ¼ tsp. pepper

MOJO SAUCE
- 1 cup orange juice
- ½ cup fresh cilantro leaves
- ¼ cup minced fresh oregano or 4 tsp. dried oregano
- ¼ cup lime juice
- 4 garlic cloves, minced
- 1 tsp. ground cumin
- ½ tsp. pepper
- ¼ tsp. salt
- ⅛ tsp. cayenne pepper
- 1 cup olive oil

1. In a large bowl, combine the first 6 ingredients. Crumble sausage over mixture and mix lightly but thoroughly.
2. With skin side down, pound breast with a meat mallet to ½-in. thickness. Sprinkle with salt and pepper. Spread with sausage mixture to within 1 in. of edges. Roll up jelly-roll style, starting with a short side; tie every 1½-2-in. with kitchen string.
3. In a large skillet, brown turkey on all sides. Place in a 5-qt. oval slow cooker.
4. In a blender, combine the first 9 sauce ingredients; cover and process until blended. While processing, gradually add oil in a steady stream.
5. Pour over turkey. Cover and cook on low 5 hours or until a thermometer inserted in center reads 165°. Remove from slow cooker; cover and let stand 10 minutes before slicing.
6. Meanwhile, skim fat from cooking juices; place juices in a small saucepan. Bring to a boil; cook until the liquid is reduced by half. Serve with turkey.

1 piece with 2 Tbsp. sauce: 719 cal., 46g fat (9g sat. fat), 174mg chol., 515mg sod., 7g carb. (4g sugars, 1g fiber), 66g pro.

SPINACH & TURKEY TURNOVERS

Here's a great way to reinvent leftovers from your holiday dinner. We serve these pastry pockets as a quick meal or snack.
—*Anjli Sabharwal, Marlboro, NJ*

PREP: 25 min. • **BAKE:** 15 min.
MAKES: 8 servings

- 1½ tsp. olive oil
- 2 green onions, chopped
- 1 garlic clove, minced
- ½ tsp. dried rosemary, crushed
- ¼ tsp. dried thyme
- 1 cup cubed cooked turkey
- 1 pkg. (10 oz.) frozen chopped spinach, thawed and squeezed dry
- ½ cup shredded Monterey Jack cheese
- ¼ cup turkey gravy
- ¼ tsp. salt
- ¼ tsp. pepper
- 1 pkg. (17.3 oz.) frozen puff pastry, thawed
- 1 large egg, lightly beaten
- 1 Tbsp. water

SAUCE
- 1 cup whole-berry cranberry sauce
- ¼ cup orange juice
- 1 Tbsp. grated orange zest

1. Preheat oven to 400°. In a large skillet, heat oil over medium-high heat. Add green onions, garlic, rosemary and thyme; cook and stir 1 minute. Remove from heat. Stir in the turkey, spinach, cheese, gravy, salt and pepper.
2. Unfold puff pastry; cut each sheet into 4 squares. Transfer to greased baking sheets. Spoon turkey mixture onto center of each square. In a small bowl, whisk egg and water; brush over edges of pastry. Fold 1 corner of the dough diagonally over filling, forming triangles; seal edges with a fork. Brush tops with egg mixture. Bake 12-14 minutes or until golden brown.
3. Meanwhile, in a small saucepan, combine the cranberry sauce and juice. Bring to a boil; cook and stir 3-4 minutes or until slightly thickened. Stir in orange zest. Serve with turnovers.

1 turnover with 2 Tbsp. sauce: 435 cal., 21g fat (6g sat. fat), 47mg chol., 397mg sod., 50g carb. (9g sugars, 6g fiber), 13g pro.

🍎 TURKEY-THYME STUFFED PEPPERS

My 3-year-old, Chloe, is a big fan of these healthy peppers, which have a great thyme flavor. She likes to help mix the ingredients and make meals with me.
—*Jennifer Kent, Philadelphia, PA*

- -

PREP: 30 min. • **COOK:** 10 min.
MAKES: 4 servings

- 1 lb. lean ground turkey
- 1 medium onion, finely chopped
- 3 garlic cloves, minced
- ½ tsp. dried thyme
- ¼ tsp. salt
- ¼ tsp. dried rosemary, crushed
- ⅛ tsp. pepper
- 1 can (14½ oz.) diced tomatoes, undrained
- 1 pkg. (8.8 oz.) ready-to-serve brown rice
- ½ cup seasoned bread crumbs
- 4 medium sweet yellow or orange peppers
- ¼ cup shredded part-skim mozzarella cheese

1. In a large skillet, cook turkey and onion over medium heat 8-10 minutes or until turkey is no longer pink and onion is tender, breaking up turkey into crumbles. Add garlic and seasonings; cook 1 minute longer. Stir in tomatoes, rice and bread crumbs.

2. Cut sweet peppers lengthwise in half; remove seeds. Arrange pepper halves in a 13x9-in. microwave-safe dish; fill with turkey mixture. Sprinkle with cheese. Microwave, covered, on high for 7-9 minutes or until peppers are crisp-tender.

2 stuffed pepper halves: 423 cal., 13g fat (3g sat. fat), 82mg chol., 670mg sod., 43g carb. (10g sugars, 6g fiber), 31g pro.
Diabetic exchanges: 3 medium-fat meat, 2 starch, 2 vegetable.

TURKEY-THYME STUFFED PEPPERS

🕐 TURKEY SALTIMBOCCA

I kept prosciutto and sage in this Italian classic, but instead of veal I use turkey. This saltimbocca is so divine, you won't believe how quick and easy it is.
—*Deirdre Cox, Kansas City, MO*

TAKES: 30 min. • **MAKES:** 2 servings

- ¼ cup all-purpose flour
- 1 turkey breast tenderloin (8 oz.)
- ⅛ tsp. pepper
- 1½ tsp. olive oil
- 2 Tbsp. butter, divided
- 1 thin slice prosciutto or deli ham, cut into thin strips
- 2 Tbsp. minced fresh sage
- ¼ cup white wine or chicken broth

1. Place flour in a large shallow bowl. Cut tenderloin horizontally in half; flatten each half with a meat mallet to ½-in. thickness. Sprinkle with pepper. Dip in flour to coat both sides; shake off excess.
2. In a large skillet, heat oil and 1 Tbsp. butter over medium heat. Add turkey; cook 3-4 minutes on each side or until no longer pink. Remove from the pan; keep warm.
3. In same pan, heat 1½ tsp. butter over medium-high heat. Add prosciutto and sage; cook and stir until slightly crisp. Add the wine to pan; increase heat to medium-high. Cook until the liquid is slightly reduced, stirring to loosen browned bits from pan. Remove from heat; stir in remaining 1½ tsp. butter. Serve with turkey.
1 serving: 300 cal., 17g fat (8g sat. fat), 92mg chol., 279mg sod., 4g carb. (0 sugars, 0 fiber), 29g pro.

TURKEY SOUP

🍲 TURKEY SOUP

I like making this soup around the holidays after the big turkey dinner. It's especially satisfying on cold winter nights when it's snowing—which happens a lot where I live!
—*Carol Brethauer, Denver, CO*

PREP: 30 min. • **COOK:** 4 hours
MAKES: 12 servings (5 qt.)

- 1 leftover turkey carcass (from a 14-lb. turkey)
- 3 qt. water
- 2 cans (14½ oz. each) reduced-sodium chicken broth
- ½ cup uncooked long grain rice
- 1 medium onion, finely chopped
- 4 celery ribs, finely chopped
- 2 medium carrots, grated
- 1 bay leaf
- Dash poultry seasoning
- ½ tsp. onion powder
- ½ tsp. garlic powder
- ¼ tsp. pepper
- Salt, optional

1. In a stockpot, place turkey carcass, water and broth. Bring to a boil. Reduce heat; cover and simmer 4-5 hours.
2. Remove carcass from stock. Remove any meat; dice. Return to stock along with rice, onion, celery, carrots, bay leaf and poultry seasoning. Add remaining seasonings to taste. Cover; simmer over medium-low heat until rice is cooked. Discard bay leaf.
1⅔ cups: 147 cal., 2g fat (0 sat. fat), 28mg chol., 412mg sod., 15g carb. (3g sugars, 1g fiber), 12g pro. **Diabetic exchanges:** 1 starch, 1 lean meat.

MARINATED THANKSGIVING TURKEY

My family enjoys this turkey because it cooks up tender, tasty and golden brown. Build up flavor by marinating the meat, then grill it to add a tempting, smoky barbecued taste.

—Ken Churches, Kailua-Kona, HI

PREP: 10 min. + marinating
GRILL: 2½ hours + standing
MAKES: 12 servings

- 2 **cups water**
- 1½ **cups chicken broth**
- 1 **cup reduced-sodium soy sauce**
- ⅔ **cup lemon juice**
- 2 **garlic cloves, minced**
- 1½ **tsp. ground ginger**
- 1 **tsp. pepper**
- 2 **turkey-size oven roasting bags**
- 1 **turkey (12 to 14 lbs.)**

1. Combine the first 7 ingredients; set aside and refrigerate 1 cup for basting. Place 1 oven roasting bag inside the other. Place turkey inside inner bag; pour in remaining marinade. Seal bags, pressing out as much air as possible; turn to coat turkey. Place in a shallow roasting pan. Refrigerate overnight, turning several times.

2. Remove the turkey; drain and discard marinade.

3. Prepare grill for indirect medium heat. Tuck wings under turkey and arrange breast side down on grill rack. Grill, covered, for 1 hour.

4. If using a charcoal grill, add 10 briquettes to coals; turn the turkey. Baste with reserved marinade. Cook, covered, for 1½-2 hours, adding 10 briquettes to maintain heat and brushing with marinade every 30 minutes until thermometer inserted in thigh reads 170°. Remove turkey from grill; tent with foil. Let stand 20 minutes before carving.

5. Conventional roasting method: Follow steps for marinating turkey overnight. Preheat oven to 325°. Place turkey on a rack in a large roaster. Bake, uncovered, 3-3½ hours or until a thermometer inserted in a thigh reads 170°. Baste frequently with reserved marinade. When turkey begins to brown, cover lightly with a tent of aluminum foil. Remove turkey from oven; tent with foil. Let stand 20 minutes before carving. If desired, skim fat and thicken pan drippings for gravy; serve with turkey.

9 oz. cooked turkey: 407 cal., 12g fat (4g sat. fat), 171mg chol., 383mg sod., 5g carb. (0 sugars, 1g fiber), 67g pro.

MARINATED THANKSGIVING TURKEY

GRILL THE HOLIDAY BIRD
Just hover your camera here.

🍲 MEXICAN TURKEY MEAT LOAF

Here's a zesty, flavorful meat loaf you can really sink your teeth into! Pair it with black beans, rice, green salad with lime vinaigrette or any of your favorite Tex-Mex sides.
—*Kristen Miller, Glendale, WI*

PREP: 25 min. • **COOK:** 3 hours + standing
MAKES: 1 loaf (6 servings)

- 2 slices white bread, torn into small pieces
- ⅓ cup 2% milk
- 1 lb. lean ground turkey
- ½ lb. fresh chorizo
- 1 medium sweet red pepper, finely chopped
- 1 small onion, finely chopped
- 1 jalapeno pepper, seeded and finely chopped
- 2 large eggs, lightly beaten
- 2 Tbsp. minced fresh cilantro
- 2 garlic cloves, minced
- 2 tsp. chili powder
- 1 tsp. salt
- 1 tsp. ground cumin
- ½ tsp. dried oregano
- ½ tsp. pepper
- ¼ tsp. cayenne pepper
- ⅔ cup salsa, divided
  Additional minced fresh cilantro
  Hot cooked Spanish rice

1. Combine bread and milk in a large bowl; let stand until liquid is absorbed. Add the next 14 ingredients and half of the salsa; mix lightly but thoroughly.
2. On an 18x7-in. piece of heavy-duty foil, shape the meat mixture into a 10x6-in. oval loaf. Lifting with foil, transfer to a 6-qt. oval slow cooker. Press the ends of the foil up sides of slow cooker.
3. Cook, covered, on low 3-4 hours or until a thermometer reads 165°. Lifting with the foil, drain fat into slow cooker before removing meat loaf to a platter;

top with remaining salsa and sprinkle with cilantro. Let stand 10 minutes before slicing. Serve with rice.
1 piece: 335 cal., 20g fat (6g sat. fat), 149mg chol., 1109mg sod., 11g carb. (4g sugars, 1g fiber), 27g pro.

🍎 SNEAKY TURKEY MEATBALLS

Like most kids, mine refuse to eat certain veggies. In order to get healthy foods into their diets, I have to be sneaky sometimes. The vegetables in this recipe keep the meat moist while providing nutrients—and I'm happy to say my kids love 'em.
—*Courtney Stultz, Weir, KS*

PREP: 15 min. • **BAKE:** 20 min.
MAKES: 6 servings

- ¼ head cauliflower, broken into florets
- ½ cup finely shredded cabbage
- 1 Tbsp. potato starch or cornstarch
- 1 Tbsp. balsamic vinegar
- 1 tsp. sea salt
- 1 tsp. dried basil
- ½ tsp. pepper
- 1 lb. ground turkey
  Optional: Barbecue sauce and fresh basil leaves

1. Preheat oven to 400°. Place the cauliflower in a food processor; pulse until finely chopped. Transfer to a large bowl. Add the cabbage, potato starch, vinegar, salt, basil and pepper.
2. Add turkey; mix lightly but thoroughly. With an ice cream scoop or with wet hands, shape mixture into 1 ½-in. balls. Place meatballs on a greased rack in a 15x10x1-in. baking pan. Bake them 20-24 minutes or until cooked through. If desired, toss with barbecue sauce and top with basil.
2 meatballs: 125 cal., 6g fat (1g sat. fat), 50mg chol., 370mg sod., 4g carb. (1g sugars, 1g fiber), 15g pro. **Diabetic exchanges:** 2 medium-fat meat.

*SNEAKY TURKEY
MEATBALLS*

⏱ TURKEY & BROCCOLI PASTRY BRAID

This meal in one is a tasty way to get kids—and adults—to eat broccoli. The puff pastry that wraps up turkey, cheese and veggies is pure, flaky goodness.
—*Jenelle Fender, Steinbach, MB*

- -

TAKES: 30 min. • **MAKES:** 4 servings

1 cup finely chopped cooked turkey (about 5 oz.)
½ cup finely chopped fresh broccoli
½ cup finely chopped sweet red pepper
½ cup shredded cheddar cheese
¼ cup Miracle Whip
¼ tsp. dill weed
1 sheet frozen puff pastry, thawed

1. Preheat oven to 400°. For filling, mix first 6 ingredients.
2. Unfold pastry onto a lightly floured surface; roll into a 15x10-in. rectangle. Transfer to baking sheet. Spoon filling down center third of rectangle. On each long side, cut 8 strips about 3 in. into the center. Starting at an end, fold alternating strips overfilling, pinching ends to join.
3. Bake until golden brown and filling is heated through, 20-25 minutes.

1 piece: 463 cal., 26g fat (7g sat. fat), 50mg chol., 435mg sod., 38g carb. (2g sugars, 5g fiber), 18g pro.

TEST KITCHEN TIPS

- After rolling out the puff pastry, loosely roll the dough up around the rolling pin to easily lift and transfer it to a baking sheet.
- Switch up the flavor by using ham and Swiss instead of turkey and cheddar.
- For a shiny appearance, brush the pastry with an egg wash before baking (whisk 1 egg with 1 Tbsp. water).

HERBED ROAST TURKEY BREAST

🍎 HERBED ROAST TURKEY BREAST

I made this turkey breast for my first formal dinner party as a newlywed. It was such a success that it's become a standby on all my entertaining menus.
—*Lisa Mahon Fluegeman, Cincinnati, OH*

PREP: 10 min. • **BAKE:** 2 hours + standing
MAKES: 12 servings

- 1 bone-in turkey breast (5 to 6 lbs.)
- 5 tsp. lemon juice
- 1 Tbsp. olive oil
- 1 to 2 tsp. pepper
- 1 tsp. dried rosemary, crushed
- 1 tsp. dried thyme
- 1 tsp. garlic salt
- 1 medium onion, cut into wedges
- 1 celery rib, cut into 2-in. pieces
- ½ cup white wine or chicken broth

1. Preheat oven to 325°. With fingers, carefully loosen the skin from both sides of turkey breast. Combine lemon juice and oil; brush under the skin. Combine pepper, rosemary, thyme and garlic salt; rub over turkey.
2. Place the onion and celery in a 3-qt. baking dish. Top with breast, skin side up. Pour wine into the dish.
3. Bake, uncovered, until a thermometer reads 170°, 2-2½ hours. (Cover loosely with foil if turkey browns too quickly.) Cover turkey and let stand 15 minutes before carving.

5 oz. cooked turkey: 285 cal., 11g fat (3g sat. fat), 102mg chol., 241mg sod., 2g carb. (1g sugars, 0 fiber), 40g pro.
Diabetic exchanges: 5 medium-fat meat.

WHY YOU'LL LOVE IT...

"I have been following an Alton Brown recipe for at least the past 5 years. NO LONGER! THIS IS PERFECT! My grandmother said it's the best turkey breast she's ever had."
—KELLYS1061, TASTEOFHOME.COM

ROAST THIS TURKEY WITH US
Just hover your camera here.

🍎 TURKEY TENDERLOIN & ROOT VEGGIE SHEET-PAN SUPPER

My family loves turkey tenderloin so I tried them in a sheet-pan supper. I used ingredients I had on hand, including bacon, which lends a nice smoky flavor. It's so quick and easy to prepare.
—*Susan Bickta, Kutztown, PA*

PREP: 15 min. • **BAKE:** 30 min.
MAKES: 6 servings

- 6   bacon strips
- 2   medium potatoes, cut into ½-in. pieces
- 4   medium carrots, peeled and cut into ½-in. pieces
- 2   medium onions, cut into ½-in. pieces
- 2   tsp. canola oil
- 1   tsp. salt, divided
- ½   tsp. pepper, divided
- 1   pkg. (20 oz.) turkey breast tenderloins
     Minced fresh parsley, optional

1. Preheat oven to 375°. Line a 15x10x1-in. baking pan with foil. Place bacon on prepared pan; bake 15 minutes.
2. Meanwhile, in a large bowl, toss potatoes, carrots and onions with oil; sprinkle with ½ tsp. salt and ¼ tsp. pepper. Sprinkle remaining salt and pepper on tenderloins.
3. Remove par-cooked bacon from baking pan. Transfer vegetables to pan, spreading evenly. Place tenderloins on top of vegetables; cover with bacon slices. Bake until a thermometer reads 165° and the vegetables are tender, 30-35 minutes. If desired, top with parsley to serve.
3 oz. cooked turkey with ⅔ cup vegetables: 238 cal., 11g fat (3g sat. fat), 42mg chol., 500mg sod., 15g carb. (3g sugars, 2g fiber), 22g pro. **Diabetic exchanges:** 3 lean meat, 1 vegetable, ½ starch.

GRILLED HULI HULI TURKEY DRUMSTICKS

GRILLED HULI HULI TURKEY DRUMSTICKS

I'm never one to do things traditionally, so when it came time to hosting Thanksgiving, I went in a completely tropical direction. Borrowing my favorite Hawaiian chicken recipe, I substituted turkey legs and have never looked back.
—*Jacyn Siebert, San Francisco, CA*

PREP: 15 min. + marinating
GRILL: 40 min. + standing
MAKES: 12 servings

- 1   cup packed brown sugar
- ¾   cup ketchup
- ¾   cup reduced-sodium soy sauce
- ⅓   cup sherry or chicken broth
- 1   Tbsp. minced fresh gingerroot
- 1   Tbsp. minced garlic
- 6   turkey drumsticks (1½ lbs. each)
- 1   bunch green onions, chopped

1. Mix the first 6 ingredients. Reserve 1⅓ cups mixture for basting; cover and refrigerate. Pour remaining marinade into a large baking dish. Add drumsticks and turn to coat. Cover and refrigerate 8 hours or overnight.
2. Drain turkey, discarding marinade. Place turkey on greased grill rack. Grill, covered, over indirect medium heat, 40-45 minutes or until a thermometer reads 175. Turn the drumsticks occasionally throughout cooking. Baste often with reserved marinade during the last 10 minutes. Let stand 15 minutes; garnish with green onions.
8 oz. cooked turkey: 486 cal., 20g fat (6g sat. fat), 171mg chol., 671mg sod., 16g carb. (15g sugars, 0 fiber), 57g pro.

🍎 TURKEY-STUFFED ACORN SQUASH

For something a little different, why not present each guest with their own beautifully prepared squash, stuffed with all the flavors that make the holidays bright—turkey, dressing and cranberry sauce. This recipe makes it easy to make just as many servings as you need.
—Cindy Romberg, Mississauga, ON

- -

PREP: 10 min. • **BAKE:** 55 min.
MAKES: 4 servings

- 2 medium acorn squash (about 1½ lbs. each)
- 1 small onion, finely chopped
- 2 cups cubed cooked turkey
- 2 cups cooked stuffing
- ½ cup whole-berry cranberry sauce
- ⅓ cup white wine or chicken broth
- ½ tsp. salt

1. Preheat oven to 350°. Cut each squash lengthwise in half; remove and discard seeds. Using a sharp knife, cut a thin slice from bottom of each half to allow them to lie flat. Place halves in a shallow roasting pan, hollow side down; add ¼ in. of hot water. Bake, uncovered, 30 minutes.
2. Meanwhile, place onion in a large microwave-safe bowl; microwave, covered, on high for 1-2 minutes or until tender. Stir in turkey, stuffing, cranberry sauce and wine.
3. Carefully remove the squash from roasting pan; drain water. Return the squash to pan, hollow side up; sprinkle with salt. Spoon turkey mixture into squash cavities. Bake, uncovered, until heated through and squash halves are is easily pierced with a fork, 25-30 minutes longer.

1 stuffed acorn squash half: 502 cal., 12g fat (3g sat. fat), 71mg chol., 875mg sod., 73g carb. (20g sugars, 9g fiber), 27g pro.

🦃 AIR-FRYER TURKEY CLUB ROULADES

Weeknights turn elegant when these short-prep roulades with familiar ingredients are on the menu. Not a fan of turkey? Substitute chicken breasts that you pound to about ¼ inch thick.
—Taste of Home *Test Kitchen*

- -

PREP: 20 min. • **COOK:** 10 min./batch
MAKES: 8 servings

- ¾ lb. fresh asparagus, trimmed
- 8 turkey breast cutlets (about 1 lb.)
- 1 Tbsp. Dijon-mayonnaise blend
- 8 slices deli ham
- 8 slices provolone cheese
- ½ tsp. poultry seasoning
- ½ tsp. pepper
- 8 bacon strips

SAUCE
- ⅔ cup Dijon-mayonnaise blend
- 4 tsp. 2% milk
- ¼ tsp. poultry seasoning

1. Preheat air fryer to 375°. Place asparagus on greased tray in air-fryer basket. Cook until crisp-tender, 4-5 minutes, tossing halfway through cooking. Set aside.
2. Spread turkey cutlets with Dijon-mayonnaise. Layer with ham, cheese and asparagus. Sprinkle with poultry seasoning and pepper. Roll up tightly and wrap with bacon.
3. In batches, arrange roulades in a single layer on greased tray in air-fryer basket. Cook until bacon is crisp and turkey is no longer pink, 8-10 minutes, turning occasionally. Combine sauce ingredients; serve with roulades.

1 roulade with 1 Tbsp. sauce: 224 cal., 11g fat (5g sat. fat), 64mg chol., 1075mg sod., 2g carb. (1g sugars, 0 fiber), 25g pro.

TURKEY-STUFFED ACORN SQUASH

🍎 🍲 MOIST ITALIAN TURKEY BREAST

This recipe makes some of the juiciest turkey I've ever eaten. High in lean protein, it's a smart entree for a special occasion.
—*Jessica Kunz, Springfield, IL*

PREP: 25 min. • **COOK:** 5 hours + standing
MAKES: 12 servings

- 1 lb. carrots, cut into 2-in. pieces
- 2 medium onions, cut into wedges
- 3 celery ribs, cut into 2-in. pieces
- 1 can (14½ oz.) chicken broth
- 1 bone-in turkey breast (6 to 7 lbs.), thawed and skin removed
- 2 Tbsp. olive oil
- 1½ tsp. seasoned salt
- 1 tsp. Italian seasoning
- ½ tsp. pepper

1. Place vegetables and broth in a 6- or 7-qt. slow cooker; top with turkey breast. Brush turkey with oil; sprinkle with seasonings.
2. Cook, covered, on low until a thermometer inserted in turkey reads at least 170°, 5-6 hours. Remove turkey from slow cooker; let stand, covered, 15 minutes before carving. Serve with vegetables. If desired, strain cooking juices and thicken for gravy.
1 serving: 360 cal., 15g fat (4g sat. fat), 123mg chol., 477mg sod., 6g carb. (3g sugars, 2g fiber), 48g pro.

TURKEY BISCUIT SKILLET

🕐 TURKEY BISCUIT SKILLET

My mother always made while we were growing up. Now I make it for my own husband and kids. I use the small size biscuits because the larger ones don't seem to brown up as nicely on the top. I also add mushrooms to this recipe because my family loves mushrooms.
—*Keri Boffeli, Monticello, IA*

TAKES: 30 min. • **MAKES:** 6 servings

- 1 Tbsp. butter
- ⅓ cup chopped onion
- ¼ cup all-purpose flour
- 1 can (10½ oz.) condensed chicken broth, undiluted
- ¼ cup fat-free milk
- ⅛ tsp. pepper
- 2 cups cubed cooked turkey breast
- 2 cups frozen peas and carrots (about 10 oz.), thawed
- 1 tube (12 oz.) refrigerated buttermilk biscuits, quartered

1. Preheat oven to 400°. Melt the butter in a 10-in. cast-iron or other ovenproof skillet over medium-high heat. Add the onion; cook and stir until tender, 2-3 minutes.
2. In a small bowl, mix flour, broth, milk and pepper until smooth; stir into pan. Bring to a boil, stirring constantly; cook and stir until thickened, 1-2 minutes. Add the turkey and frozen vegetables; heat through. Arrange biscuits over stew. Bake until biscuits are golden brown, 15-20 minutes.
1 serving: 319 cal., 10g fat (4g sat. fat), 43mg chol., 878mg sod., 36g carb. (4g sugars, 2g fiber), 22g pro.

WHY YOU'LL LOVE IT...

"I used chicken instead of turkey. This recipe is to die for. My husband and I both loved it. Eating the leftovers today."
—KAREN-KITTYBANKS, TASTEOFHOME.COM

RECIPE INDEX

CUTS OF POULTRY

QR CODE INDEX

Dozens of QR codes lead you to instructional videos, cooking tips, insider tricks and bonus recipes.

WATCH US MAKE...

BAKED LEMON CHICKEN

BUFFALO CHICKEN DIP

CHICKEN & DUMPLINGS

CHICKEN ALFREDO LASAGNA

CHICKEN BURRITO SKILLET

CHICKEN CORDON BLEU STROMBOLI

CHICKEN PICCATA MEATBALLS

CHICKEN POTPIE GALETTE WITH CHEDDAR-THYME CRUST

COUNTRY CHICKEN WITH GRAVY

EASY CHICKEN ENCHILADAS

FAVORITE CHICKEN POTPIE

FILIPINO CHICKEN ADOBO

HERBED ROAST TURKEY BREAST

PAN-ROASTED CHICKEN & VEGETABLES

SLOW-COOKER CHICKEN PARMESAN

SUPER QUICK CHICKEN FRIED RICE

THE ULTIMATE CHICKEN NOODLE SOUP

TROPICAL CHICKEN CAULIFLOWER RICE BOWLS

WHITE BEAN CHICKEN CHILI

LEARN MORE ABOUT...

AIR-FRYING CHICKEN

BAKING JUICY CHICKEN BREASTS

CARVING A CHICKEN

CARVING A TURKEY

DEBONING A CHICKEN

DEFROSTING CHICKEN

ETHNIC CHICKEN DISHES

FROZEN CHICKEN IN INSTANT POT

FRYING CHICKEN

GRILL CLEANING

GRILLING JUICY CHICKEN

GRILLING SPATCHCOCKED CHICKEN

GRILLING TURKEY

MAKING CHICKEN STOCK

POACHING CHICKEN

REVIVING OLD CAST IRON

RINSING POULTRY

ROASTING CHICKEN

SHREDDING CHICKEN

SLOW-COOKER MEAL PLAN

SMOKING ON THE GRILL

SPATCHCOCKING A CHICKEN

STIR-FRY SECRET

UNCOOKED CHICKEN SAFETY

WING RECIPES